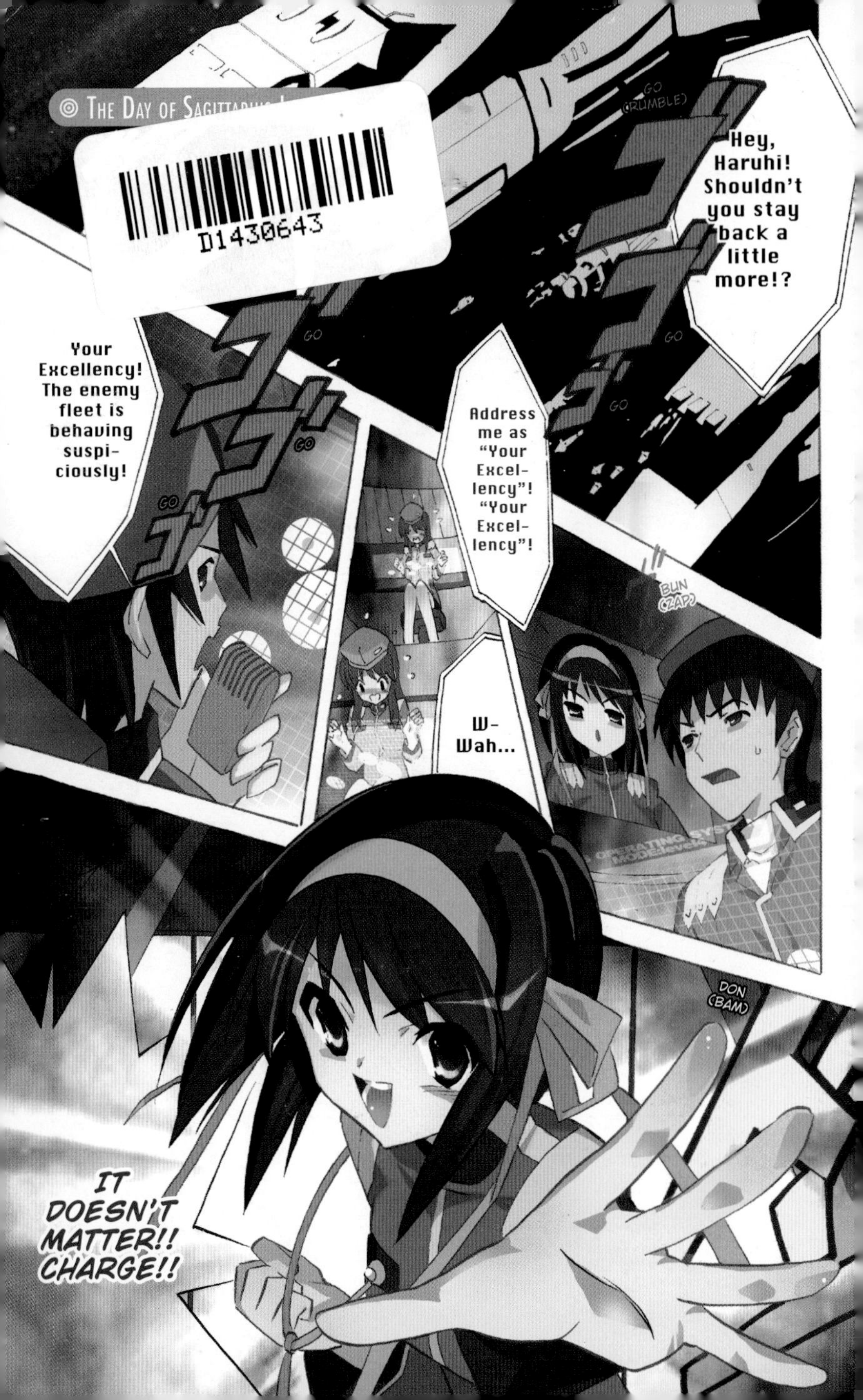
GO (RUMBLE)
Hey, Haruhi! Shouldn't you stay back a little more!?
GO
GO
GO
GO
GO
BUN (ZAP)
Address me as "Your Excel-lency"! "Your Excel-lency"!
W-Wah...
Your Excellency! The enemy fleet is behaving suspi-ciously!
DON (BAM)
IT DOESN'T MATTER!! CHARGE!!

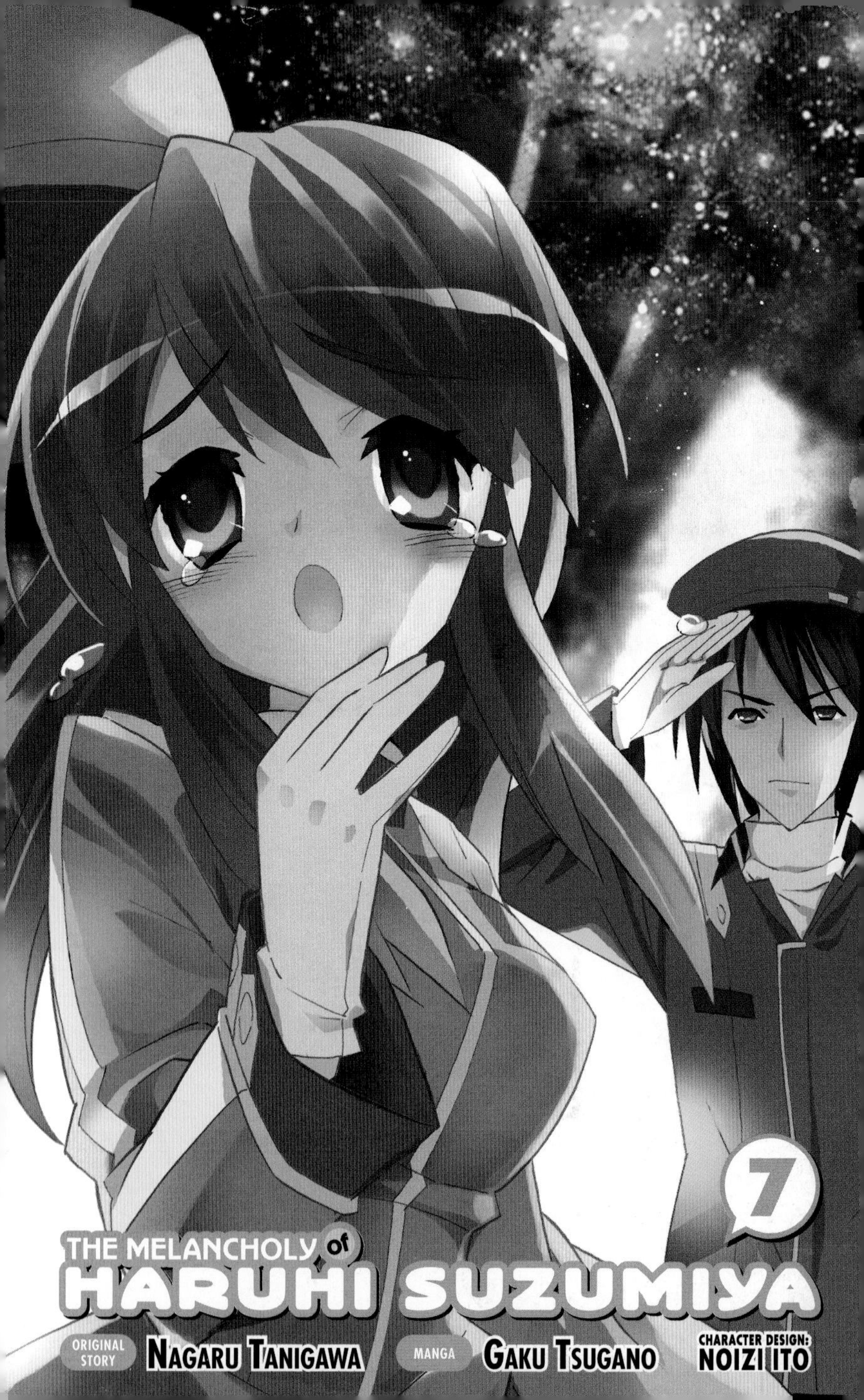
7
THE MELANCHOLY of
HARUHI SUZUMIYA
ORIGINAL STORY
NAGARU TANIGAWA
MANGA
GAKU TSUGANO
CHARACTER DESIGN:
NOIZI ITO

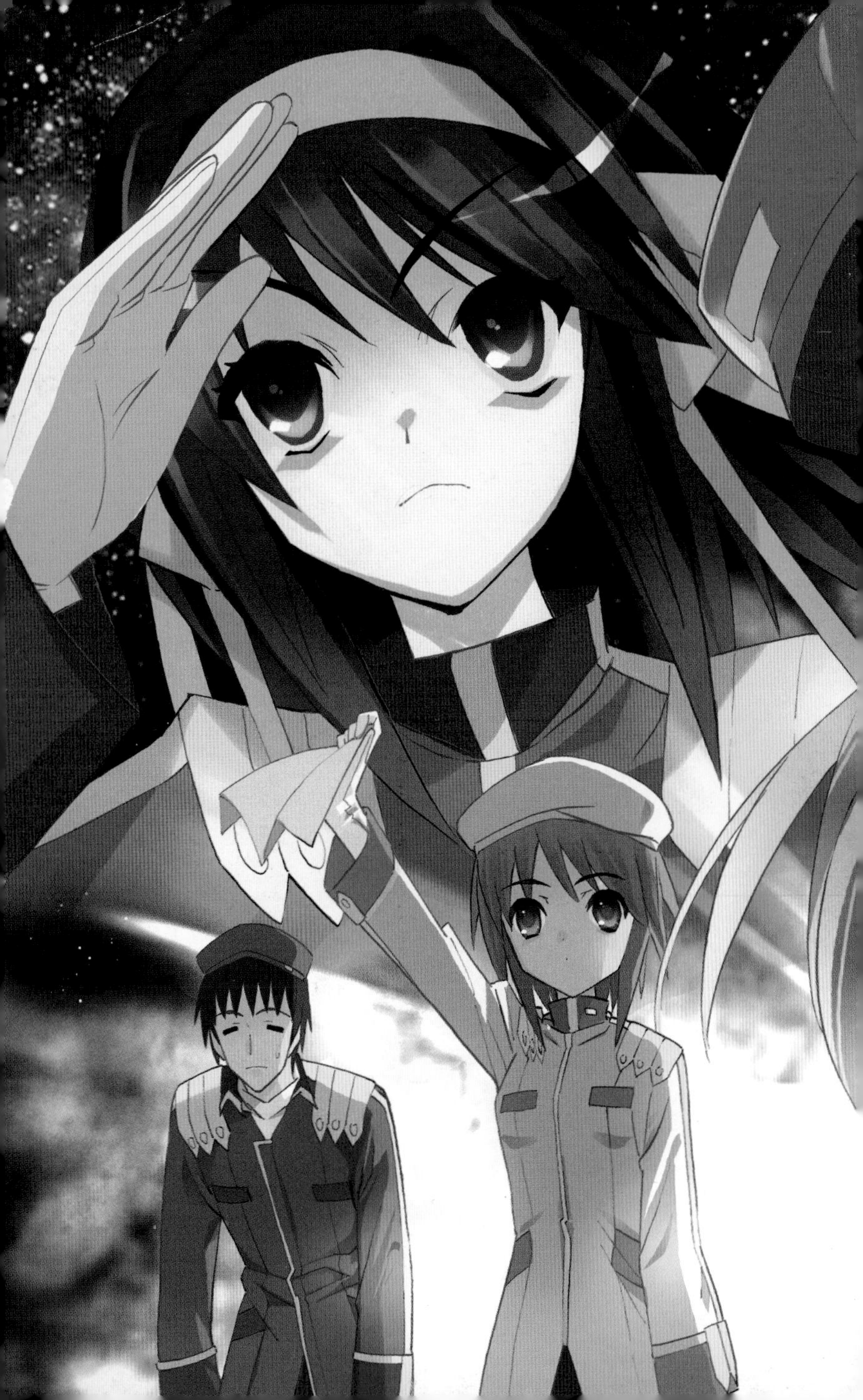

CONTENTS

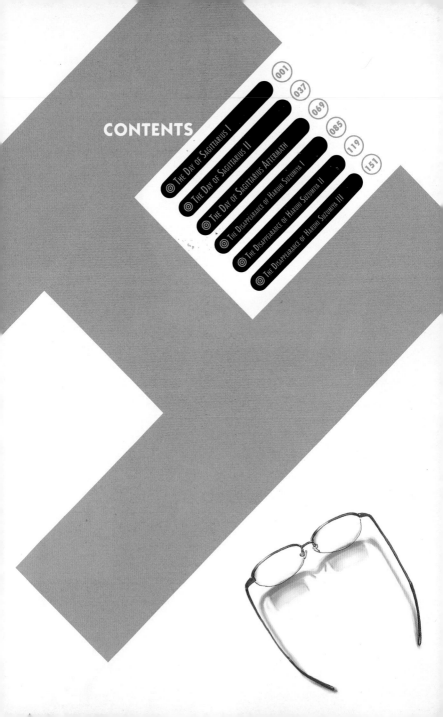

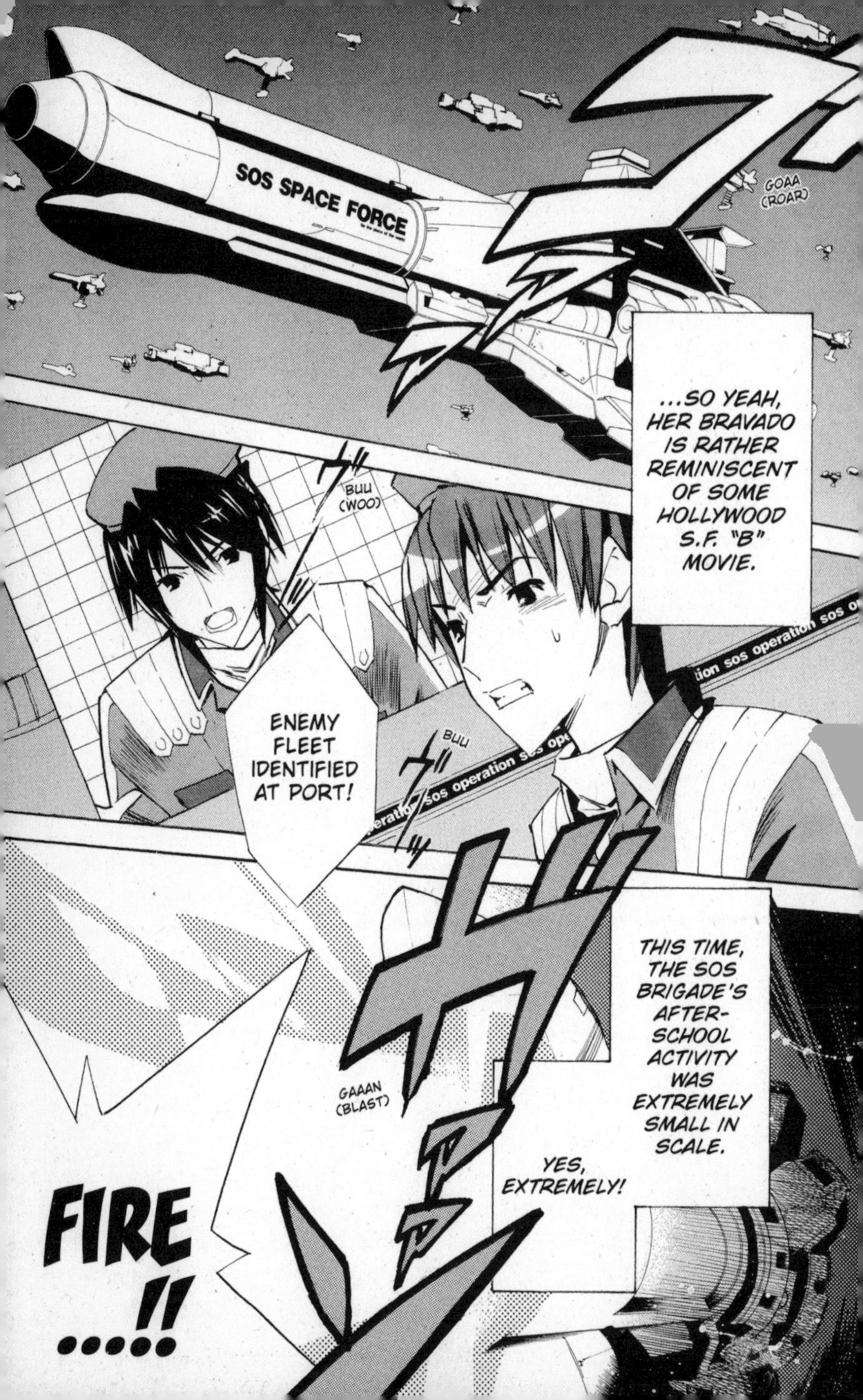
SOS SPACE FORCE
GOAA (ROAR)
...SO YEAH, HER BRAVADO IS RATHER REMINISCENT OF SOME HOLLYWOOD S.F. "B" MOVIE.
BUU (WOO)
ENEMY FLEET IDENTIFIED AT PORT!
BUU
THIS TIME, THE SOS BRIGADE'S AFTER-SCHOOL ACTIVITY WAS EXTREMELY SMALL IN SCALE.
YES, EXTREMELY!
GAAAN (BLAST)
FIRE.....!!

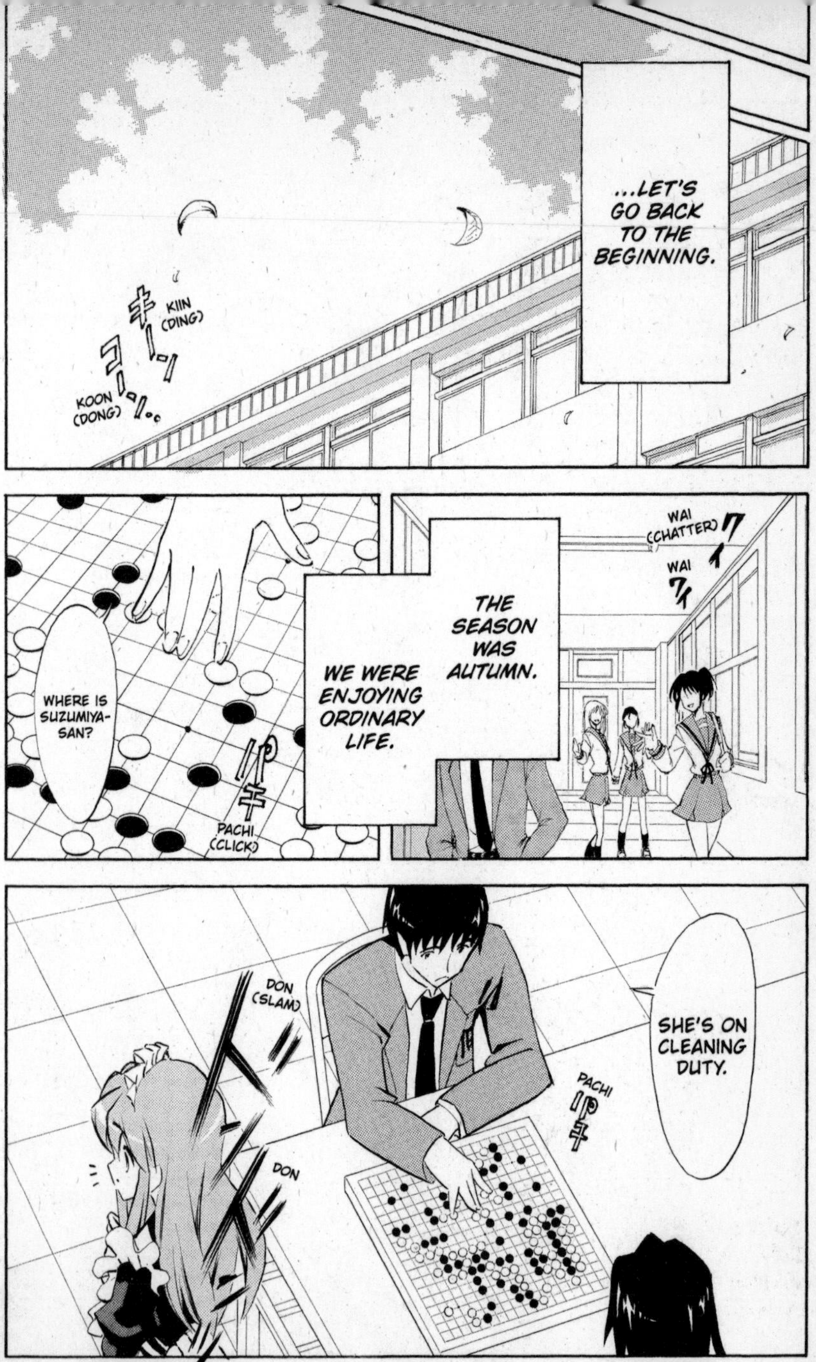

...LET'S GO BACK TO THE BEGINNING.
KIIN (DING)
KOON (DONG)
WAI (CHATTER)
WAI
THE SEASON WAS AUTUMN.
WE WERE ENJOYING ORDINARY LIFE.
WHERE IS SUZUMIYA-SAN?
PACHI (CLICK)
SHE'S ON CLEANING DUTY.
PACHI
DON (SLAM)
DON

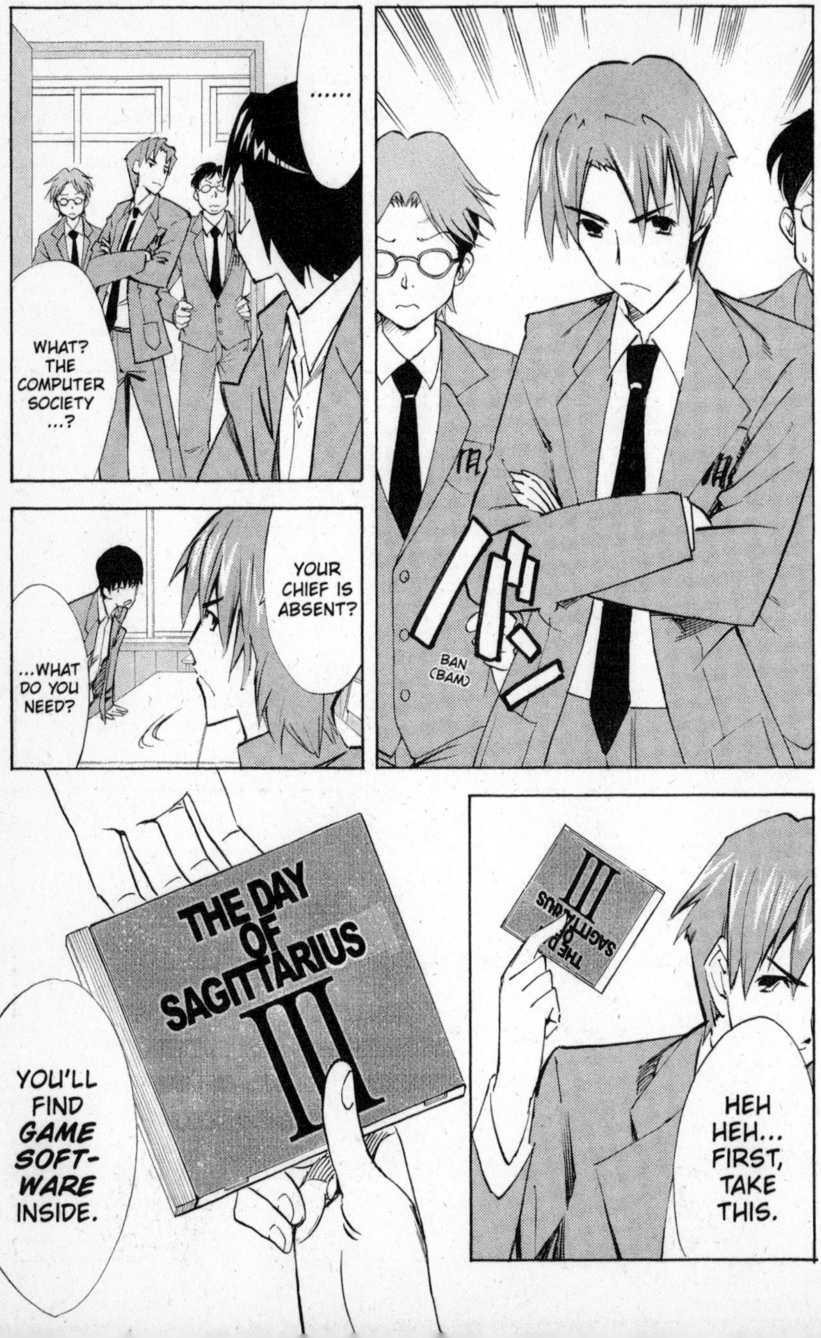
BAN (BAM)
......
WHAT? THE COMPUTER SOCIETY ...?
YOUR CHIEF IS ABSENT?
...WHAT DO YOU NEED?
HEH HEH... FIRST, TAKE THIS.
THE DAY OF SAGITTARIUS III
YOU'LL FIND GAME SOFTWARE INSIDE.

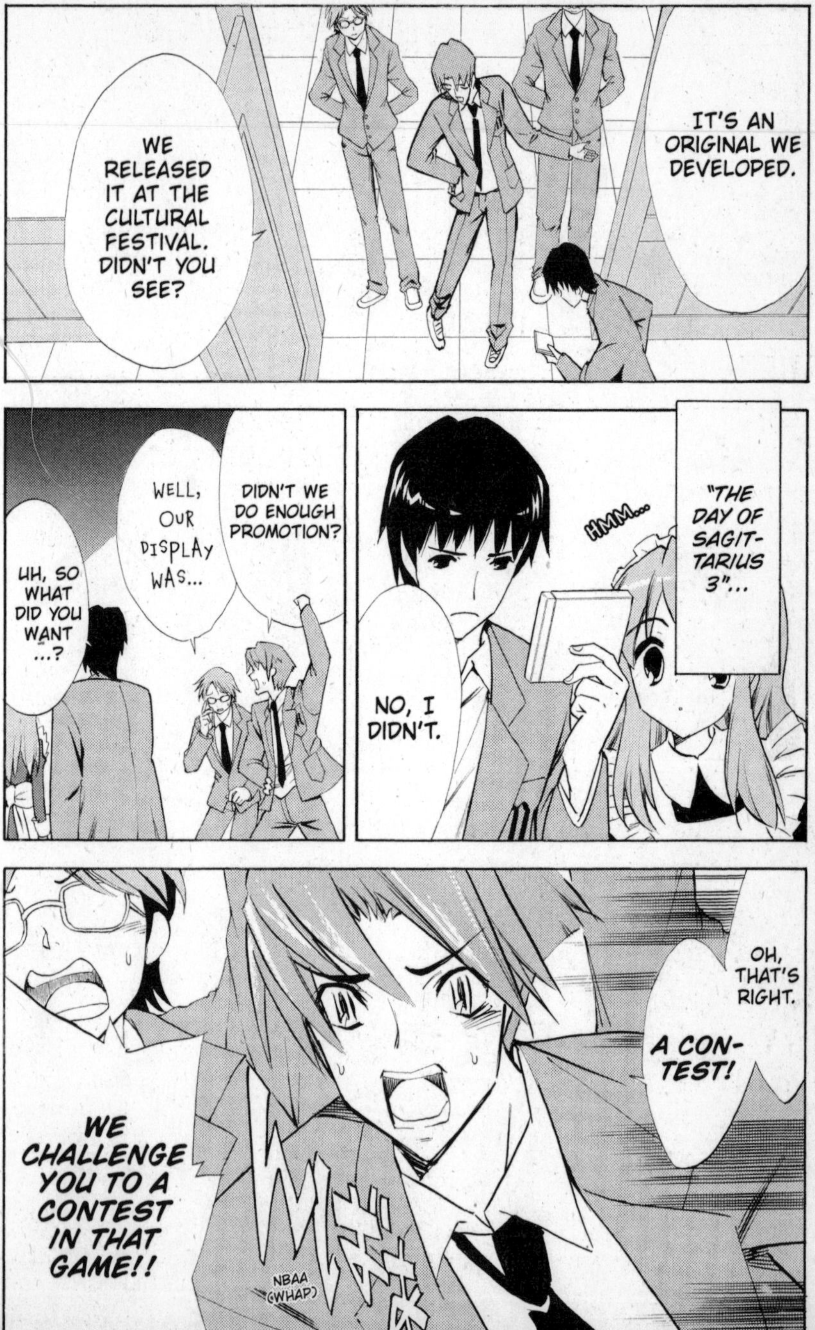
IT'S AN ORIGINAL WE DEVELOPED.
WE RELEASED IT AT THE CULTURAL FESTIVAL. DIDN'T YOU SEE?
"THE DAY OF SAGIT-TARIUS 3"...
HMM...
NO, I DIDN'T.
DIDN'T WE DO ENOUGH PROMOTION?
WELL, OUR DISPLAY WAS...
UH, SO WHAT DID YOU WANT ...?
OH, THAT'S RIGHT.
A CON-TEST!
WE CHALLENGE YOU TO A CONTEST IN THAT GAME!!
NBAA (WHAP)

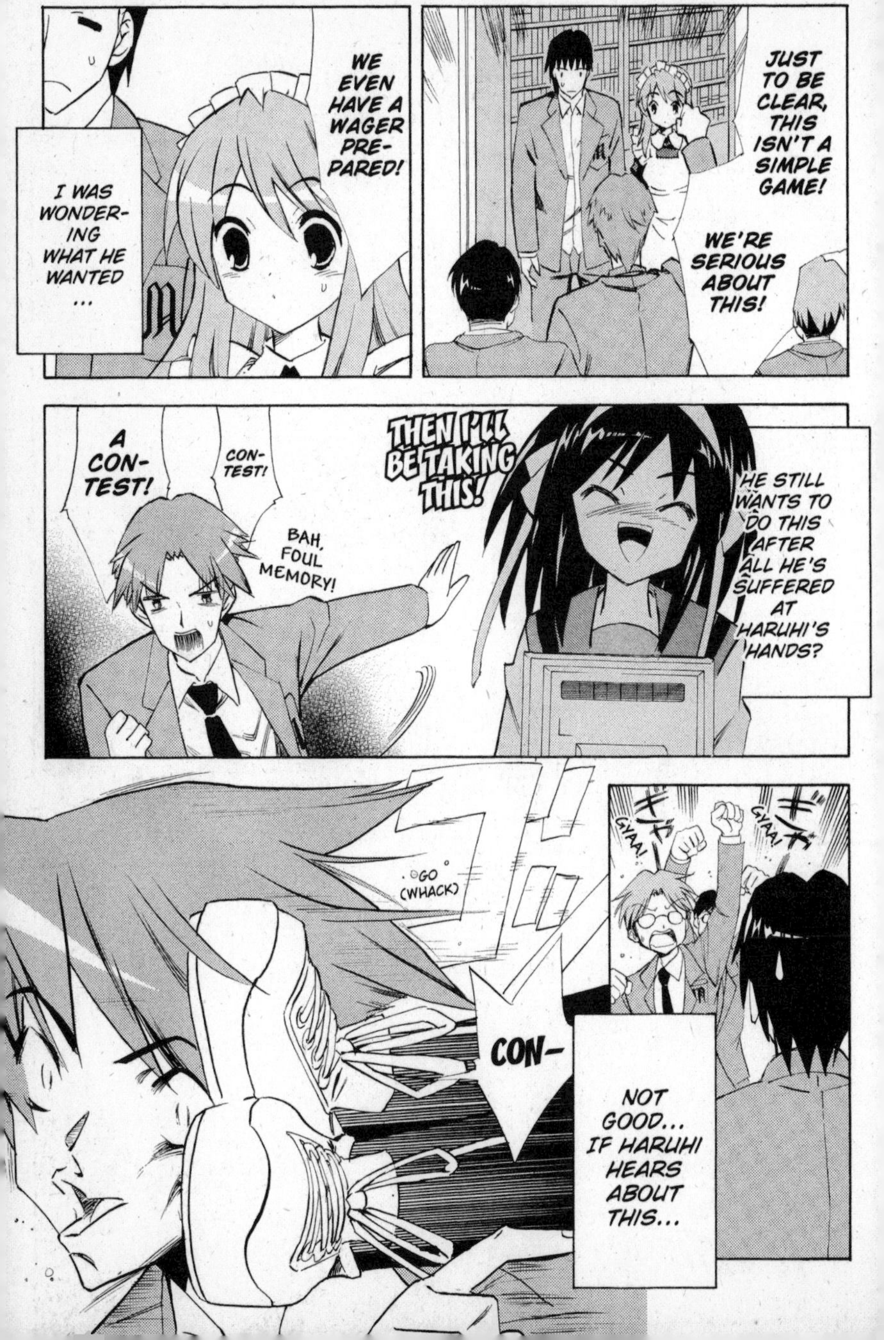
JUST TO BE CLEAR, THIS ISN'T A SIMPLE GAME!
WE'RE SERIOUS ABOUT THIS!
WE EVEN HAVE A WAGER PRE-PARED!
I WAS WONDER-ING WHAT HE WANTED...
HE STILL WANTS TO DO THIS AFTER ALL HE'S SUFFERED AT HARUHI'S HANDS?
THEN I'LL BE TAKING THIS!
A CON-TEST!
CON-TEST!
BAH, FOUL MEMORY!
GYAA!
GYAA!
NOT GOOD... IF HARUHI HEARS ABOUT THIS...
GO (WHACK)
CON-

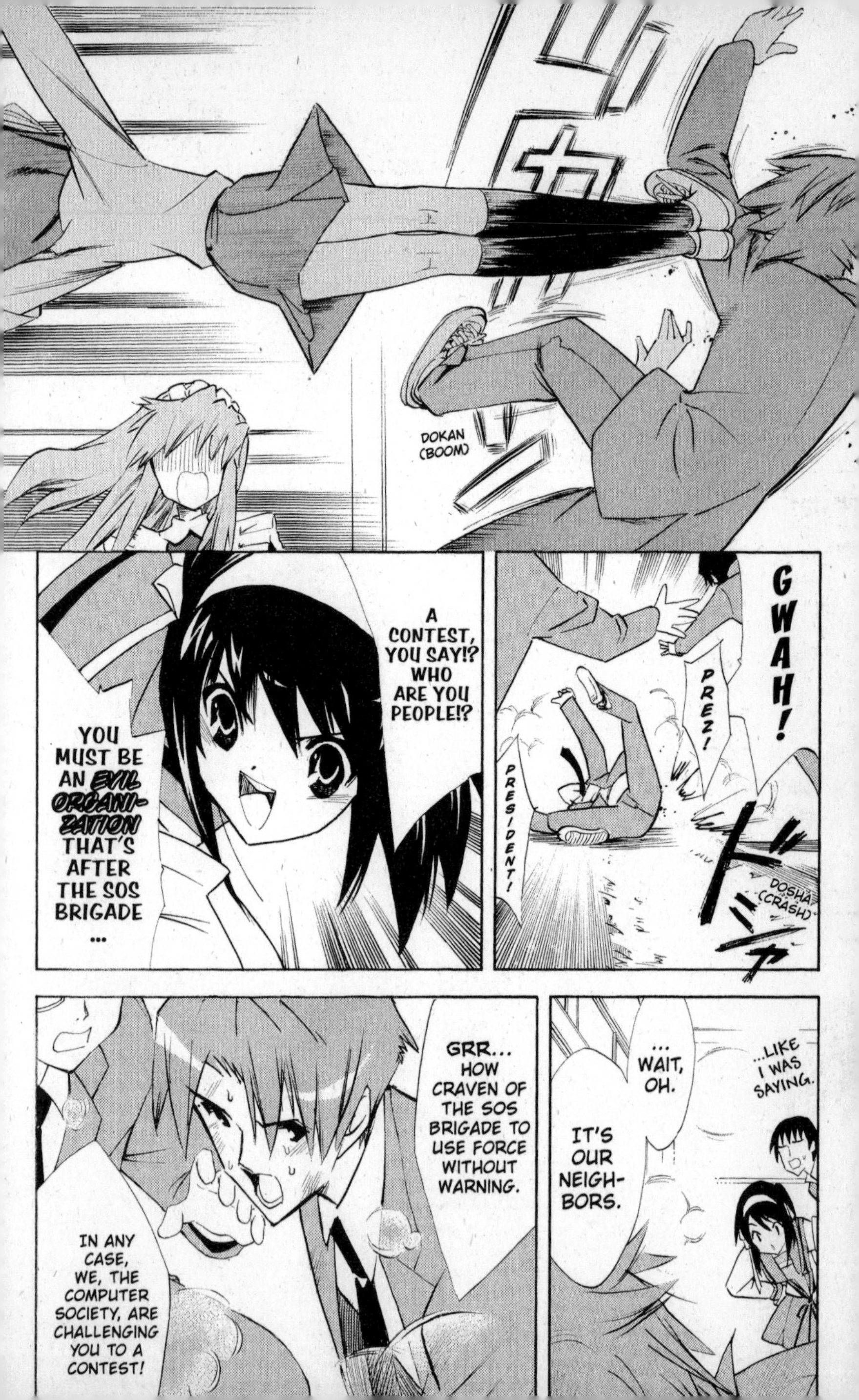
DOKAN (BOOM)
GWAH!
PREZ!
PRESIDENT!
DOSHA (CRASH)
A CONTEST, YOU SAY!? WHO ARE YOU PEOPLE!?
YOU MUST BE AN EVIL ORGANIZATION THAT'S AFTER THE SOS BRIGADE...
...LIKE I WAS SAYING.
...WAIT, OH.
IT'S OUR NEIGHBORS.
GRR... HOW CRAVEN OF THE SOS BRIGADE TO USE FORCE WITHOUT WARNING.
IN ANY CASE, WE, THE COMPUTER SOCIETY, ARE CHALLENGING YOU TO A CONTEST!

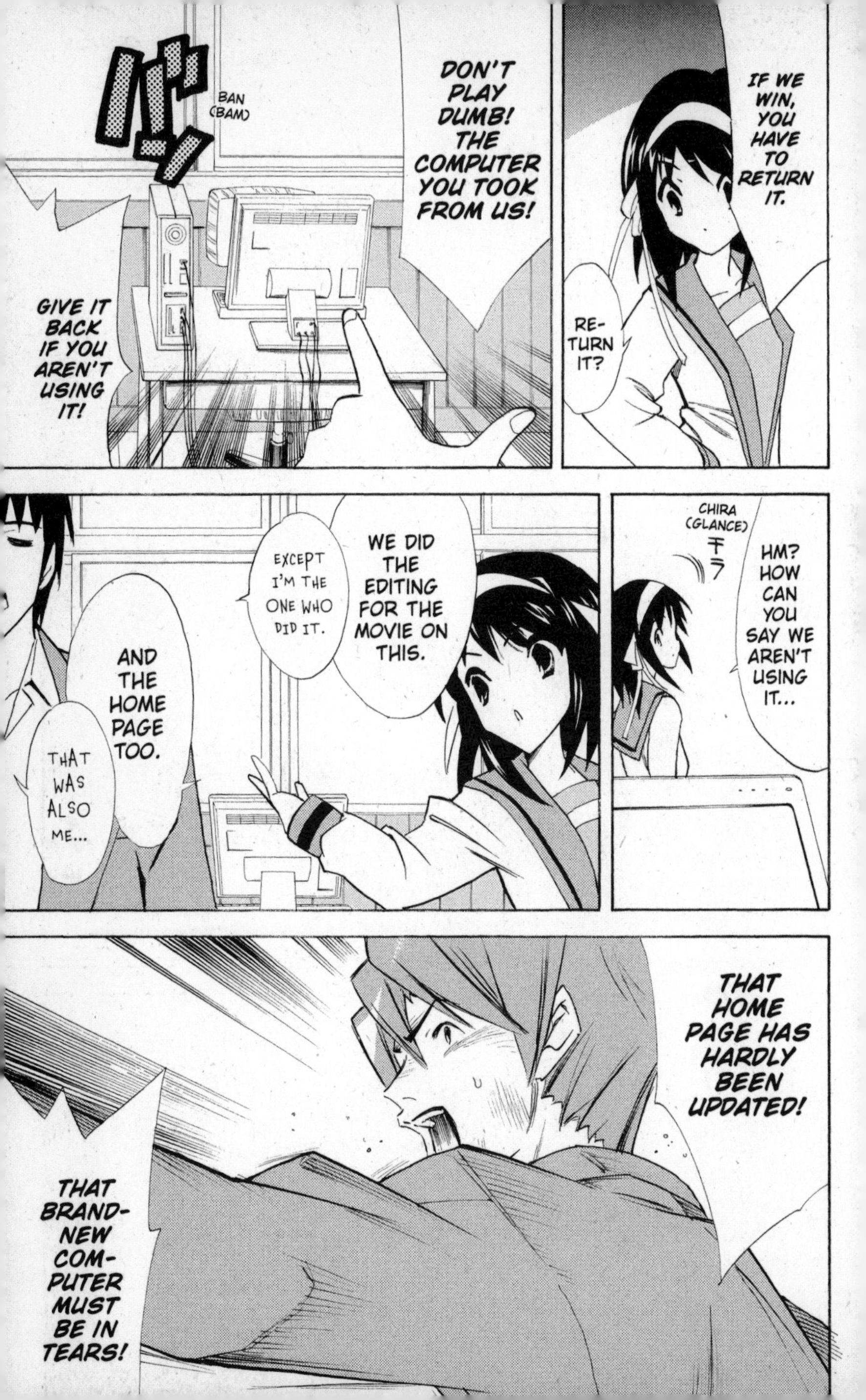
IF WE WIN, YOU HAVE TO RETURN IT.
RE-TURN IT?
DON'T PLAY DUMB! THE COMPUTER YOU TOOK FROM US!
BAN (BAM)
GIVE IT BACK IF YOU AREN'T USING IT!
CHIRA (GLANCE)
チラ
HM? HOW CAN YOU SAY WE AREN'T USING IT...
WE DID THE EDITING FOR THE MOVIE ON THIS.
EXCEPT I'M THE ONE WHO DID IT.
AND THE HOME PAGE TOO.
THAT WAS ALSO ME...
THAT HOME PAGE HAS HARDLY BEEN UPDATED!
THAT BRAND-NEW COMPUTER MUST BE IN TEARS!

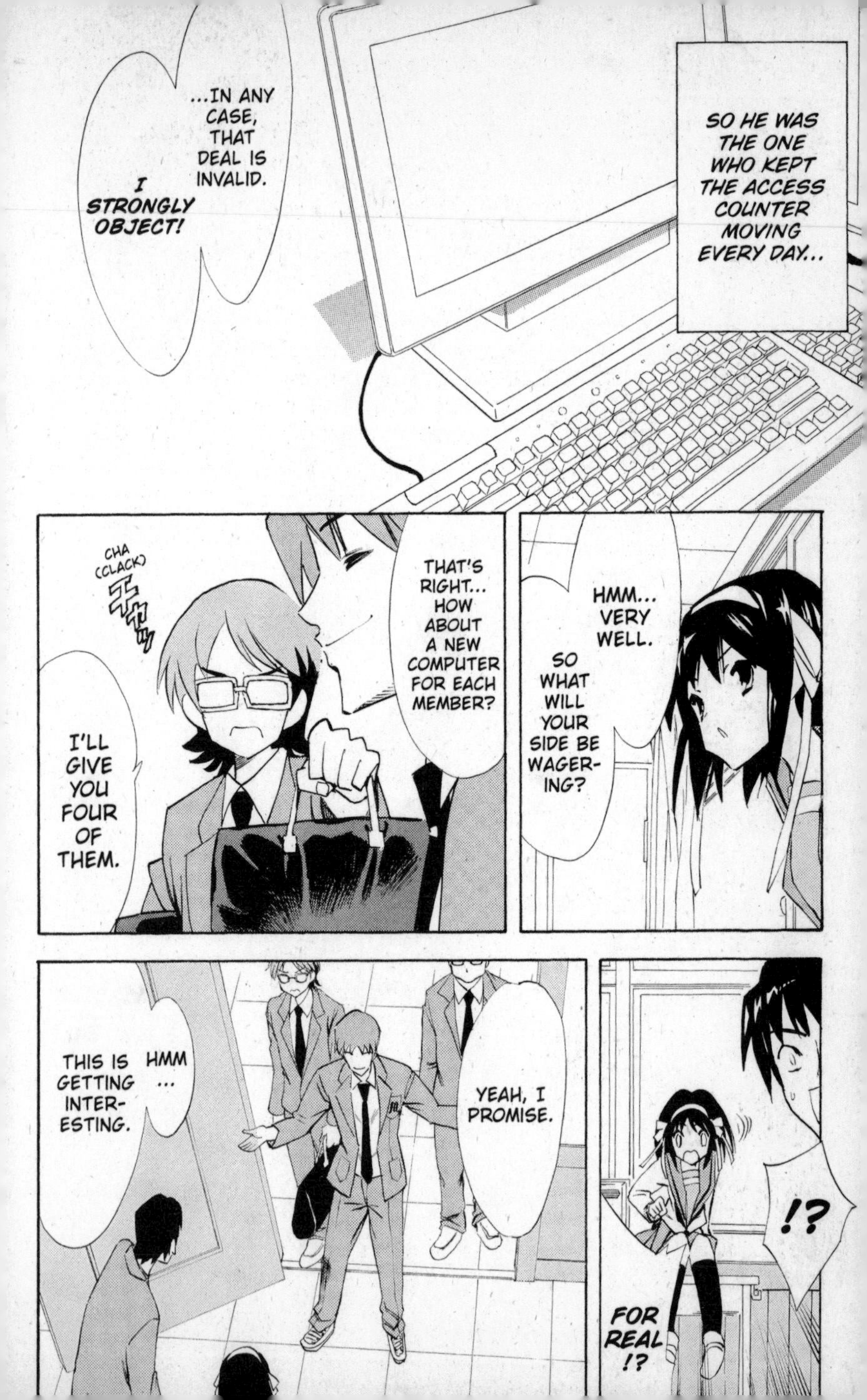
SO HE WAS THE ONE WHO KEPT THE ACCESS COUNTER MOVING EVERY DAY...
...IN ANY CASE, THAT DEAL IS INVALID.
I STRONGLY OBJECT!
HMM... VERY WELL.
SO WHAT WILL YOUR SIDE BE WAGER-ING?
THAT'S RIGHT... HOW ABOUT A NEW COMPUTER FOR EACH MEMBER?
CHA (CLACK)
I'LL GIVE YOU FOUR OF THEM.
!?
FOR REAL !?
YEAH, I PROMISE.
HMM ...
THIS IS GETTING INTER-ESTING.

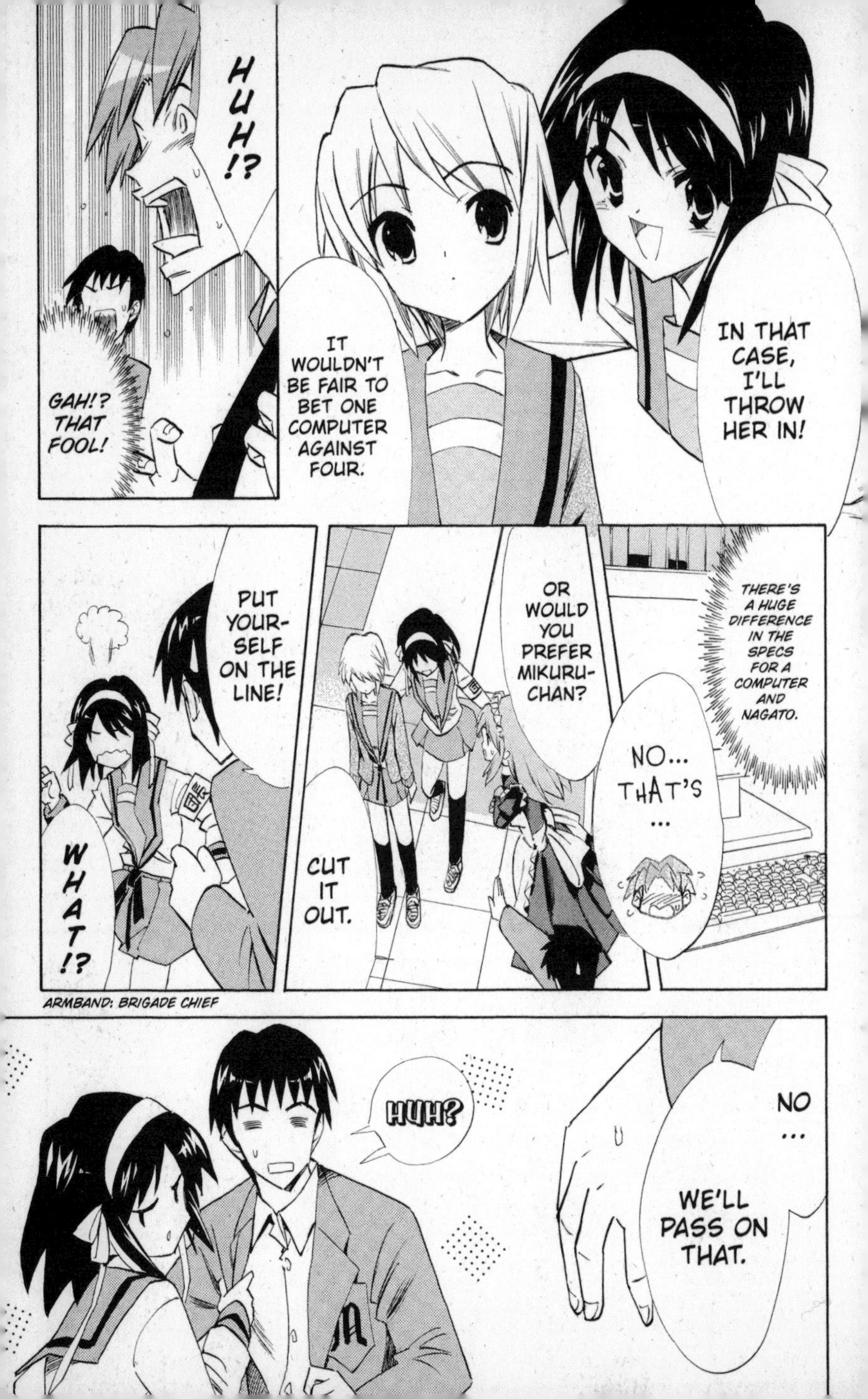
IN THAT CASE, I'LL THROW HER IN!
IT WOULDN'T BE FAIR TO BET ONE COMPUTER AGAINST FOUR.
HUH!?
GAH!? THAT FOOL!
THERE'S A HUGE DIFFERENCE IN THE SPECS FOR A COMPUTER AND NAGATO.
NO... THAT'S ...
OR WOULD YOU PREFER MIKURU-CHAN?
CUT IT OUT.
PUT YOURSELF ON THE LINE!
WHAT!?
ARMBAND: BRIGADE CHIEF
NO ...
WE'LL PASS ON THAT.
HUH?

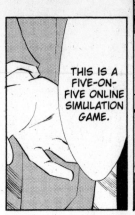

CHA (CLACK)
チャッ
THIS IS A FIVE-ON-FIVE ONLINE SIMULATION GAME.
THE BATTLE WILL COMMENCE ONE WEEK FROM NOW AT 4 P.M.... WE'LL LEND YOU THOSE UNTIL THEN.
POLISH UP YOUR SKILLS.
SURE THING, CHIEF.
I HOPE YOU'LL PROVE TO BE A FORMIDABLE OPPONENT.
DON'T DISAPPOINT ME.
HOW GENEROUS OF YOU TO GIVE US OUR PRIZE BEFORE THE CONTEST.
I'LL ENJOY HAVING A COMPUTER FOR EACH BRIGADE MEMBER!

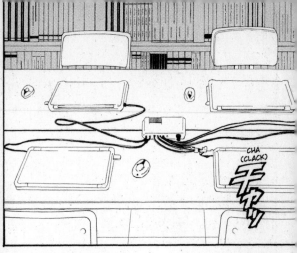

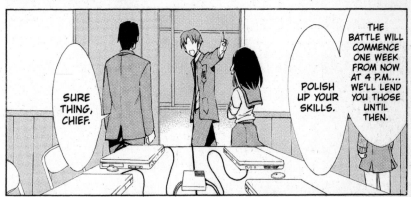

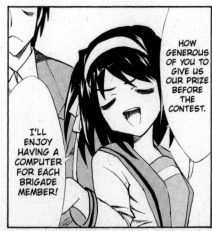

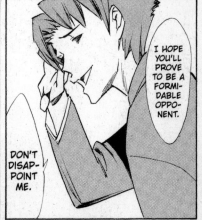

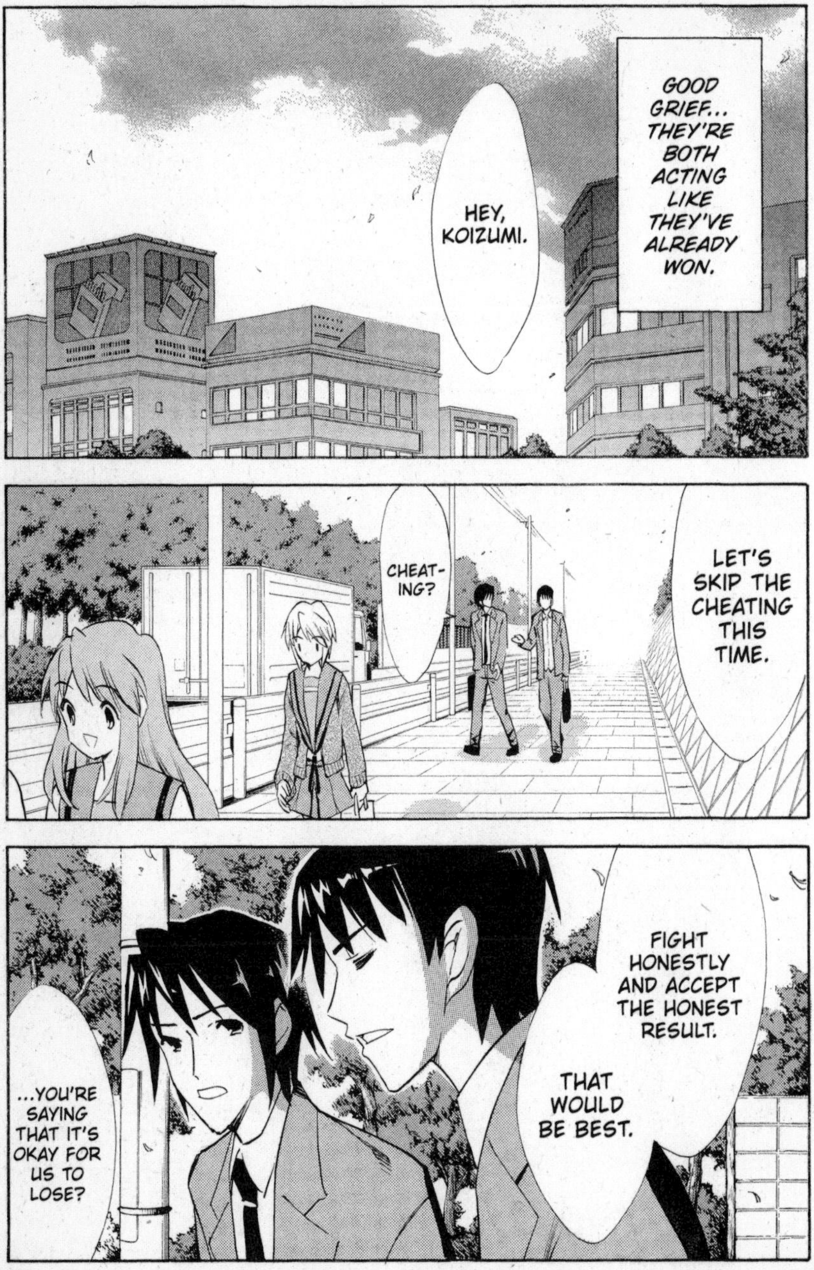
GOOD GRIEF... THEY'RE BOTH ACTING LIKE THEY'VE ALREADY WON.
HEY, KOIZUMI.
LET'S SKIP THE CHEATING THIS TIME.
CHEAT-ING?
FIGHT HONESTLY AND ACCEPT THE HONEST RESULT.
THAT WOULD BE BEST.
...YOU'RE SAYING THAT IT'S OKAY FOR US TO LOSE?

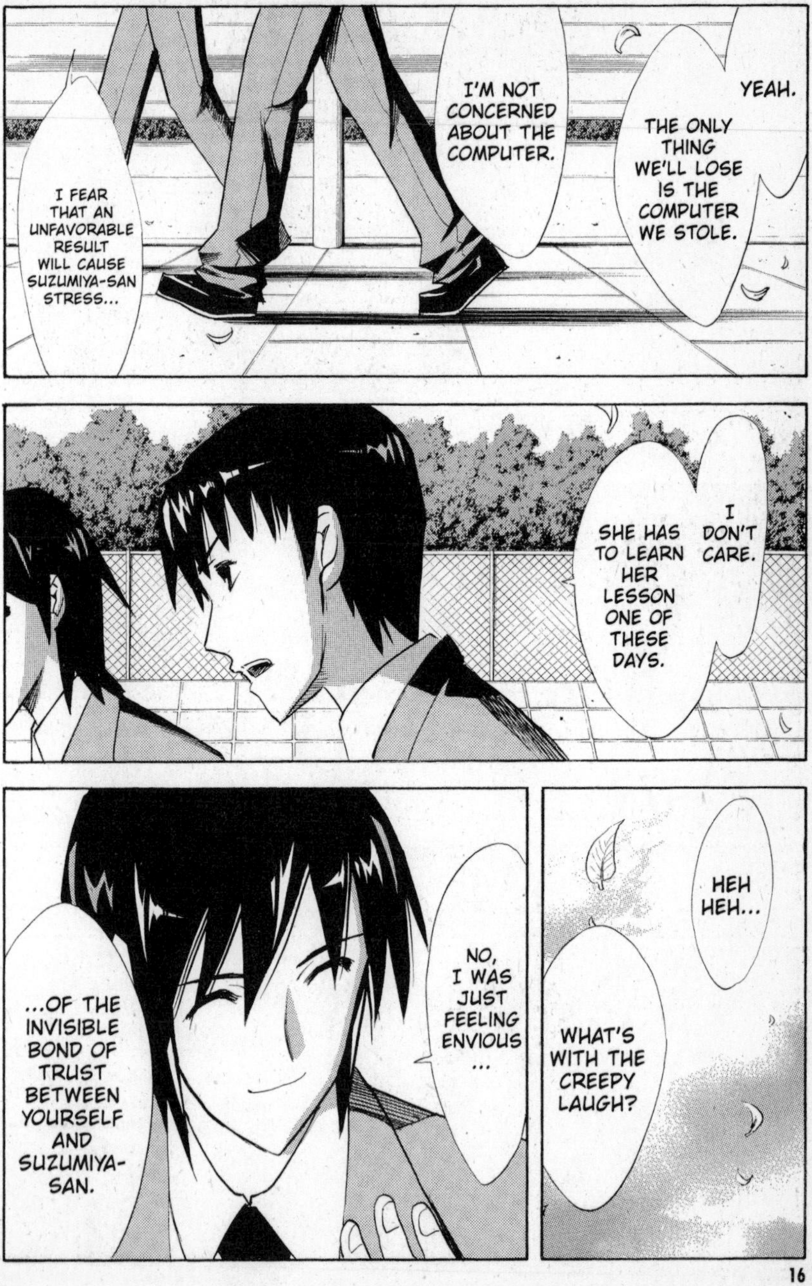

YEAH.
THE ONLY THING WE'LL LOSE IS THE COMPUTER WE STOLE.
I'M NOT CONCERNED ABOUT THE COMPUTER.
I FEAR THAT AN UNFAVORABLE RESULT WILL CAUSE SUZUMIYA-SAN STRESS...
I DON'T CARE.
SHE HAS TO LEARN HER LESSON ONE OF THESE DAYS.
HEH HEH...
WHAT'S WITH THE CREEPY LAUGH?
NO, I WAS JUST FEELING ENVIOUS...
...OF THE INVISIBLE BOND OF TRUST BETWEEN YOURSELF AND SUZUMIYA-SAN.

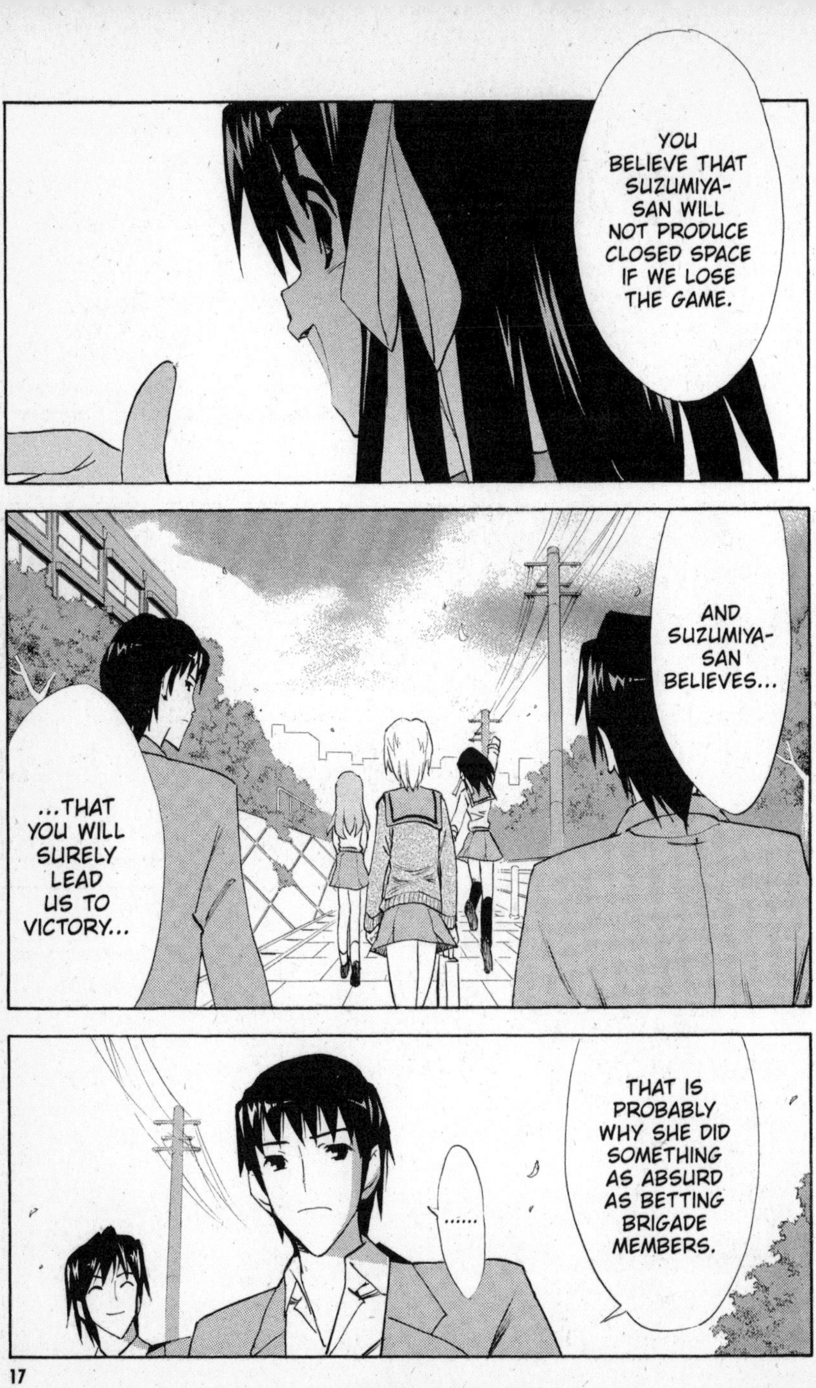
YOU BELIEVE THAT SUZUMIYA-SAN WILL NOT PRODUCE CLOSED SPACE IF WE LOSE THE GAME.
AND SUZUMIYA-SAN BELIEVES...
...THAT YOU WILL SURELY LEAD US TO VICTORY...
THAT IS PROBABLY WHY SHE DID SOMETHING AS ABSURD AS BETTING BRIGADE MEMBERS.
......

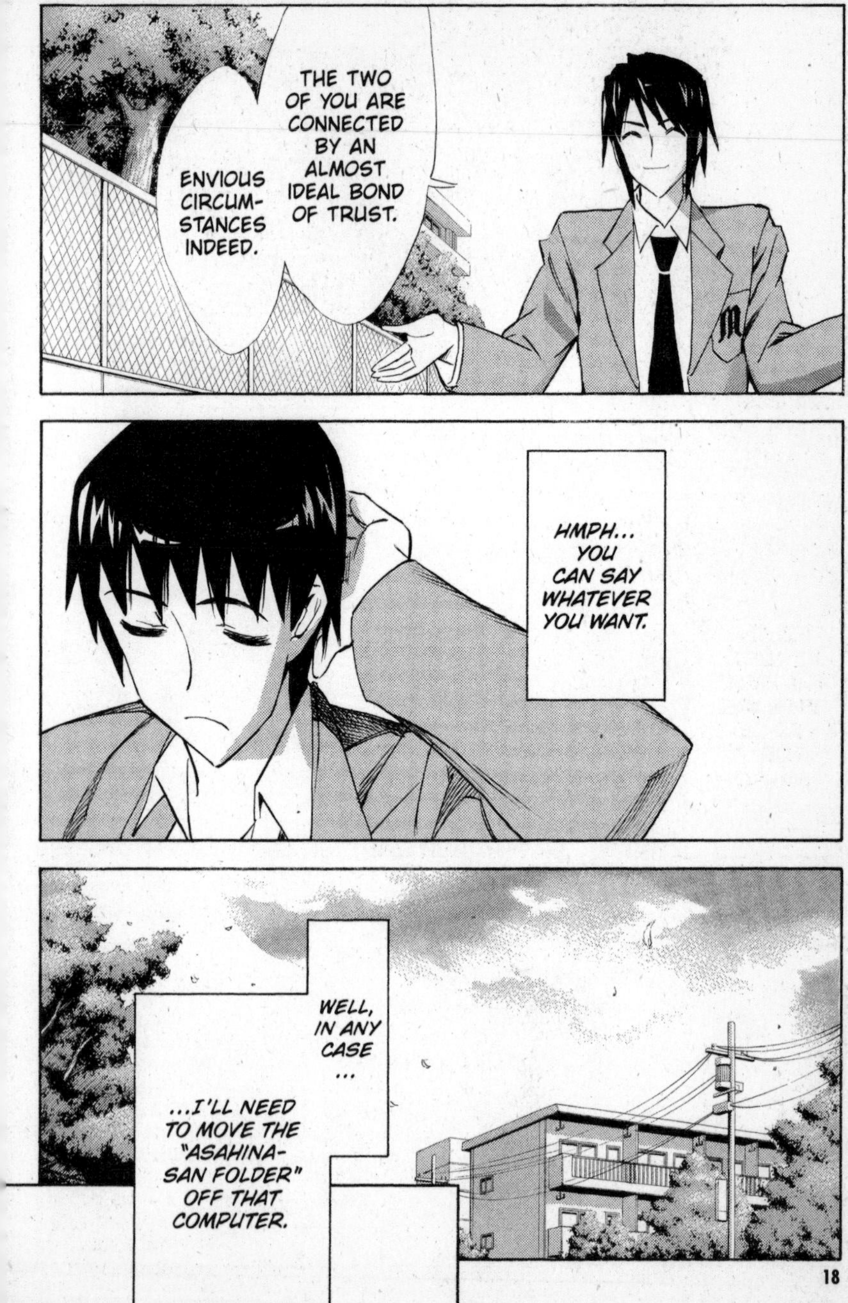
THE TWO OF YOU ARE CONNECTED BY AN ALMOST IDEAL BOND OF TRUST.
ENVIOUS CIRCUM-STANCES INDEED.
HMPH... YOU CAN SAY WHATEVER YOU WANT.
WELL, IN ANY CASE ...
...I'LL NEED TO MOVE THE "ASAHINA-SAN FOLDER" OFF THAT COMPUTER.

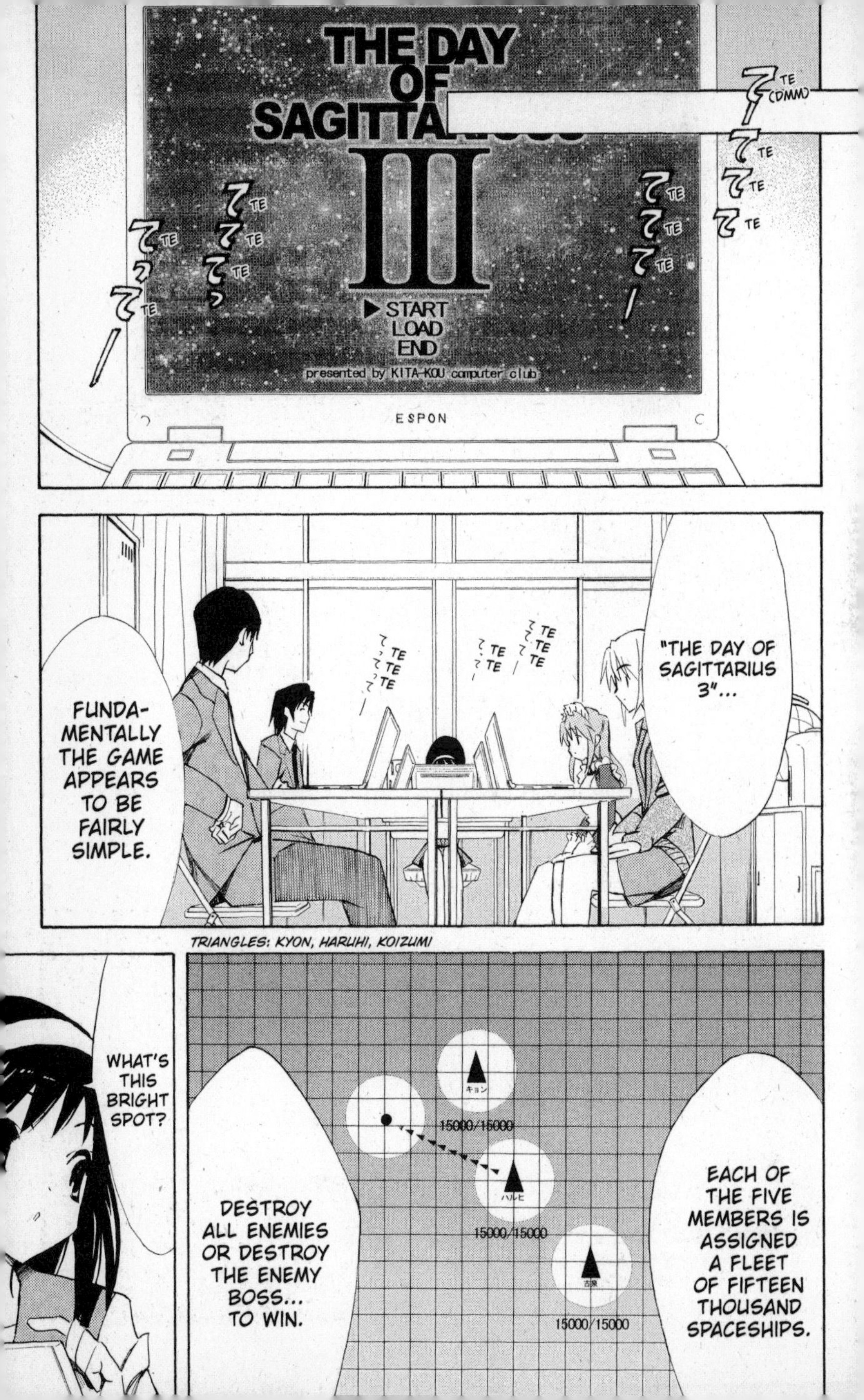
THE DAY OF SAGITTA
III
▶START
LOAD
END
presented by KITA-KOU computer club
ESPON
TE (DMM)
TE TE TE TE
TE TE TE
TE TE TE
TE TE
"THE DAY OF SAGITTARIUS 3"...
TE TE TE TE TE TE TE TE
FUNDAMENTALLY THE GAME APPEARS TO BE FAIRLY SIMPLE.
TRIANGLES: KYON, HARUHI, KOIZUMI
EACH OF THE FIVE MEMBERS IS ASSIGNED A FLEET OF FIFTEEN THOUSAND SPACESHIPS.
キョン
15000/15000
ハルヒ
15000/15000
古泉
15000/15000
DESTROY ALL ENEMIES OR DESTROY THE ENEMY BOSS... TO WIN.
WHAT'S THIS BRIGHT SPOT?

TRIANGLES: HARUHI, KYON

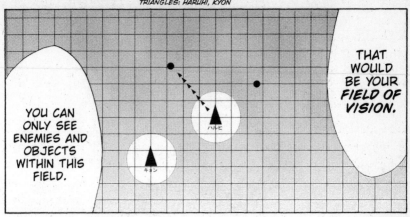

THAT WOULD BE YOUR ***FIELD OF VISION.***
ハルヒ
キョン
YOU CAN ONLY SEE ENEMIES AND OBJECTS WITHIN THIS FIELD.
YOU MUST SEND OUT SCOUTS TO EXPAND YOUR FIELD.
IT WILL BE CRUCIAL TO SWIFTLY DETERMINE THE POSITION OF THE ENEMY.
attack!
shift+A
ハルヒ
キョン
UM... I DON'T REALLY UNDER-STAND THIS KIND OF STUFF...
...BUT YOU CAN'T SEE THE ENEMY IN THE BEGINNING?
THAT'S HOW IT WORKS.

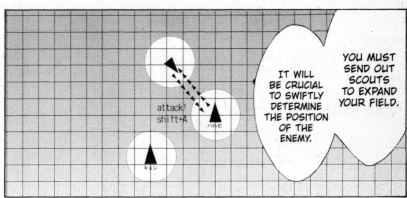

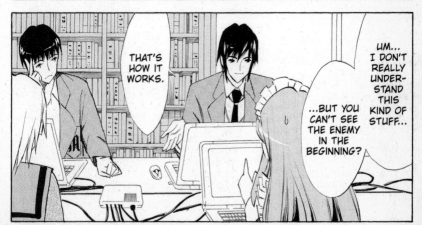

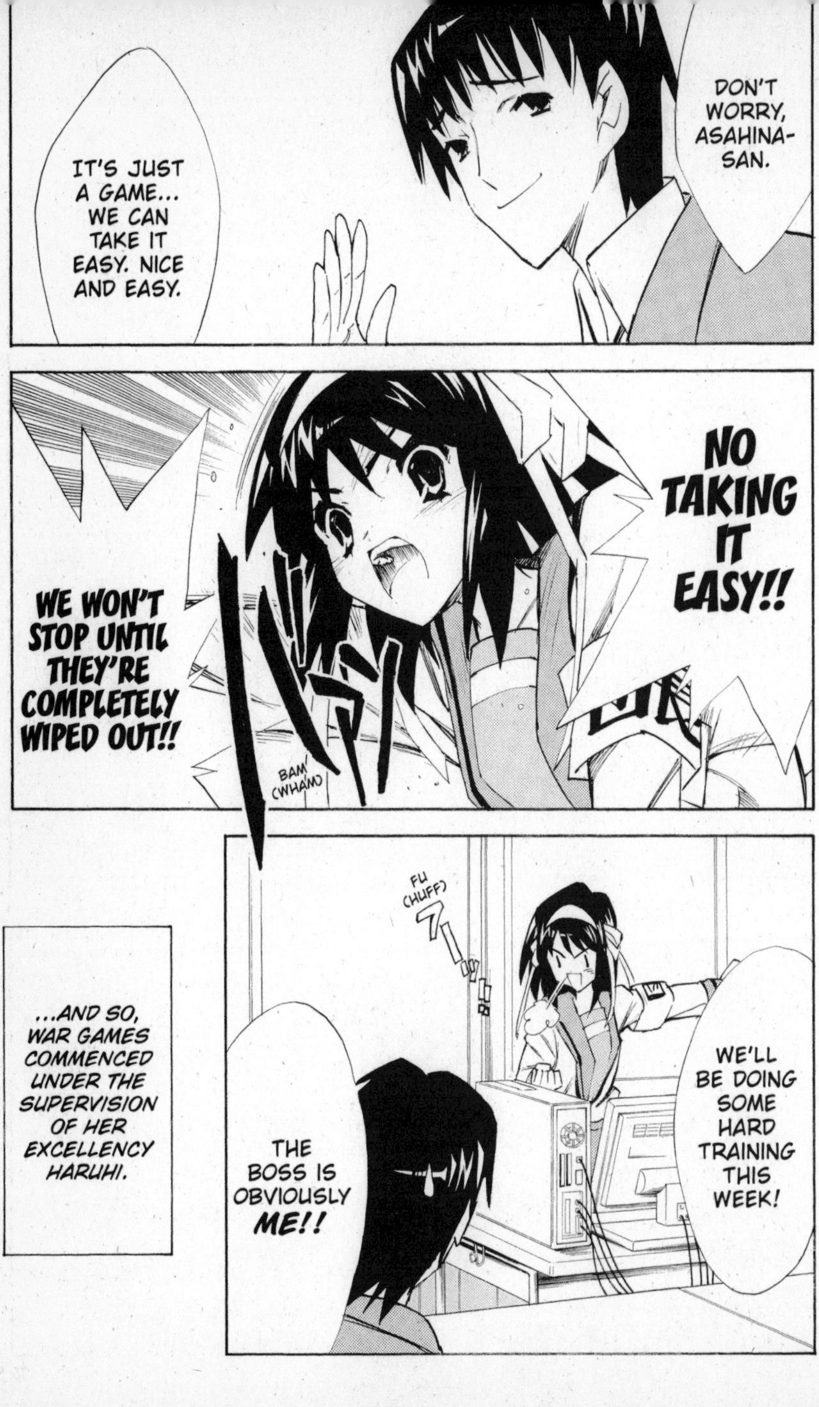
DON'T WORRY, ASAHINA-SAN.
IT'S JUST A GAME... WE CAN TAKE IT EASY. NICE AND EASY.
NO TAKING IT EASY!!
WE WON'T STOP UNTIL THEY'RE COMPLETELY WIPED OUT!!
BAM (WHAM)
WE'LL BE DOING SOME HARD TRAINING THIS WEEK!
FU (HUFF)
THE BOSS IS OBVIOUSLY ME!!
...AND SO, WAR GAMES COMMENCED UNDER THE SUPERVISION OF HER EXCELLENCY HARUHI.

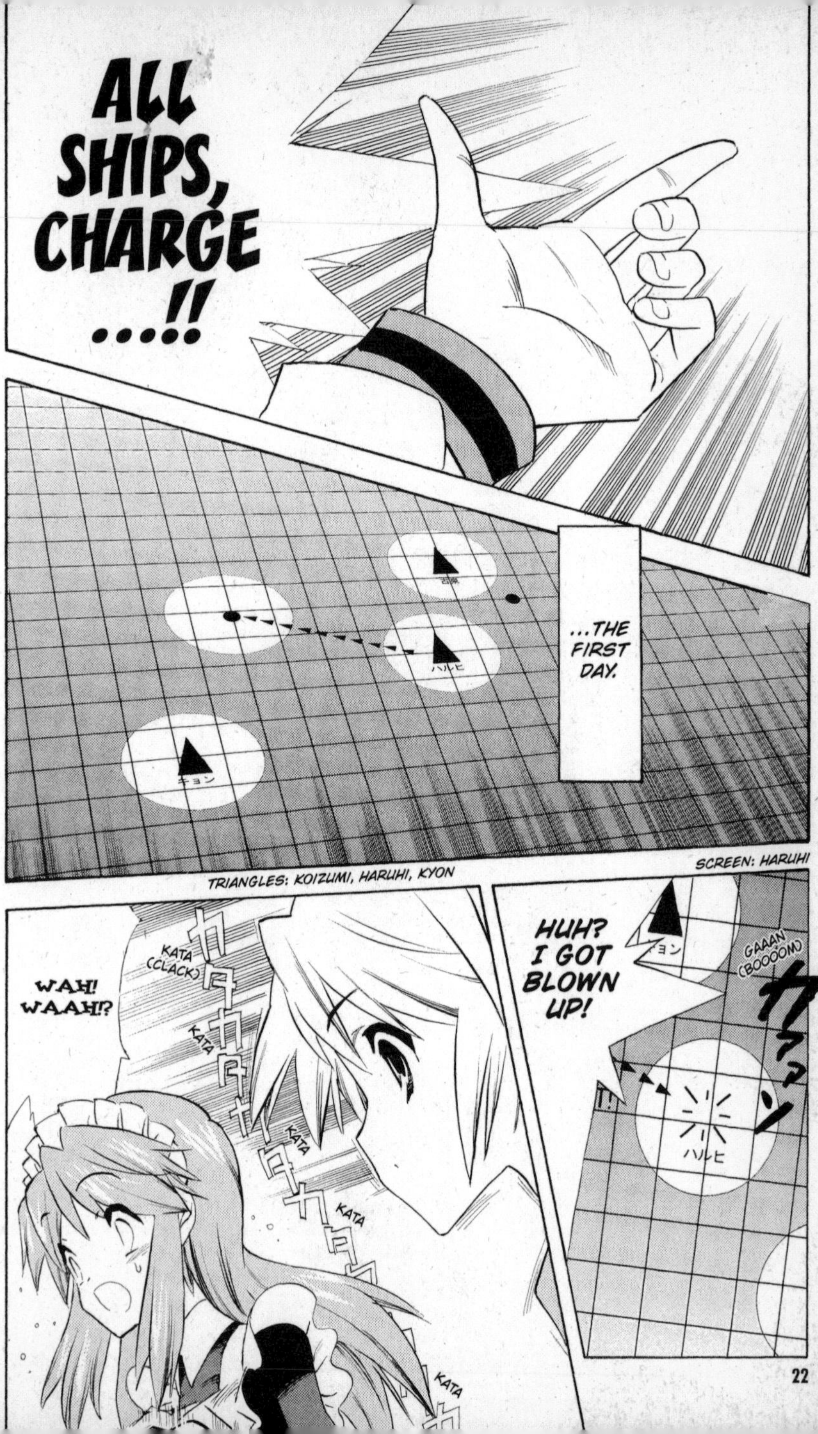
ALL SHIPS, CHARGE....!!
...THE FIRST DAY.
ハルヒ
キョン
SCREEN: HARUHI
TRIANGLES: KOIZUMI, HARUHI, KYON
キョン
HUH? I GOT BLOWN UP!
GAAAN (BOOOOM)
ハルヒ
KATA (CLACK)
WAH! WAAH!?
KATA
KATA
KATA
KATA

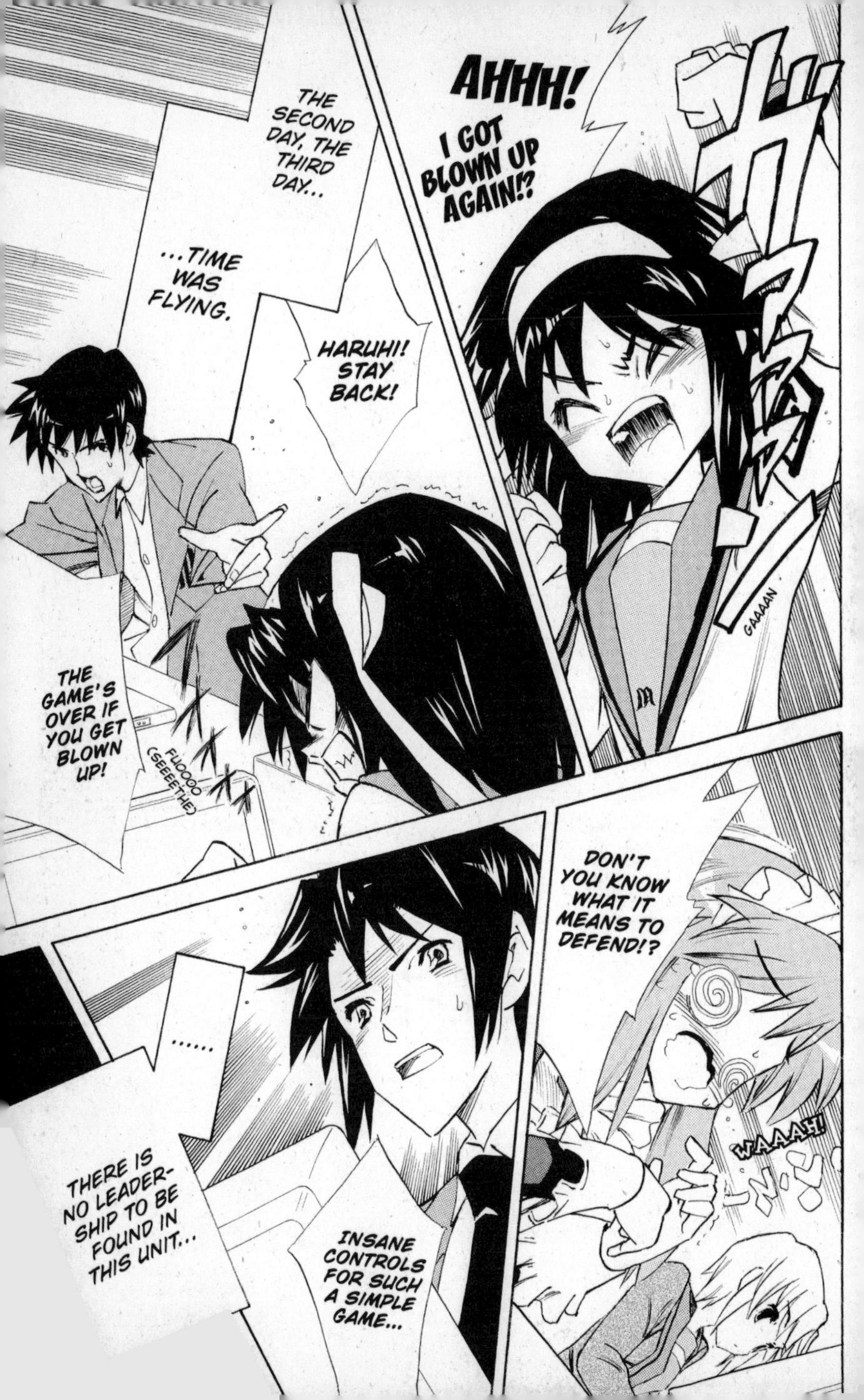
AHHHH!
I GOT BLOWN UP AGAIN!?
GAAAAN
THE SECOND DAY, THE THIRD DAY...
...TIME WAS FLYING.
HARUHI! STAY BACK!
THE GAME'S OVER IF YOU GET BLOWN UP!
FUOOOO (SEEEETHE)
DON'T YOU KNOW WHAT IT MEANS TO DEFEND!?
WAAAH!
......
INSANE CONTROLS FOR SUCH A SIMPLE GAME...
THERE IS NO LEADER-SHIP TO BE FOUND IN THIS UNIT...

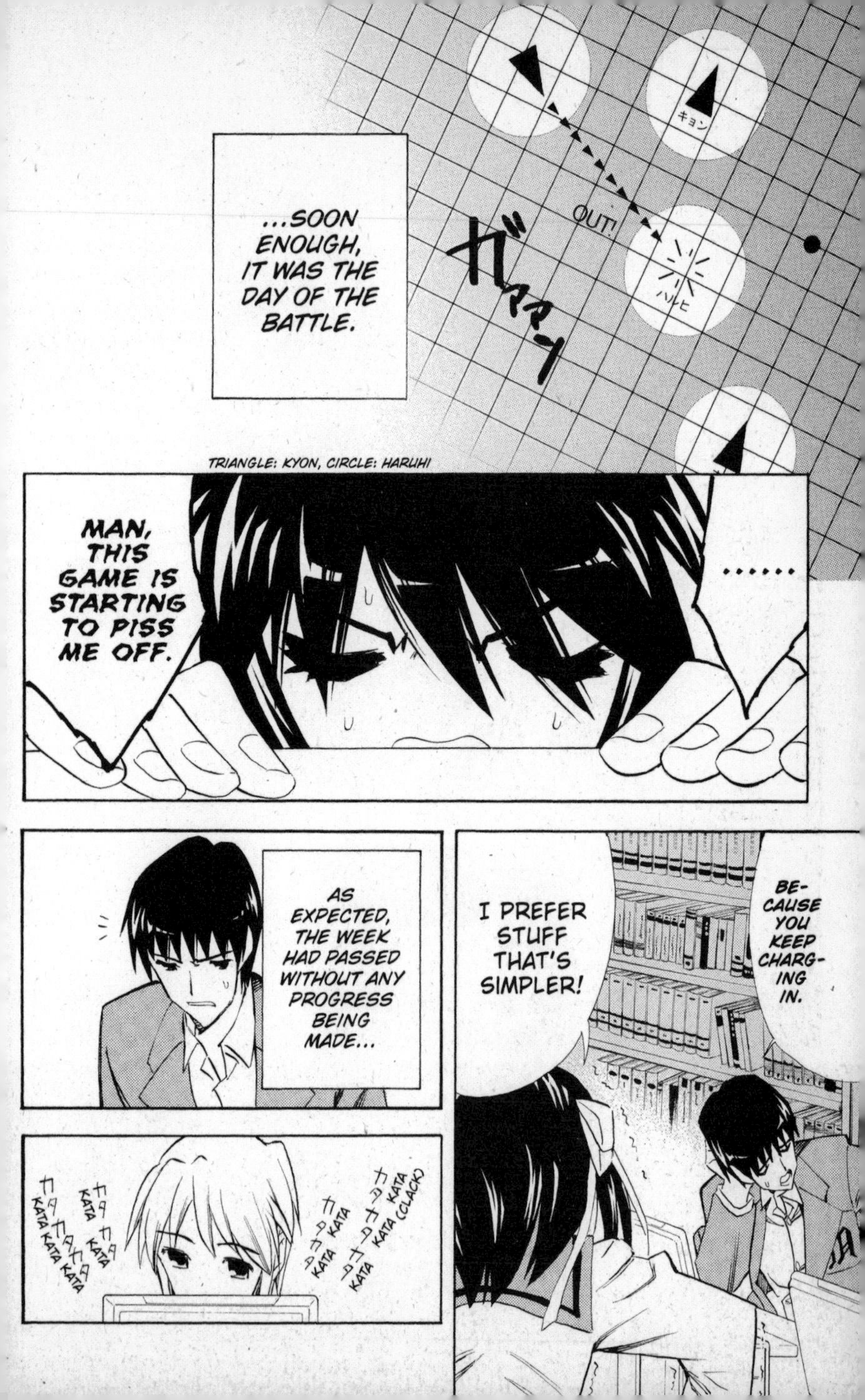
キョン
OUT!
ハルヒ
...SOON ENOUGH, IT WAS THE DAY OF THE BATTLE.
TRIANGLE: KYON, CIRCLE: HARUHI
......
MAN, THIS GAME IS STARTING TO PISS ME OFF.
BE-CAUSE YOU KEEP CHARG-ING IN.
I PREFER STUFF THAT'S SIMPLER!
AS EXPECTED, THE WEEK HAD PASSED WITHOUT ANY PROGRESS BEING MADE...
KATA KATA (CLACK)
KATA KATA
KATA KATA
KATA KATA KATA

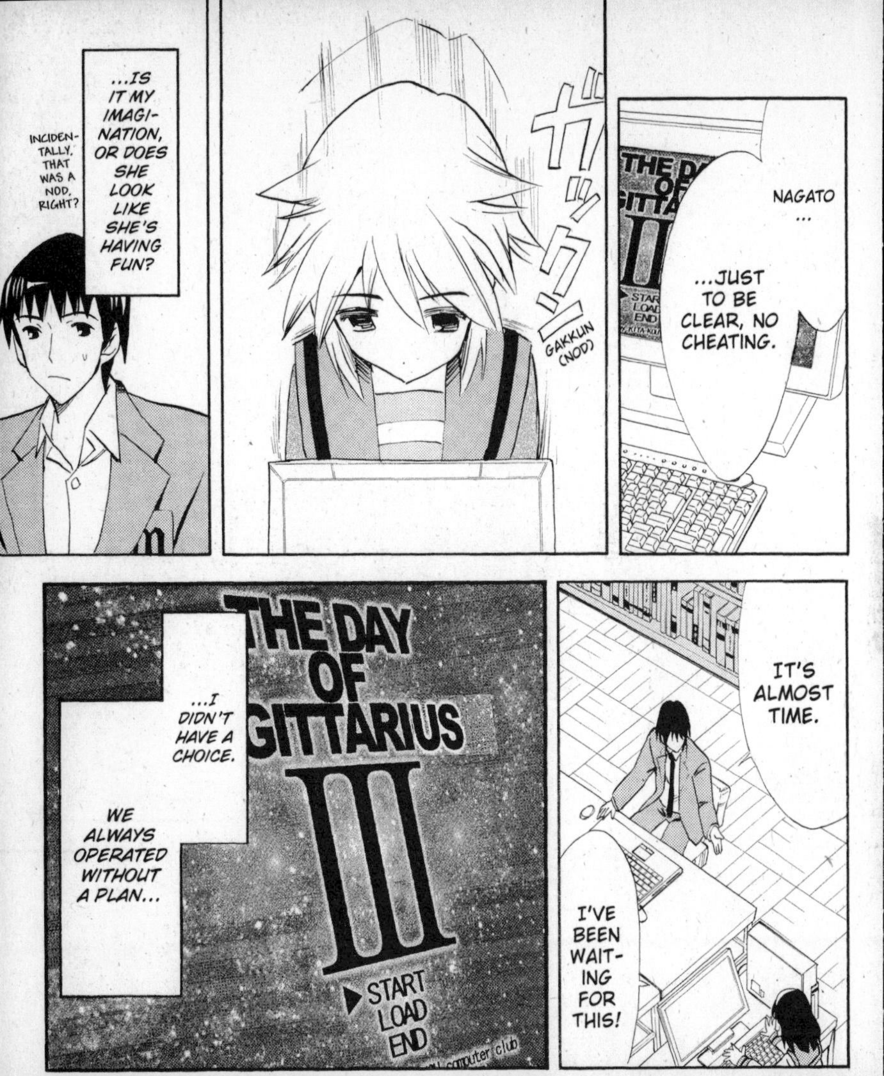
NAGATO...
...JUST TO BE CLEAR, NO CHEATING.
THE DAY OF GITTARIUS III
START LOAD END
GAKKUN (NOD)
...IS IT MY IMAGINATION, OR DOES SHE LOOK LIKE SHE'S HAVING FUN?
INCIDENTALLY, THAT WAS A NOD, RIGHT?
IT'S ALMOST TIME.
I'VE BEEN WAITING FOR THIS!
THE DAY OF GITTARIUS III
START
LOAD
END
computer club
...I DIDN'T HAVE A CHOICE.
WE ALWAYS OPERATED WITHOUT A PLAN...

1600 HOURS:
BATTLE START

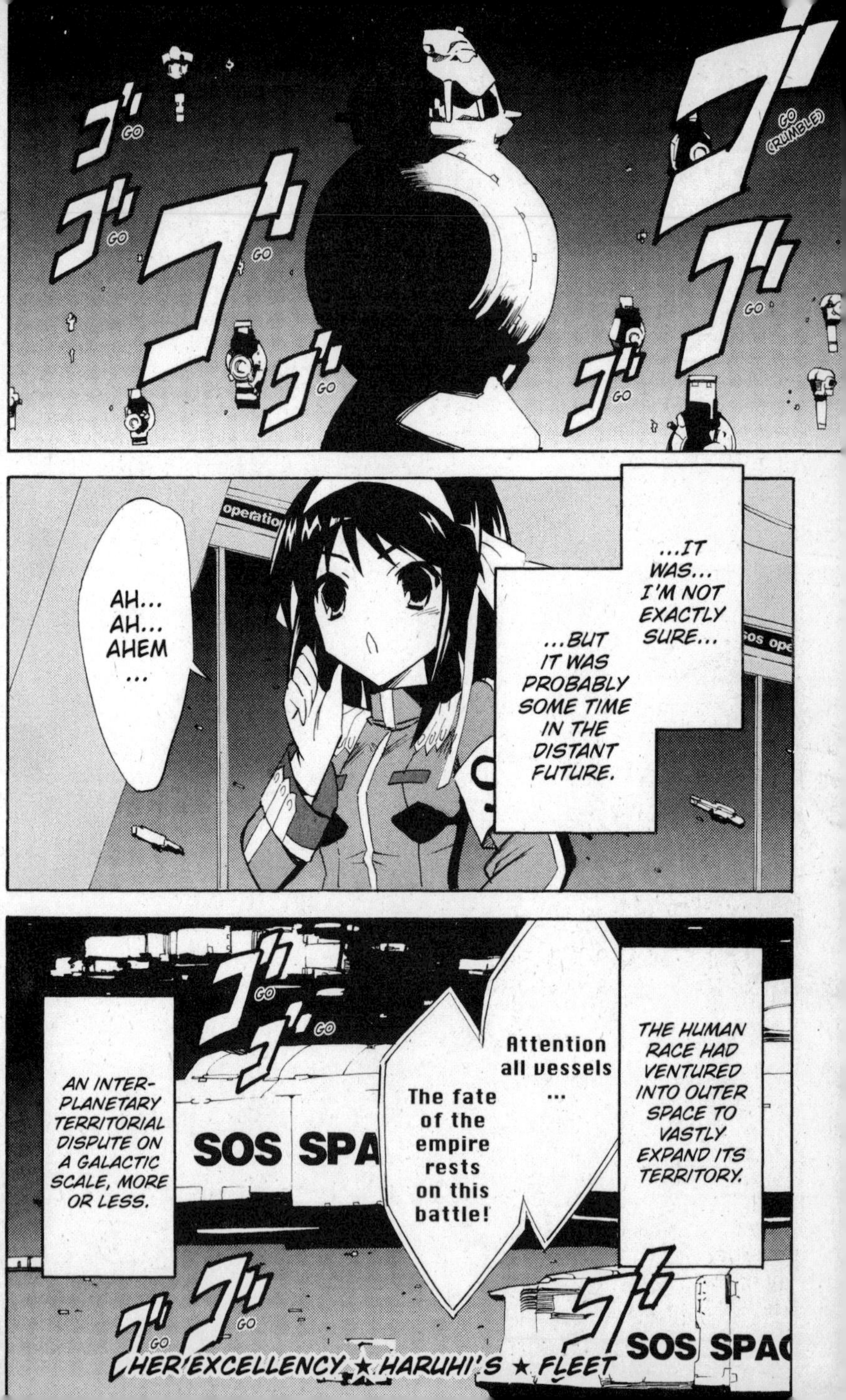
GO (RUMBLE)
GO
GO
GO
GO
GO
GO
GO
...IT WAS... I'M NOT EXACTLY SURE...
...BUT IT WAS PROBABLY SOME TIME IN THE DISTANT FUTURE.
AH... AH... AHEM ...
GO
GO
THE HUMAN RACE HAD VENTURED INTO OUTER SPACE TO VASTLY EXPAND ITS TERRITORY.
Attention all vessels ...
The fate of the empire rests on this battle!
AN INTER-PLANETARY TERRITORIAL DISPUTE ON A GALACTIC SCALE, MORE OR LESS.
GO
GO
HER EXCELLENCY ★ HARUHI'S ★ FLEET

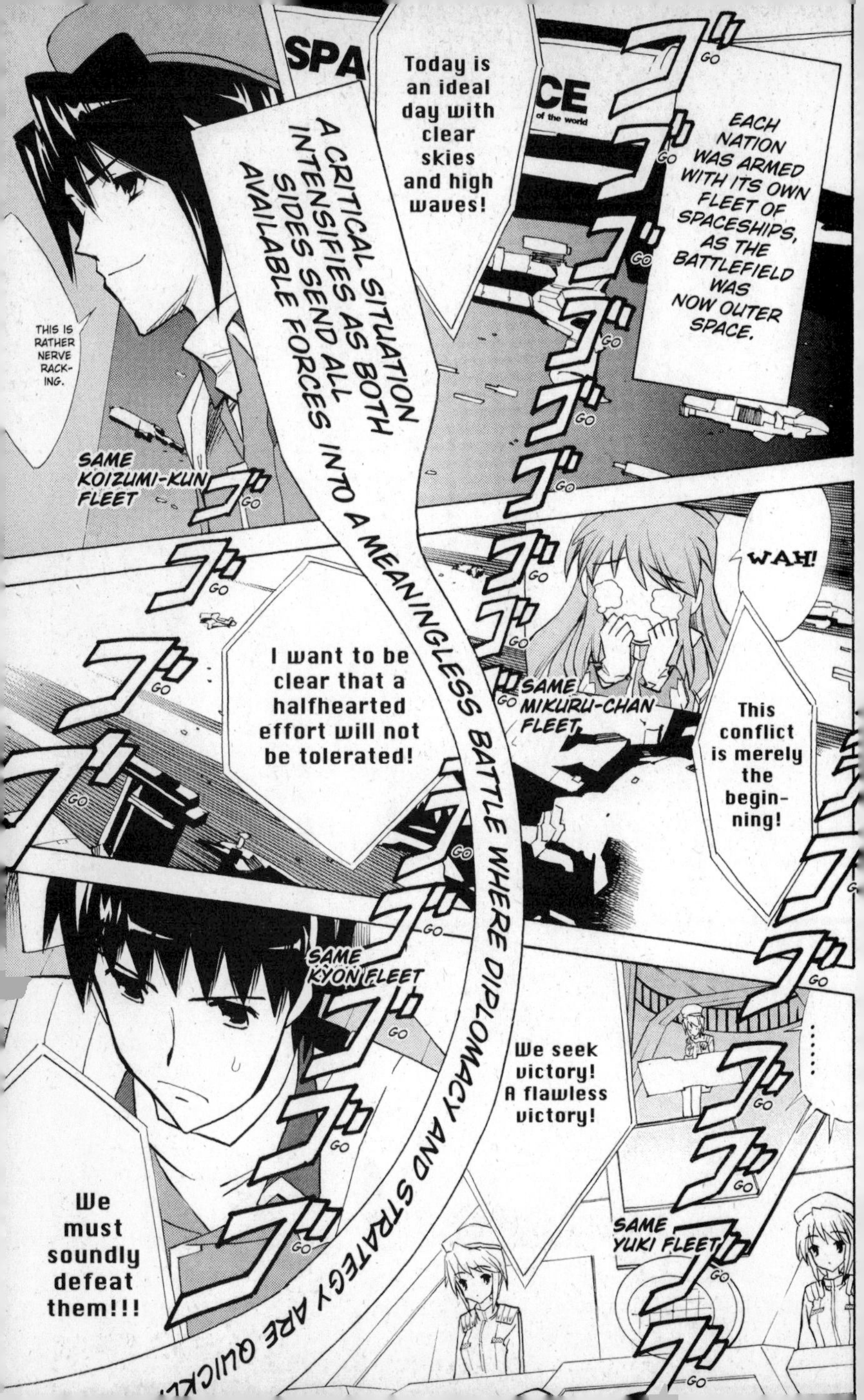
EACH NATION WAS ARMED WITH ITS OWN FLEET OF SPACESHIPS, AS THE BATTLEFIELD WAS NOW OUTER SPACE.
GO
Today is an ideal day with clear skies and high waves!
A CRITICAL SITUATION INTENSIFIES AS BOTH SIDES SEND ALL AVAILABLE FORCES INTO A MEANINGLESS BATTLE WHERE DIPLOMACY AND STRATEGY ARE QUICKL
THIS IS RATHER NERVE RACK-ING.
SAME KOIZUMI-KUN FLEET
GO
WAH!
This conflict is merely the begin-ning!
SAME MIKURU-CHAN FLEET
I want to be clear that a halfhearted effort will not be tolerated!
GO
......
SAME YUKI FLEET
We seek victory! A flawless victory!
SAME KYON FLEET
We must soundly defeat them!!!
GO

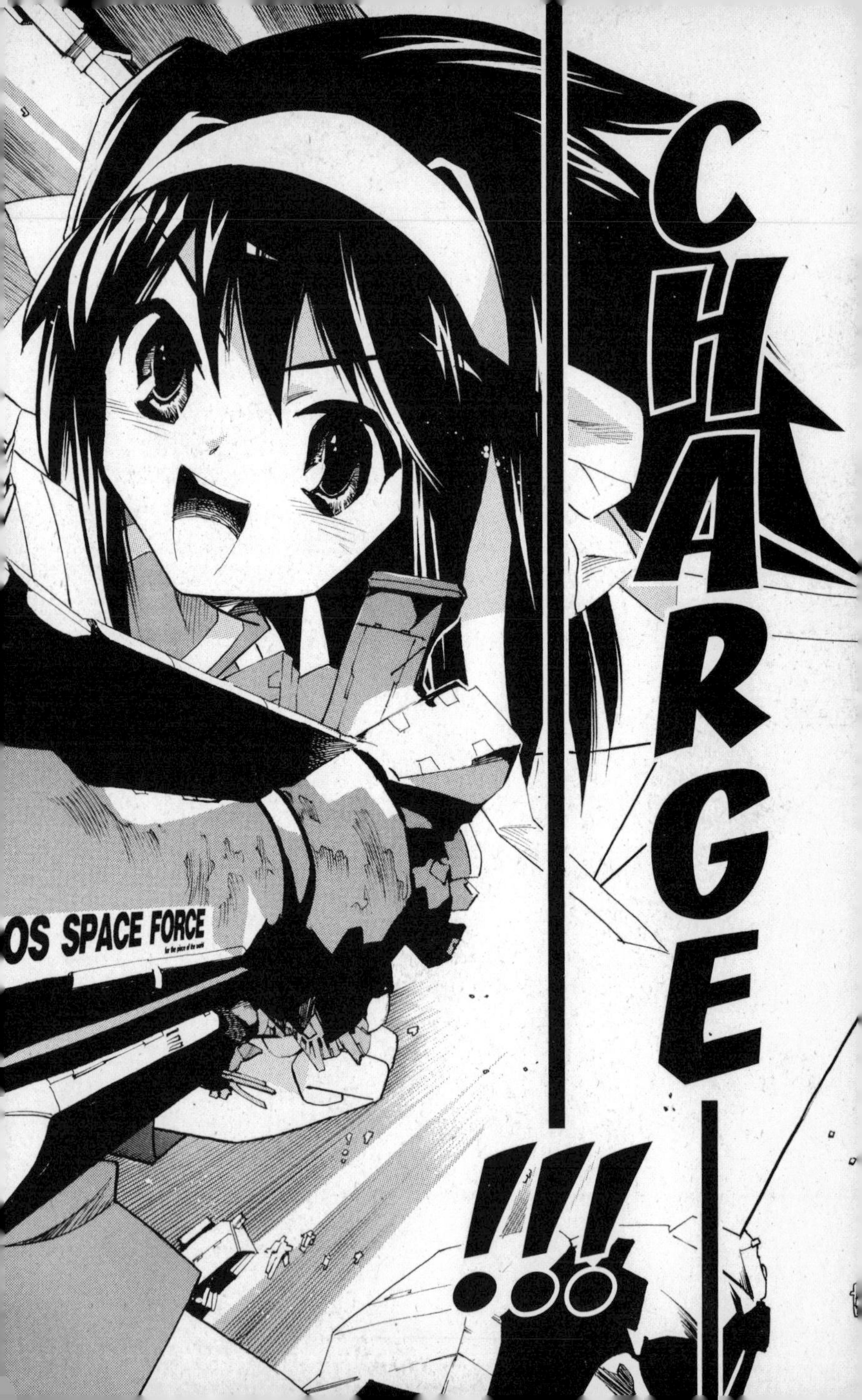
CHARGE!!!...
OS SPACE FORCE

1600 HOURS:
HER EXCELLENCY ★ HARUHI'S ★ FLEET
AND THE REST OF THE SOS
BRIGADE SPACE FORCE
ADVANCE INTO COMPUTER SOCIETY
SPACE FORCE TERRITORY!!!
DESTROY THEM ALL!!!

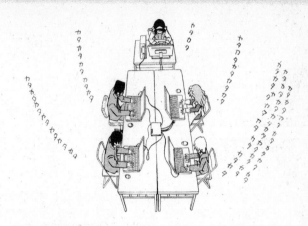

SFX: KATA (CLACK) KATA KATA KATA KATA KATA KATA KATA KATA KATA KATA KATA KATA KATA

AND SO, THE EXTREMELY SIMPLE BATTLE BEGAN.

WE WERE ABLE TO LOCATE THE ENEMY RIGHT OFF THE BAT.

WHOA...

NATURALLY, ALL CREDIT WENT TO NAGATO'S SCOUTING.

YO!

YO!

ASAHINA-SAN AND HARUHI ARE USELESS.

AH!

SHIT!

WE'RE ALREADY AT A FIVE-THREE DISADVANTAGE, SO I HAD TO MAKE UP THE DIFFERENCE...

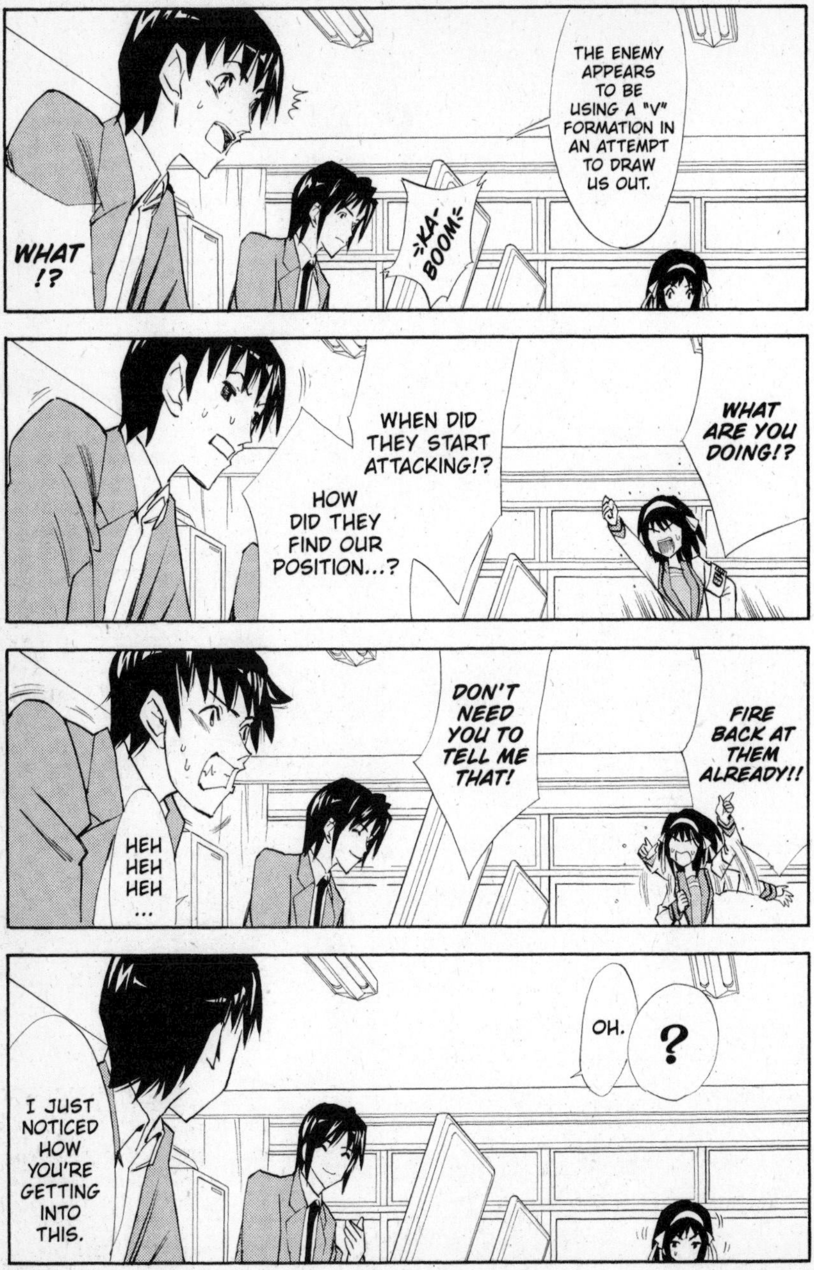
THE ENEMY APPEARS TO BE USING A "V" FORMATION IN AN ATTEMPT TO DRAW US OUT.
KA-BOOM
WHAT!?
WHAT ARE YOU DOING!?
WHEN DID THEY START ATTACKING!?
HOW DID THEY FIND OUR POSITION...?
FIRE BACK AT THEM ALREADY!!
DON'T NEED YOU TO TELL ME THAT!
HEH HEH HEH...
?
OH.
I JUST NOTICED HOW YOU'RE GETTING INTO THIS.

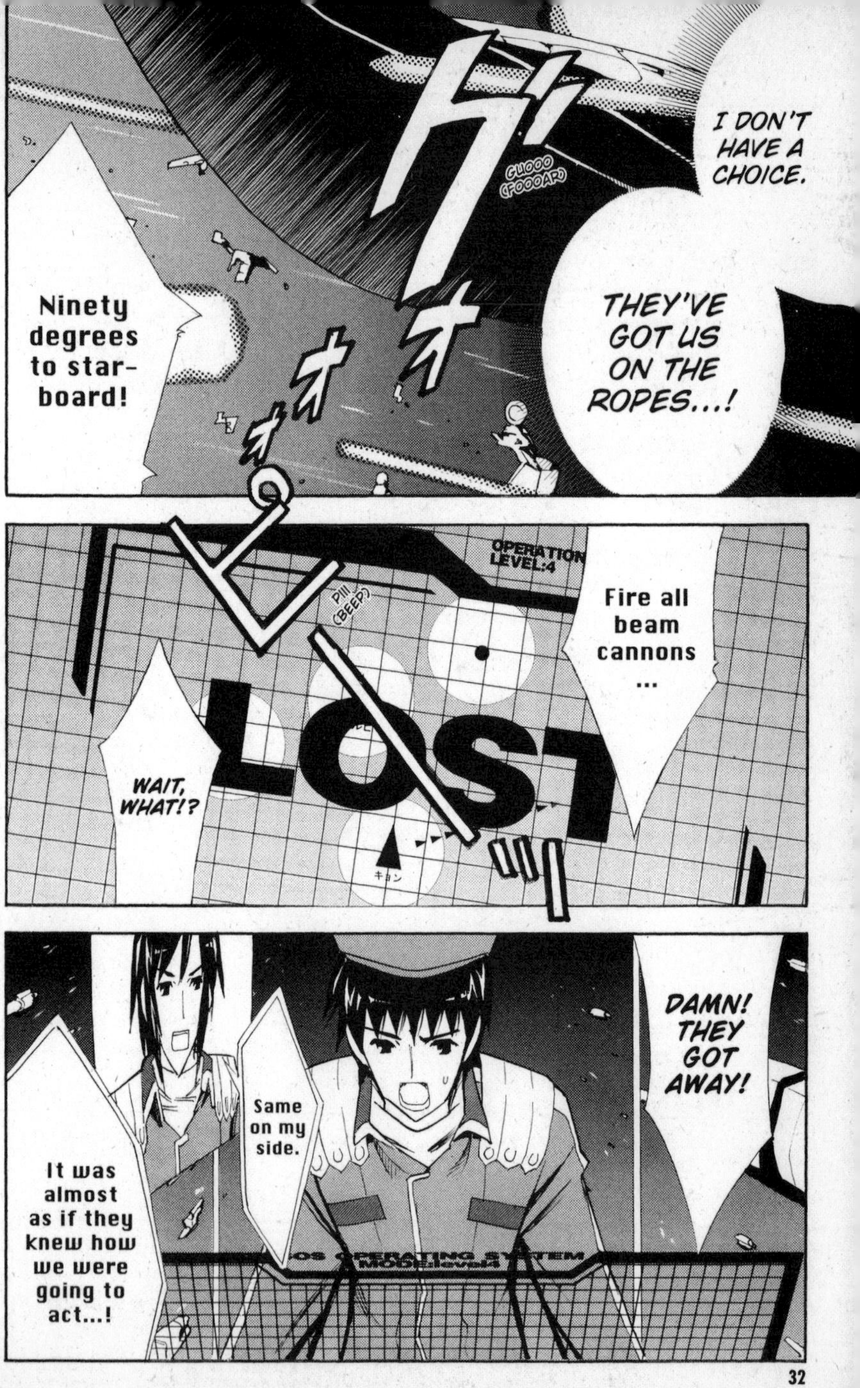
I DON'T HAVE A CHOICE.
THEY'VE GOT US ON THE ROPES...!
GUOOO (FOOOAR)
Ninety degrees to starboard!
OPERATION LEVEL:4
Fire all beam cannons ...
PIII (BEEP)
LOST
WAIT, WHAT!?
DAMN! THEY GOT AWAY!
Same on my side.
It was almost as if they knew how we were going to act...!

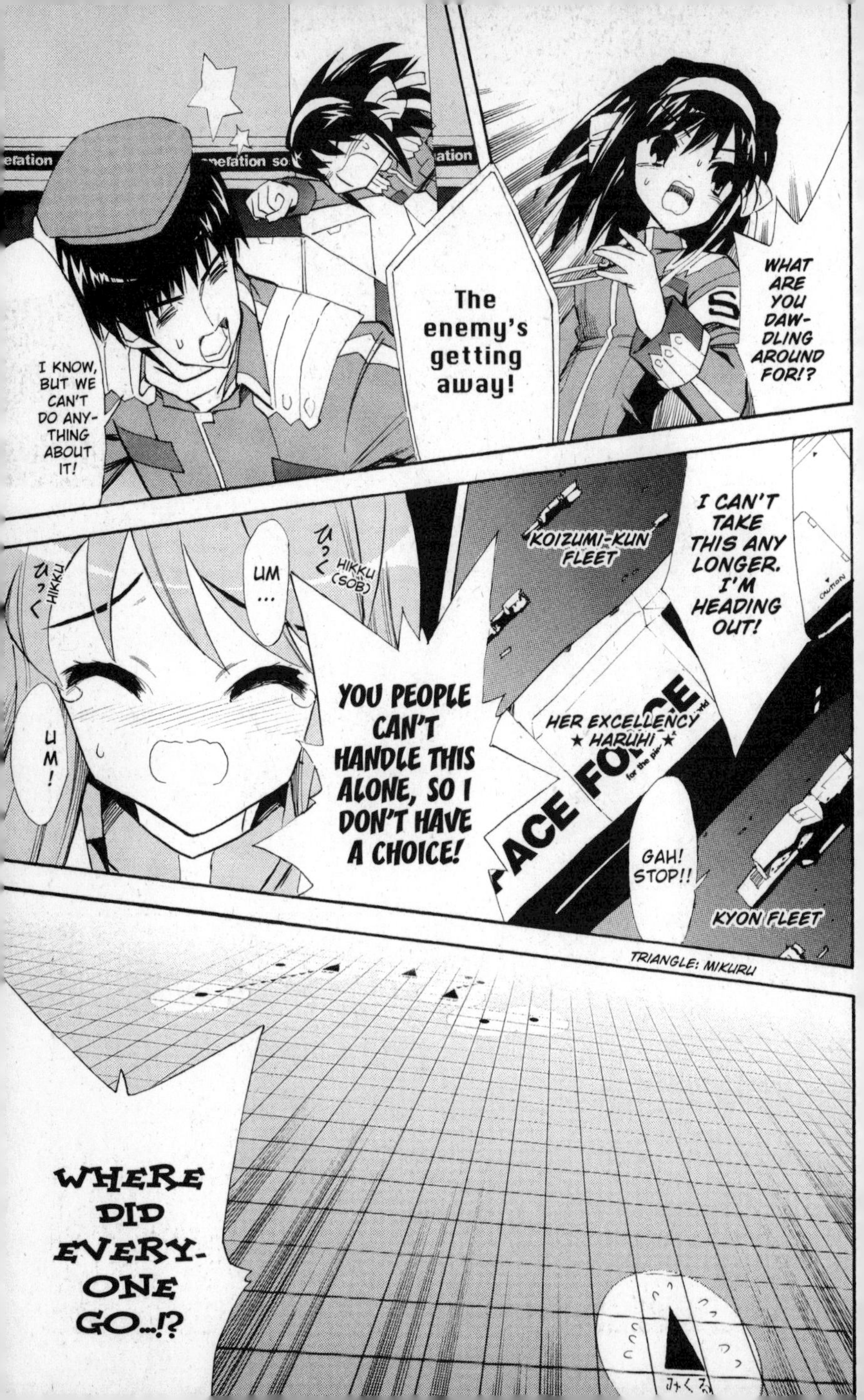
WHAT ARE YOU DAWDLING AROUND FOR!?
The enemy's getting away!
I KNOW, BUT WE CAN'T DO ANYTHING ABOUT IT!
I CAN'T TAKE THIS ANY LONGER. I'M HEADING OUT!
KOIZUMI-KUN FLEET
HER EXCELLENCY ★ HARUHI ★
YOU PEOPLE CAN'T HANDLE THIS ALONE, SO I DON'T HAVE A CHOICE!
GAH! STOP!!
KYON FLEET
HIKKU (SOB)
UM ...
HIKKU
UM!
TRIANGLE: MIKURU
WHERE DID EVERY-ONE GO...!?

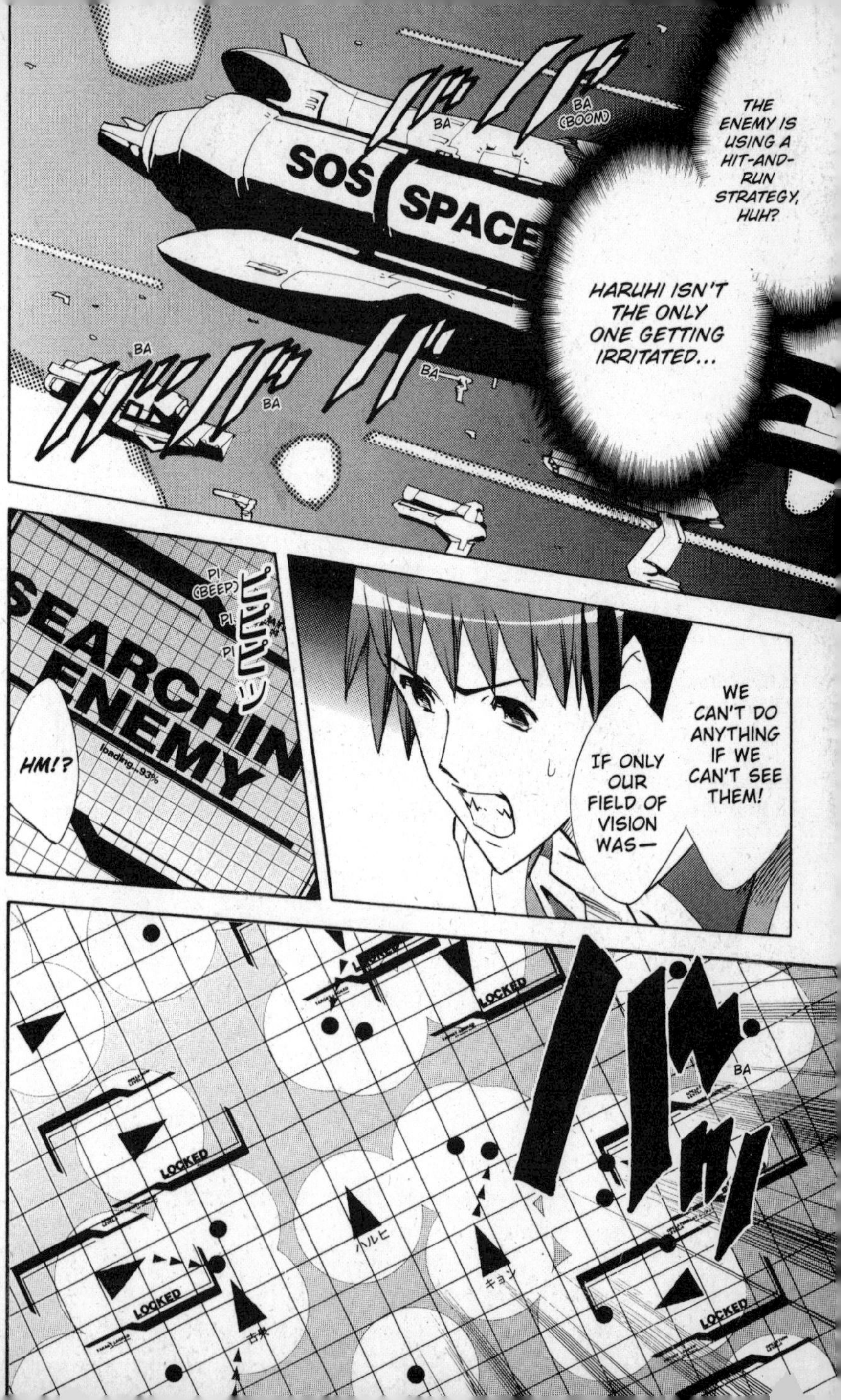
THE ENEMY IS USING A HIT-AND-RUN STRATEGY, HUH?
HARUHI ISN'T THE ONLY ONE GETTING IRRITATED...
BA (BOOM)
BA
SOS SPACE
BA
BA
BA
WE CAN'T DO ANYTHING IF WE CAN'T SEE THEM!
IF ONLY OUR FIELD OF VISION WAS—
PI (BEEP)
PI
PI
SEARCHIN ENEMY
loading...93%
HM!?
BA
LOCKED
LOCKED
LOCKED
LOCKED
ハルヒ
キョン
古泉

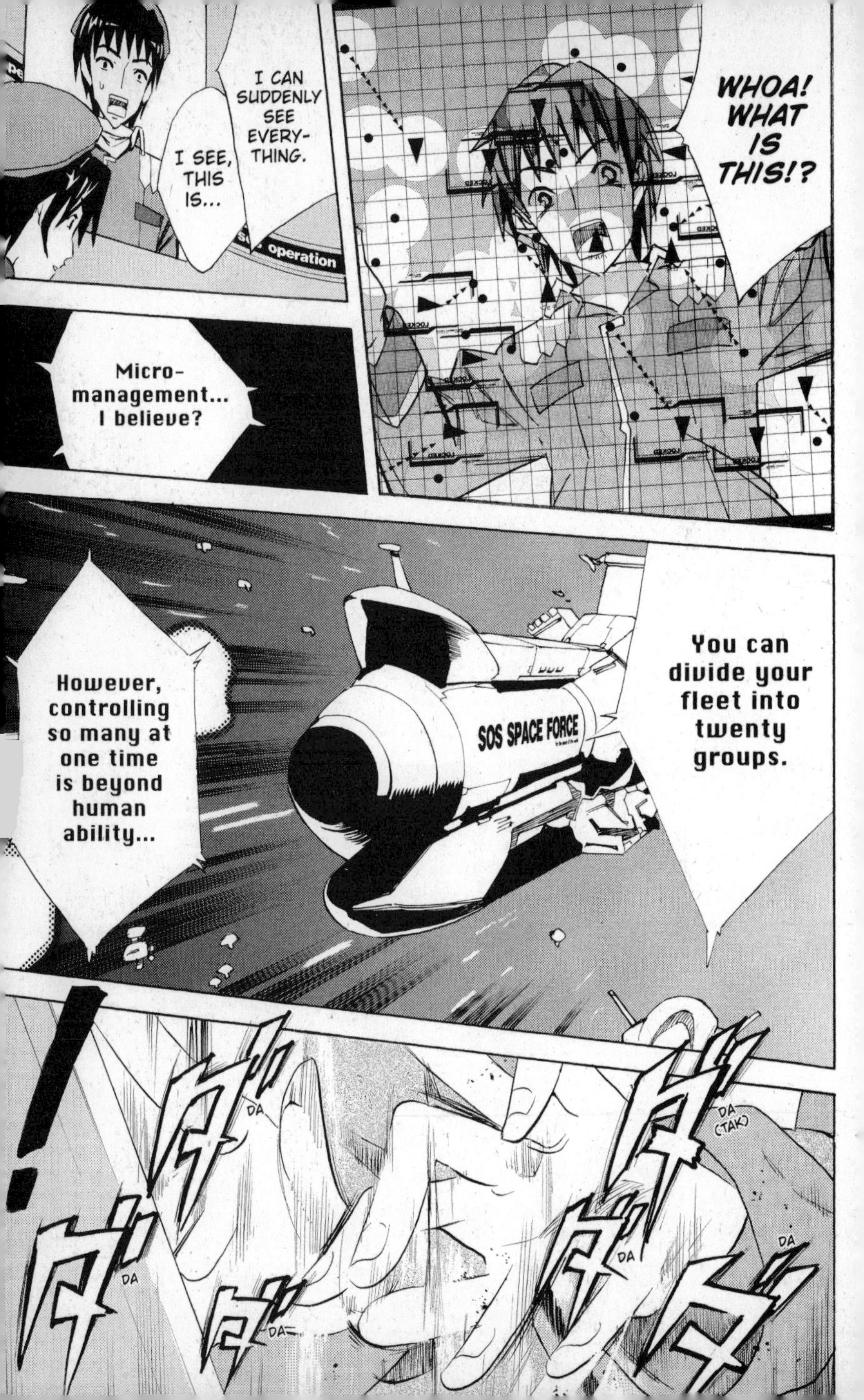
WHOA! WHAT IS THIS!?
I CAN SUDDENLY SEE EVERYTHING.
I SEE, THIS IS...
operation
Micro-management... I believe?
You can divide your fleet into twenty groups.
SOS SPACE FORCE
However, controlling so many at one time is beyond human ability...
DA (TAK)
DA
DA
DA
DA
DA...

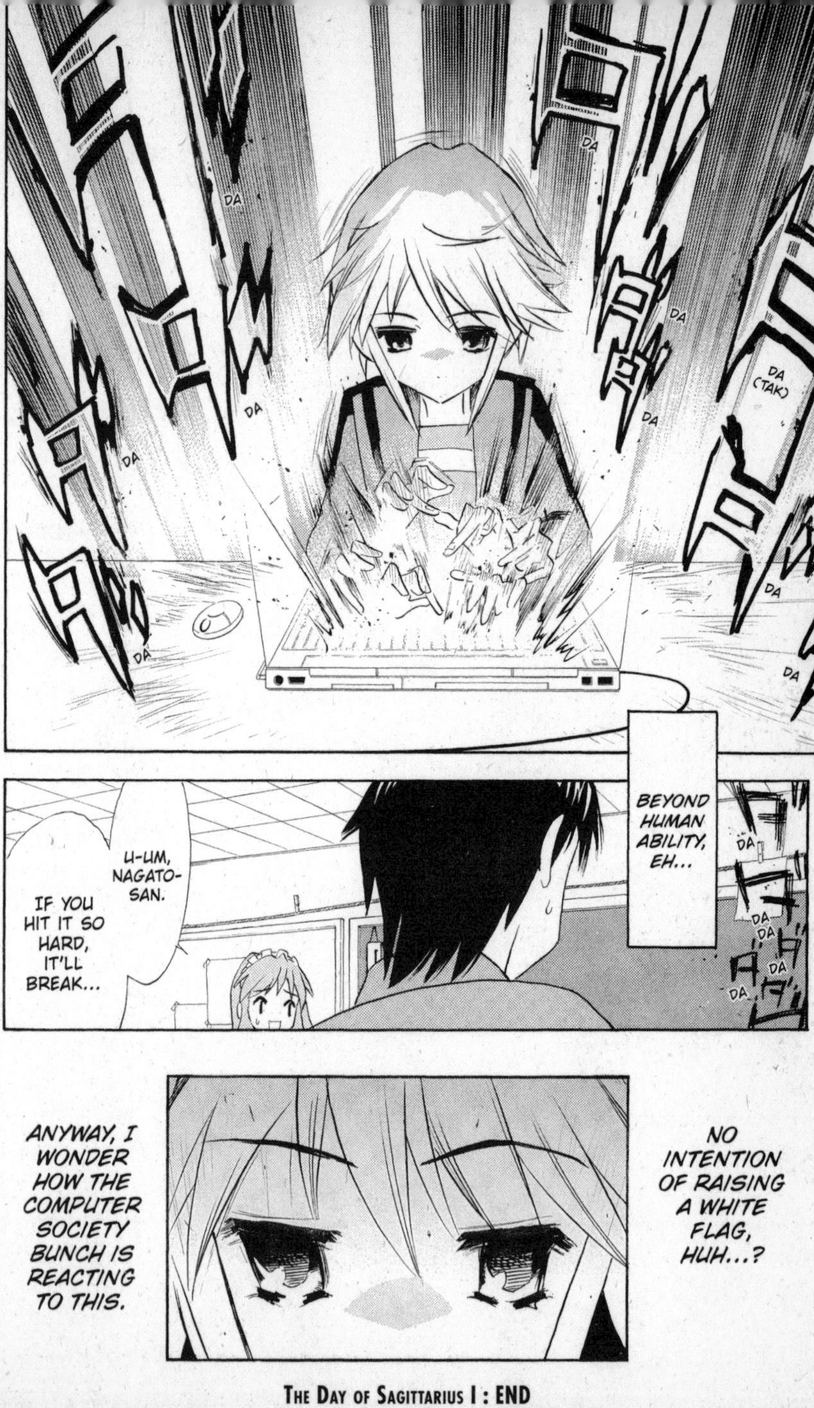
DA
DA (TAK)
DA
DA
DA
DA
DA
DA
DA
BEYOND HUMAN ABILITY, EH...
DA
DA
DA
DA
DA
U-UM, NAGATO-SAN.
IF YOU HIT IT SO HARD, IT'LL BREAK...
NO INTENTION OF RAISING A WHITE FLAG, HUH...?
ANYWAY, I WONDER HOW THE COMPUTER SOCIETY BUNCH IS REACTING TO THIS.

The Day of Sagittarius I : END

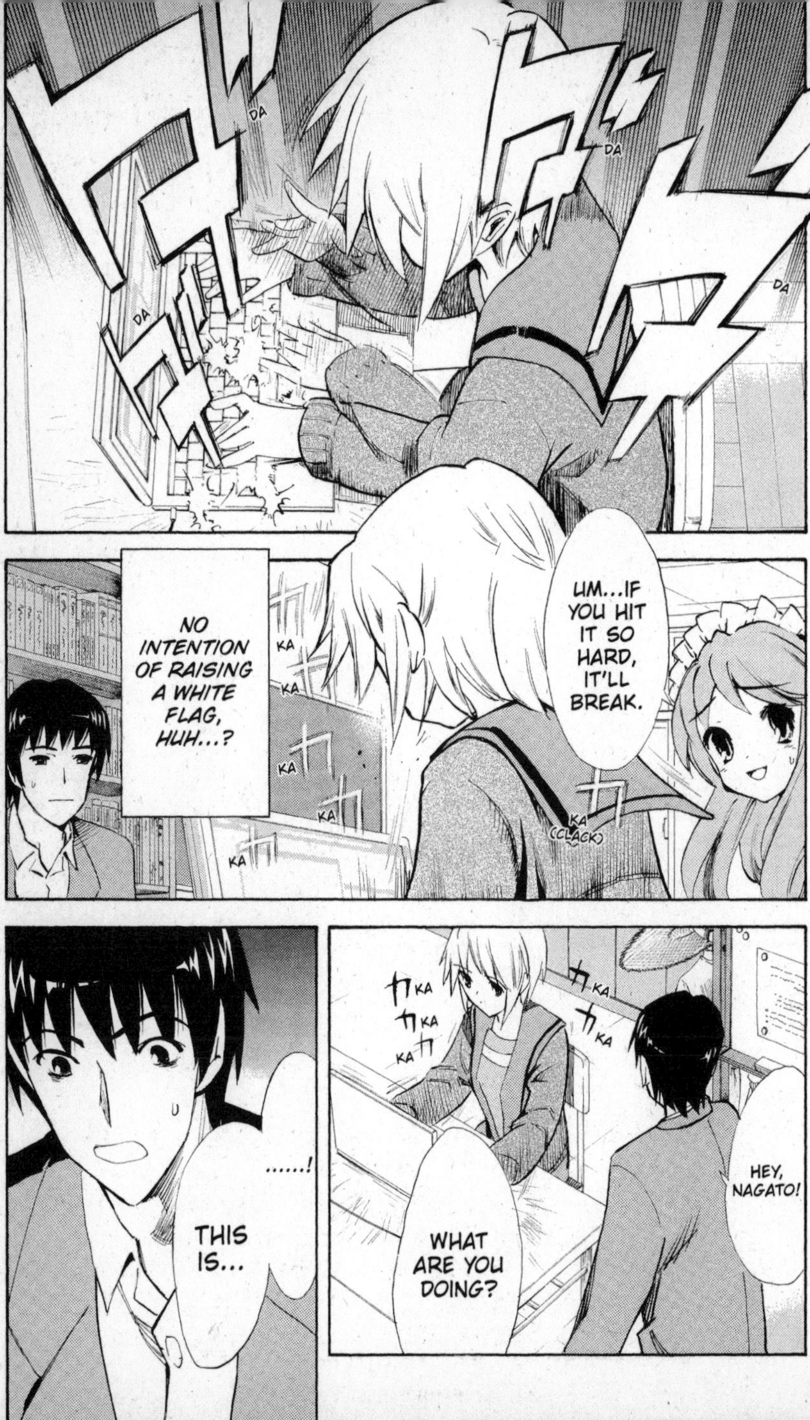
DA
DA
DA
DA
UM...IF YOU HIT IT SO HARD, IT'LL BREAK.
NO INTENTION OF RAISING A WHITE FLAG, HUH...?
KA (CLACK)
KA
KA
KA
KA
KA
HEY, NAGATO!
WHAT ARE YOU DOING?
KA
KA
KA
KA
KA
......!
THIS IS...

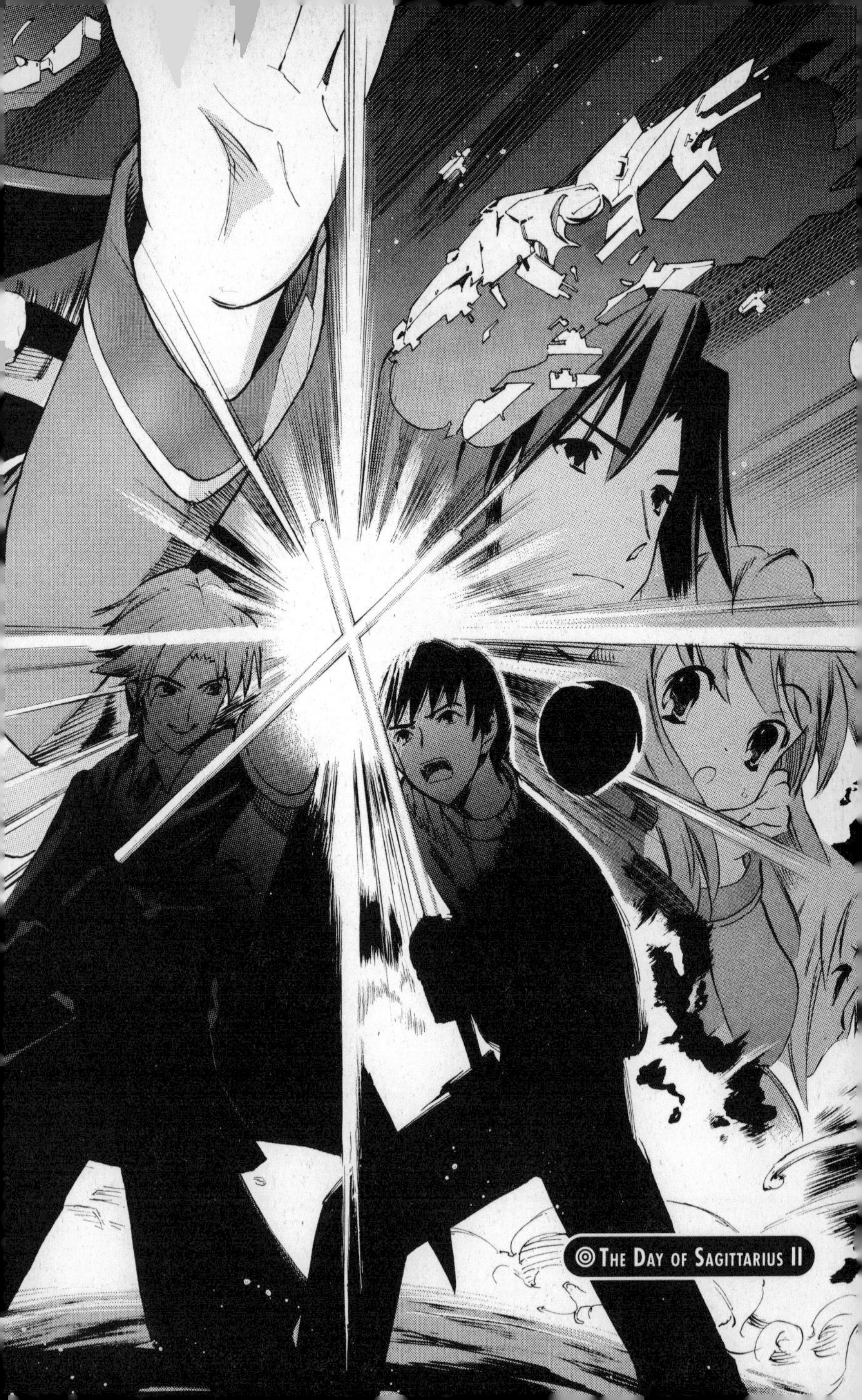
◎The Day of Sagittarius II

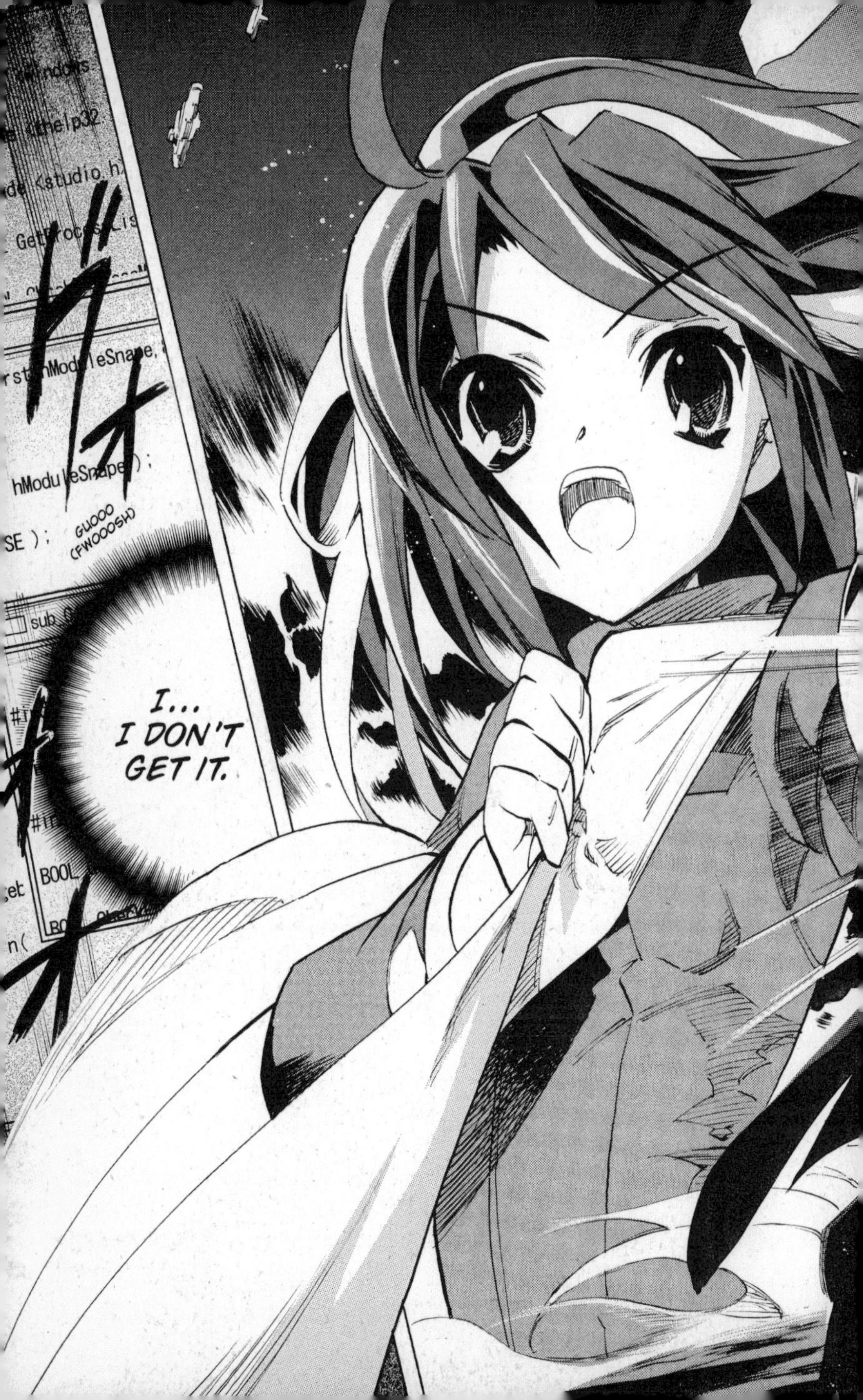
GUOOO (FWOOOSH)
I... I DON'T GET IT.

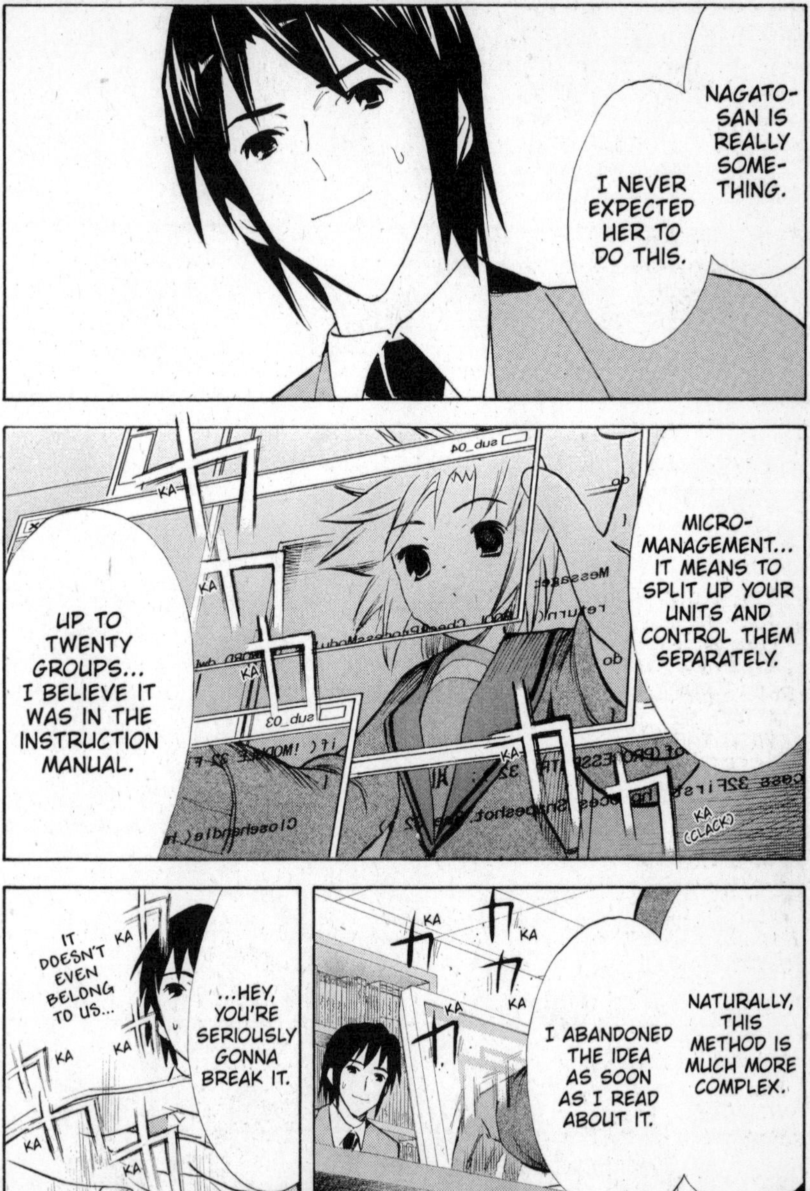
NAGATO-SAN IS REALLY SOMETHING.
I NEVER EXPECTED HER TO DO THIS.
MICRO-MANAGEMENT... IT MEANS TO SPLIT UP YOUR UNITS AND CONTROL THEM SEPARATELY.
KA (CLACK)
KA
UP TO TWENTY GROUPS... I BELIEVE IT WAS IN THE INSTRUCTION MANUAL.
NATURALLY, THIS METHOD IS MUCH MORE COMPLEX.
I ABANDONED THE IDEA AS SOON AS I READ ABOUT IT.
KA
...HEY, YOU'RE SERIOUSLY GONNA BREAK IT.
IT DOESN'T EVEN BELONG TO US...
KA

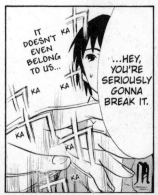

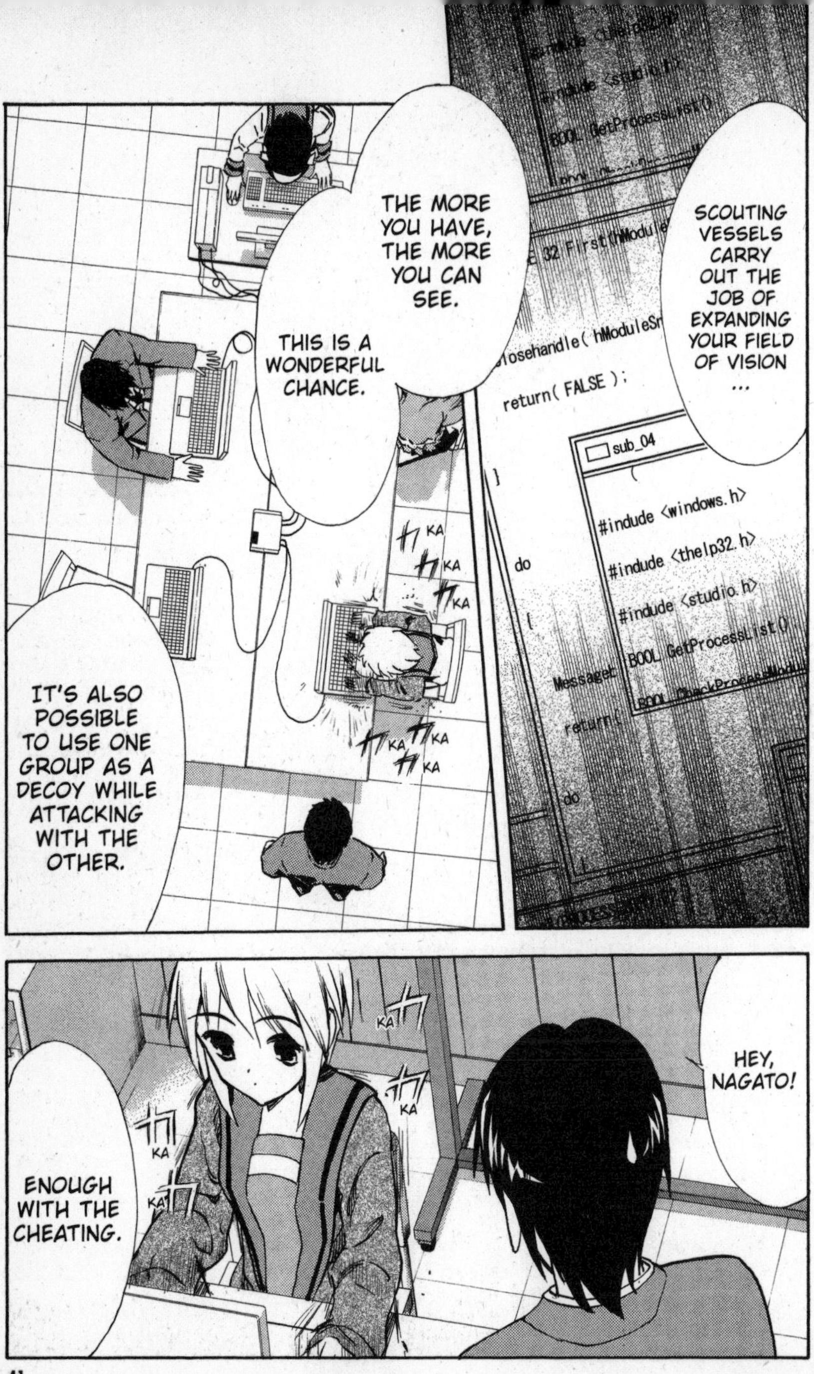
SCOUTING VESSELS CARRY OUT THE JOB OF EXPANDING YOUR FIELD OF VISION ...
return(FALSE);
sub_04
#indude <windows.h>
#indude <thelp32.h>
#indude <studio.h>
BOOL GetProcessList()
do
THE MORE YOU HAVE, THE MORE YOU CAN SEE.
THIS IS A WONDERFUL CHANCE.
KA KA KA
KA KA KA
IT'S ALSO POSSIBLE TO USE ONE GROUP AS A DECOY WHILE ATTACKING WITH THE OTHER.
HEY, NAGATO!
KA KA
KA KA
ENOUGH WITH THE CHEATING.

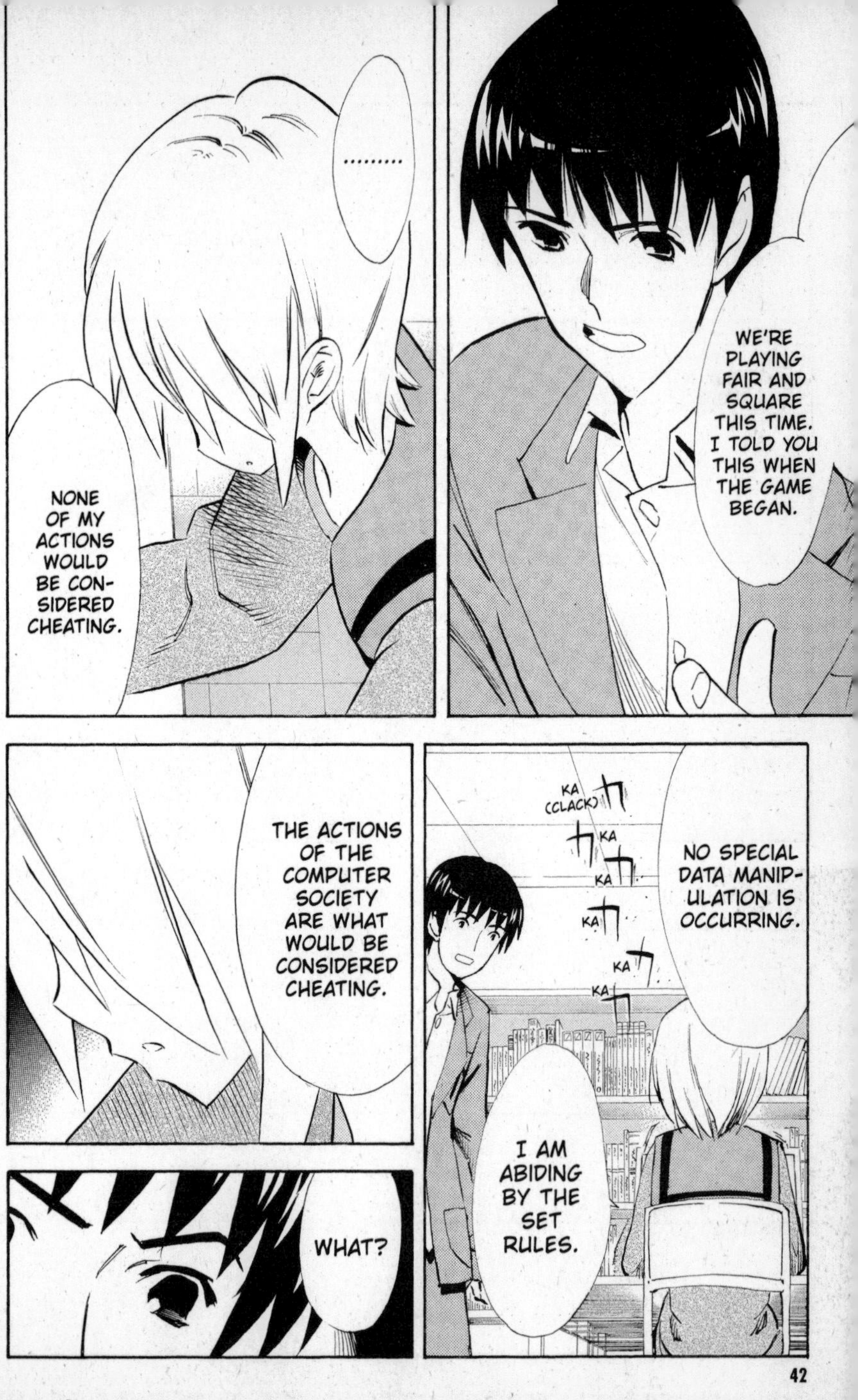
WE'RE PLAYING FAIR AND SQUARE THIS TIME. I TOLD YOU THIS WHEN THE GAME BEGAN.
....
NONE OF MY ACTIONS WOULD BE CON-SIDERED CHEATING.
NO SPECIAL DATA MANIP-ULATION IS OCCURRING.
KA (CLACK)
KA
KA
KA
KA
KA
I AM ABIDING BY THE SET RULES.
THE ACTIONS OF THE COMPUTER SOCIETY ARE WHAT WOULD BE CONSIDERED CHEATING.
WHAT?

THEIR FOG OF WAR HAS BEEN TURNED **OFF.**

THE ENTIRE MAP WAS VISIBLE FROM THE BEGINNING.

THAT IS NOT ALL.

WHAT!?

DOTS: YUKI, TRIANGLES: HARUHI, KOIZUMI

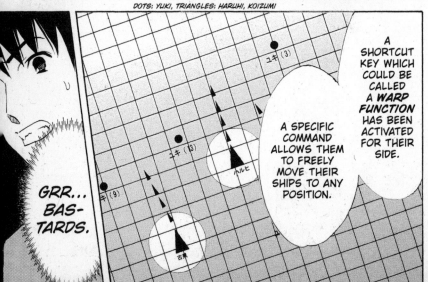

A SHORTCUT KEY WHICH COULD BE CALLED A **WARP FUNCTION** HAS BEEN ACTIVATED FOR THEIR SIDE.

A SPECIFIC COMMAND ALLOWS THEM TO FREELY MOVE THEIR SHIPS TO ANY POSITION.

GRR... BAS-TARDS.

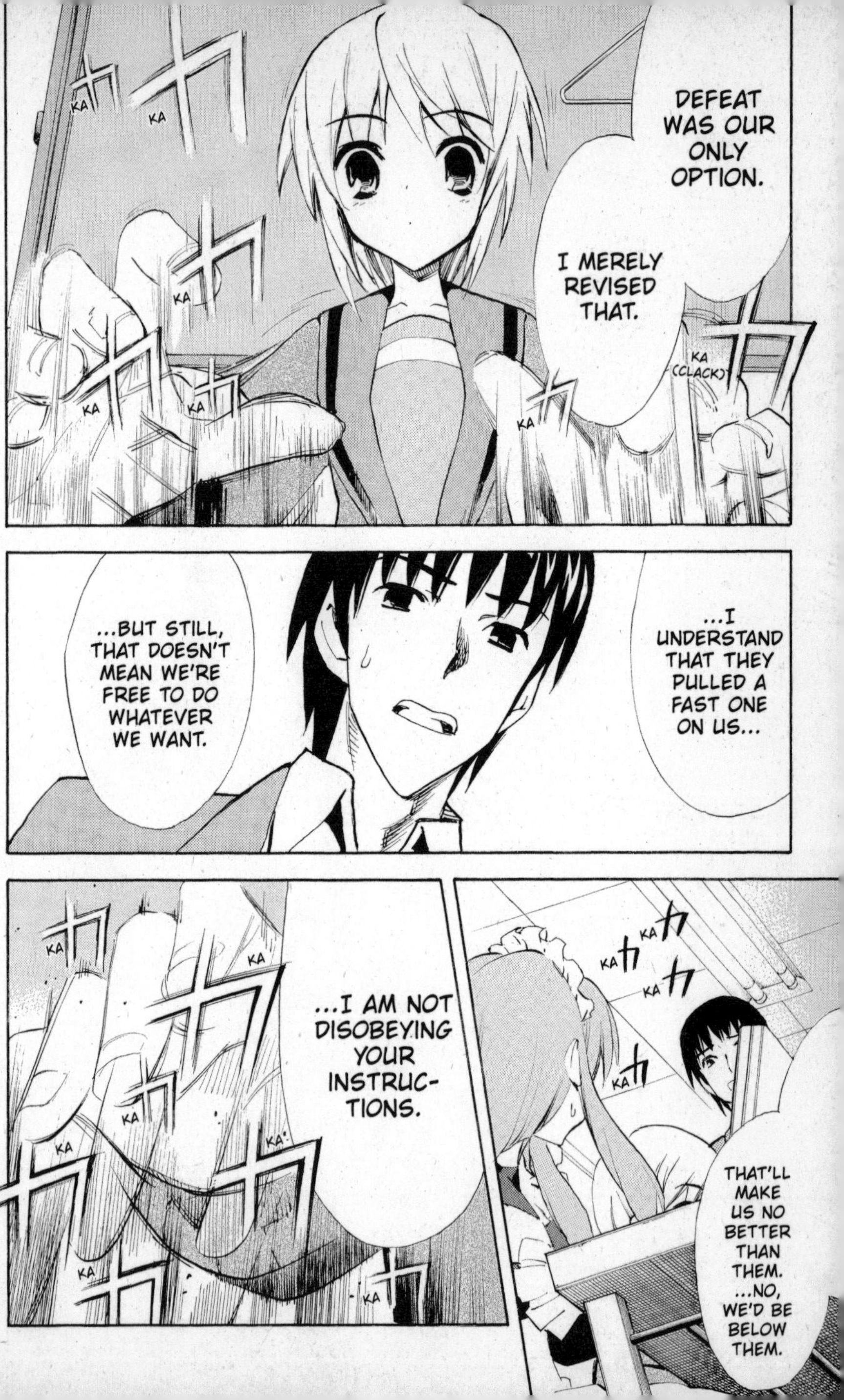
DEFEAT WAS OUR ONLY OPTION.
I MERELY REVISED THAT.
KA (CLACK)
KA
KA
KA
KA
KA
KA
...I UNDERSTAND THAT THEY PULLED A FAST ONE ON US...
...BUT STILL, THAT DOESN'T MEAN WE'RE FREE TO DO WHATEVER WE WANT.
KA
KA
KA
KA
THAT'LL MAKE US NO BETTER THAN THEM. ...NO, WE'D BE BELOW THEM.
KA
KA
KA
KA
KA
KA
KA
...I AM NOT DISOBEYING YOUR INSTRUCTIONS.

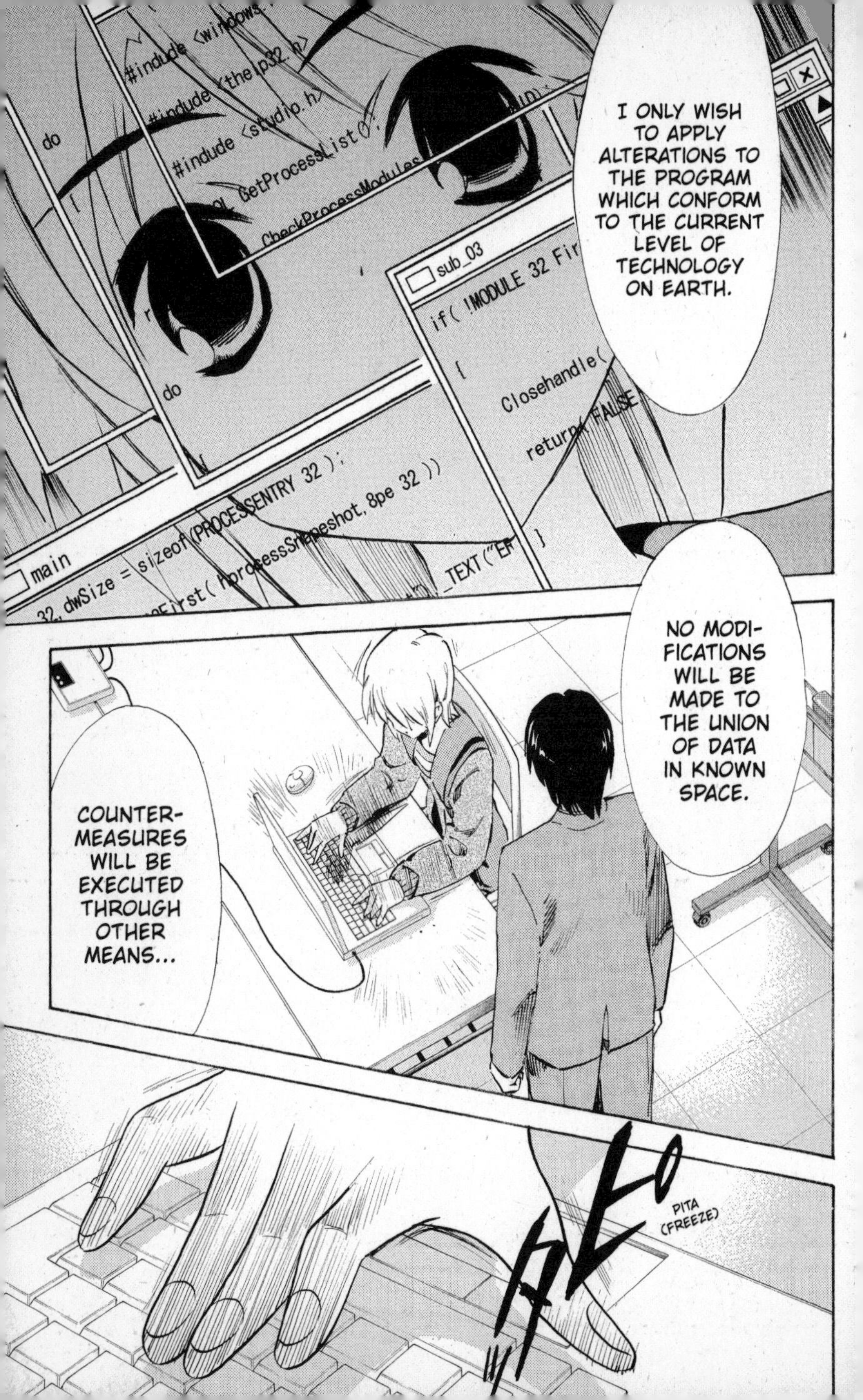
I ONLY WISH TO APPLY ALTERATIONS TO THE PROGRAM WHICH CONFORM TO THE CURRENT LEVEL OF TECHNOLOGY ON EARTH.
NO MODIFICATIONS WILL BE MADE TO THE UNION OF DATA IN KNOWN SPACE.
COUNTER-MEASURES WILL BE EXECUTED THROUGH OTHER MEANS...
PITA (FREEZE)

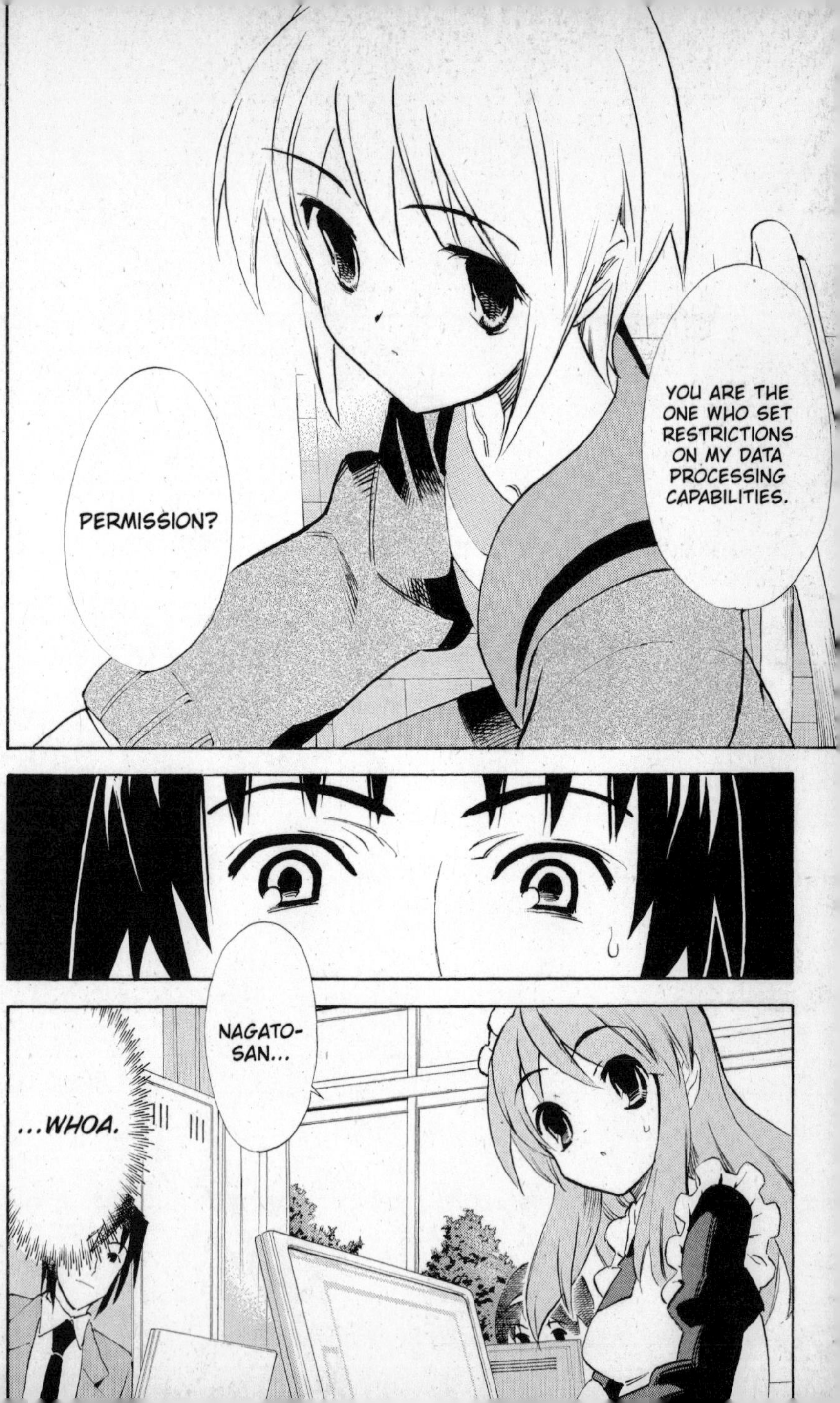
YOU ARE THE ONE WHO SET RESTRICTIONS ON MY DATA PROCESSING CAPABILITIES.
PERMISSION?
NAGATO-SAN...
...WHOA.

IT'S BEEN OVER HALF A YEAR SINCE WE FIRST MET...

...BUT I'VE NEVER SEEN SUCH DETERMINATION IN HER EYES.

COULD IT BE THAT... YOU WANT TO WIN?

...HEH.

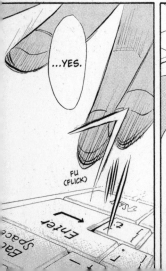

...YES.

FU (FLICK)

OKAY.

GO FOR IT... KNOCK YOURSELF OUT.

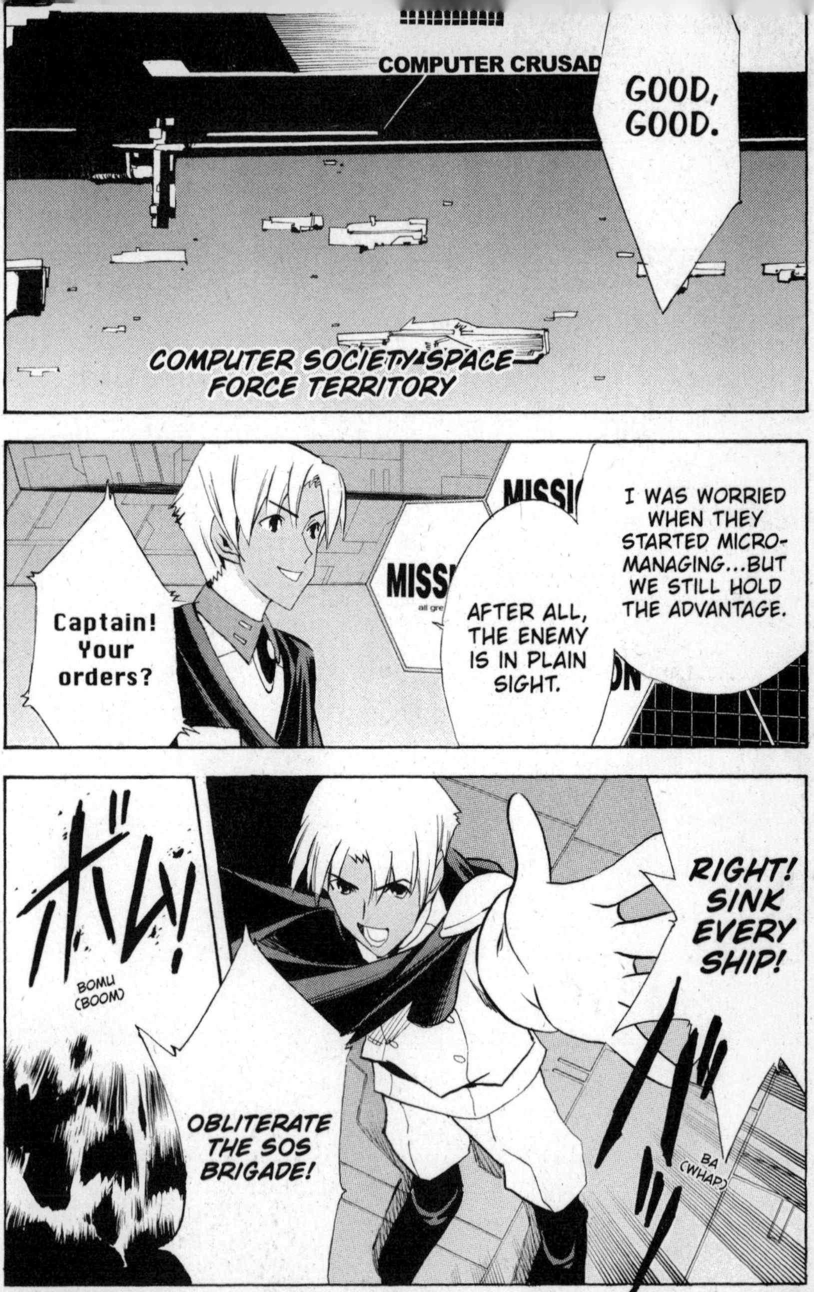
GOOD, GOOD.
COMPUTER CRUSAD
COMPUTER SOCIETY SPACE FORCE TERRITORY
I WAS WORRIED WHEN THEY STARTED MICRO-MANAGING...BUT WE STILL HOLD THE ADVANTAGE.
AFTER ALL, THE ENEMY IS IN PLAIN SIGHT.
Captain! Your orders?
RIGHT! SINK EVERY SHIP!
BA (WHAP)
OBLITERATE THE SOS BRIGADE!
BOMU (BOOM)

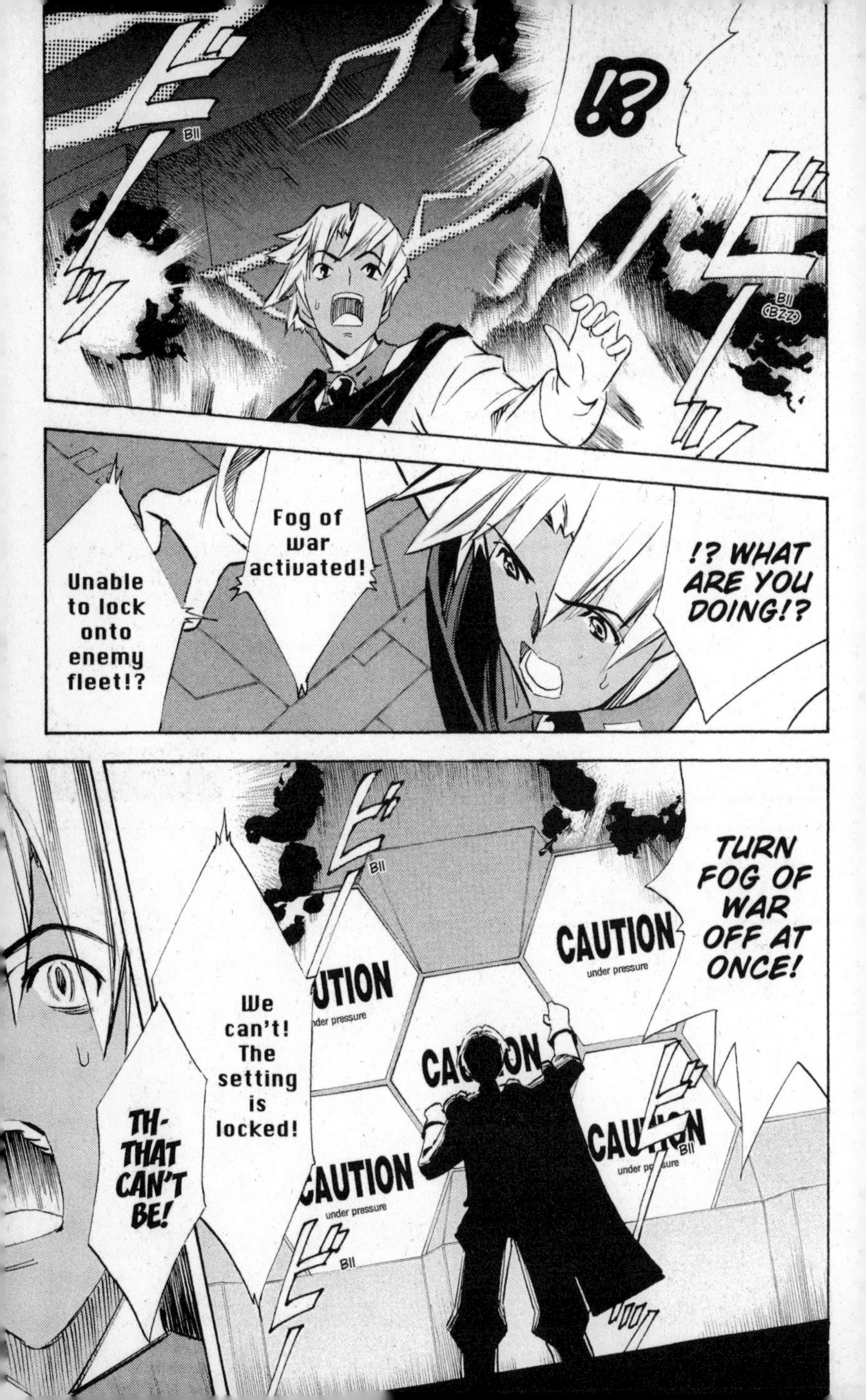
!?
BII
BII (BZZ)
!? WHAT ARE YOU DOING!?
Fog of war activated!
Unable to lock onto enemy fleet!?
TURN FOG OF WAR OFF AT ONCE!
CAUTION under pressure
BII
We can't! The setting is locked!
TH-THAT CAN'T BE!
BII
BII

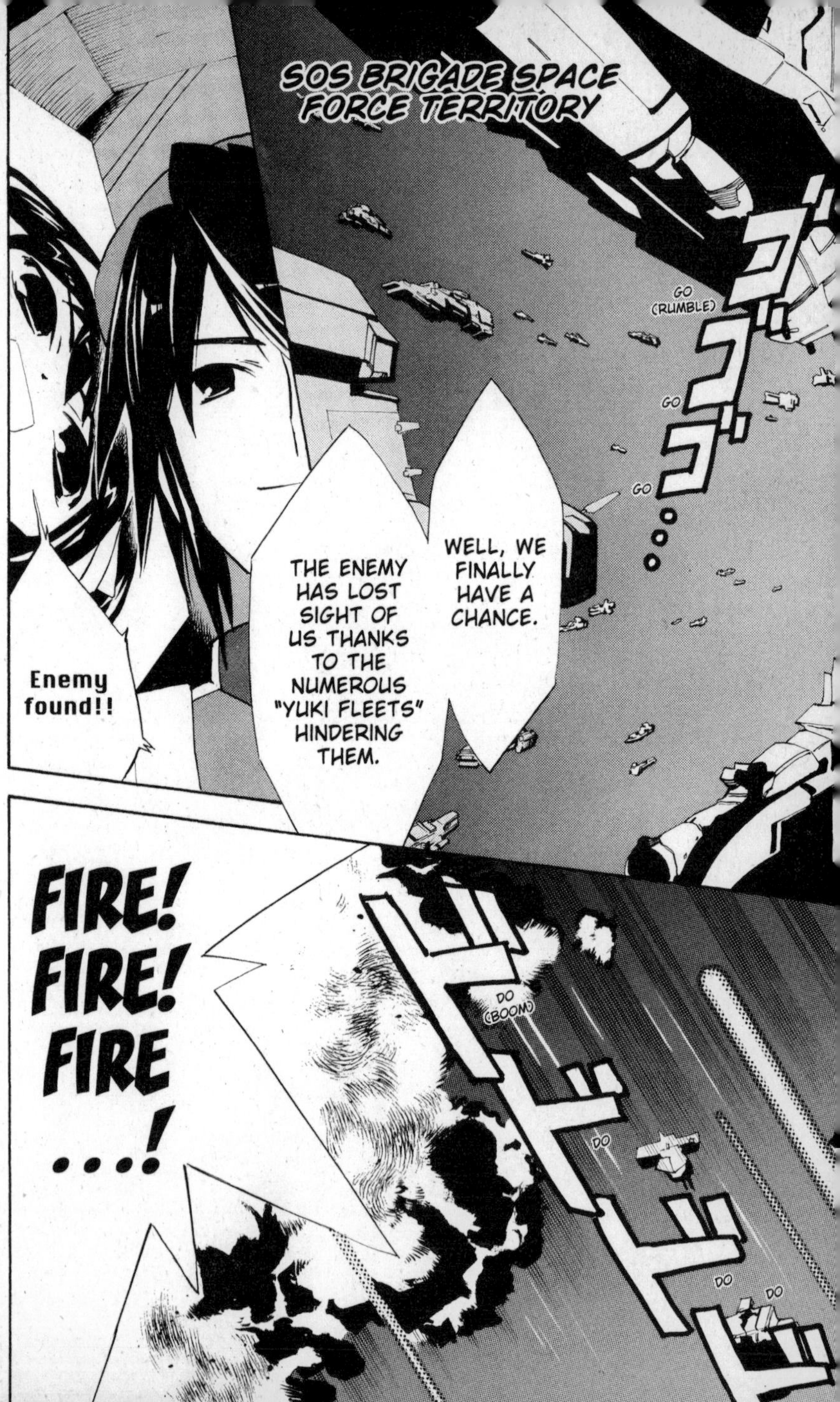
SOS BRIGADE SPACE FORCE TERRITORY
GO (RUMBLE)
GO
GO
WELL, WE FINALLY HAVE A CHANCE.
THE ENEMY HAS LOST SIGHT OF US THANKS TO THE NUMEROUS "YUKI FLEETS" HINDERING THEM.
Enemy found!!
DO (BOOM)
DO
DO
DO
FIRE! FIRE! FIRE ...!

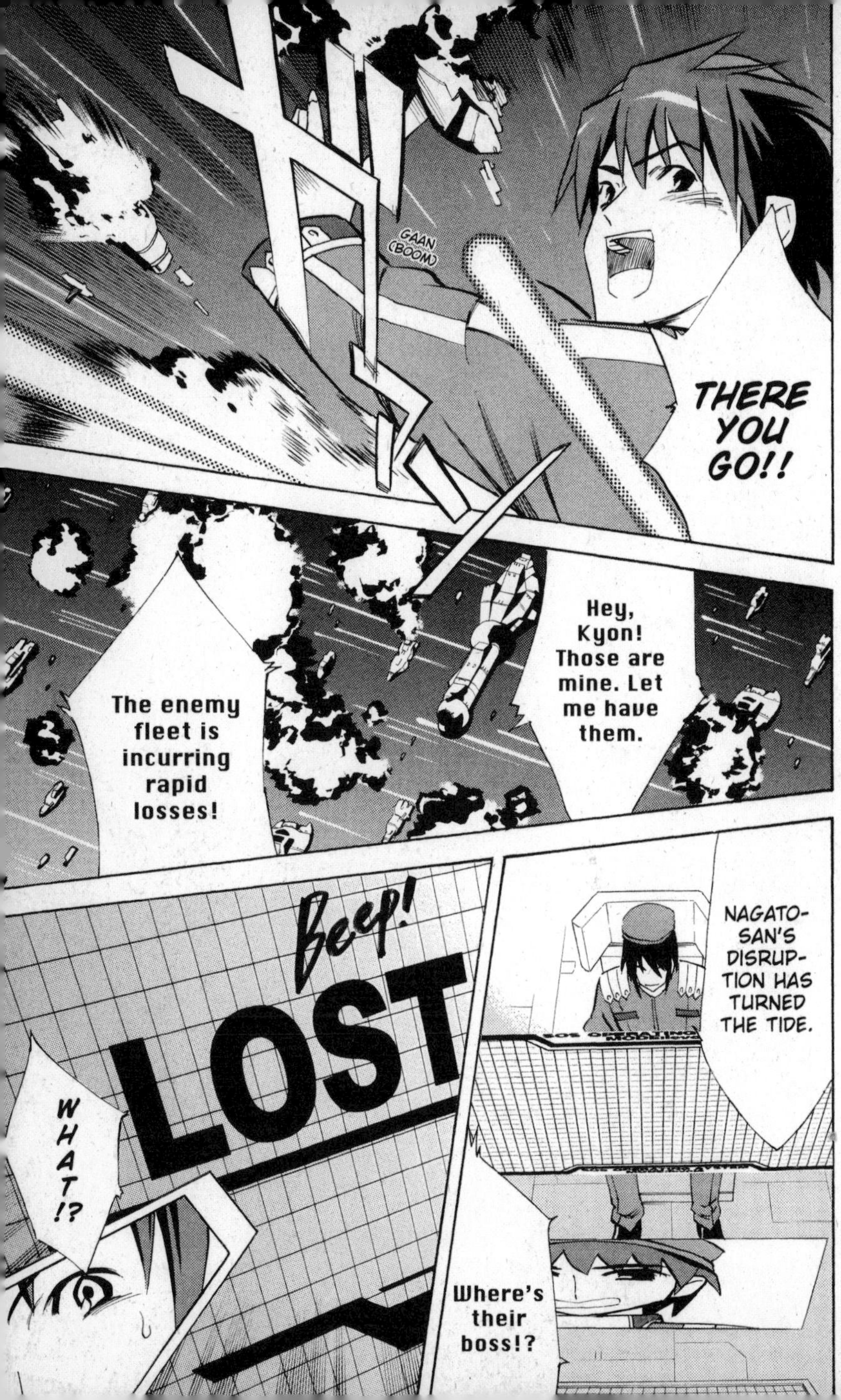
GAAN (BOOM)
THERE YOU GO!!
Hey, Kyon! Those are mine. Let me have them.
The enemy fleet is incurring rapid losses!
NAGATO-SAN'S DISRUPTION HAS TURNED THE TIDE.
Where's their boss!?
Beep!
LOST
WHAT!?

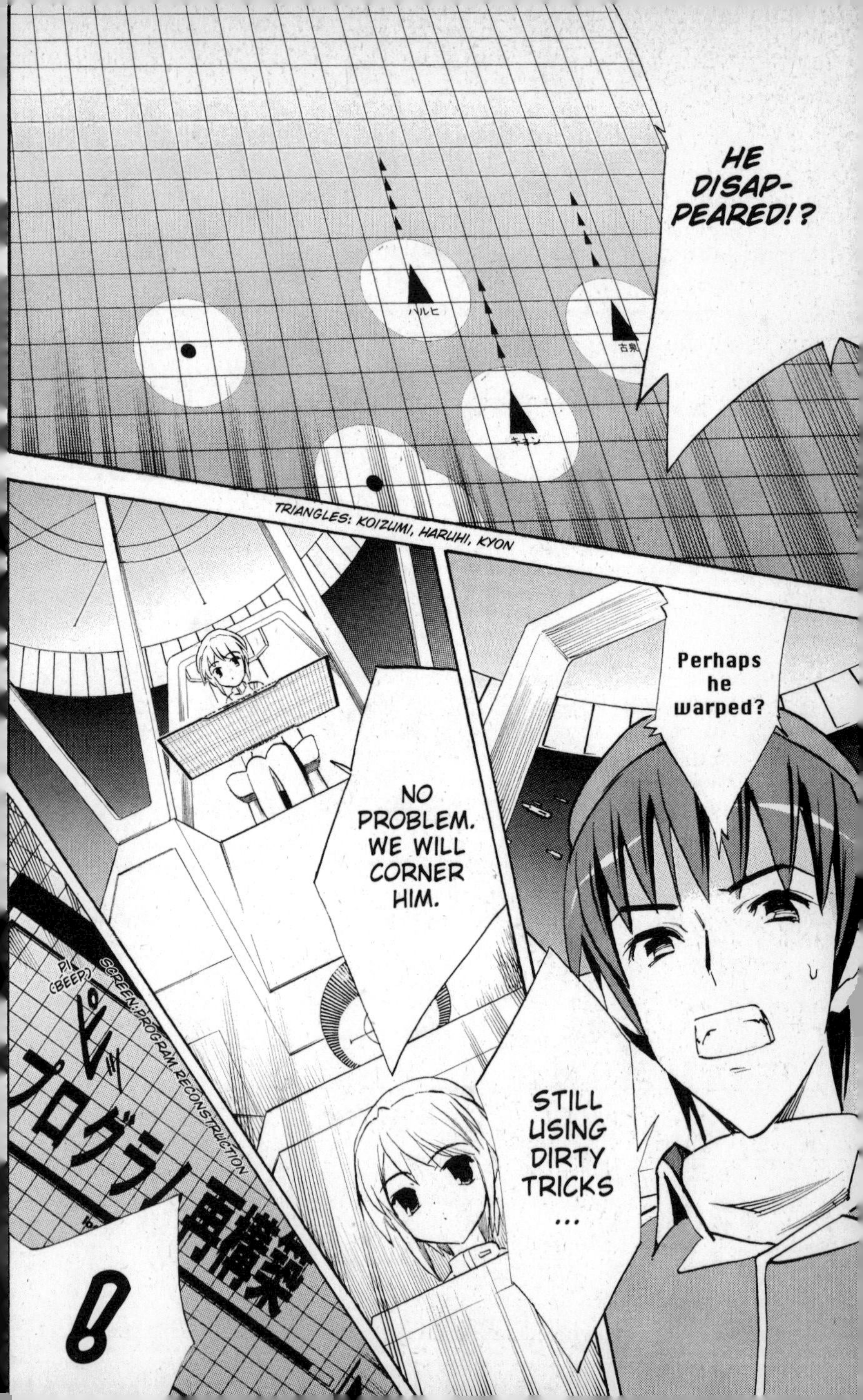
HE DISAP-
PEARED!?
ハルヒ
古泉
キョン
TRIANGLES: KOIZUMI, HARUHI, KYON
Perhaps he warped?
NO PROBLEM. WE WILL CORNER HIM.
STILL USING DIRTY TRICKS ...
PI (BEEP)
ピッ
SCREEN: PROGRAM RECONSTRUCTION
プログラム再構築
!

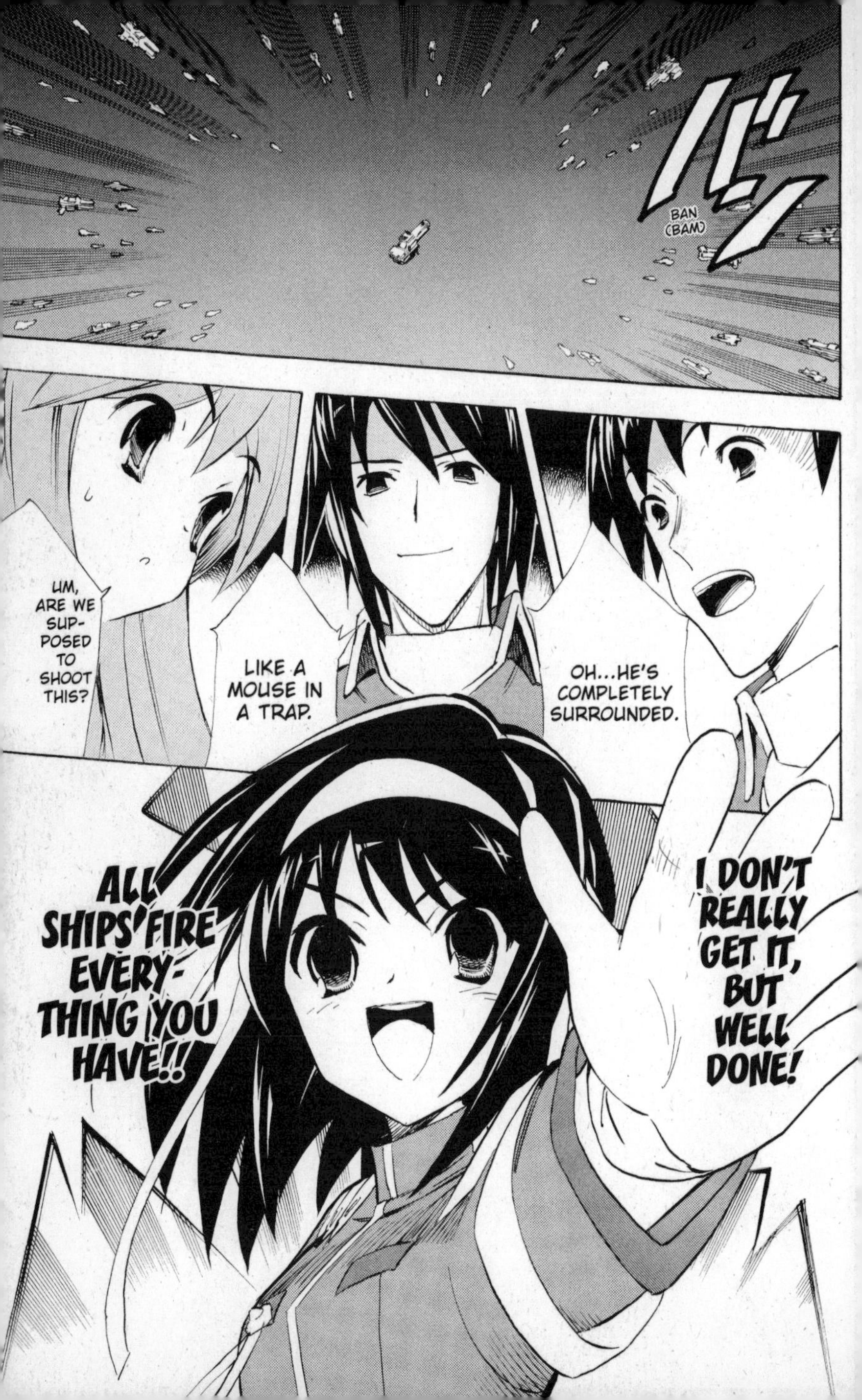
BAN (BAM)
OH...HE'S COMPLETELY SURROUNDED.
LIKE A MOUSE IN A TRAP.
UM, ARE WE SUP-POSED TO SHOOT THIS?
I DON'T REALLY GET IT, BUT WELL DONE!
ALL SHIPS' FIRE EVERY-THING YOU HAVE!!

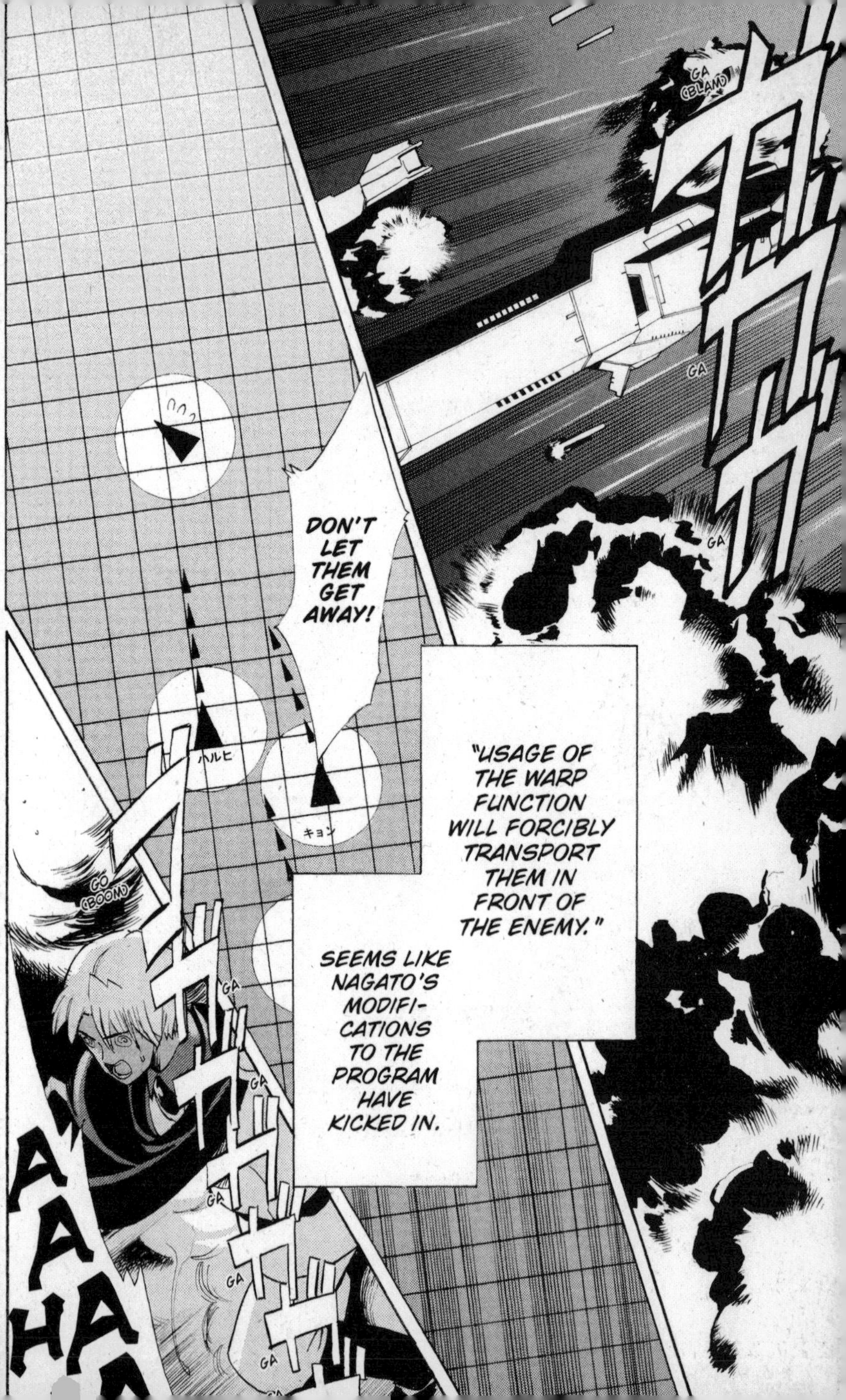
GA (BLAM)
GA
GA
DON'T LET THEM GET AWAY!
ハルヒ
キョン
"USAGE OF THE WARP FUNCTION WILL FORCIBLY TRANSPORT THEM IN FRONT OF THE ENEMY."
SEEMS LIKE NAGATO'S MODIFI-CATIONS TO THE PROGRAM HAVE KICKED IN.
GO (BOOM)
GA
GA
GA
GA
GA
AAAHA

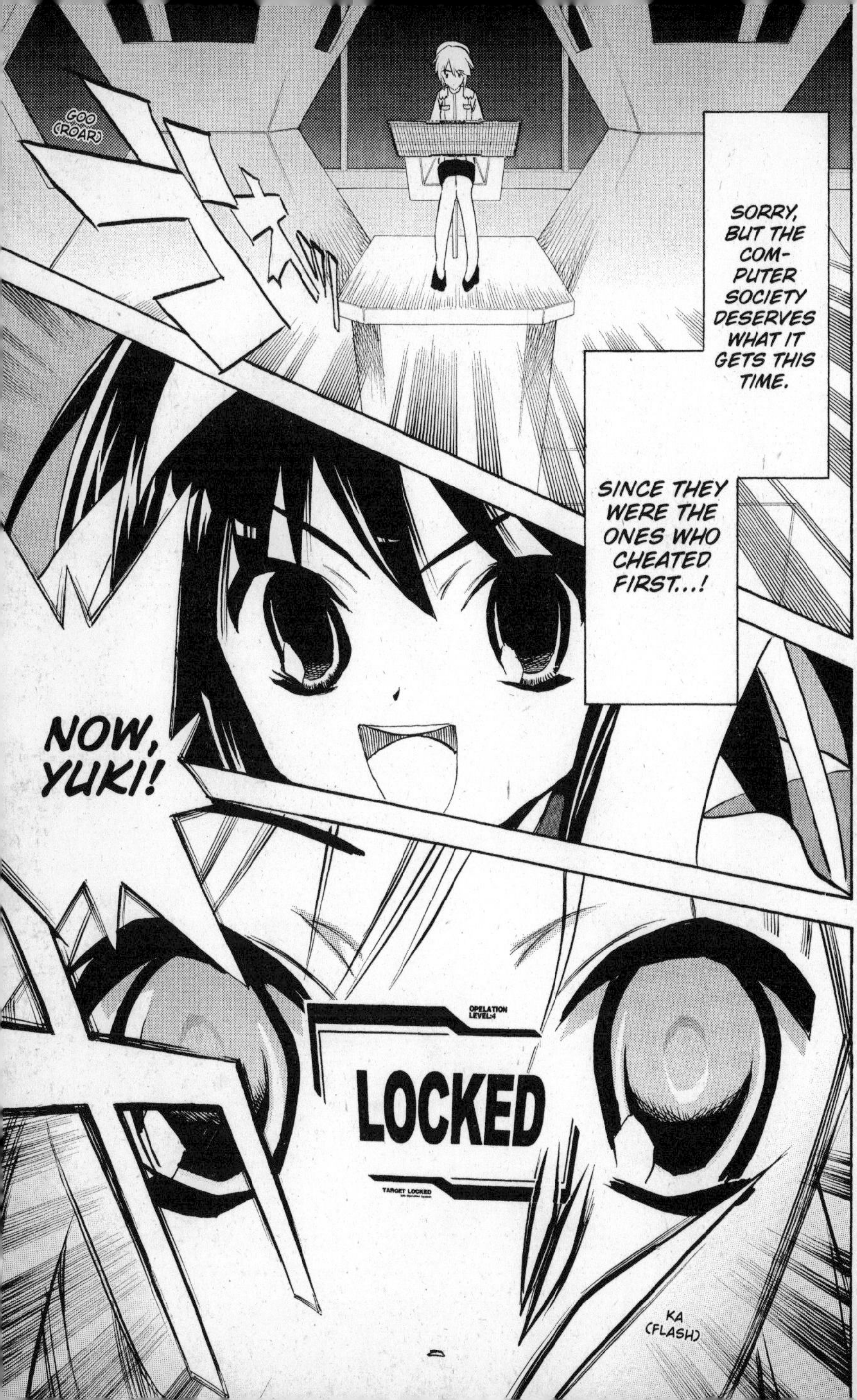
SORRY, BUT THE COM-PUTER SOCIETY DESERVES WHAT IT GETS THIS TIME.
SINCE THEY WERE THE ONES WHO CHEATED FIRST...!
GOO (ROAR)
NOW, YUKI!
OPELATION LEVEL:4
LOCKED
TARGET LOCKED
KA (FLASH)

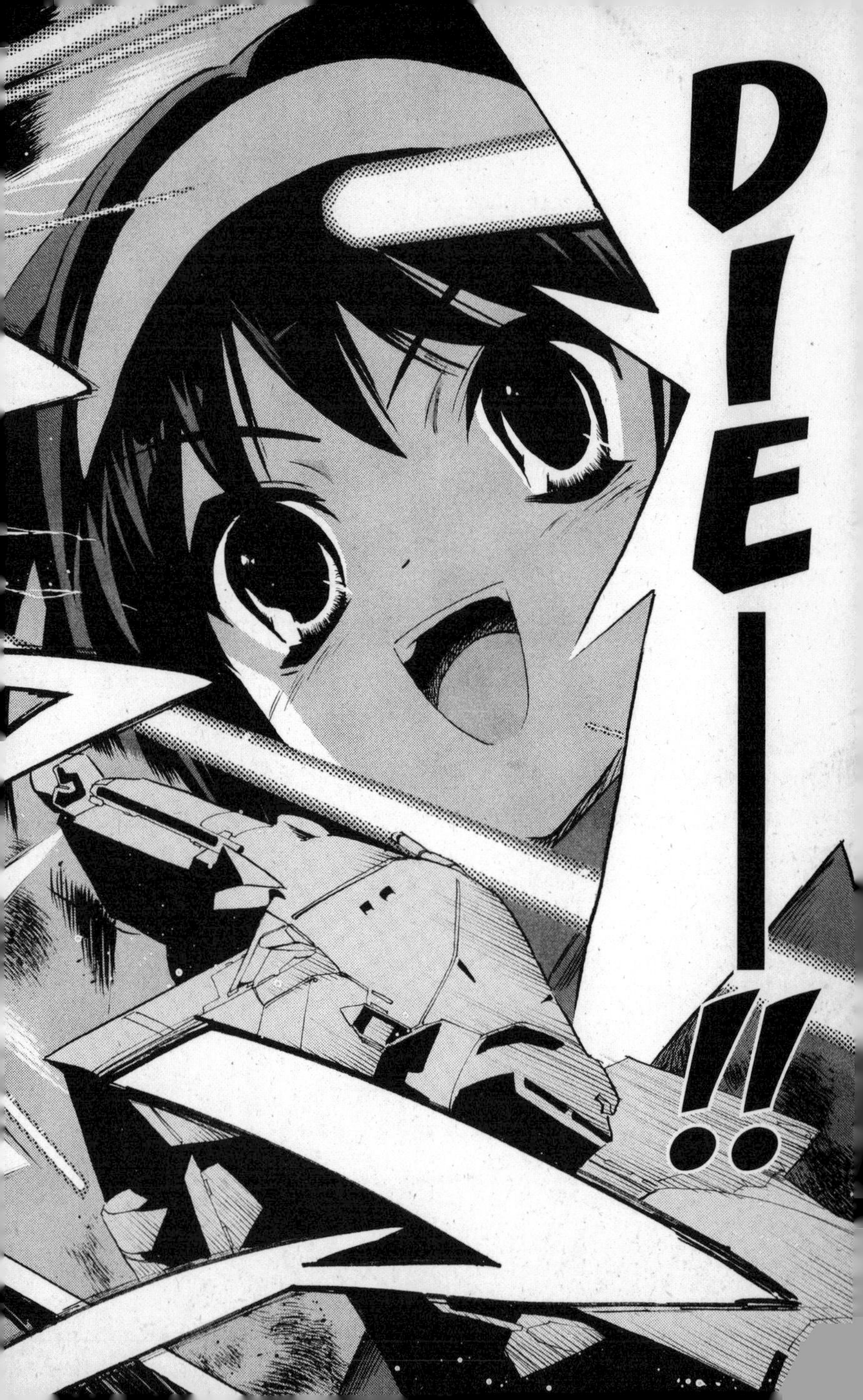
DIE—!!

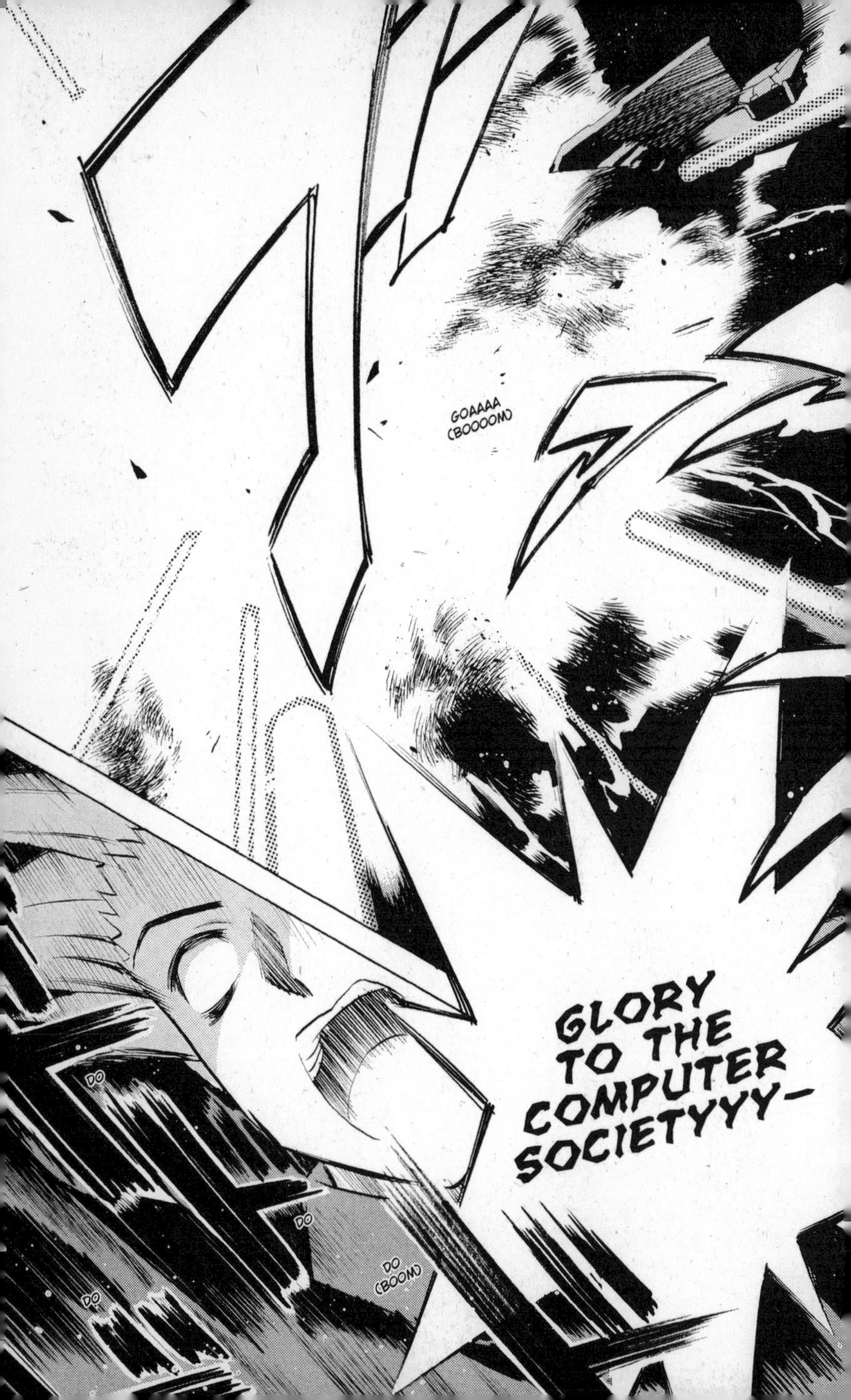
GOAAAA (BOOOOM)
GLORY TO THE COMPUTER SOCIETYYY-
DO
DO
DO (BOOM)
DO

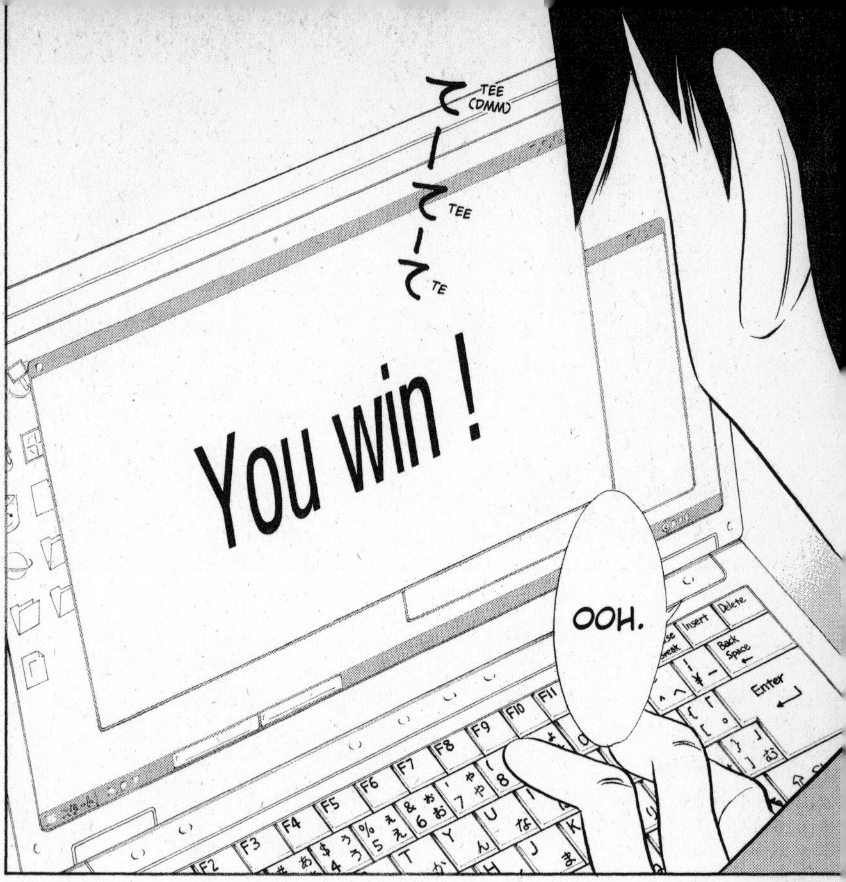
てーてーて
TEE (DMM) TEE TE
You win !
OOH.

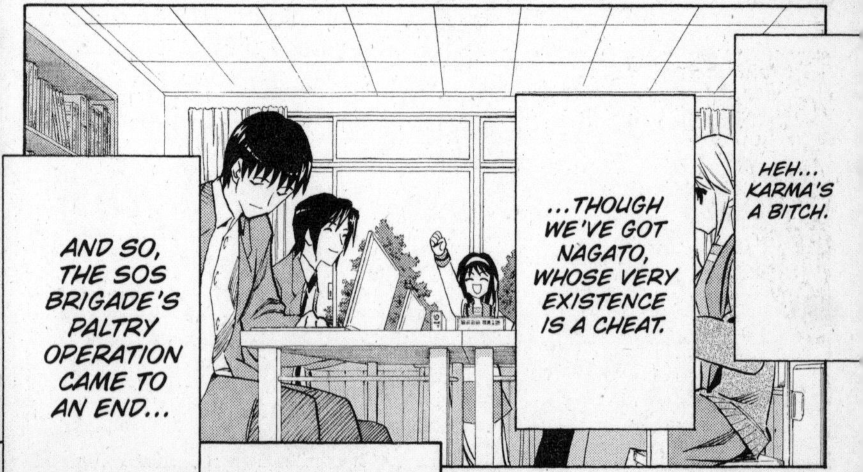
HEH... KARMA'S A BITCH.
...THOUGH WE'VE GOT NAGATO, WHOSE VERY EXISTENCE IS A CHEAT.
AND SO, THE SOS BRIGADE'S PALTRY OPERATION CAME TO AN END...

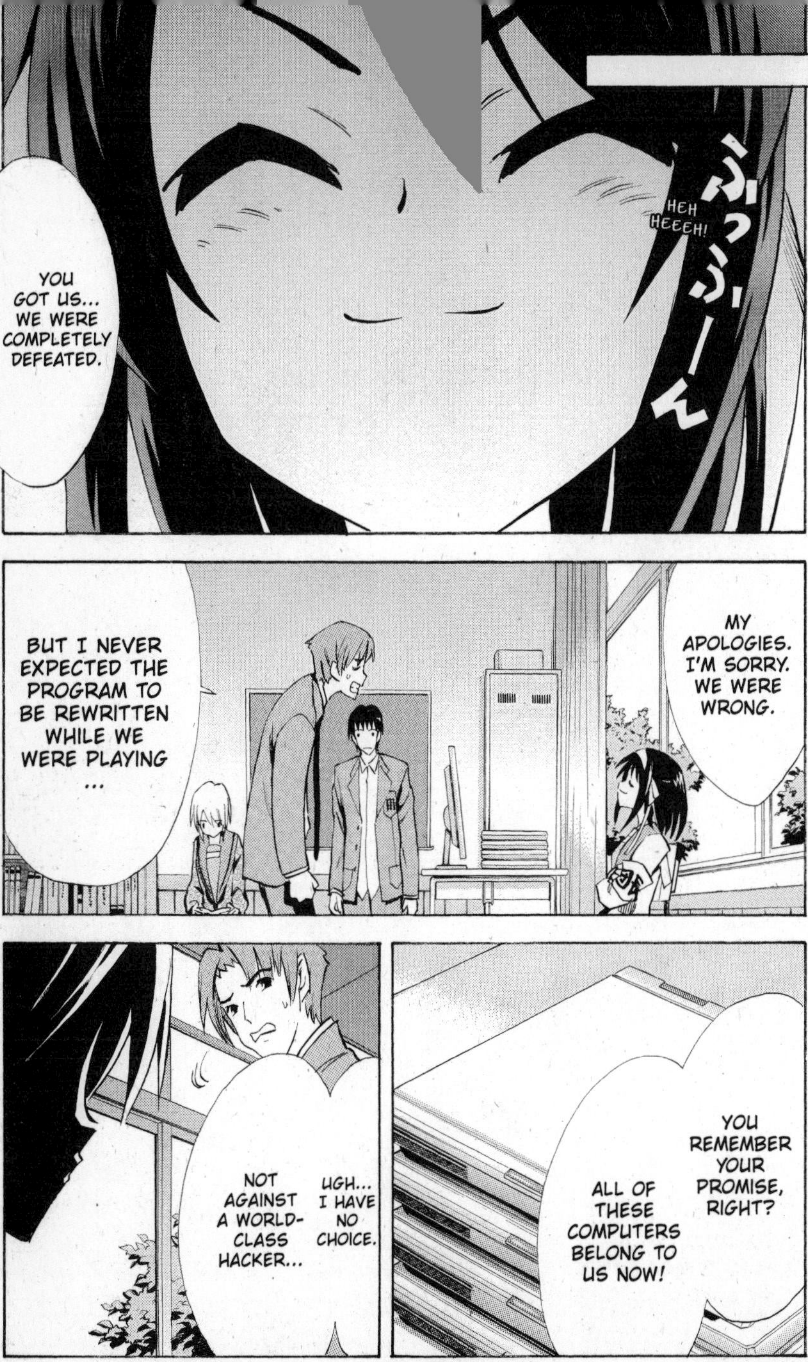
ふっふーん
HEH HEEEH!
YOU GOT US... WE WERE COMPLETELY DEFEATED.
MY APOLOGIES. I'M SORRY. WE WERE WRONG.
BUT I NEVER EXPECTED THE PROGRAM TO BE REWRITTEN WHILE WE WERE PLAYING ...
YOU REMEMBER YOUR PROMISE, RIGHT?
ALL OF THESE COMPUTERS BELONG TO US NOW!
UGH... I HAVE NO CHOICE.
NOT AGAINST A WORLD-CLASS HACKER...

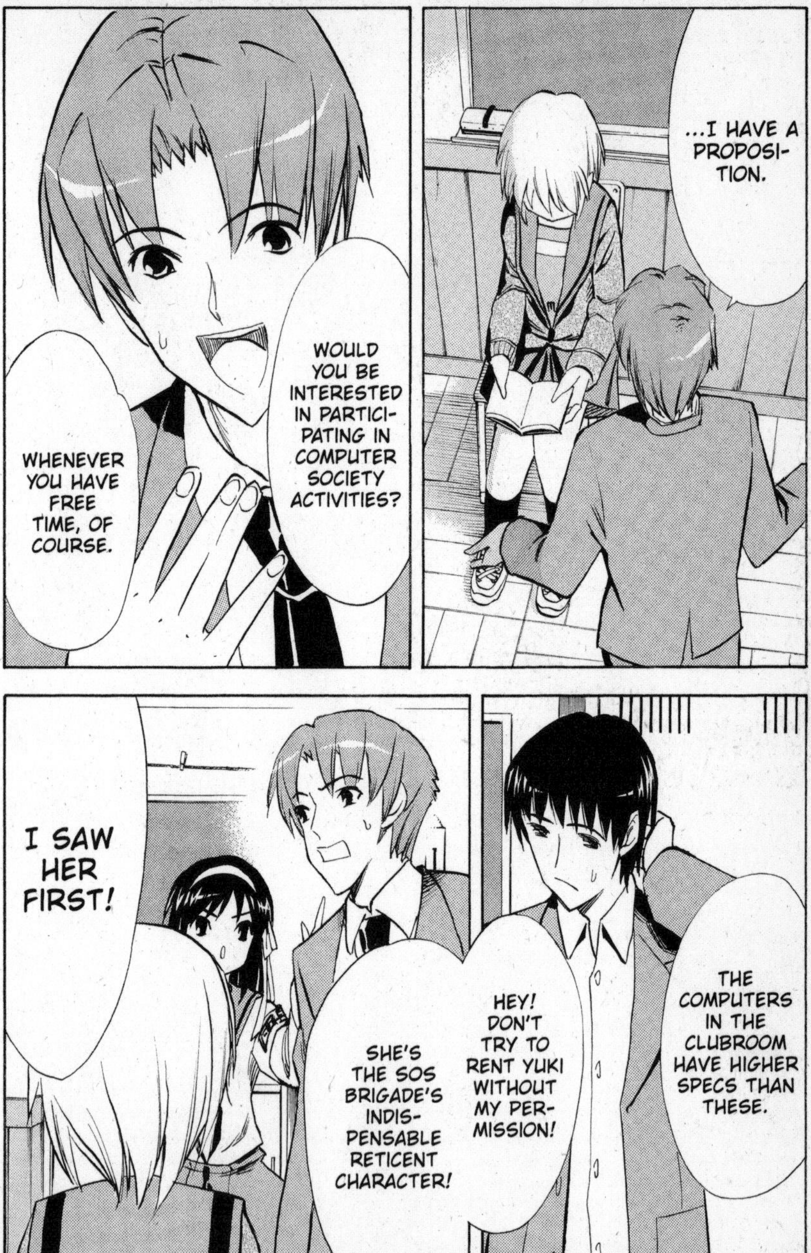
...I HAVE A PROPOSI-TION.
WOULD YOU BE INTERESTED IN PARTICI-PATING IN COMPUTER SOCIETY ACTIVITIES?
WHENEVER YOU HAVE FREE TIME, OF COURSE.
THE COMPUTERS IN THE CLUBROOM HAVE HIGHER SPECS THAN THESE.
HEY! DON'T TRY TO RENT YUKI WITHOUT MY PER-MISSION!
SHE'S THE SOS BRIGADE'S INDIS-PENSABLE RETICENT CHARACTER!
I SAW HER FIRST!

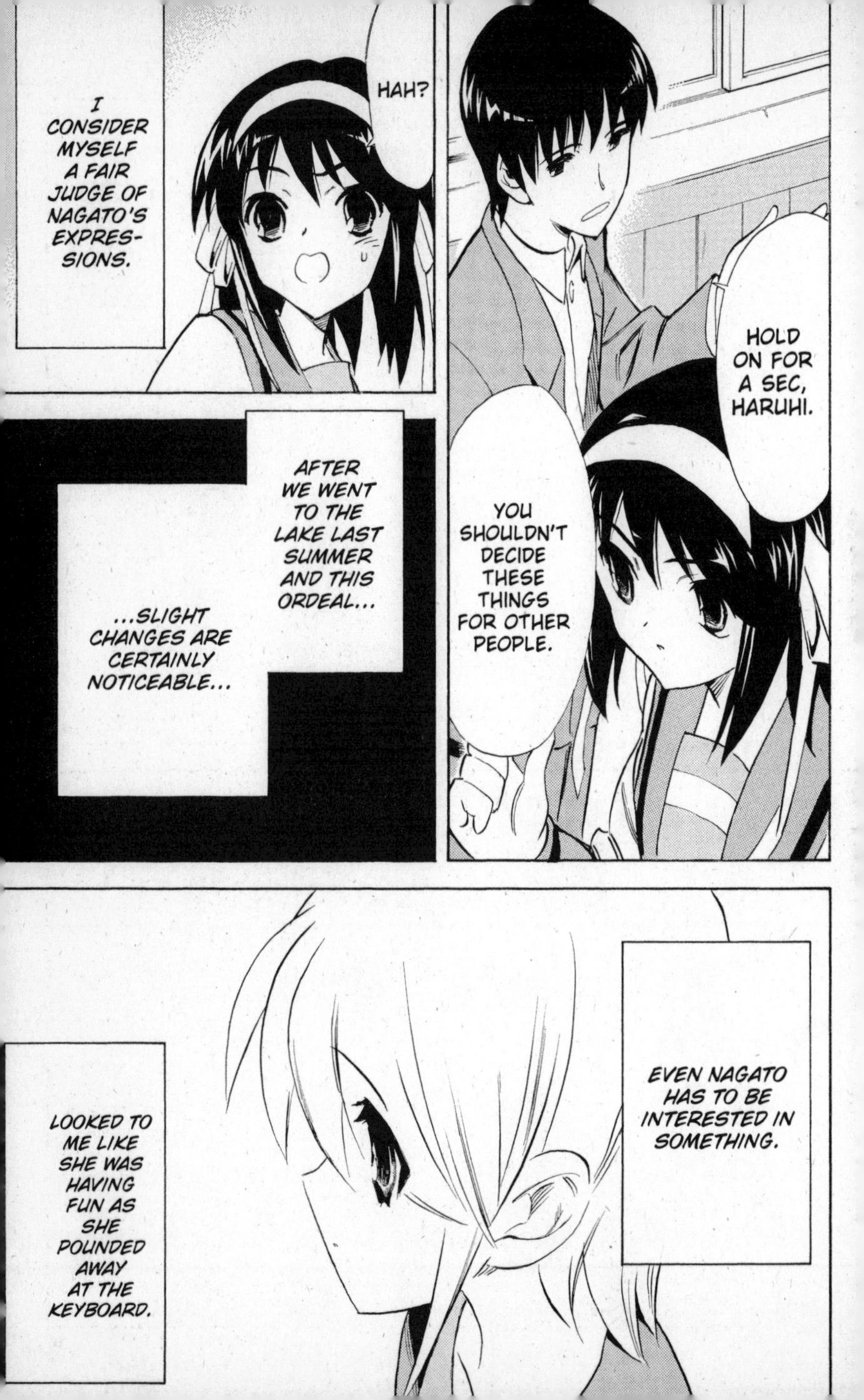
HOLD ON FOR A SEC, HARUHI.
YOU SHOULDN'T DECIDE THESE THINGS FOR OTHER PEOPLE.
HAH?
I CONSIDER MYSELF A FAIR JUDGE OF NAGATO'S EXPRES-SIONS.
AFTER WE WENT TO THE LAKE LAST SUMMER AND THIS ORDEAL...
...SLIGHT CHANGES ARE CERTAINLY NOTICEABLE...
EVEN NAGATO HAS TO BE INTERESTED IN SOMETHING.
LOOKED TO ME LIKE SHE WAS HAVING FUN AS SHE POUNDED AWAY AT THE KEYBOARD.

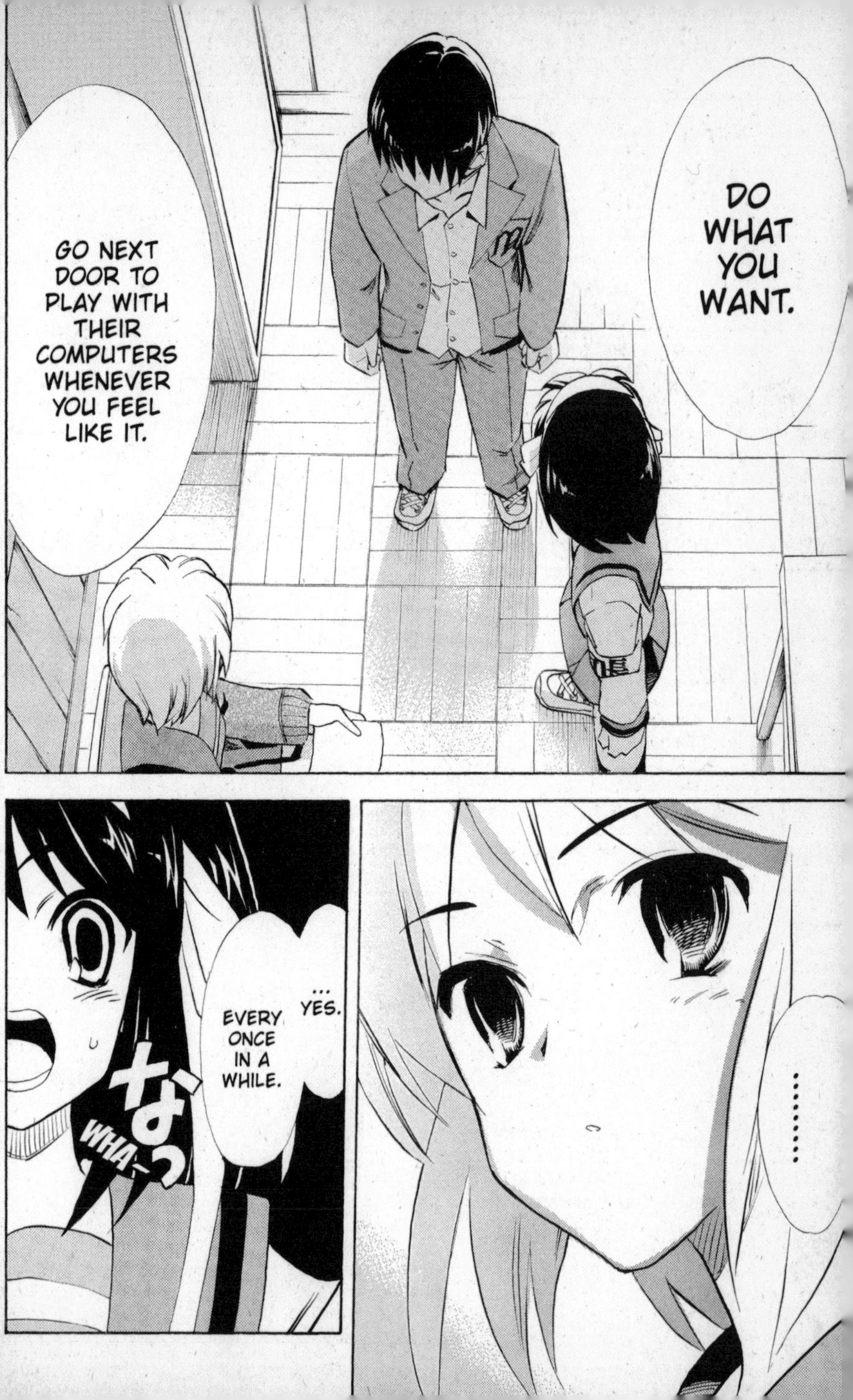
DO WHAT YOU WANT.
GO NEXT DOOR TO PLAY WITH THEIR COMPUTERS WHENEVER YOU FEEL LIKE IT.
......
...YES.
EVERY ONCE IN A WHILE.
なっ
WHA—

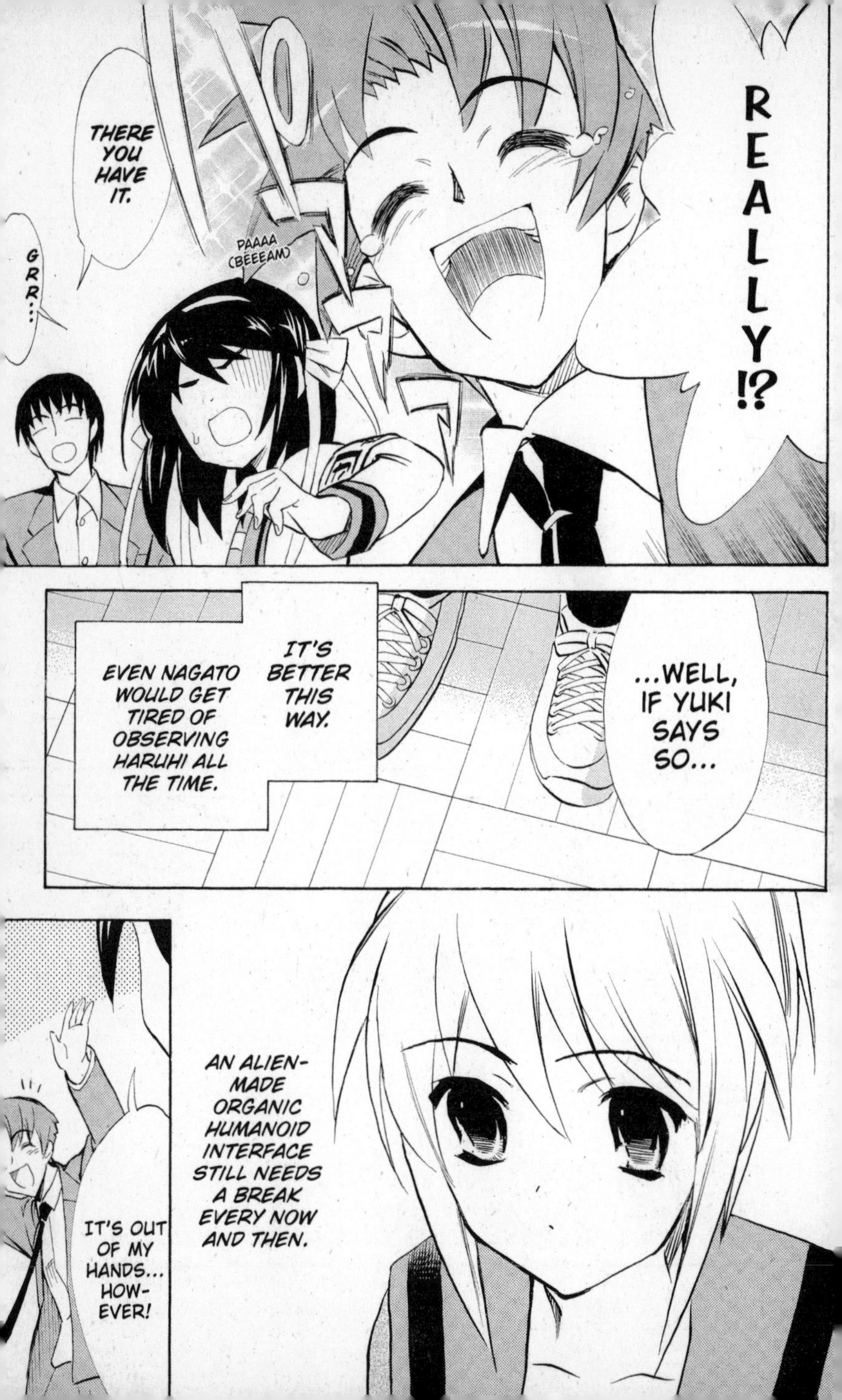
REALLY!?
PAAAA (BEEEAM)
THERE YOU HAVE IT.
GRR...
...WELL, IF YUKI SAYS SO...
IT'S BETTER THIS WAY.
EVEN NAGATO WOULD GET TIRED OF OBSERVING HARUHI ALL THE TIME.
AN ALIEN-MADE ORGANIC HUMANOID INTERFACE STILL NEEDS A BREAK EVERY NOW AND THEN.
IT'S OUT OF MY HANDS... HOW-EVER!

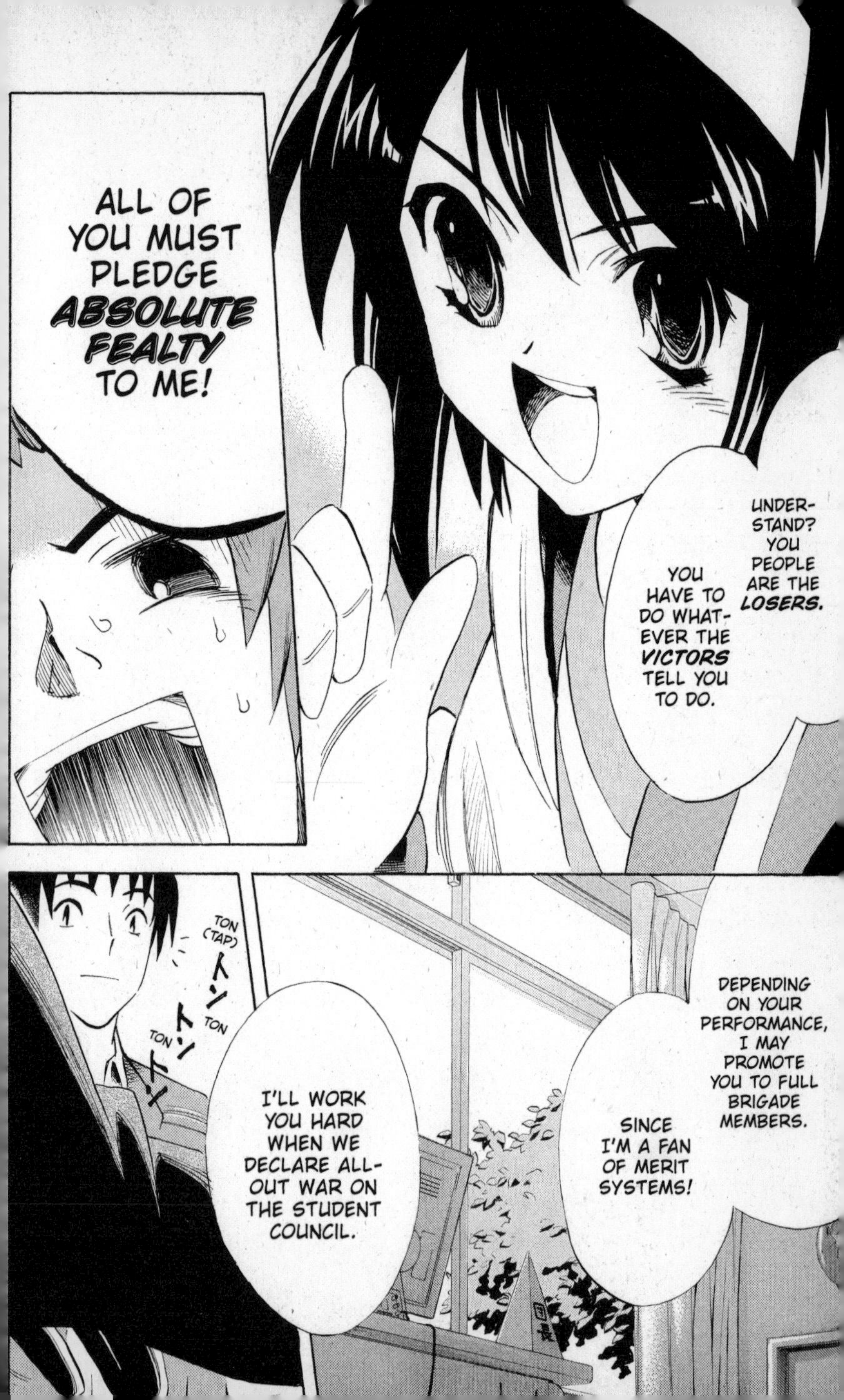
UNDER-STAND? YOU PEOPLE ARE THE LOSERS.
YOU HAVE TO DO WHAT-EVER THE VICTORS TELL YOU TO DO.
ALL OF YOU MUST PLEDGE ABSOLUTE FEALTY TO ME!
DEPENDING ON YOUR PERFORMANCE, I MAY PROMOTE YOU TO FULL BRIGADE MEMBERS.
SINCE I'M A FAN OF MERIT SYSTEMS!
I'LL WORK YOU HARD WHEN WE DECLARE ALL-OUT WAR ON THE STUDENT COUNCIL.
TON (TAP)
TON
TON

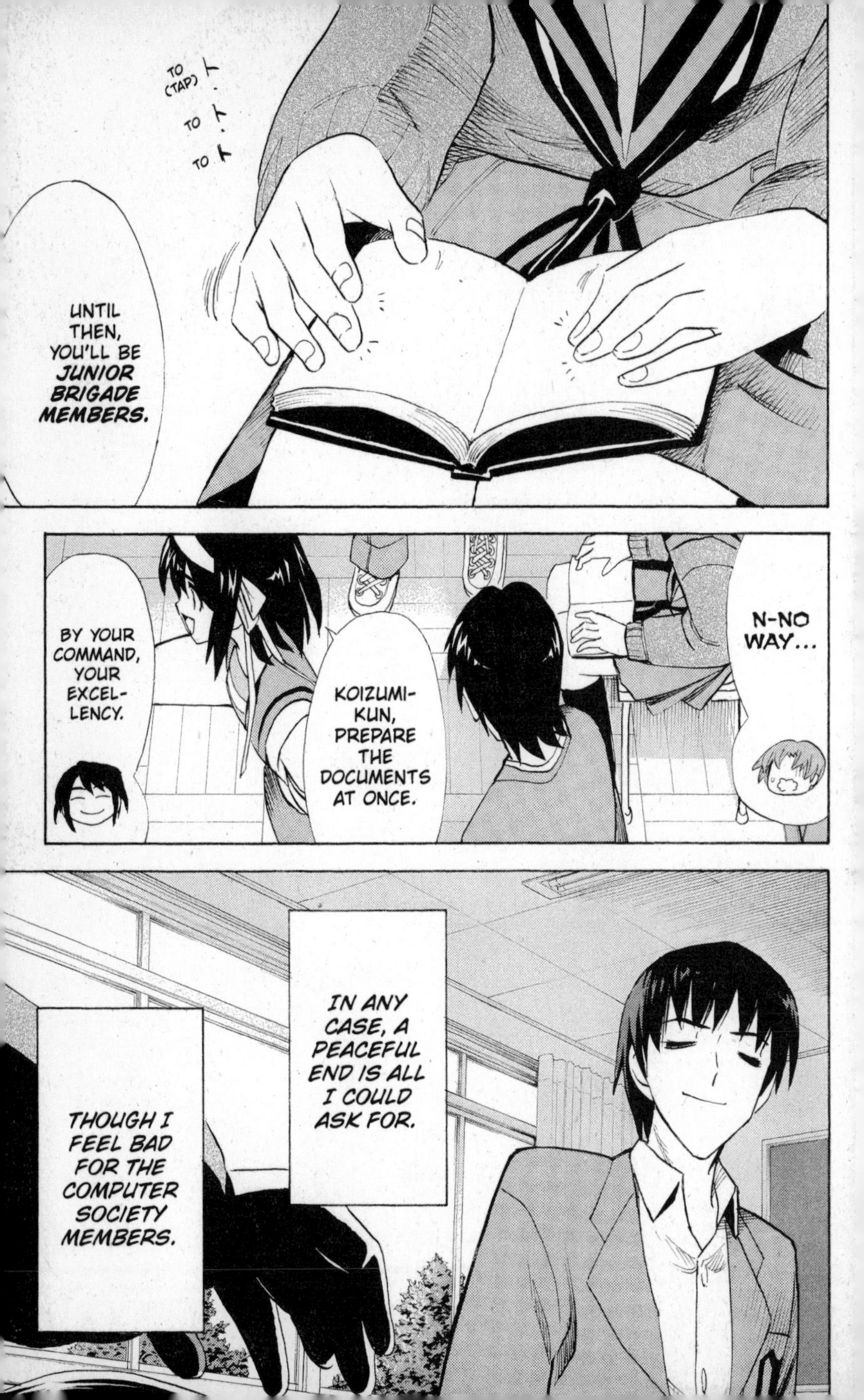
TO (TAP) ト
TO ト
TO ト
UNTIL THEN, YOU'LL BE JUNIOR BRIGADE MEMBERS.
N-NO WAY...
KOIZUMI-KUN, PREPARE THE DOCUMENTS AT ONCE.
BY YOUR COMMAND, YOUR EXCEL-LENCY.
IN ANY CASE, A PEACEFUL END IS ALL I COULD ASK FOR.
THOUGH I FEEL BAD FOR THE COMPUTER SOCIETY MEMBERS.

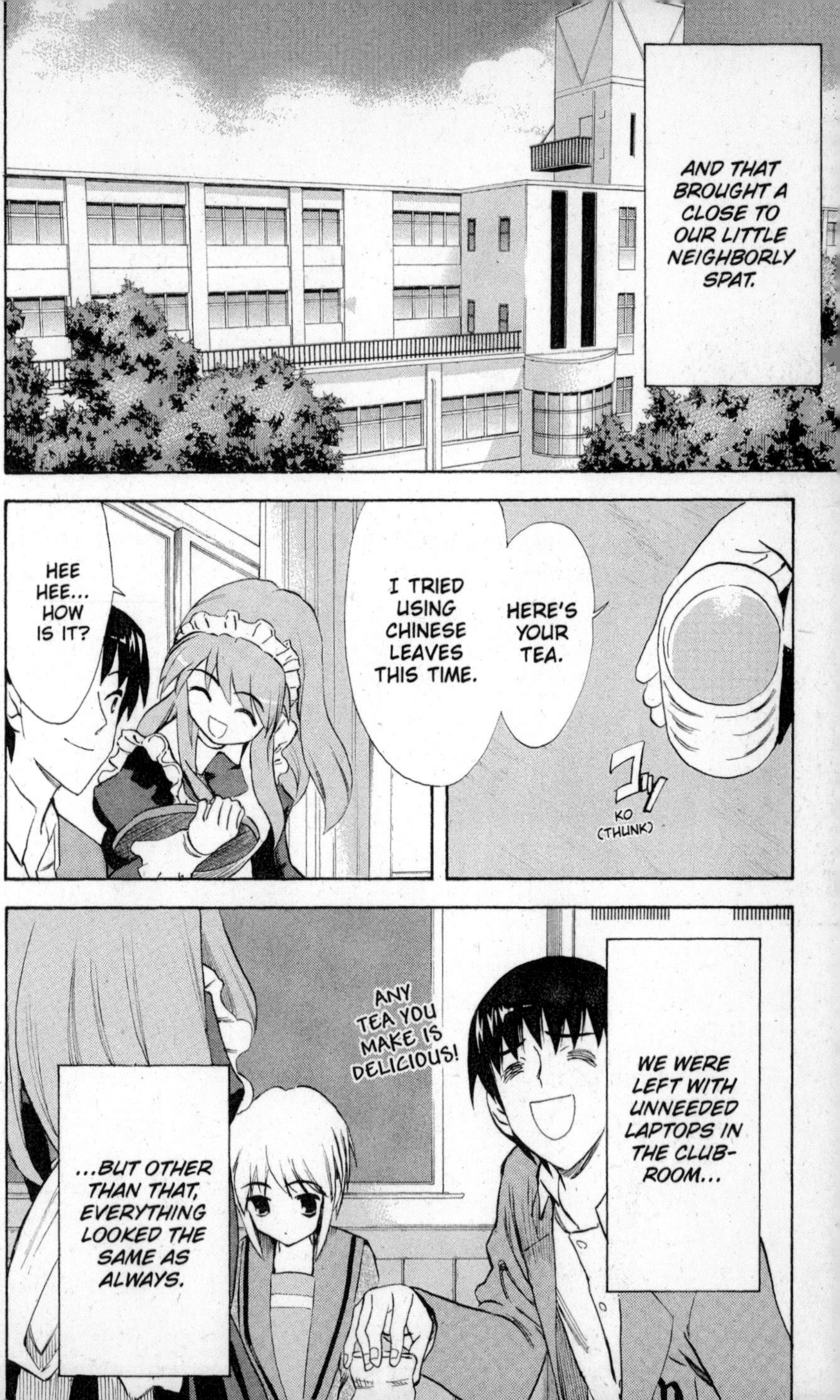
AND THAT BROUGHT A CLOSE TO OUR LITTLE NEIGHBORLY SPAT.
コッ
KO (THUNK)
HERE'S YOUR TEA.
I TRIED USING CHINESE LEAVES THIS TIME.
HEE HEE... HOW IS IT?
WE WERE LEFT WITH UNNEEDED LAPTOPS IN THE CLUB-ROOM...
ANY TEA YOU MAKE IS DELICIOUS!
...BUT OTHER THAN THAT, EVERYTHING LOOKED THE SAME AS ALWAYS.

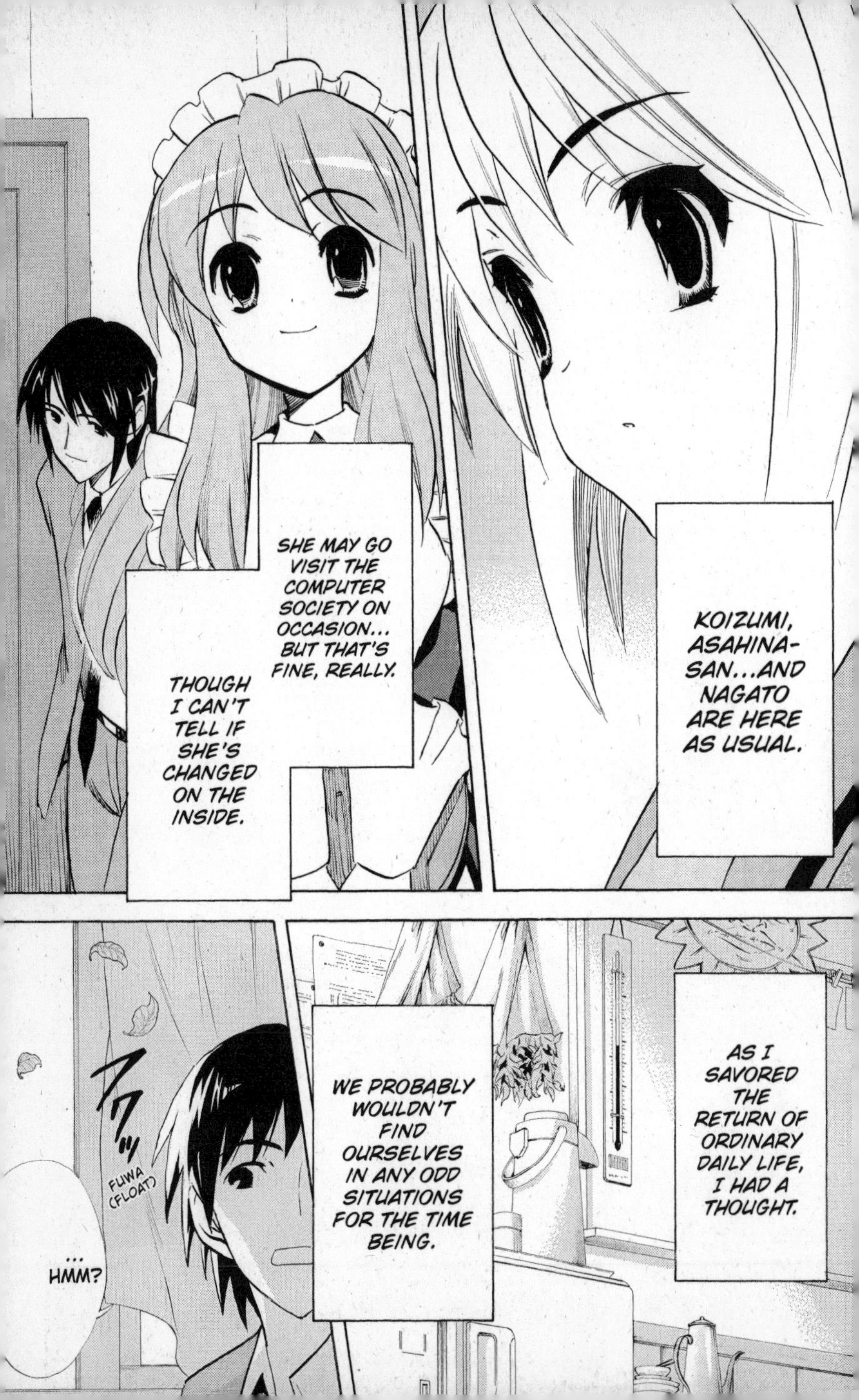
KOIZUMI, ASAHINA-SAN...AND NAGATO ARE HERE AS USUAL.
SHE MAY GO VISIT THE COMPUTER SOCIETY ON OCCASION... BUT THAT'S FINE, REALLY.
THOUGH I CAN'T TELL IF SHE'S CHANGED ON THE INSIDE.
AS I SAVORED THE RETURN OF ORDINARY DAILY LIFE, I HAD A THOUGHT.
WE PROBABLY WOULDN'T FIND OURSELVES IN ANY ODD SITUATIONS FOR THE TIME BEING.
FUWA (FLOAT)
...HMM?

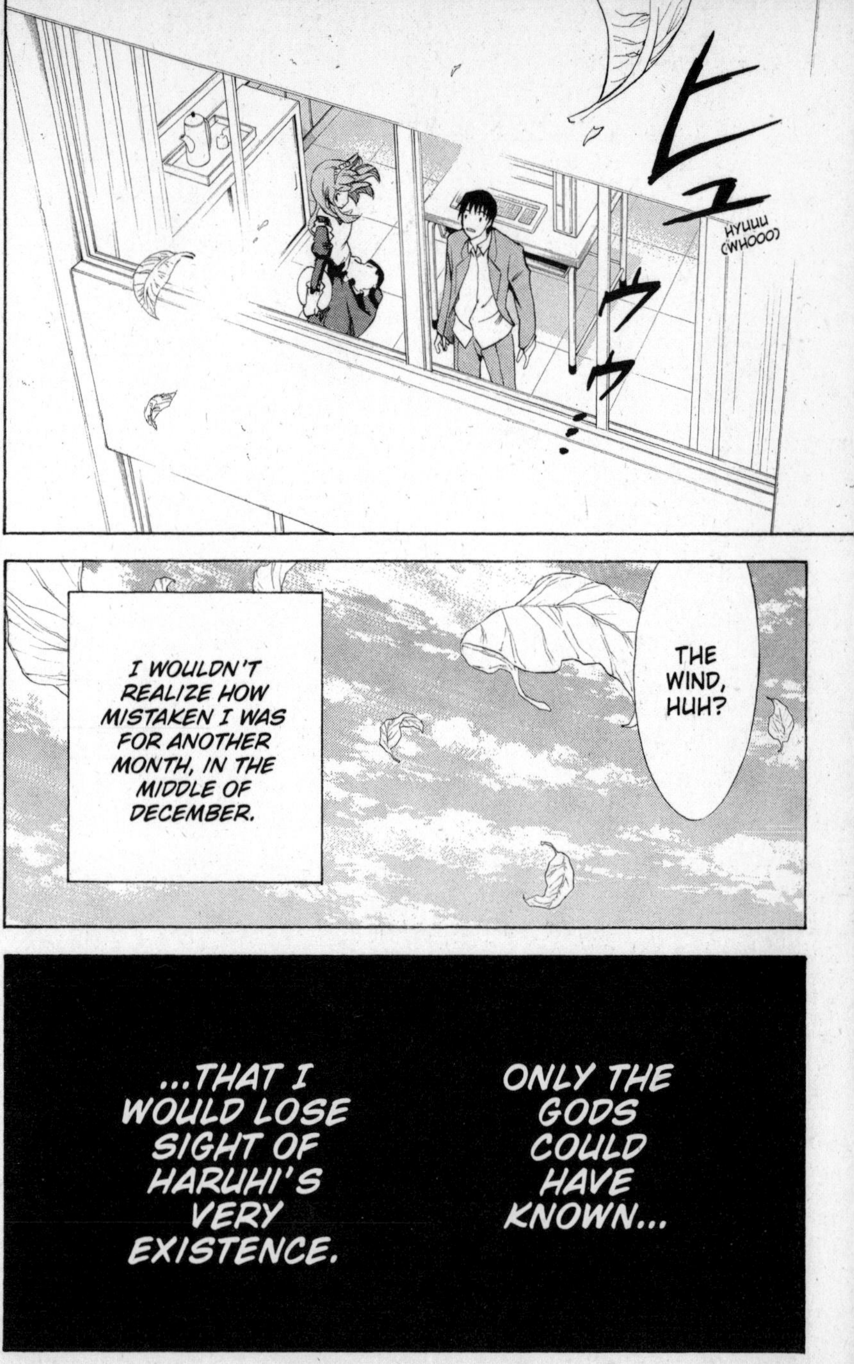
ヒュウウ…
HYUUU (WHOOO)
THE WIND, HUH?
I WOULDN'T REALIZE HOW MISTAKEN I WAS FOR ANOTHER MONTH, IN THE MIDDLE OF DECEMBER.
ONLY THE GODS COULD HAVE KNOWN...
...THAT I WOULD LOSE SIGHT OF HARUHI'S VERY EXISTENCE.

The Day of Sagittarius II : END

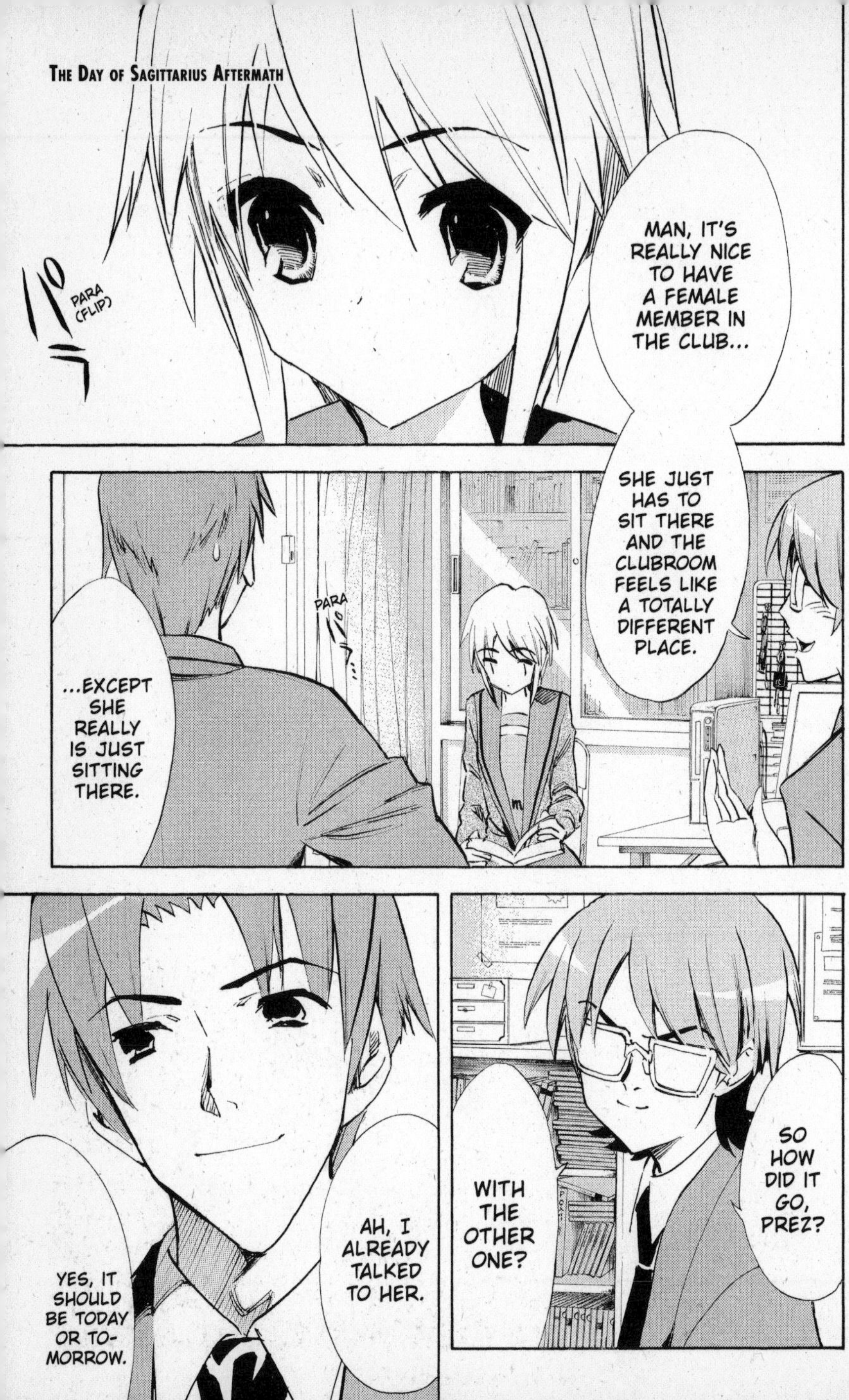
MAN, IT'S REALLY NICE TO HAVE A FEMALE MEMBER IN THE CLUB...
PARA (FLIP)
SHE JUST HAS TO SIT THERE AND THE CLUBROOM FEELS LIKE A TOTALLY DIFFERENT PLACE.
PARA
...EXCEPT SHE REALLY IS JUST SITTING THERE.
SO HOW DID IT GO, PREZ?
WITH THE OTHER ONE?
AH, I ALREADY TALKED TO HER.
YES, IT SHOULD BE TODAY OR TO-MORROW.

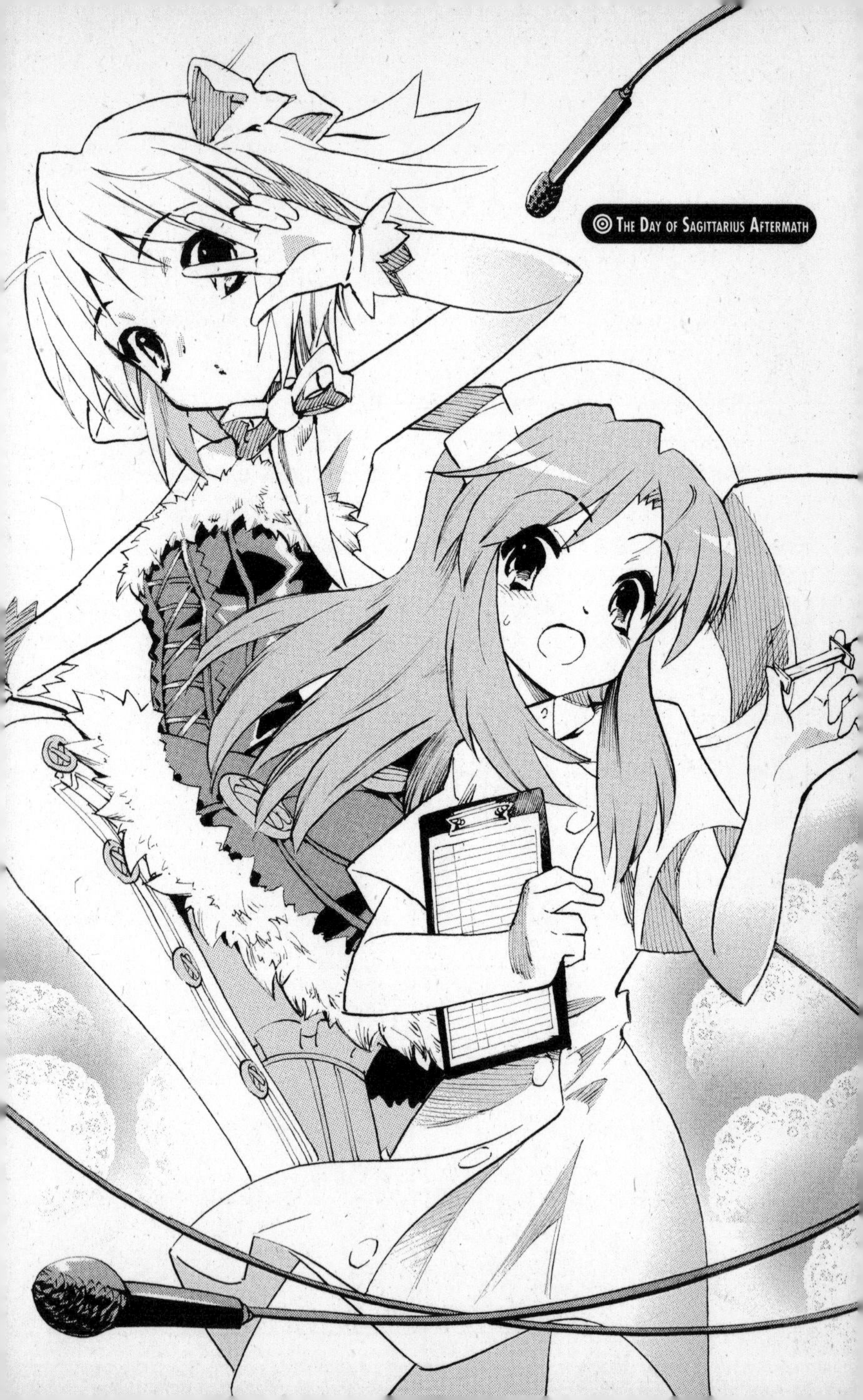
The Day of Sagittarius Aftermath

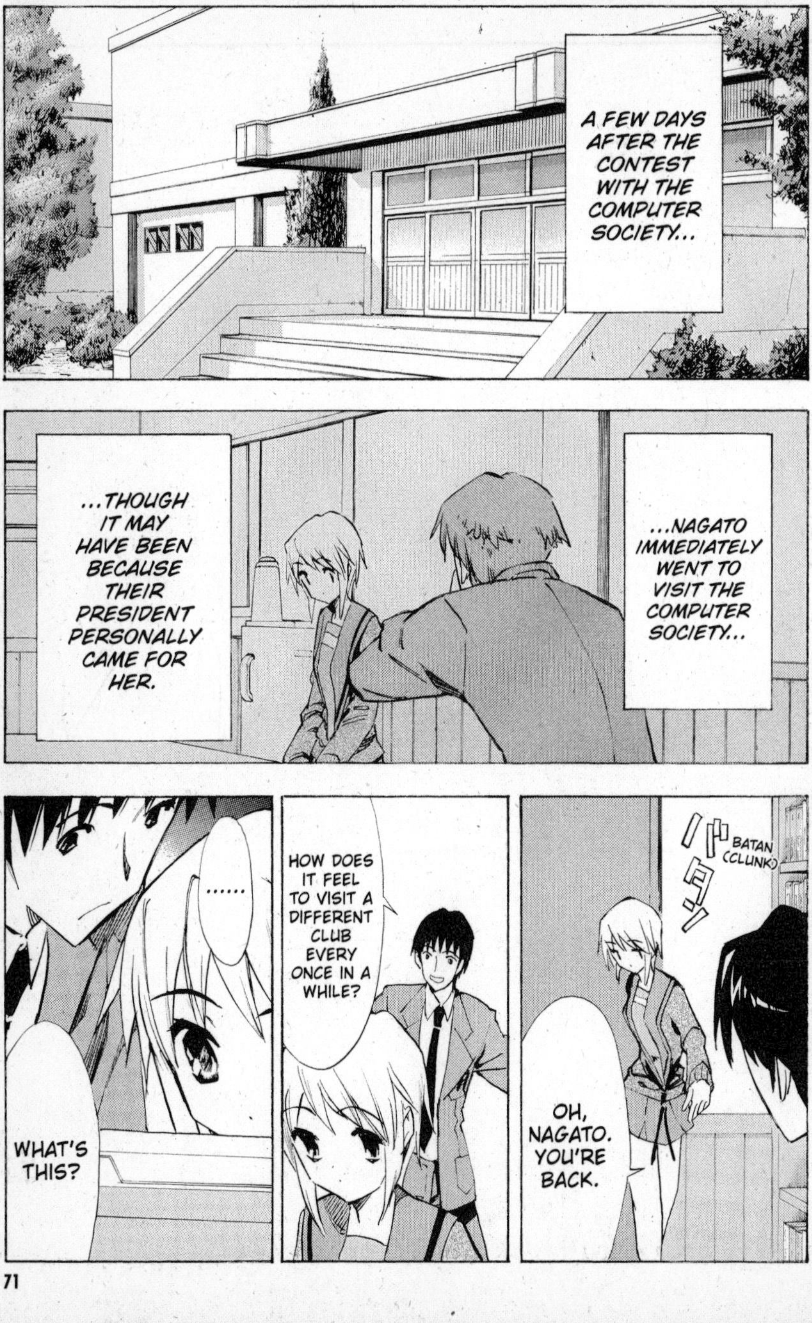
A FEW DAYS AFTER THE CONTEST WITH THE COMPUTER SOCIETY...
...NAGATO IMMEDIATELY WENT TO VISIT THE COMPUTER SOCIETY...
...THOUGH IT MAY HAVE BEEN BECAUSE THEIR PRESIDENT PERSONALLY CAME FOR HER.
バタン
BATAN (CLUNK)
OH, NAGATO. YOU'RE BACK.
HOW DOES IT FEEL TO VISIT A DIFFERENT CLUB EVERY ONCE IN A WHILE?
......
WHAT'S THIS?

E-MAIL: FROM: NORTH_HIGH_COMPUTER_RESEARCH_SOCIETY_PRESIDENT, SUBJECT: COMPY MAGAZINE VOL. 102, NORTH HIGH COMPUTER SOCIETY INFORMATION VOL., HOT NEWS FROM NORTH HIGH! COMPUTER SOCIETY INFORMATION!, COMPY MAGAZINE VOL, HELLO. I AM PRESIDENT OF THE NORTH HIGH COMPUTER SOCIETY. THIS E-MAIL IS A NEWSLETTER FOR THE SAKE OF KEEPING EVERYBODY UPDATED ON THE NEWEST NORTH HIGH COMPUTER SOCIETY NEWS. IF YOU WISH TO STOP RECEIVING THIS NEWSLETTER, PLEASE READ BELOW.

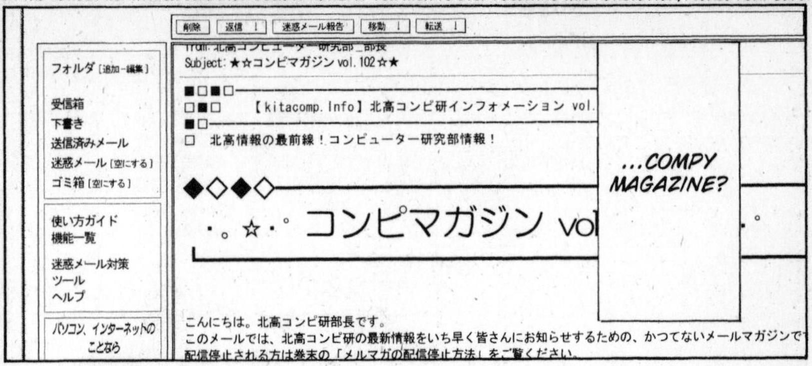

削除
返信
迷惑メール報告
移動
転送
Subject: ★☆コンピマガジン vol.102☆★
フォルダ [追加・編集]
受信箱
下書き
送信済みメール
迷惑メール [空にする]
ゴミ箱 [空にする]
【kitacomp.Info】北高コンピ研インフォメーション vol.
北高情報の最前線！コンピューター研究部情報！
コンピマガジン vol
使い方ガイド
機能一覧
迷惑メール対策
ツール
ヘルプ
こんにちは。北高コンピ研部長です。
...COMPY MAGAZINE?

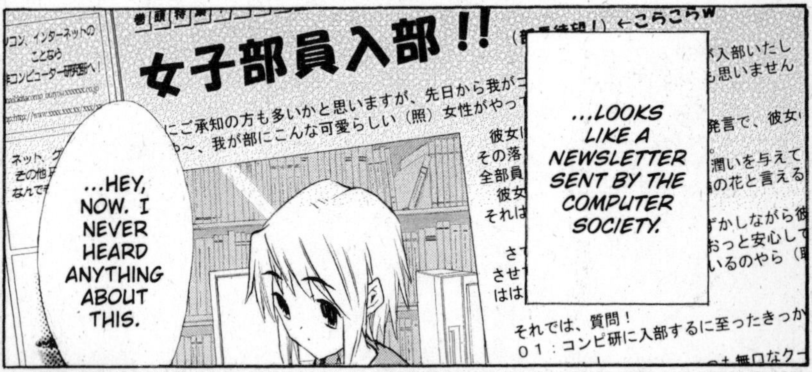

女子部員入部!!
←こらこらw
...LOOKS LIKE A NEWSLETTER SENT BY THE COMPUTER SOCIETY.
...HEY, NOW. I NEVER HEARD ANYTHING ABOUT THIS.
それでは、質問！
01：コンピ研に入部するに至ったきっか

EMAIL: FEMALE MEMBER HAS JOINED THE CLUB!! I'M SURE THAT MANY OF YOU ARE ALREADY AWARE THAT A FEW DAYS AGO...

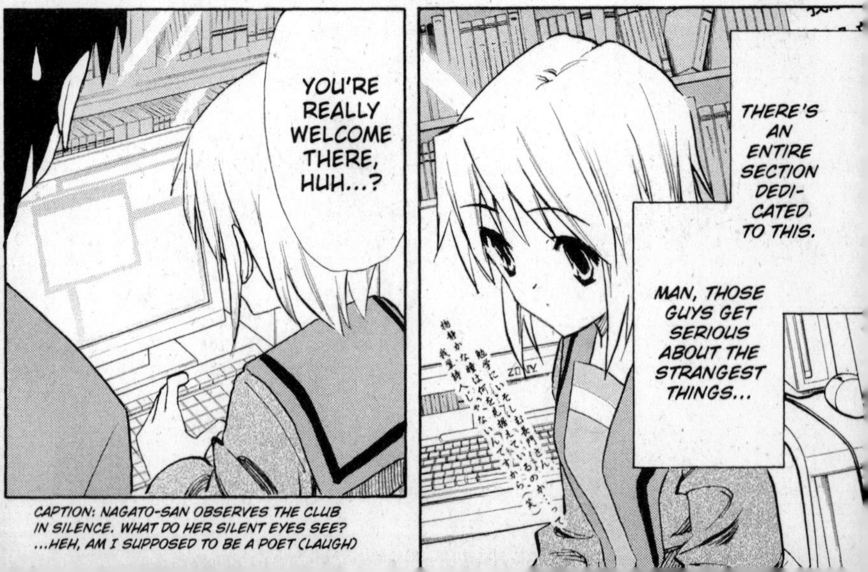

THERE'S AN ENTIRE SECTION DEDI-CATED TO THIS.
MAN, THOSE GUYS GET SERIOUS ABOUT THE STRANGEST THINGS...
YOU'RE REALLY WELCOME THERE, HUH...?

CAPTION: NAGATO-SAN OBSERVES THE CLUB IN SILENCE. WHAT DO HER SILENT EYES SEE? ...HEH, AM I SUPPOSED TO BE A POET (LAUGH)

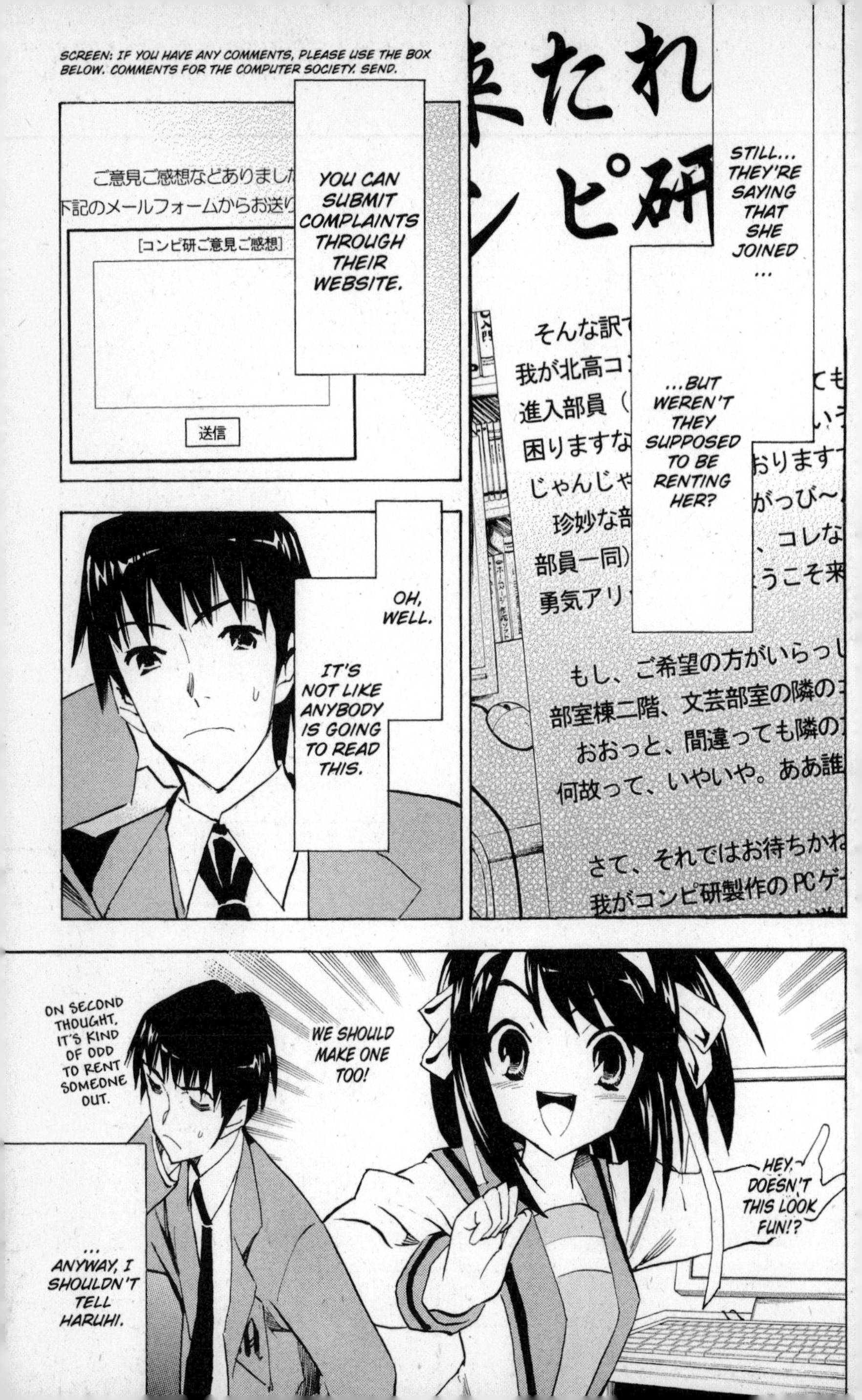
来たれ
ンピ研
STILL... THEY'RE SAYING THAT SHE JOINED...
そんな訳で
我が北高コ
進入部員（
困りますな
じゃんじゃ
珍妙な部
部員一同）
勇気アリ
...BUT WEREN'T THEY SUPPOSED TO BE RENTING HER?
ても
おります
がっぴ～
、コレな
ようこそ来
もし、ご希望の方がいらっし
部室棟二階、文芸部室の隣の
おおっと、間違っても隣の
何故って、いやいや。ああ誰
さて、それではお待ちかね
我がコンピ研製作のPCゲ
SCREEN: IF YOU HAVE ANY COMMENTS, PLEASE USE THE BOX BELOW. COMMENTS FOR THE COMPUTER SOCIETY. SEND.
ご意見ご感想などありました
下記のメールフォームからお送り
[コンピ研ご意見ご感想]
送信
YOU CAN SUBMIT COMPLAINTS THROUGH THEIR WEBSITE.
OH, WELL.
IT'S NOT LIKE ANYBODY IS GOING TO READ THIS.
HEY, DOESN'T THIS LOOK FUN!?
WE SHOULD MAKE ONE TOO!
ON SECOND THOUGHT, IT'S KIND OF ODD TO RENT SOMEONE OUT.
...ANYWAY, I SHOULDN'T TELL HARUHI.

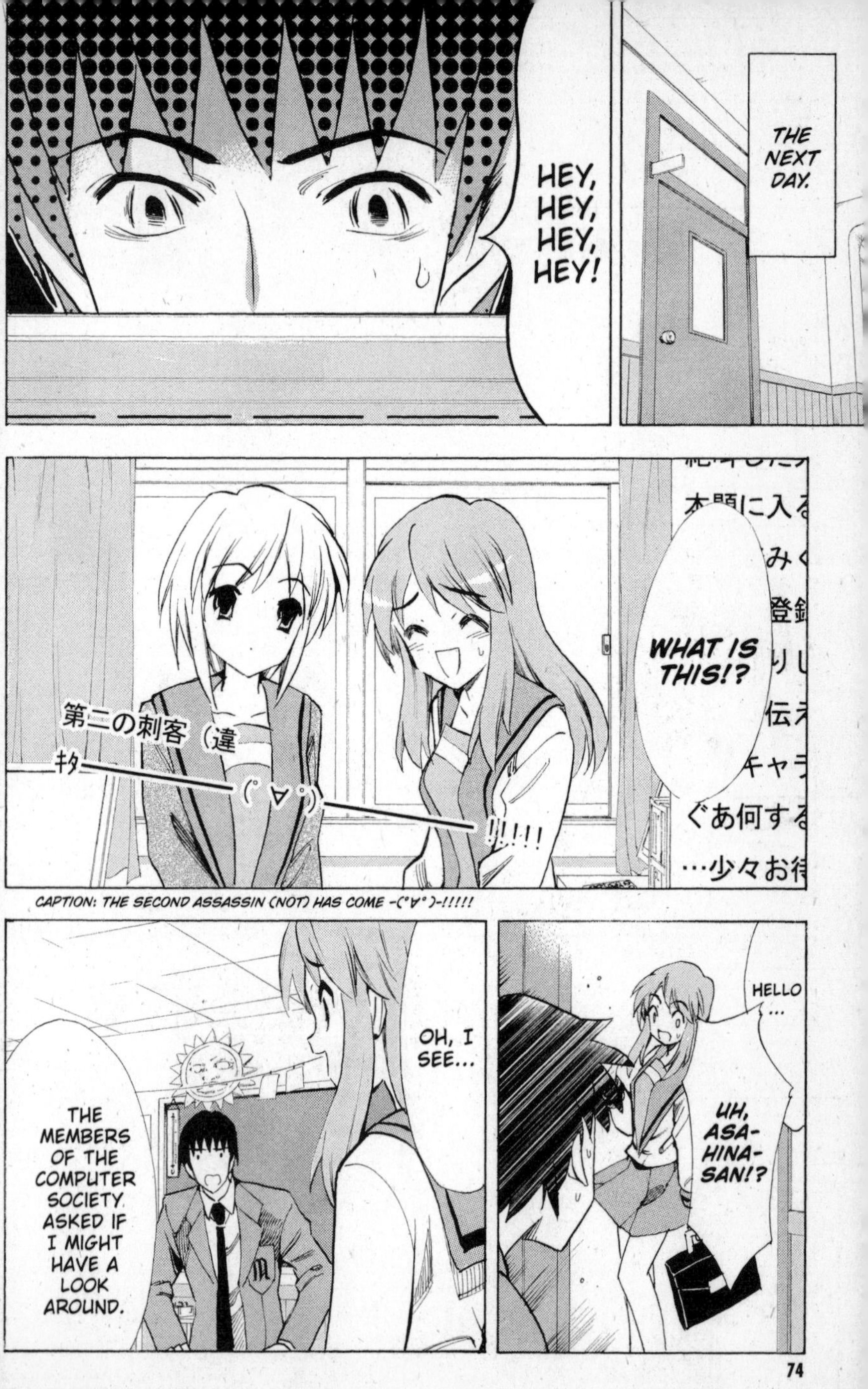
THE NEXT DAY.
HEY, HEY, HEY, HEY!
WHAT IS THIS!?
第二の刺客（違
キタ━━━━━━(ﾟ∀ﾟ)━━━━━━!!!!!
CAPTION: THE SECOND ASSASSIN (NOT) HAS COME -(ﾟ∀ﾟ)-!!!!!
HELLO...
UH, ASA-HINA-SAN!?
OH, I SEE...
THE MEMBERS OF THE COMPUTER SOCIETY ASKED IF I MIGHT HAVE A LOOK AROUND.

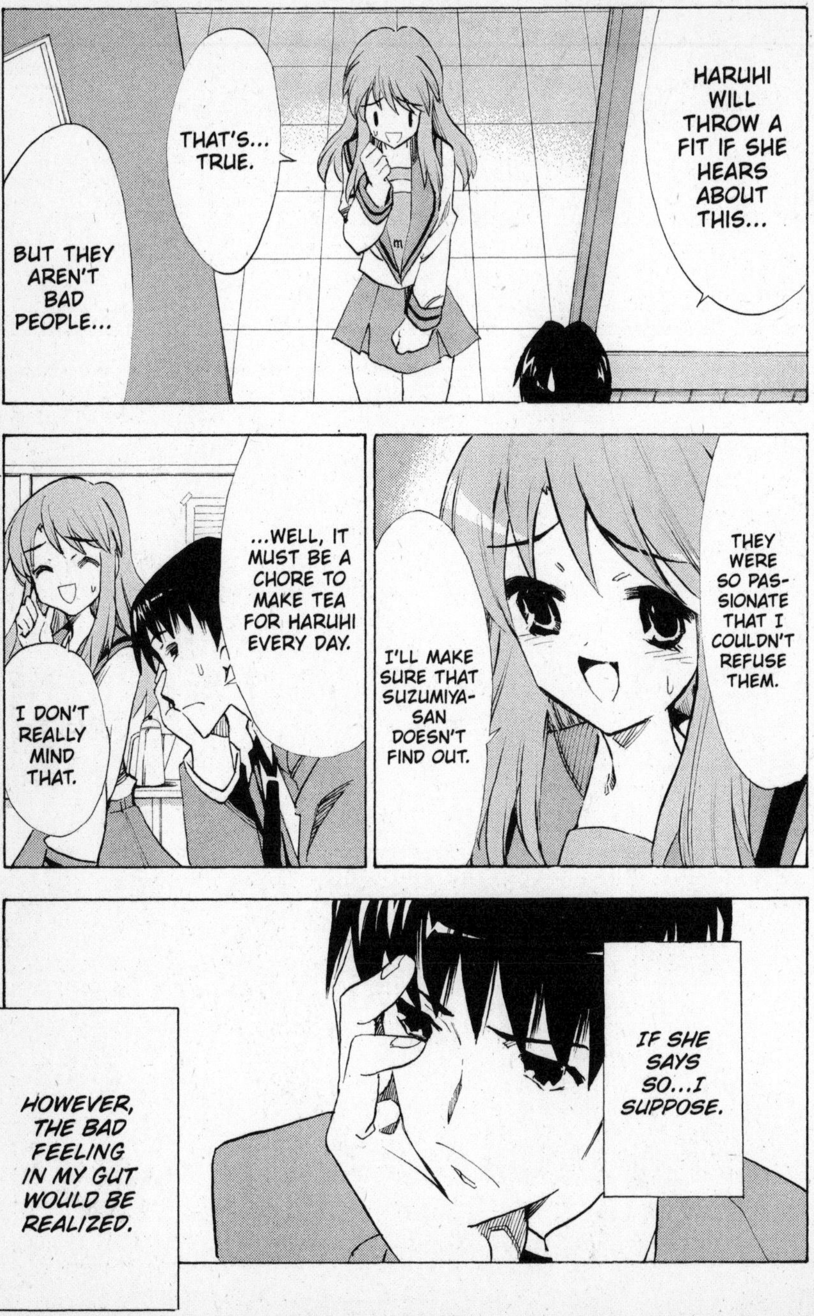
HARUHI WILL THROW A FIT IF SHE HEARS ABOUT THIS...
THAT'S... TRUE.
BUT THEY AREN'T BAD PEOPLE...
THEY WERE SO PASSIONATE THAT I COULDN'T REFUSE THEM.
I'LL MAKE SURE THAT SUZUMIYA-SAN DOESN'T FIND OUT.
...WELL, IT MUST BE A CHORE TO MAKE TEA FOR HARUHI EVERY DAY.
I DON'T REALLY MIND THAT.
IF SHE SAYS SO...I SUPPOSE.
HOWEVER, THE BAD FEELING IN MY GUT WOULD BE REALIZED.

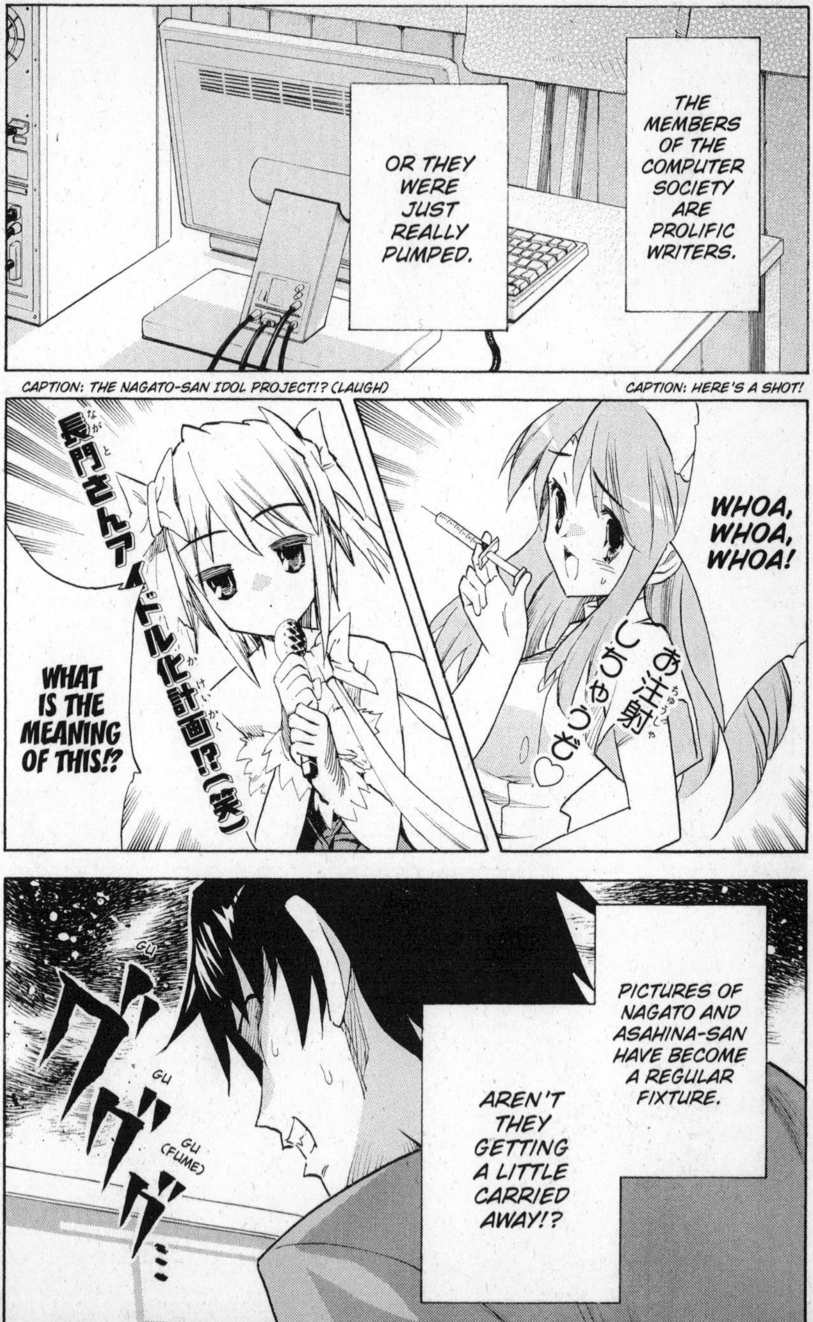
THE MEMBERS OF THE COMPUTER SOCIETY ARE PROLIFIC WRITERS.
OR THEY WERE JUST REALLY PUMPED.
CAPTION: HERE'S A SHOT!
WHOA, WHOA, WHOA!
お注射しちゃうぞ♡
CAPTION: THE NAGATO-SAN IDOL PROJECT!? (LAUGH)
長門さんアイドル化計画!?（笑）
WHAT IS THE MEANING OF THIS!?
PICTURES OF NAGATO AND ASAHINA-SAN HAVE BECOME A REGULAR FIXTURE.
AREN'T THEY GETTING A LITTLE CARRIED AWAY!?
GU
GU
GU (FUME)

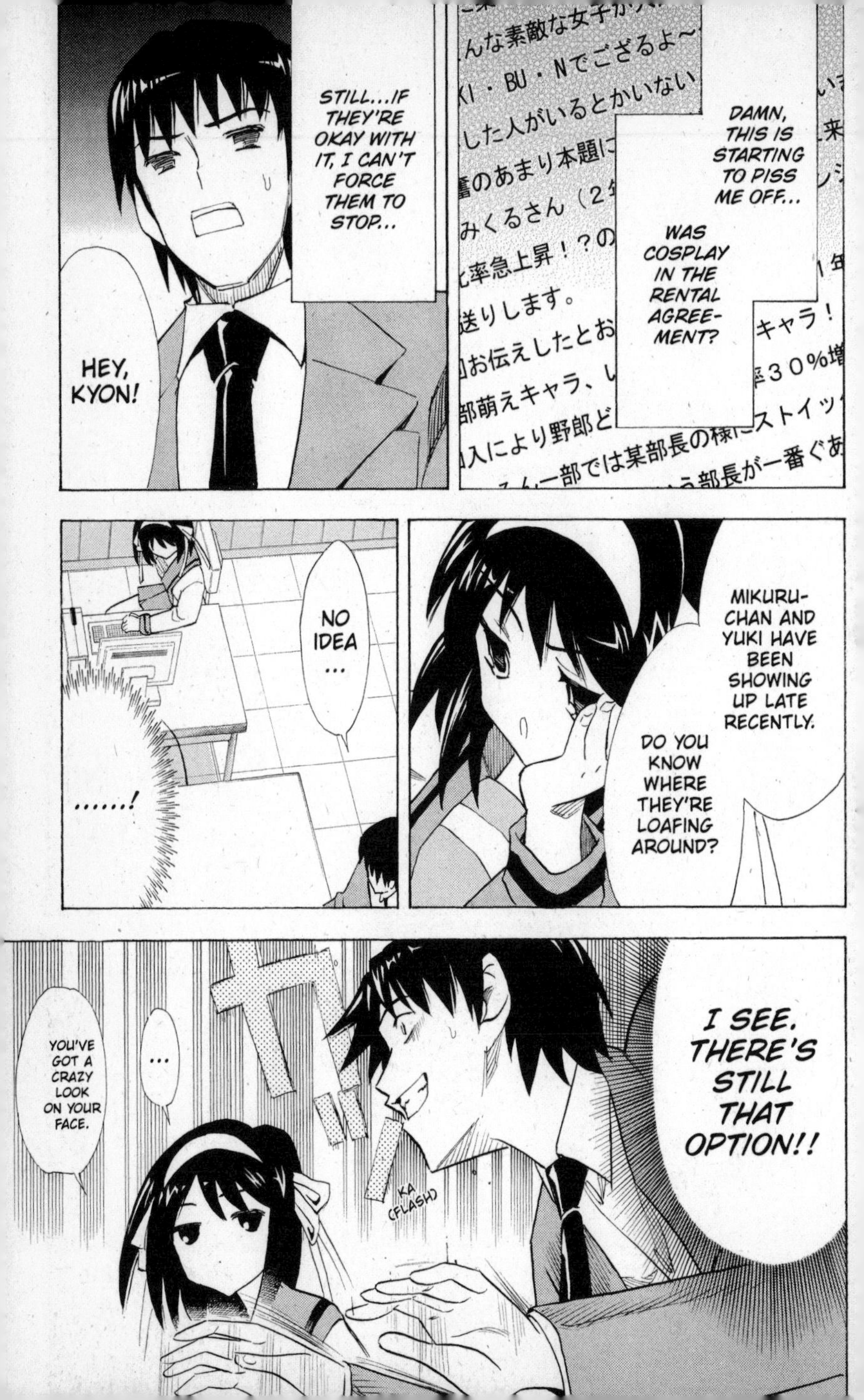
DAMN, THIS IS STARTING TO PISS ME OFF...
WAS COSPLAY IN THE RENTAL AGREE-MENT?
STILL...IF THEY'RE OKAY WITH IT, I CAN'T FORCE THEM TO STOP...
HEY, KYON!
MIKURU-CHAN AND YUKI HAVE BEEN SHOWING UP LATE RECENTLY.
DO YOU KNOW WHERE THEY'RE LOAFING AROUND?
NO IDEA ...
......!
I SEE. THERE'S STILL THAT OPTION!!
KA (FLASH)
...
YOU'VE GOT A CRAZY LOOK ON YOUR FACE.

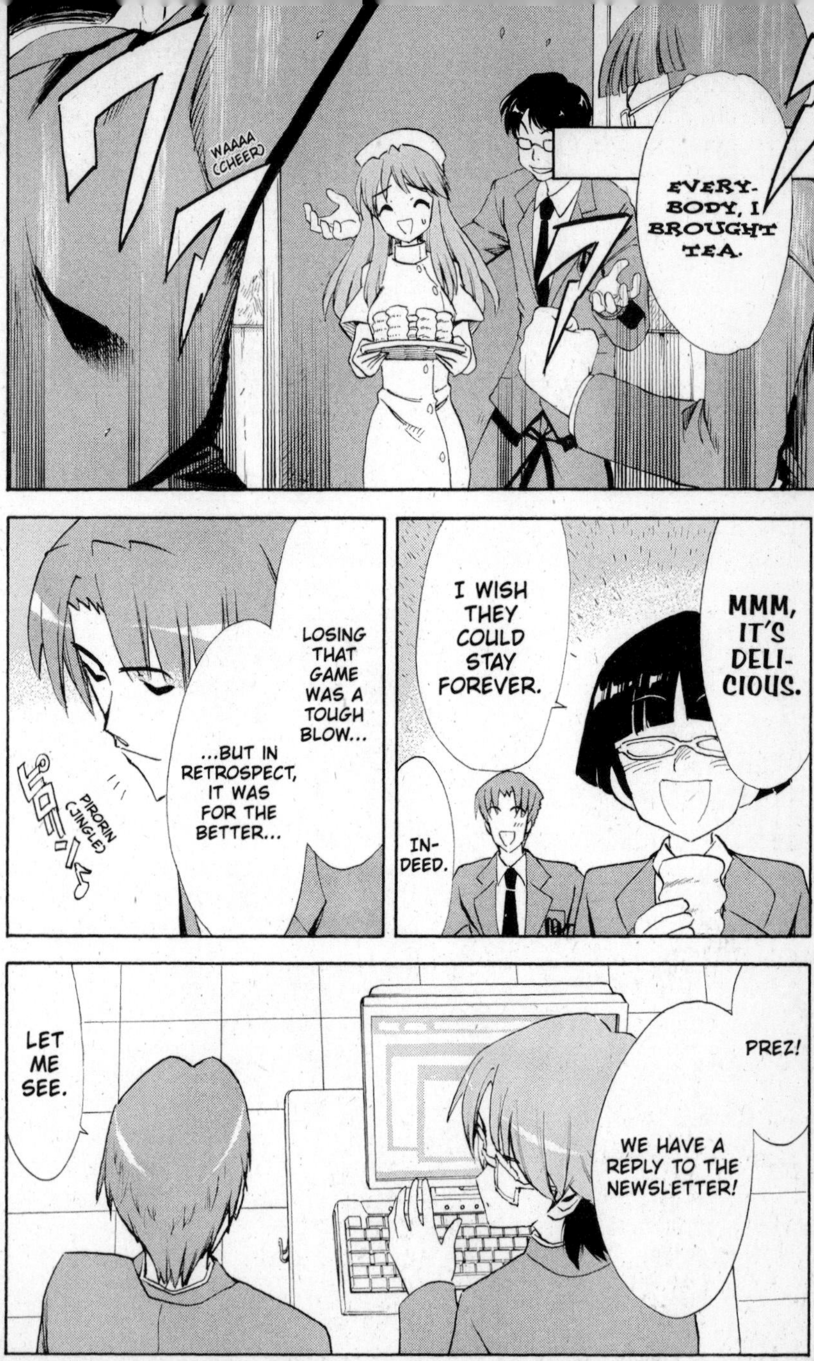
EVERY-BODY, I BROUGHT TEA.
WAAAA (CHEER)
MMM, IT'S DELICIOUS.
I WISH THEY COULD STAY FOREVER.
IN-DEED.
LOSING THAT GAME WAS A TOUGH BLOW...
...BUT IN RETROSPECT, IT WAS FOR THE BETTER...
PIRORIN (JINGLE)
PREZ!
WE HAVE A REPLY TO THE NEWSLETTER!
LET ME SEE.

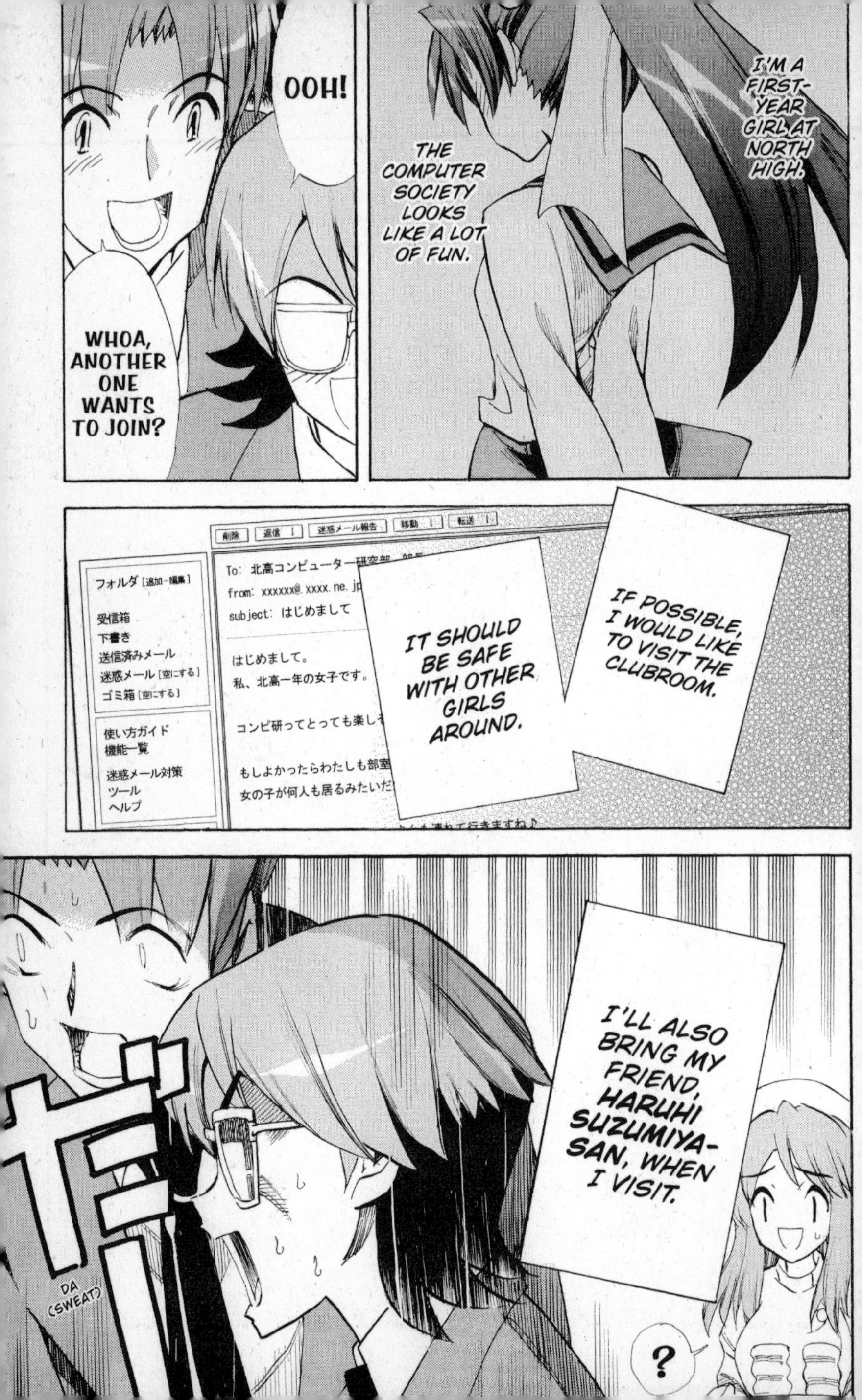

I'M A FIRST-YEAR GIRL AT NORTH HIGH.
THE COMPUTER SOCIETY LOOKS LIKE A LOT OF FUN.
OOH!
WHOA, ANOTHER ONE WANTS TO JOIN?
削除 返信 迷惑メール報告 移動 転送
フォルダ [追加・編集]
受信箱
下書き
送信済みメール
迷惑メール [空にする]
ゴミ箱 [空にする]
使い方ガイド
機能一覧
迷惑メール対策
ツール
ヘルプ
To: 北高コンピューター研究部
from: xxxxxx@.xxxx.ne.jp
subject: はじめまして
はじめまして。
私、北高一年の女子です。
IF POSSIBLE, I WOULD LIKE TO VISIT THE CLUBROOM.
IT SHOULD BE SAFE WITH OTHER GIRLS AROUND.
I'LL ALSO BRING MY FRIEND, HARUHI SUZUMIYA-SAN, WHEN I VISIT.
DA (SWEAT)
?

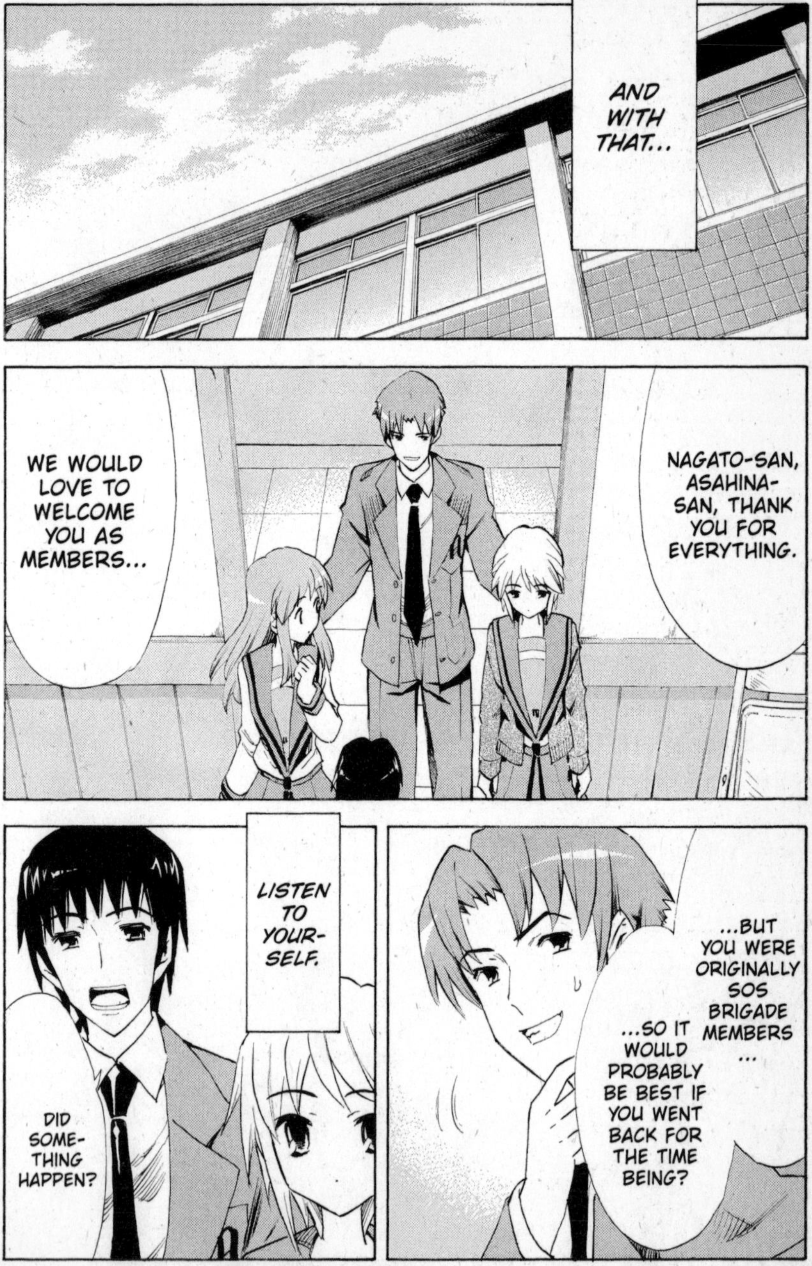
AND WITH THAT...
NAGATO-SAN, ASAHINA-SAN, THANK YOU FOR EVERYTHING.
WE WOULD LOVE TO WELCOME YOU AS MEMBERS...
...BUT YOU WERE ORIGINALLY SOS BRIGADE MEMBERS...
...SO IT WOULD PROBABLY BE BEST IF YOU WENT BACK FOR THE TIME BEING?
LISTEN TO YOURSELF.
DID SOMETHING HAPPEN?

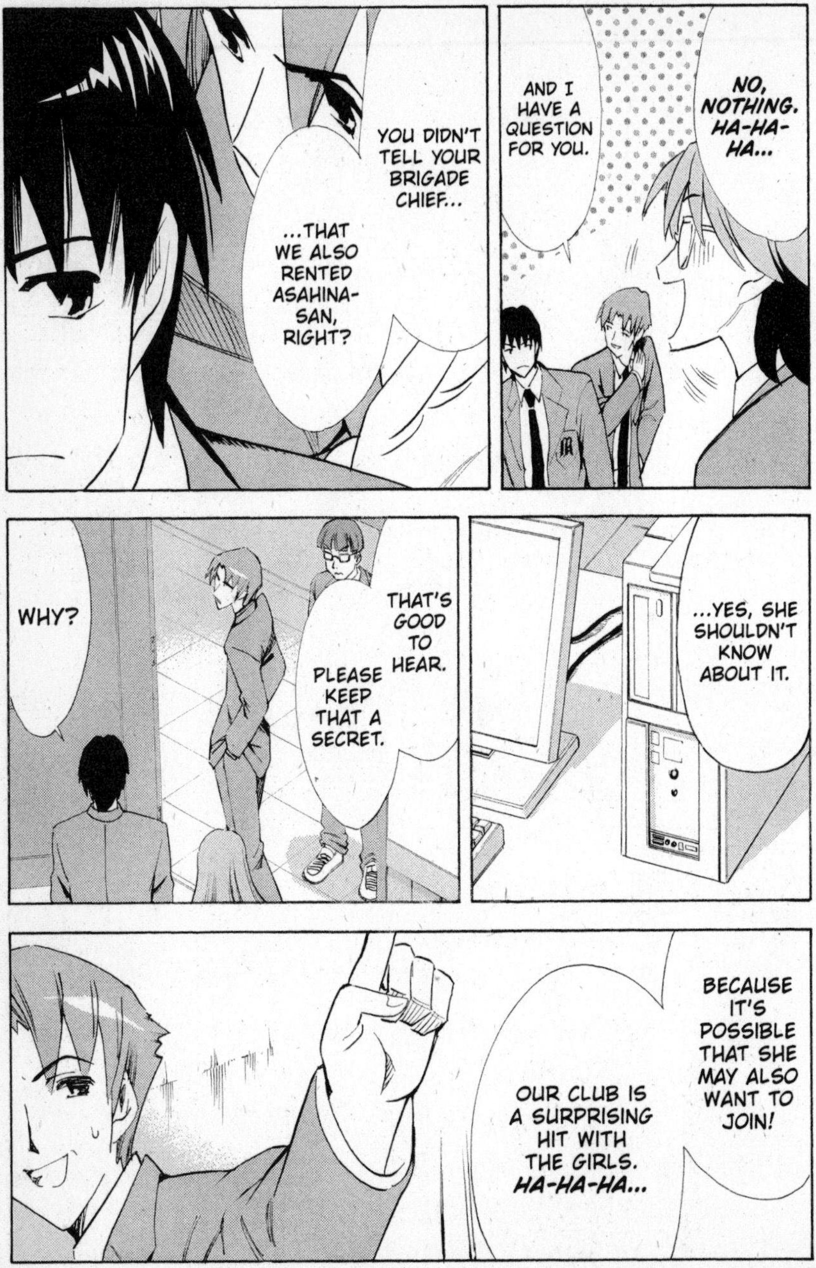
NO, NOTHING. HA-HA-HA...
AND I HAVE A QUESTION FOR YOU.
YOU DIDN'T TELL YOUR BRIGADE CHIEF...
...THAT WE ALSO RENTED ASAHINA-SAN, RIGHT?
...YES, SHE SHOULDN'T KNOW ABOUT IT.
THAT'S GOOD TO HEAR.
PLEASE KEEP THAT A SECRET.
WHY?
BECAUSE IT'S POSSIBLE THAT SHE MAY ALSO WANT TO JOIN!
OUR CLUB IS A SURPRISING HIT WITH THE GIRLS. HA-HA-HA...

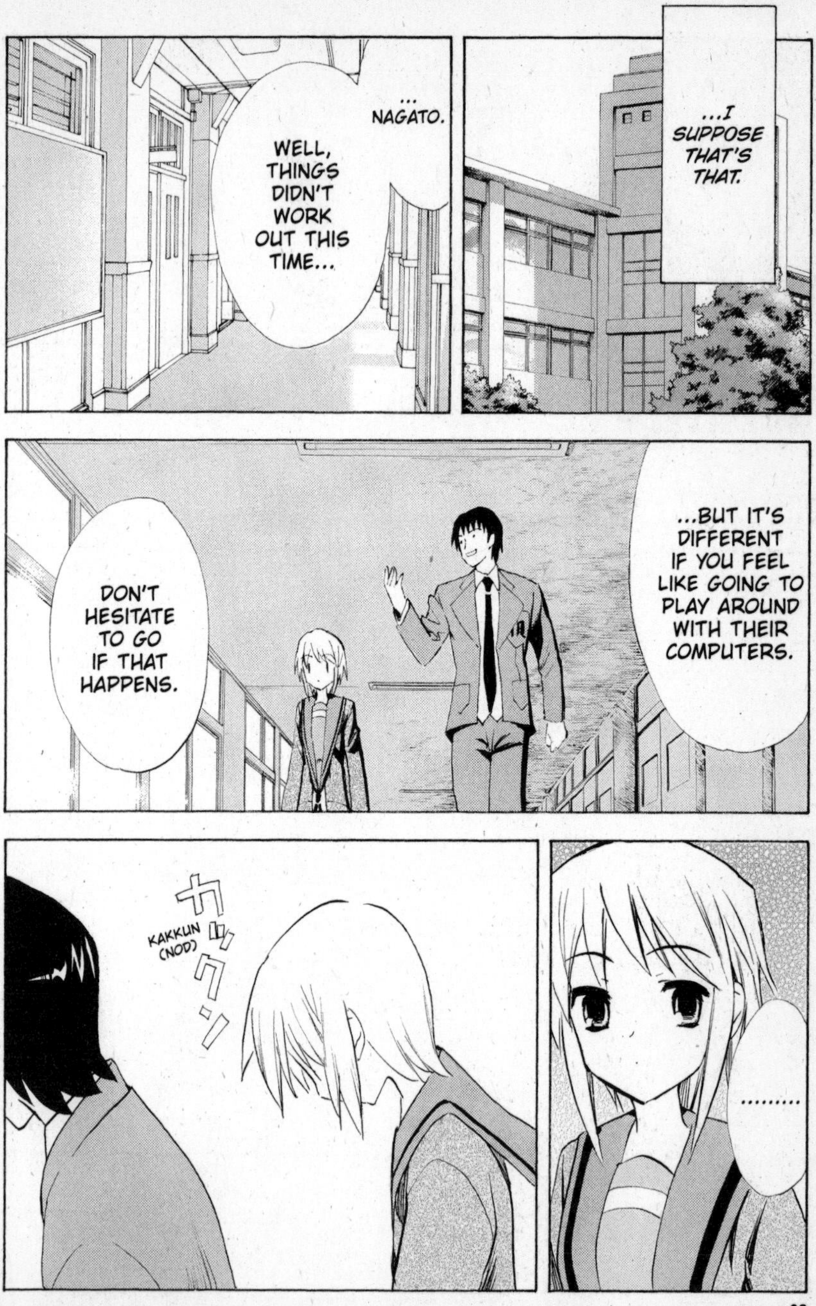
...I SUPPOSE THAT'S THAT.
... NAGATO.
WELL, THINGS DIDN'T WORK OUT THIS TIME...
...BUT IT'S DIFFERENT IF YOU FEEL LIKE GOING TO PLAY AROUND WITH THEIR COMPUTERS.
DON'T HESITATE TO GO IF THAT HAPPENS.
....
カックン
KAKKUN (NOD)

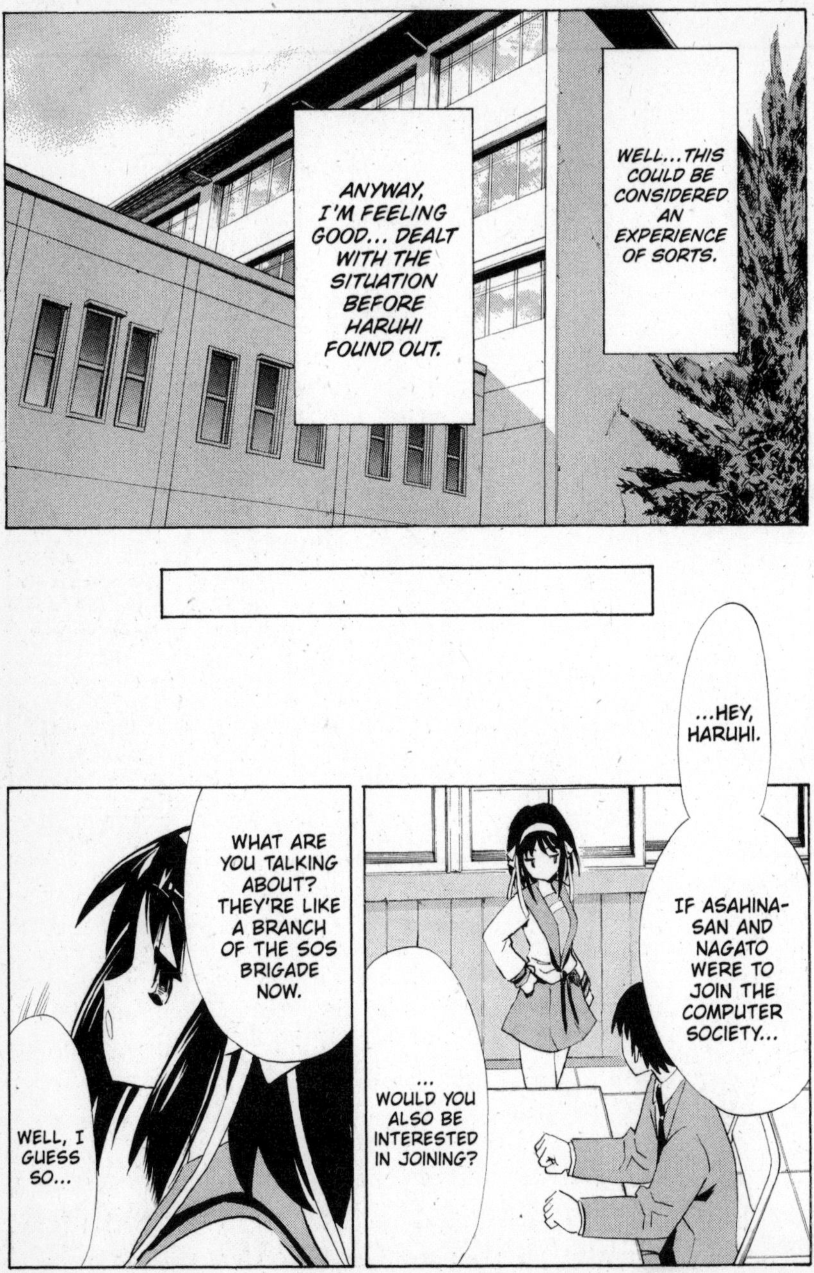
WELL...THIS COULD BE CONSIDERED AN EXPERIENCE OF SORTS.
ANYWAY, I'M FEELING GOOD... DEALT WITH THE SITUATION BEFORE HARUHI FOUND OUT.
...HEY, HARUHI.
IF ASAHINA-SAN AND NAGATO WERE TO JOIN THE COMPUTER SOCIETY...
... WOULD YOU ALSO BE INTERESTED IN JOINING?
WHAT ARE YOU TALKING ABOUT? THEY'RE LIKE A BRANCH OF THE SOS BRIGADE NOW.
WELL, I GUESS SO...

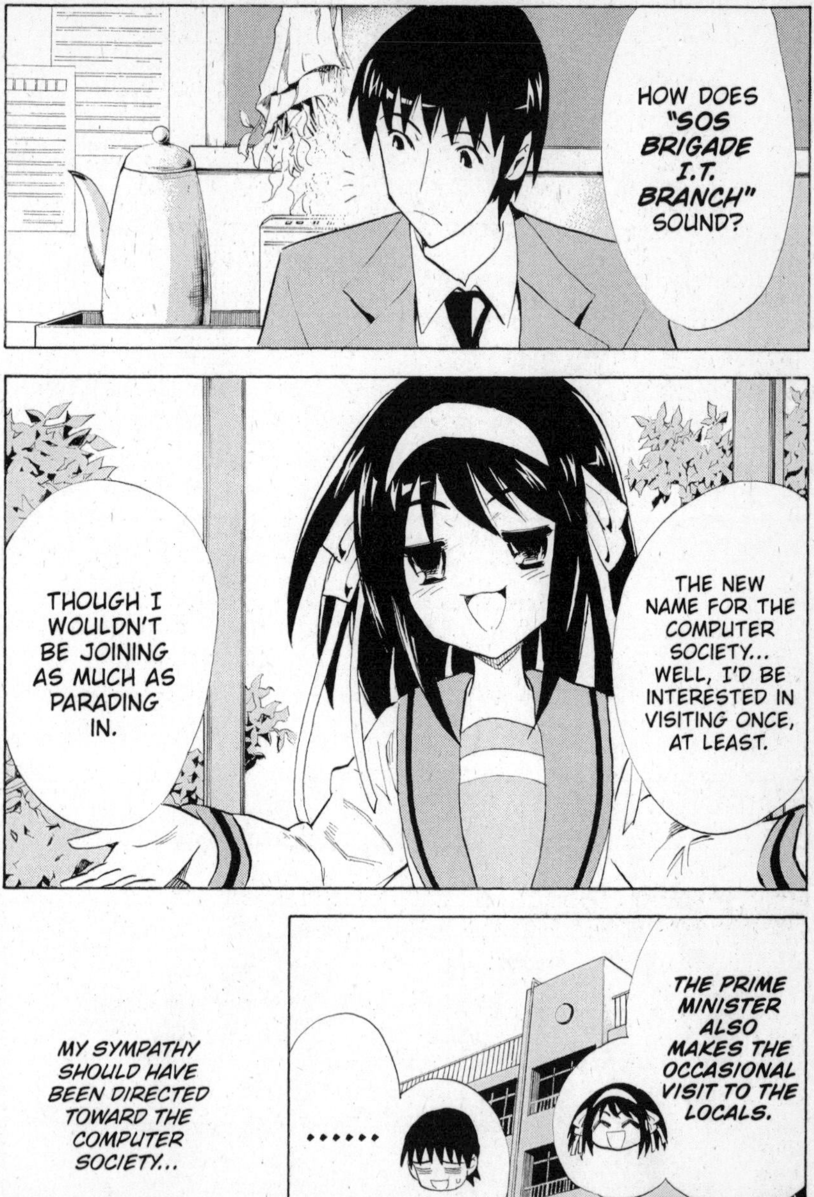
HOW DOES "SOS BRIGADE I.T. BRANCH" SOUND?
THE NEW NAME FOR THE COMPUTER SOCIETY... WELL, I'D BE INTERESTED IN VISITING ONCE, AT LEAST.
THOUGH I WOULDN'T BE JOINING AS MUCH AS PARADING IN.
THE PRIME MINISTER ALSO MAKES THE OCCASIONAL VISIT TO THE LOCALS.
......
MY SYMPATHY SHOULD HAVE BEEN DIRECTED TOWARD THE COMPUTER SOCIETY...

THE DAY OF SAGITTARIUS AFTERMATH : END

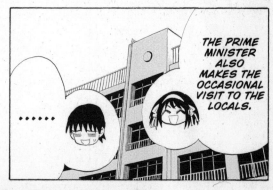

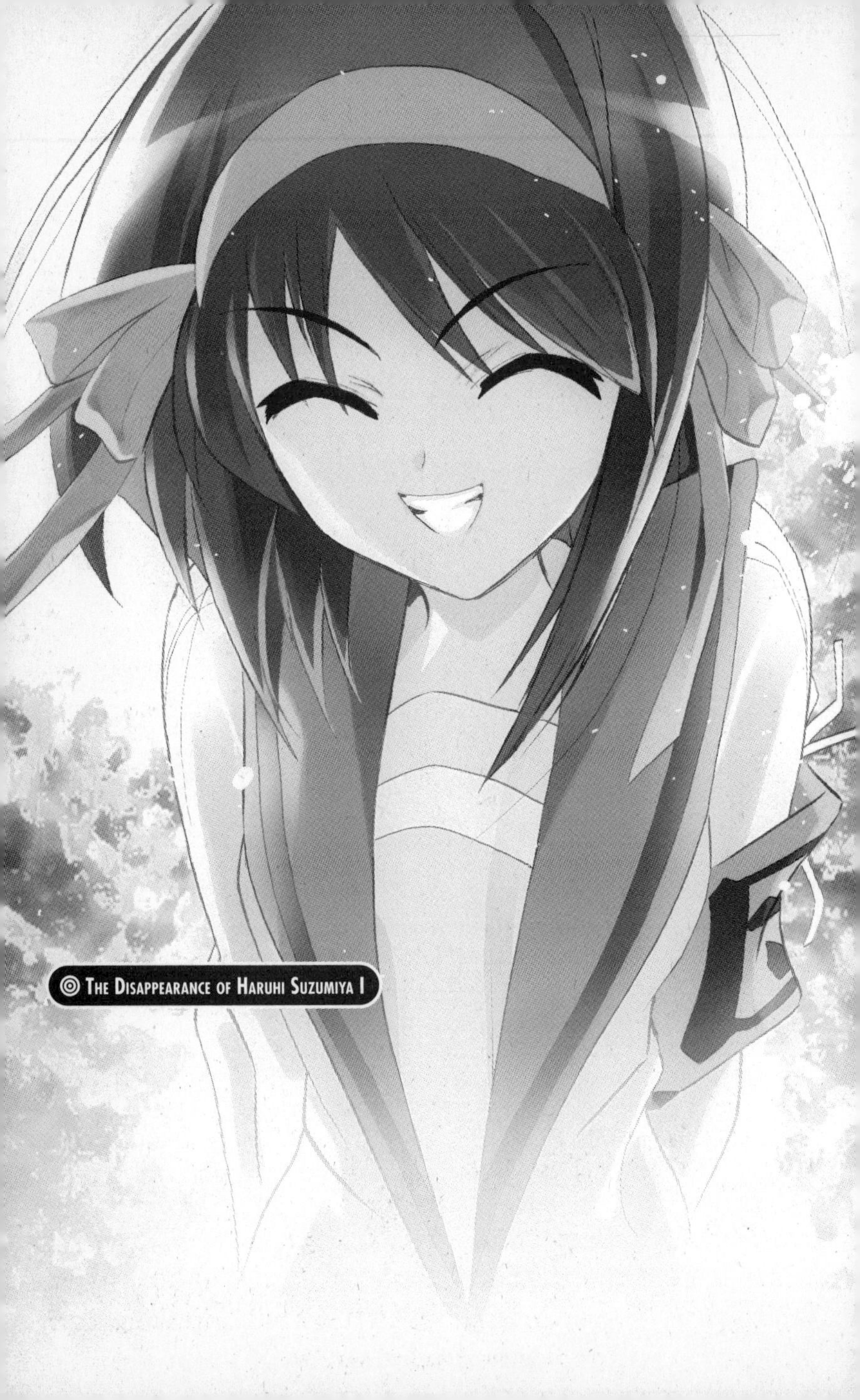
◎ The Disappearance of Haruhi Suzumiya I

THE MELANCHOLY OF HARUHI SUZUMIYA

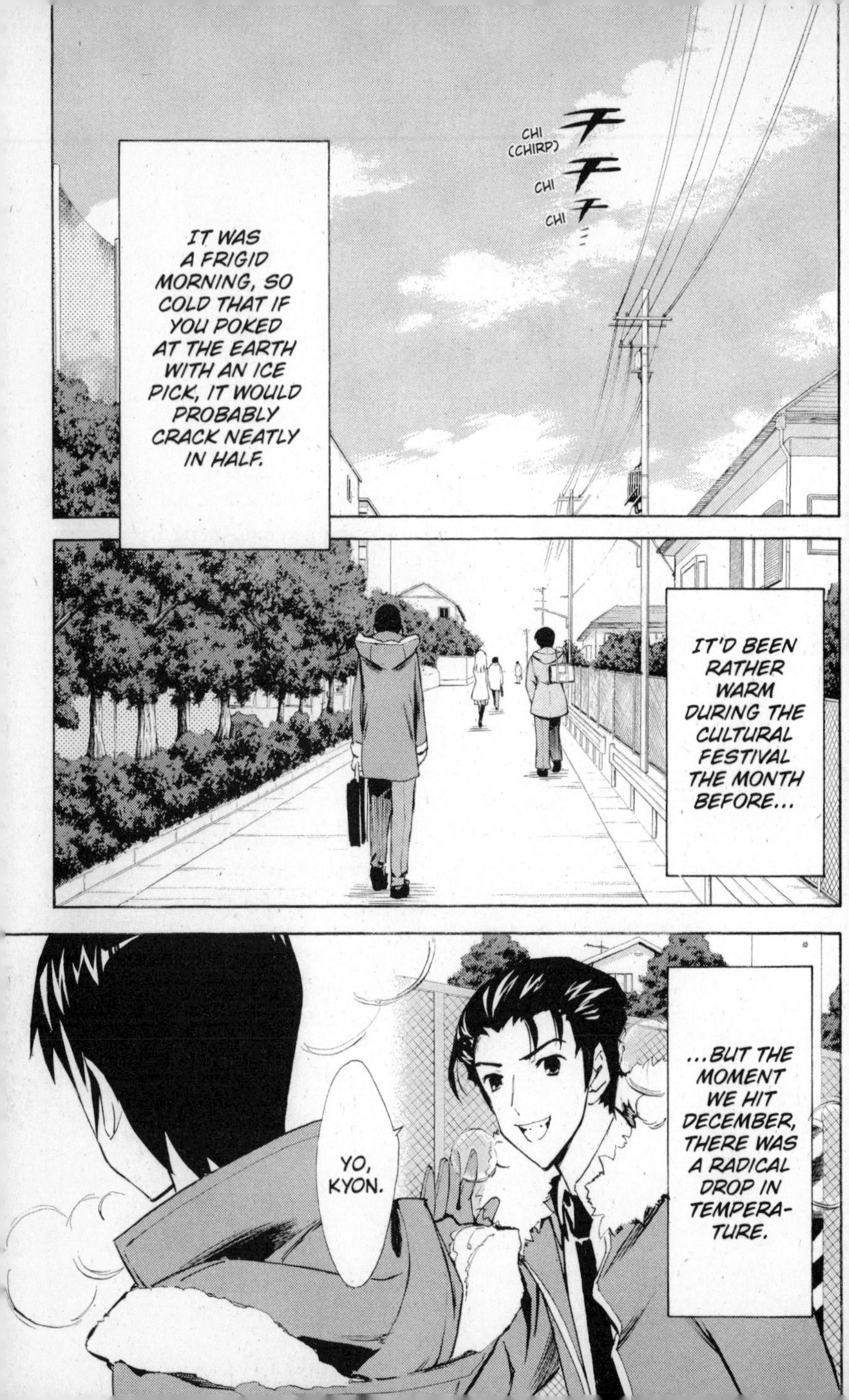
CHI (CHIRP)
CHI
CHI
IT WAS A FRIGID MORNING, SO COLD THAT IF YOU POKED AT THE EARTH WITH AN ICE PICK, IT WOULD PROBABLY CRACK NEATLY IN HALF.
IT'D BEEN RATHER WARM DURING THE CULTURAL FESTIVAL THE MONTH BEFORE...
...BUT THE MOMENT WE HIT DECEMBER, THERE WAS A RADICAL DROP IN TEMPERA-TURE.
YO, KYON.

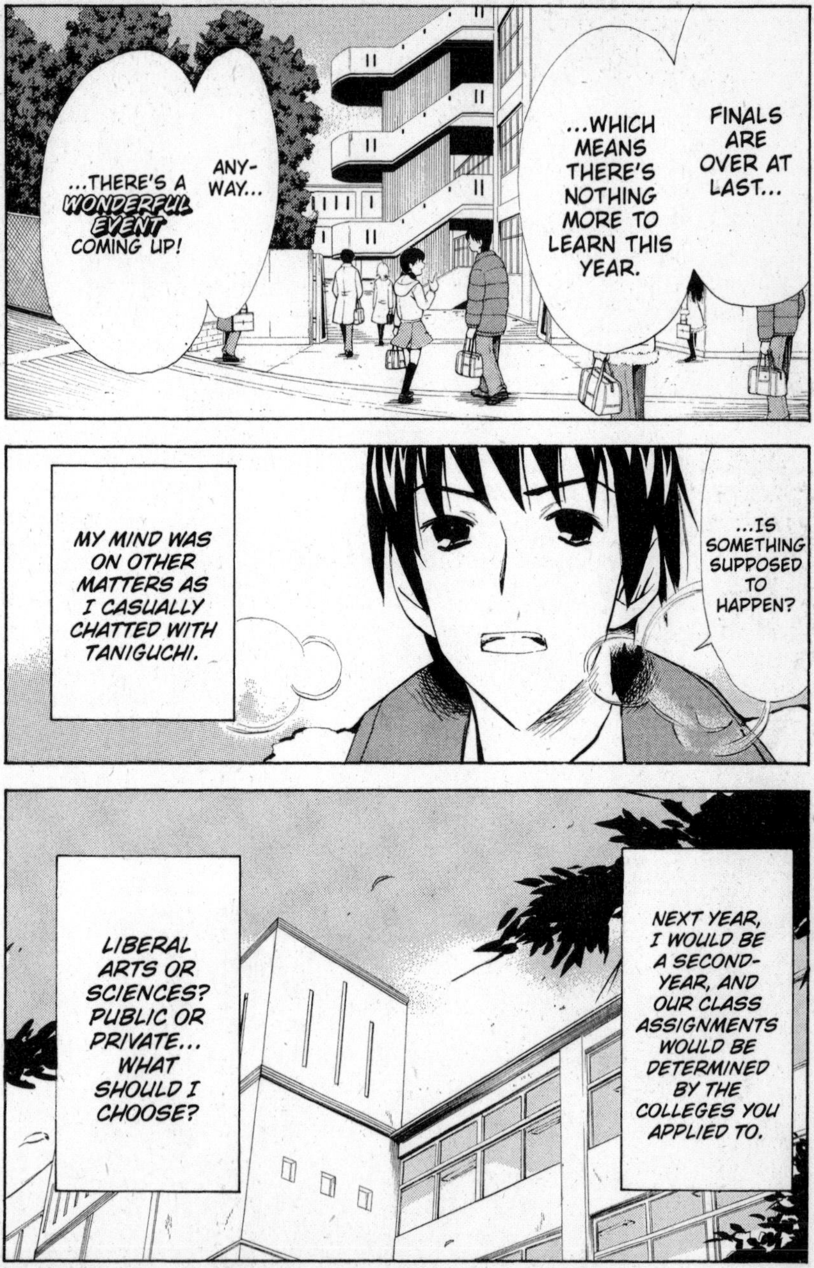
FINALS ARE OVER AT LAST...
...WHICH MEANS THERE'S NOTHING MORE TO LEARN THIS YEAR.
ANYWAY...
...THERE'S A WONDERFUL EVENT COMING UP!
...IS SOMETHING SUPPOSED TO HAPPEN?
MY MIND WAS ON OTHER MATTERS AS I CASUALLY CHATTED WITH TANIGUCHI.
NEXT YEAR, I WOULD BE A SECOND-YEAR, AND OUR CLASS ASSIGNMENTS WOULD BE DETERMINED BY THE COLLEGES YOU APPLIED TO.
LIBERAL ARTS OR SCIENCES? PUBLIC OR PRIVATE... WHAT SHOULD I CHOOSE?

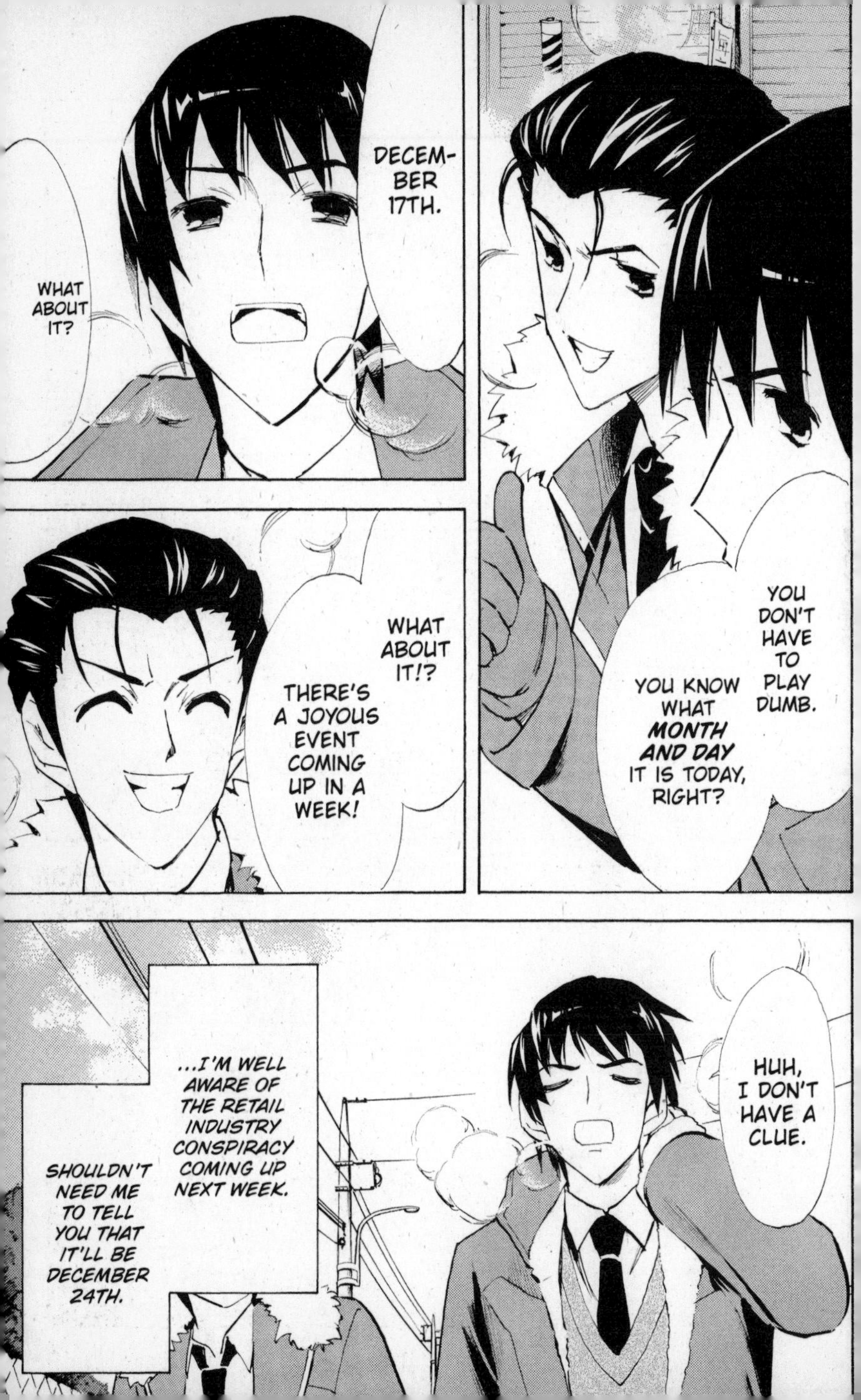

YOU DON'T HAVE TO PLAY DUMB.
YOU KNOW WHAT MONTH AND DAY IT IS TODAY, RIGHT?
DECEMBER 17TH.
WHAT ABOUT IT?
WHAT ABOUT IT!?
THERE'S A JOYOUS EVENT COMING UP IN A WEEK!
HUH, I DON'T HAVE A CLUE.
...I'M WELL AWARE OF THE RETAIL INDUSTRY CONSPIRACY COMING UP NEXT WEEK.
SHOULDN'T NEED ME TO TELL YOU THAT IT'LL BE DECEMBER 24TH.

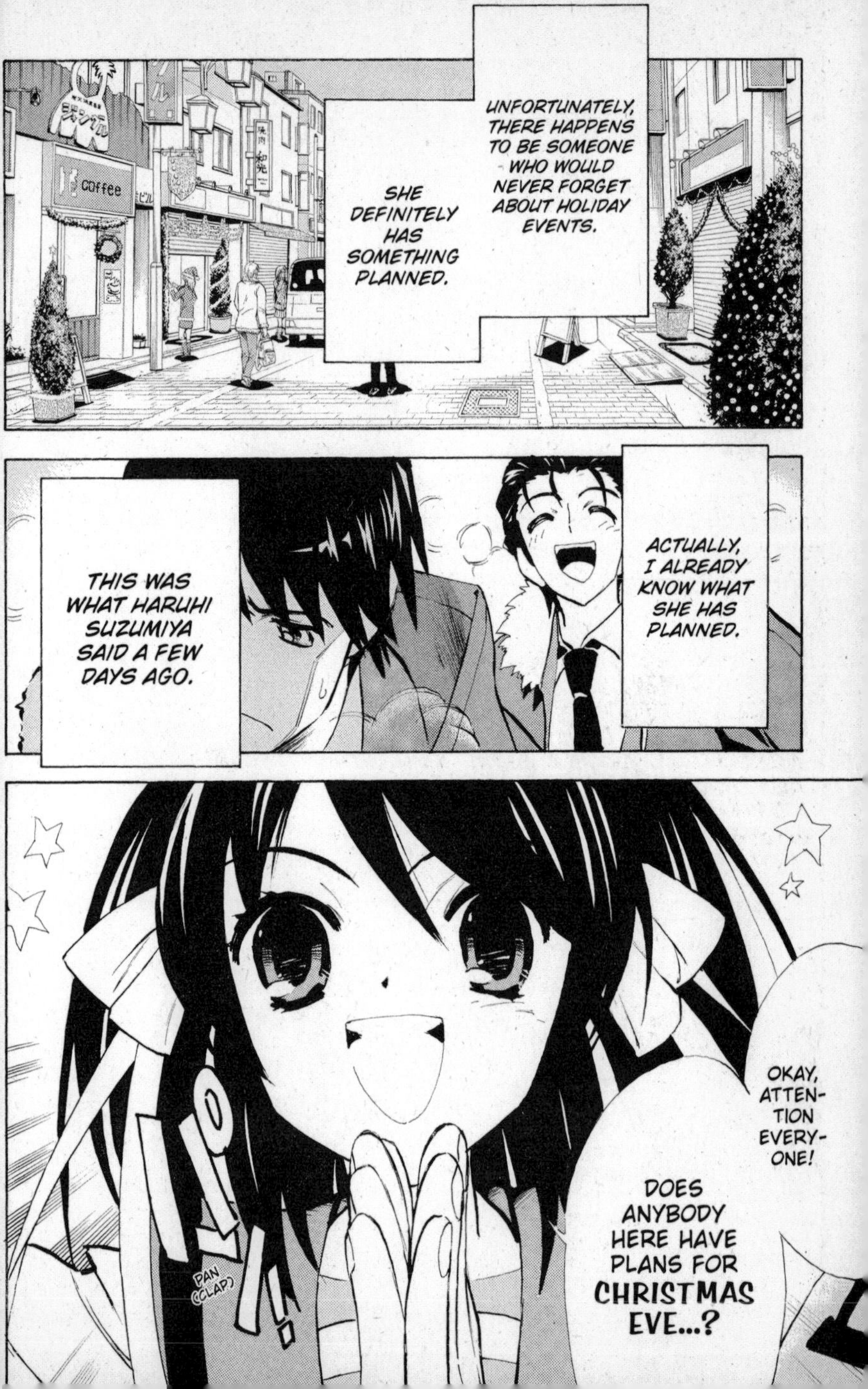
UNFORTUNATELY, THERE HAPPENS TO BE SOMEONE WHO WOULD NEVER FORGET ABOUT HOLIDAY EVENTS.
SHE DEFINITELY HAS SOMETHING PLANNED.
coffee
ACTUALLY, I ALREADY KNOW WHAT SHE HAS PLANNED.
THIS WAS WHAT HARUHI SUZUMIYA SAID A FEW DAYS AGO.
OKAY, ATTEN-TION EVERY-ONE!
DOES ANYBODY HERE HAVE PLANS FOR CHRISTMAS EVE...?
PAN (CLAP)

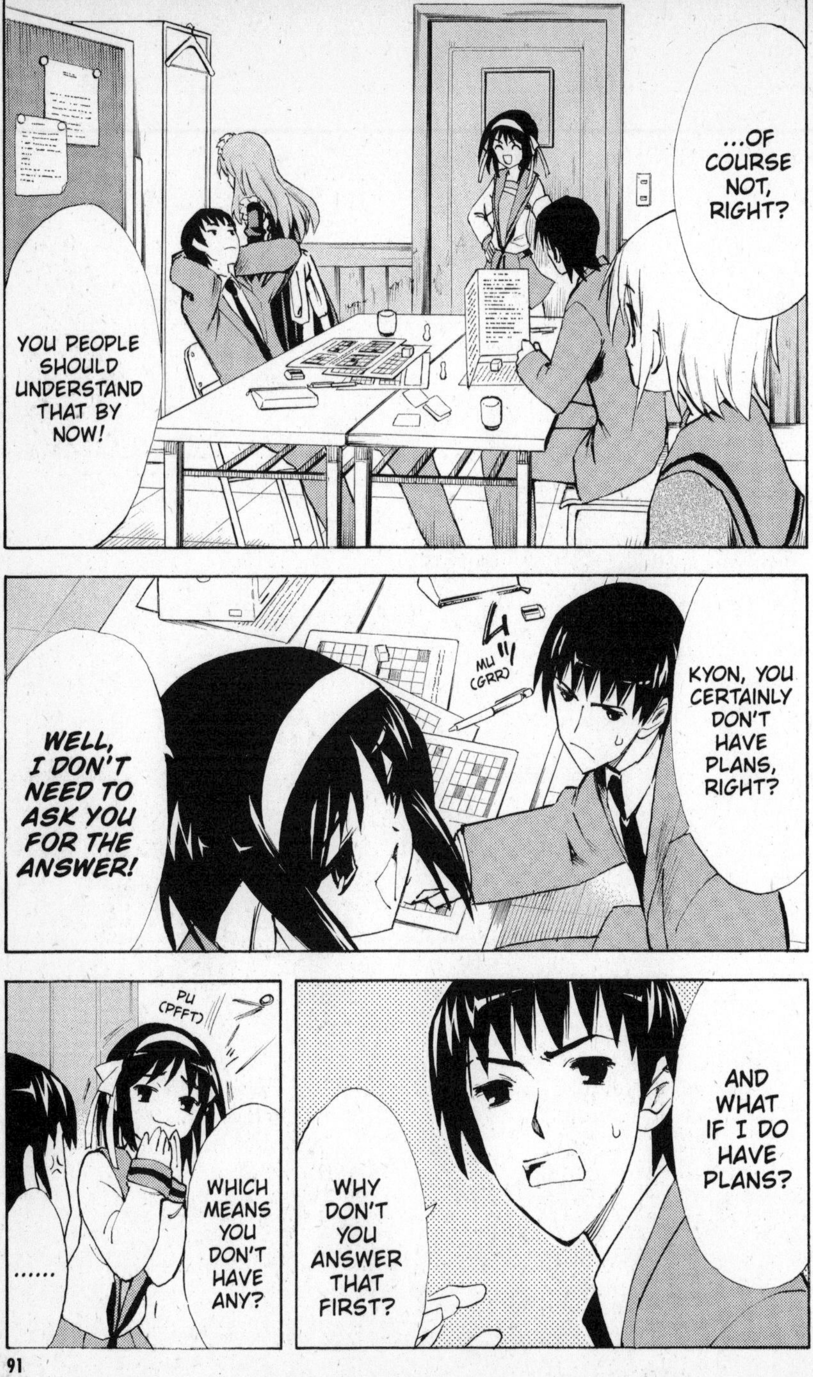
...OF COURSE NOT, RIGHT?
YOU PEOPLE SHOULD UNDERSTAND THAT BY NOW!
KYON, YOU CERTAINLY DON'T HAVE PLANS, RIGHT?
MU (GRR)
WELL, I DON'T NEED TO ASK YOU FOR THE ANSWER!
AND WHAT IF I DO HAVE PLANS?
WHY DON'T YOU ANSWER THAT FIRST?
PU (PFFT)
WHICH MEANS YOU DON'T HAVE ANY?
......

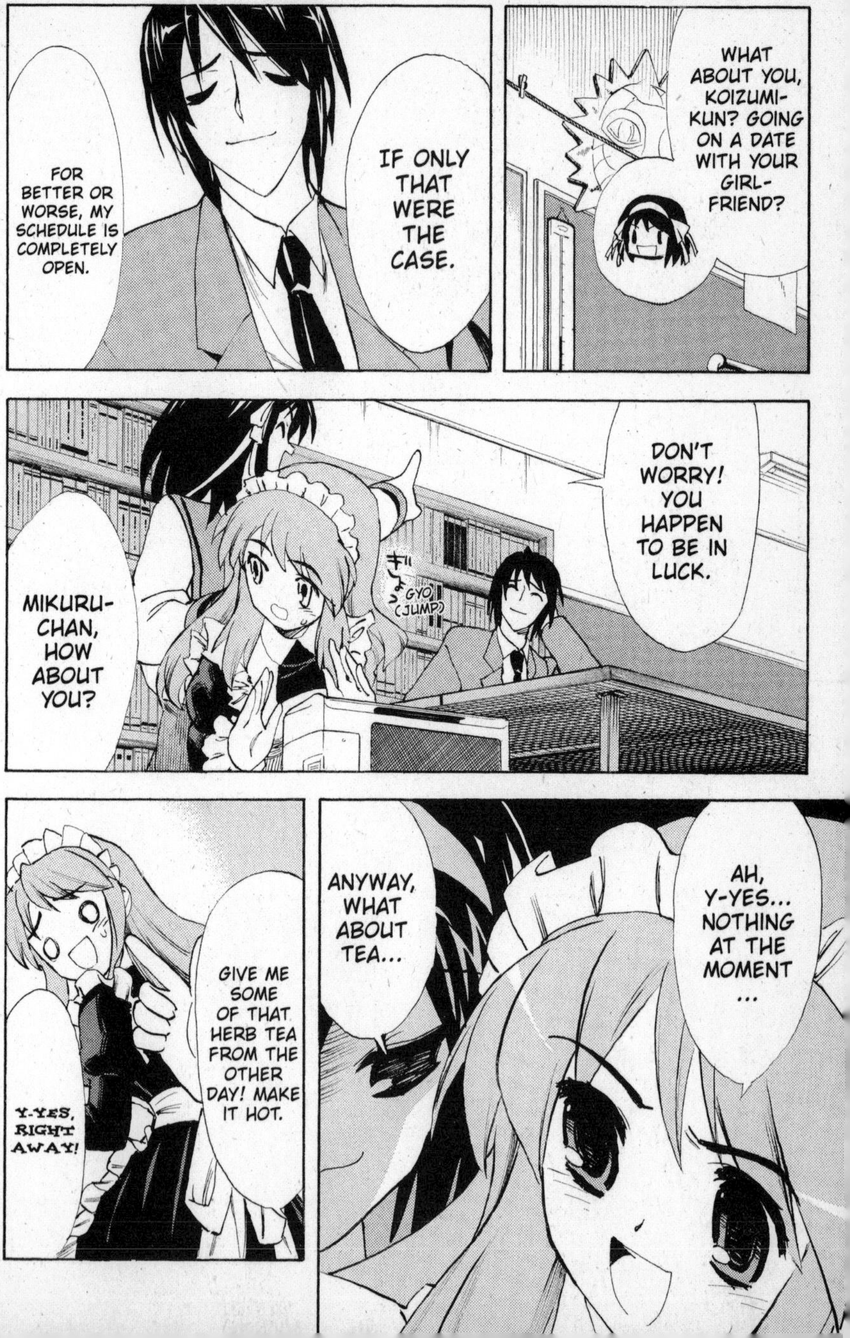
WHAT ABOUT YOU, KOIZUMI-KUN? GOING ON A DATE WITH YOUR GIRL-FRIEND?
IF ONLY THAT WERE THE CASE.
FOR BETTER OR WORSE, MY SCHEDULE IS COMPLETELY OPEN.
DON'T WORRY! YOU HAPPEN TO BE IN LUCK.
MIKURU-CHAN, HOW ABOUT YOU?
ぎょっ GYO (JUMP)
AH, Y-YES... NOTHING AT THE MOMENT ...
ANYWAY, WHAT ABOUT TEA...
GIVE ME SOME OF THAT HERB TEA FROM THE OTHER DAY! MAKE IT HOT.
Y-YES, RIGHT AWAY!

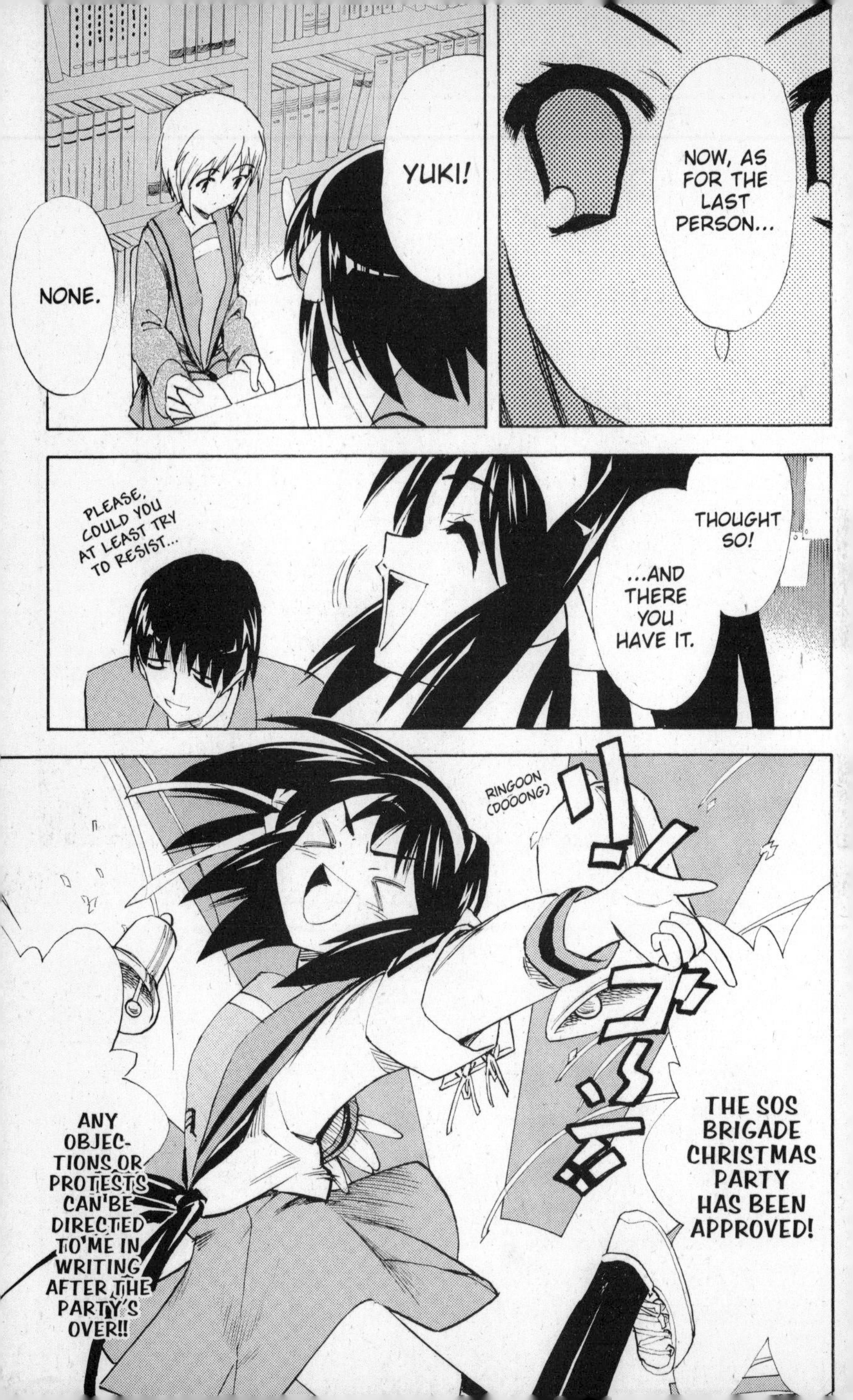
NOW, AS FOR THE LAST PERSON...
YUKI!
NONE.
THOUGHT SO!
...AND THERE YOU HAVE IT.
PLEASE, COULD YOU AT LEAST TRY TO RESIST...
RINGOON (DOOONG)
THE SOS BRIGADE CHRISTMAS PARTY HAS BEEN APPROVED!
ANY OBJECTIONS OR PROTESTS CAN BE DIRECTED TO ME IN WRITING AFTER THE PARTY'S OVER!!

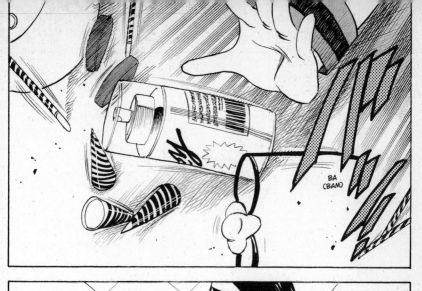

BA
(BAM)

TO
(TAP)

TO

TO

SINCE IT'S THE CHRISTMAS SEASON AND ALL, WE HAVE TO BE PREPARED.

SO WITH THAT IN MIND, I BROUGHT SOME SPECIAL ITEMS.

YOU HAVE TO START BY CREATING THE HOLIDAY ATMOSPHERE.

WASSHA WASSHA

WASSHA (WHIRR)

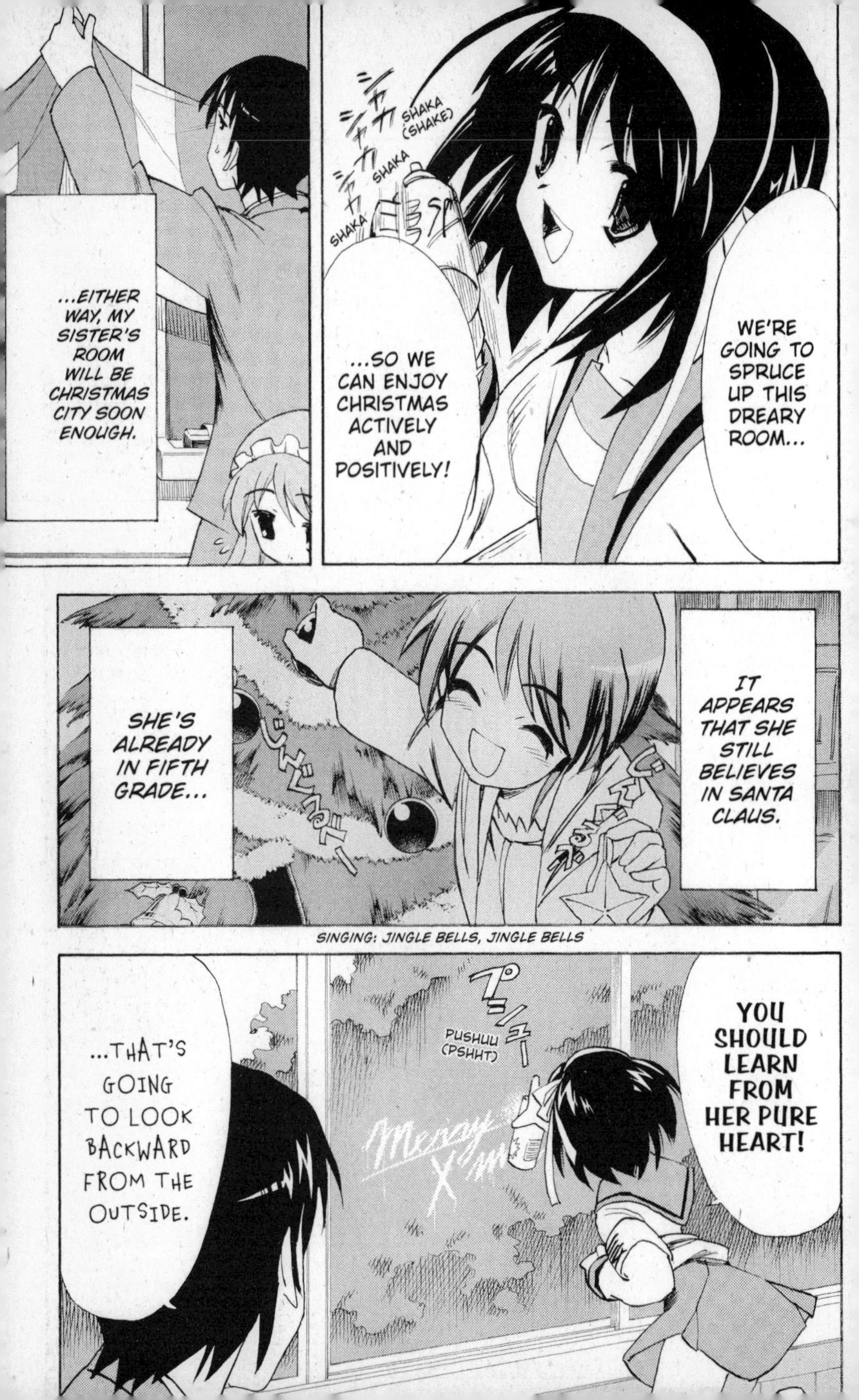
WE'RE GOING TO SPRUCE UP THIS DREARY ROOM...
SHAKA (SHAKE)
SHAKA
SHAKA
...SO WE CAN ENJOY CHRISTMAS ACTIVELY AND POSITIVELY!
...EITHER WAY, MY SISTER'S ROOM WILL BE CHRISTMAS CITY SOON ENOUGH.
IT APPEARS THAT SHE STILL BELIEVES IN SANTA CLAUS.
SHE'S ALREADY IN FIFTH GRADE...
SINGING: JINGLE BELLS, JINGLE BELLS
YOU SHOULD LEARN FROM HER PURE HEART!
PUSHUU (PSHHT)
...THAT'S GOING TO LOOK BACKWARD FROM THE OUTSIDE.

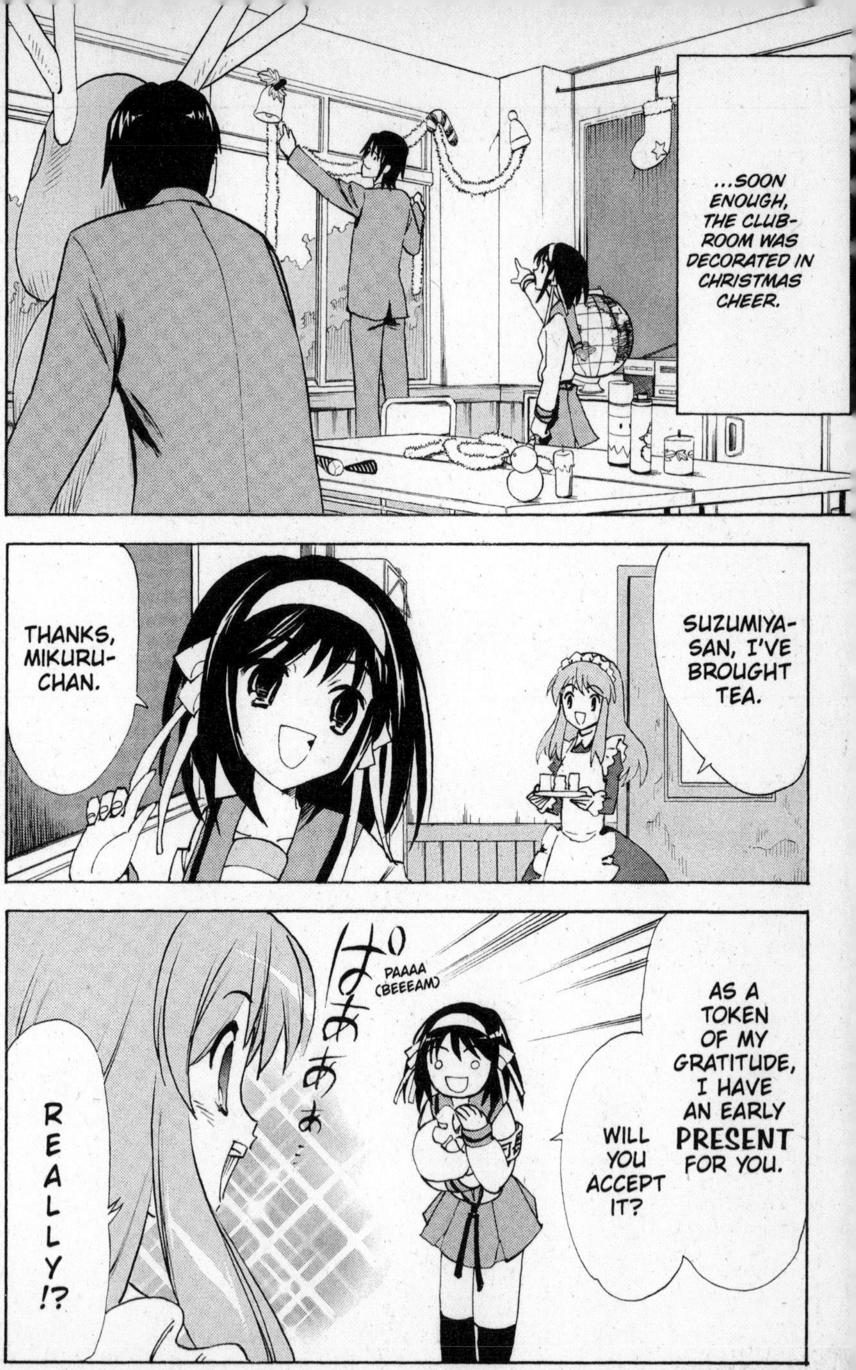
...SOON ENOUGH, THE CLUB-ROOM WAS DECORATED IN CHRISTMAS CHEER.
SUZUMIYA-SAN, I'VE BROUGHT TEA.
THANKS, MIKURU-CHAN.
AS A TOKEN OF MY GRATITUDE, I HAVE AN EARLY PRESENT FOR YOU.
ぱあああ
PAAAA (BEEEAM)
WILL YOU ACCEPT IT?
REALLY!?

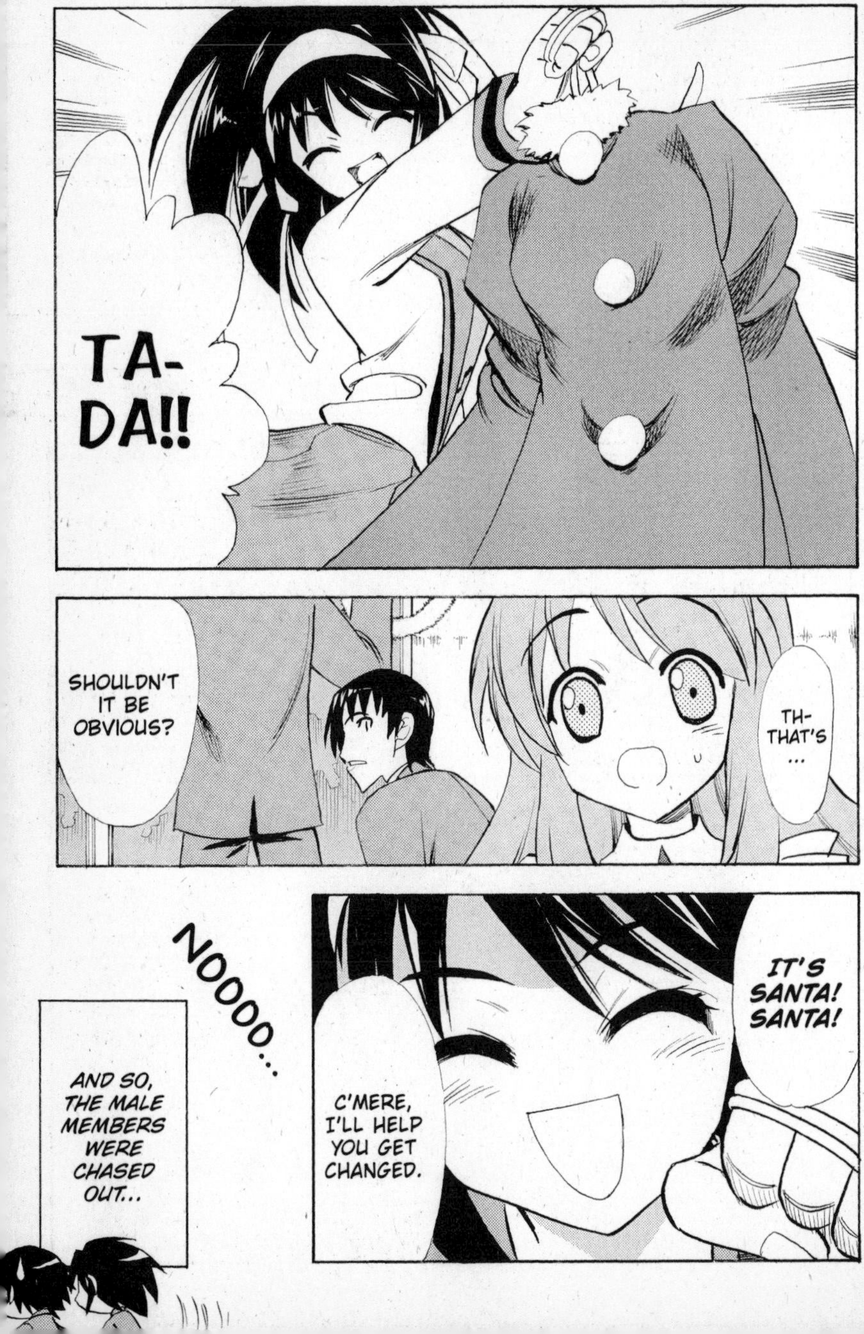
TA-DA!!
TH-THAT'S ...
SHOULDN'T IT BE OBVIOUS?
IT'S SANTA! SANTA!
C'MERE, I'LL HELP YOU GET CHANGED.
NOOOO...
AND SO, THE MALE MEMBERS WERE CHASED OUT...

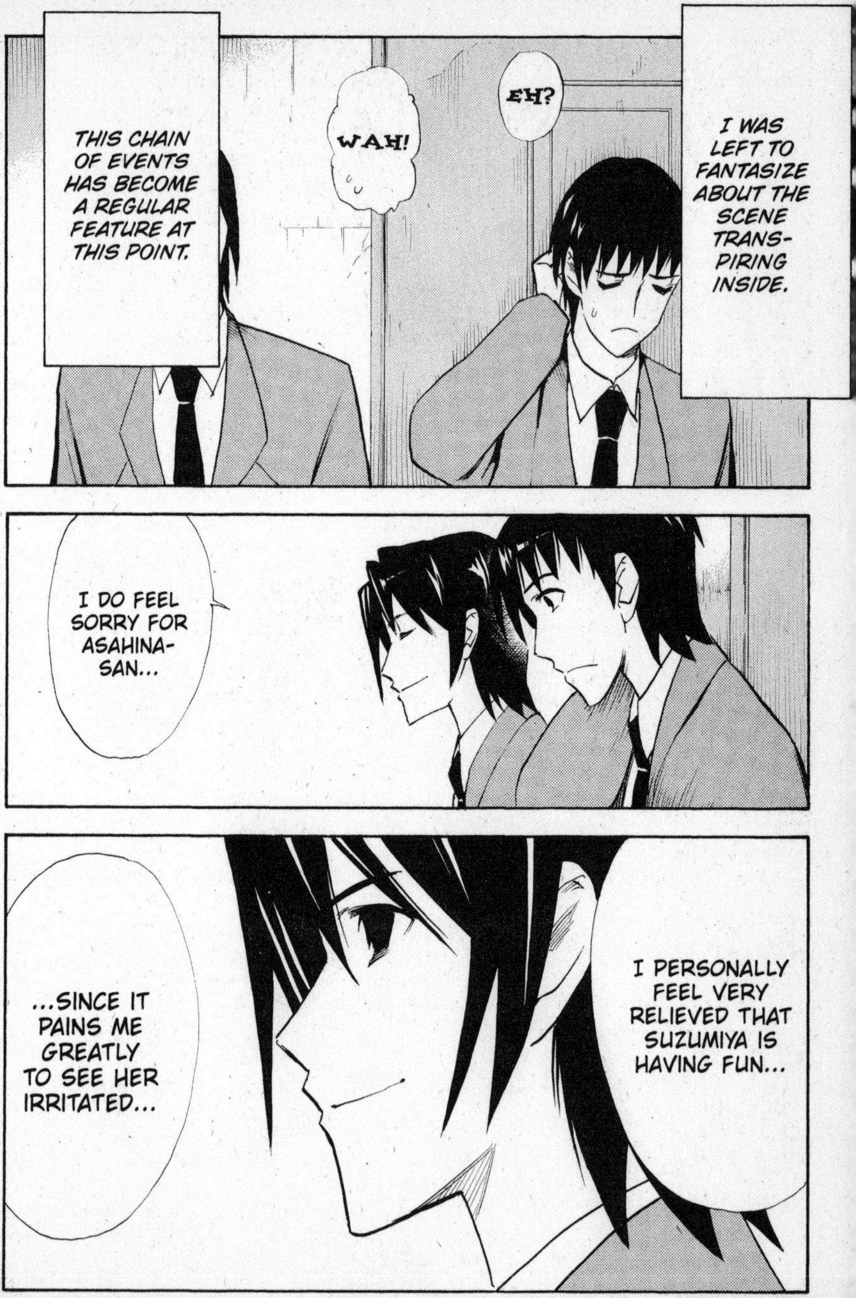
I WAS LEFT TO FANTASIZE ABOUT THE SCENE TRANS-PIRING INSIDE.
EH?
WAH!
THIS CHAIN OF EVENTS HAS BECOME A REGULAR FEATURE AT THIS POINT.
I DO FEEL SORRY FOR ASAHINA-SAN...
I PERSONALLY FEEL VERY RELIEVED THAT SUZUMIYA IS HAVING FUN...
...SINCE IT PAINS ME GREATLY TO SEE HER IRRITATED...

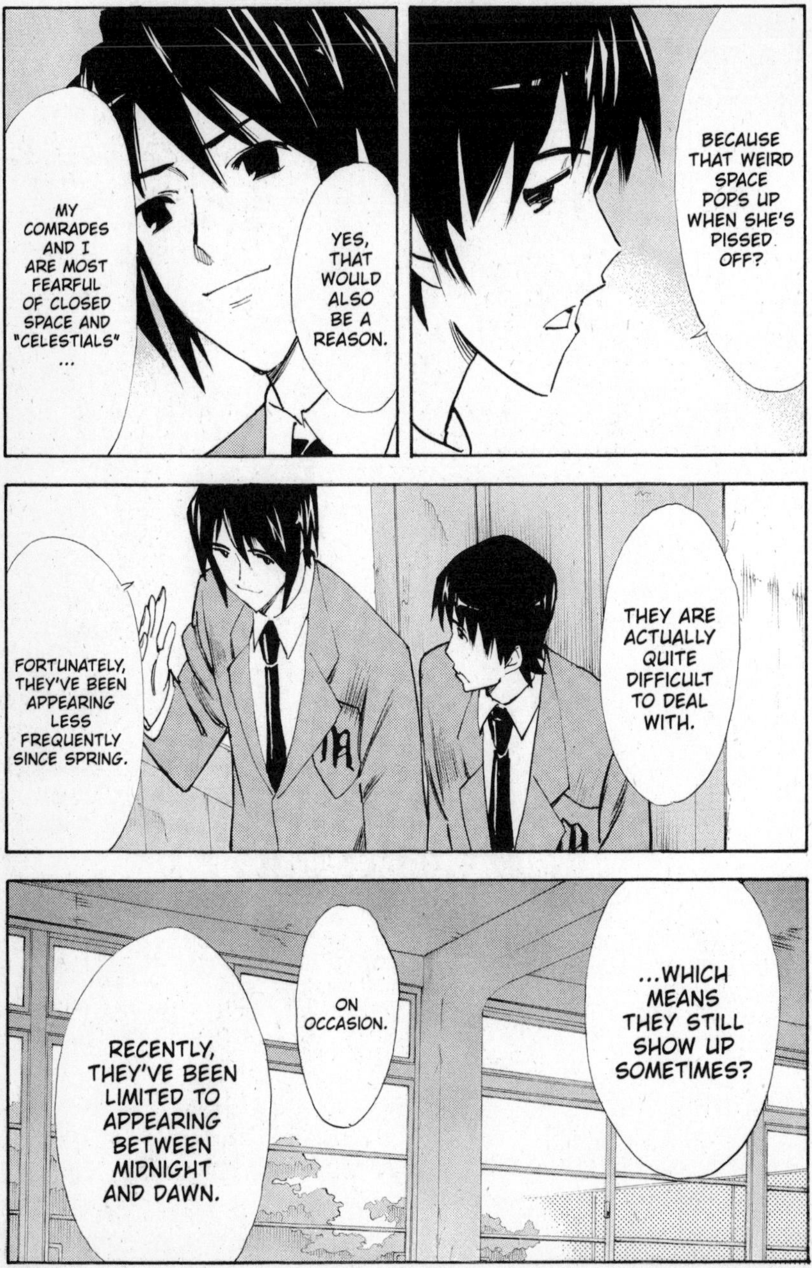
BECAUSE THAT WEIRD SPACE POPS UP WHEN SHE'S PISSED OFF?
YES, THAT WOULD ALSO BE A REASON.
MY COMRADES AND I ARE MOST FEARFUL OF CLOSED SPACE AND "CELESTIALS"...
THEY ARE ACTUALLY QUITE DIFFICULT TO DEAL WITH.
FORTUNATELY, THEY'VE BEEN APPEARING LESS FREQUENTLY SINCE SPRING.
...WHICH MEANS THEY STILL SHOW UP SOMETIMES?
ON OCCASION.
RECENTLY, THEY'VE BEEN LIMITED TO APPEARING BETWEEN MIDNIGHT AND DAWN.

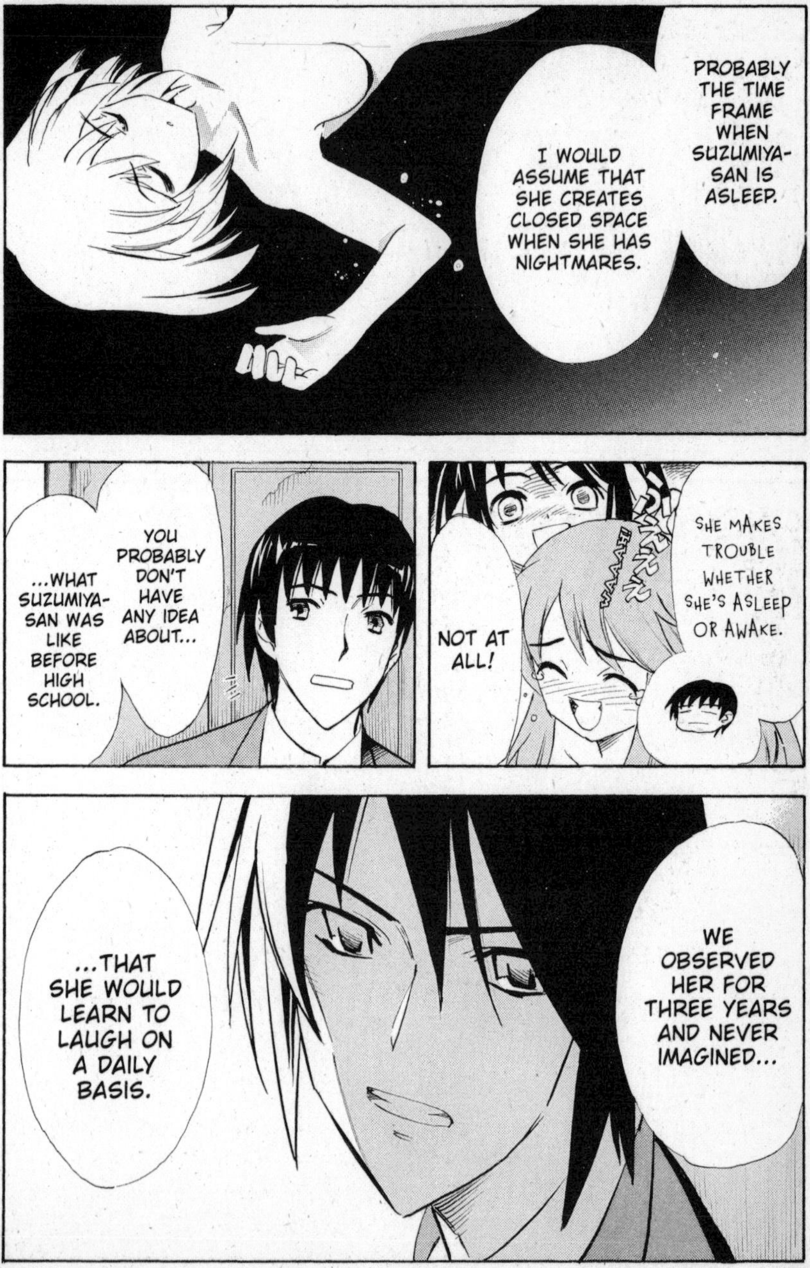
PROBABLY THE TIME FRAME WHEN SUZUMIYA-SAN IS ASLEEP.
I WOULD ASSUME THAT SHE CREATES CLOSED SPACE WHEN SHE HAS NIGHTMARES.
SHE MAKES TROUBLE WHETHER SHE'S ASLEEP OR AWAKE.
NOT AT ALL!
YOU PROBABLY DON'T HAVE ANY IDEA ABOUT...
...WHAT SUZUMIYA-SAN WAS LIKE BEFORE HIGH SCHOOL.
WE OBSERVED HER FOR THREE YEARS AND NEVER IMAGINED...
...THAT SHE WOULD LEARN TO LAUGH ON A DAILY BASIS.

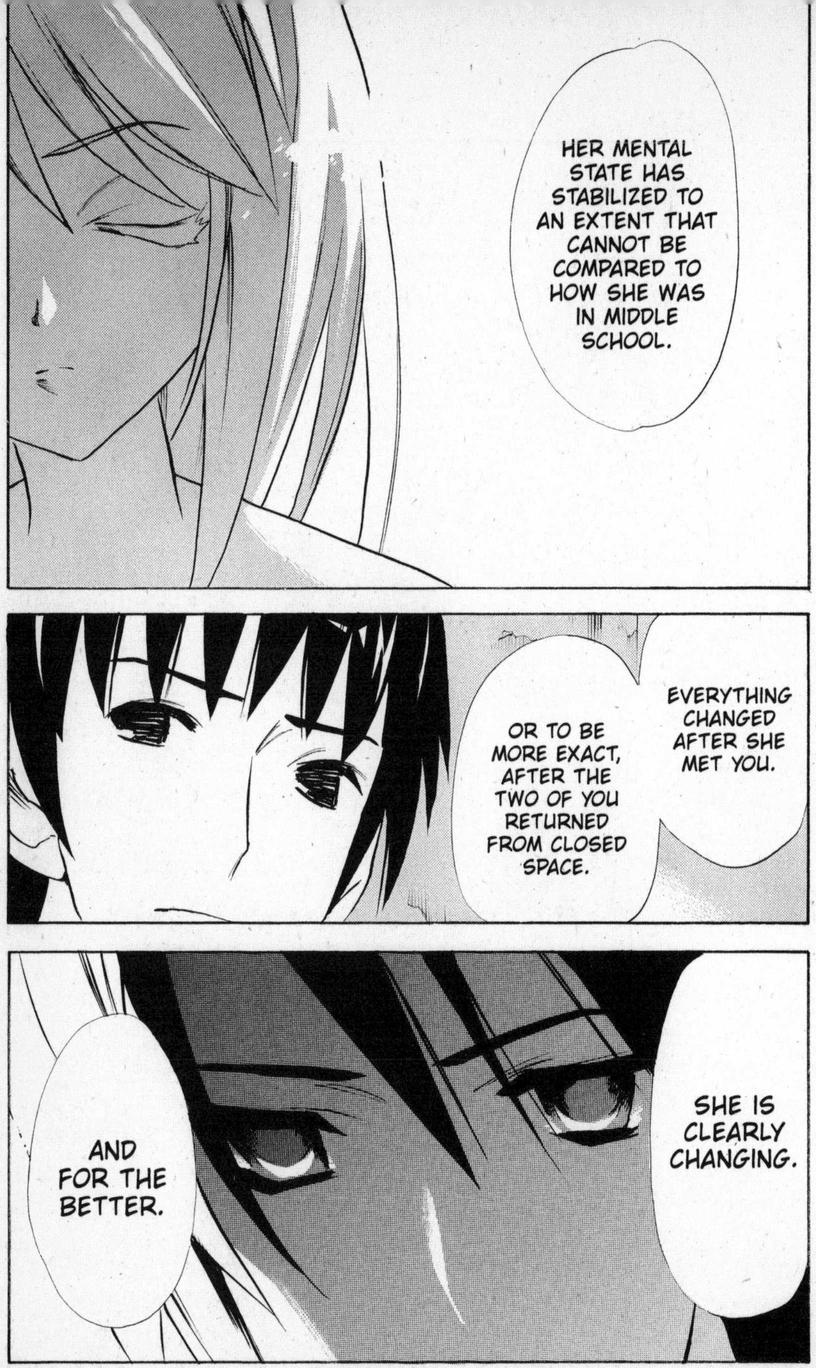
HER MENTAL STATE HAS STABILIZED TO AN EXTENT THAT CANNOT BE COMPARED TO HOW SHE WAS IN MIDDLE SCHOOL.
EVERYTHING CHANGED AFTER SHE MET YOU.
OR TO BE MORE EXACT, AFTER THE TWO OF YOU RETURNED FROM CLOSED SPACE.
SHE IS CLEARLY CHANGING.
AND FOR THE BETTER.

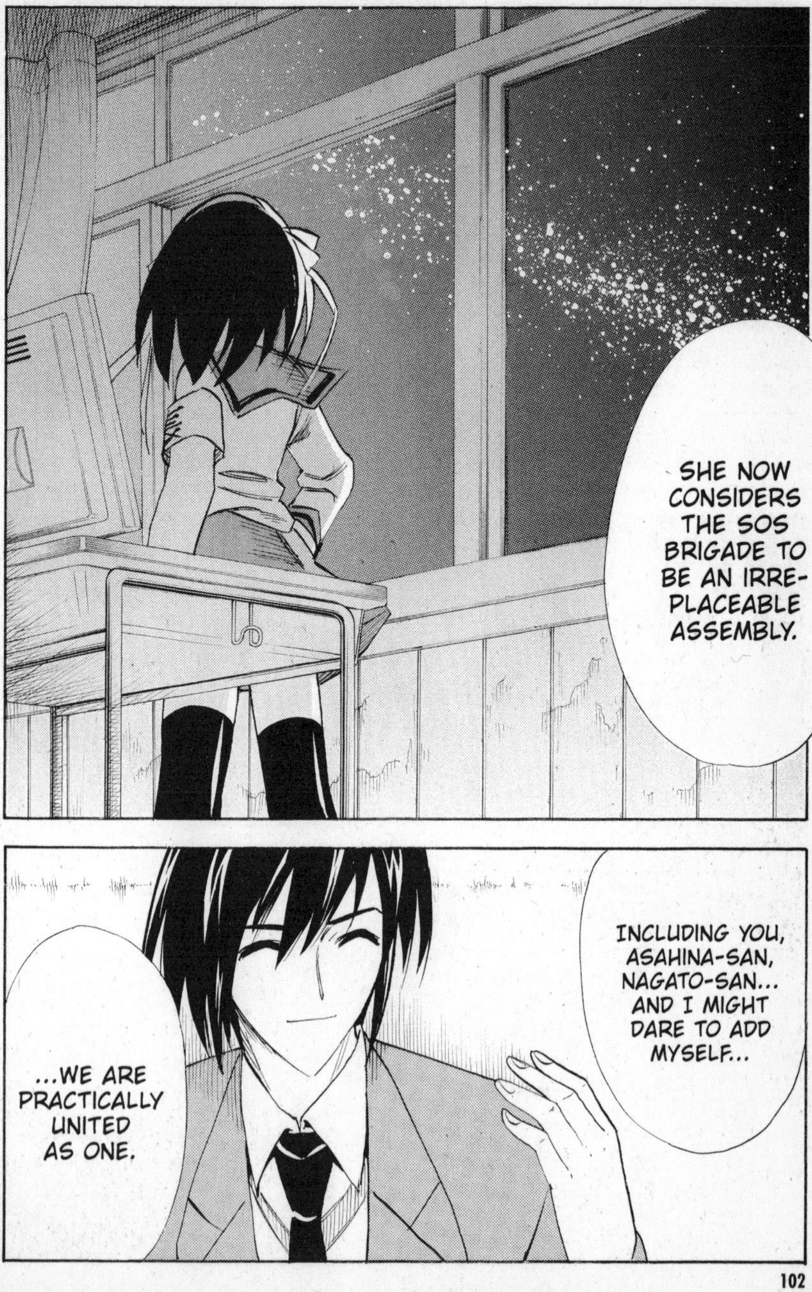
SHE NOW CONSIDERS THE SOS BRIGADE TO BE AN IRRE-PLACEABLE ASSEMBLY.
INCLUDING YOU, ASAHINA-SAN, NAGATO-SAN... AND I MIGHT DARE TO ADD MYSELF...
...WE ARE PRACTICALLY UNITED AS ONE.

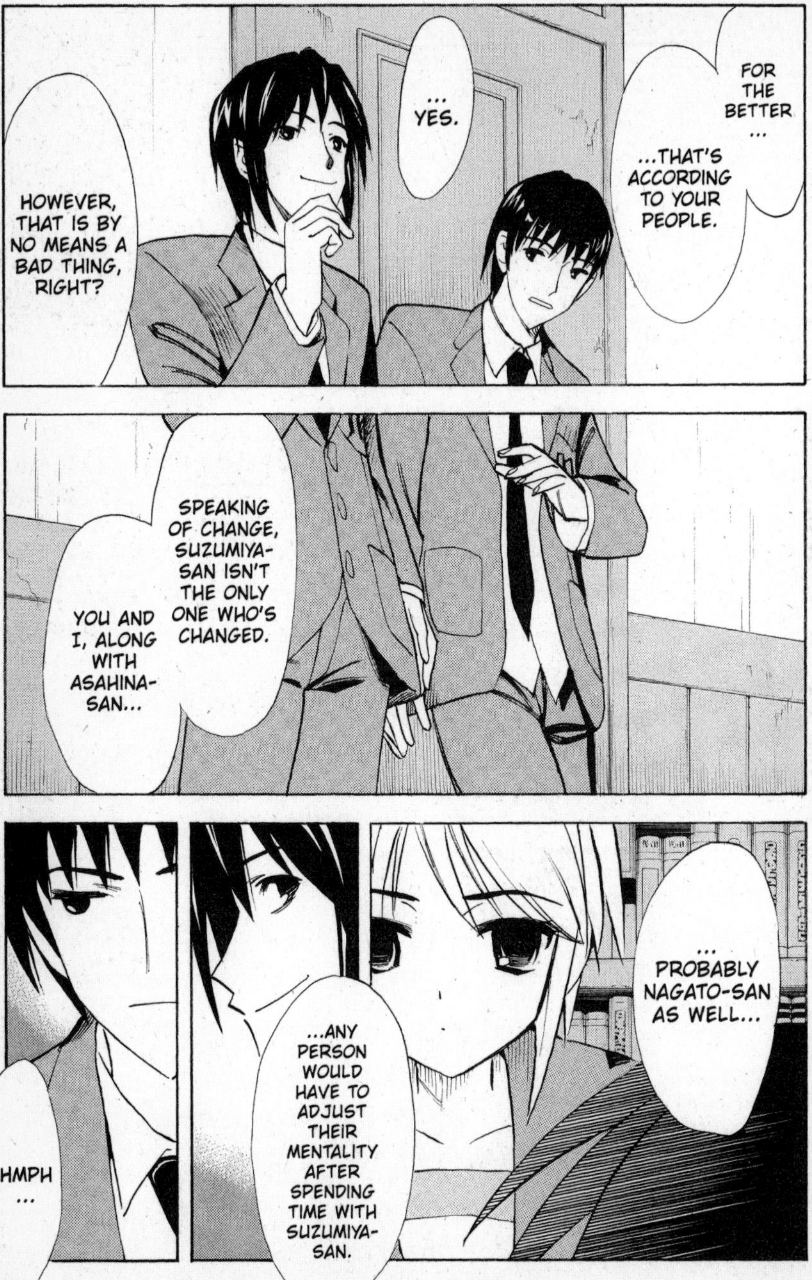
FOR THE BETTER ... ...THAT'S ACCORDING TO YOUR PEOPLE.
... YES.
HOWEVER, THAT IS BY NO MEANS A BAD THING, RIGHT?
SPEAKING OF CHANGE, SUZUMIYA-SAN ISN'T THE ONLY ONE WHO'S CHANGED.
YOU AND I, ALONG WITH ASAHINA-SAN...
... PROBABLY NAGATO-SAN AS WELL...
...ANY PERSON WOULD HAVE TO ADJUST THEIR MENTALITY AFTER SPENDING TIME WITH SUZUMIYA-SAN.
HMPH ...

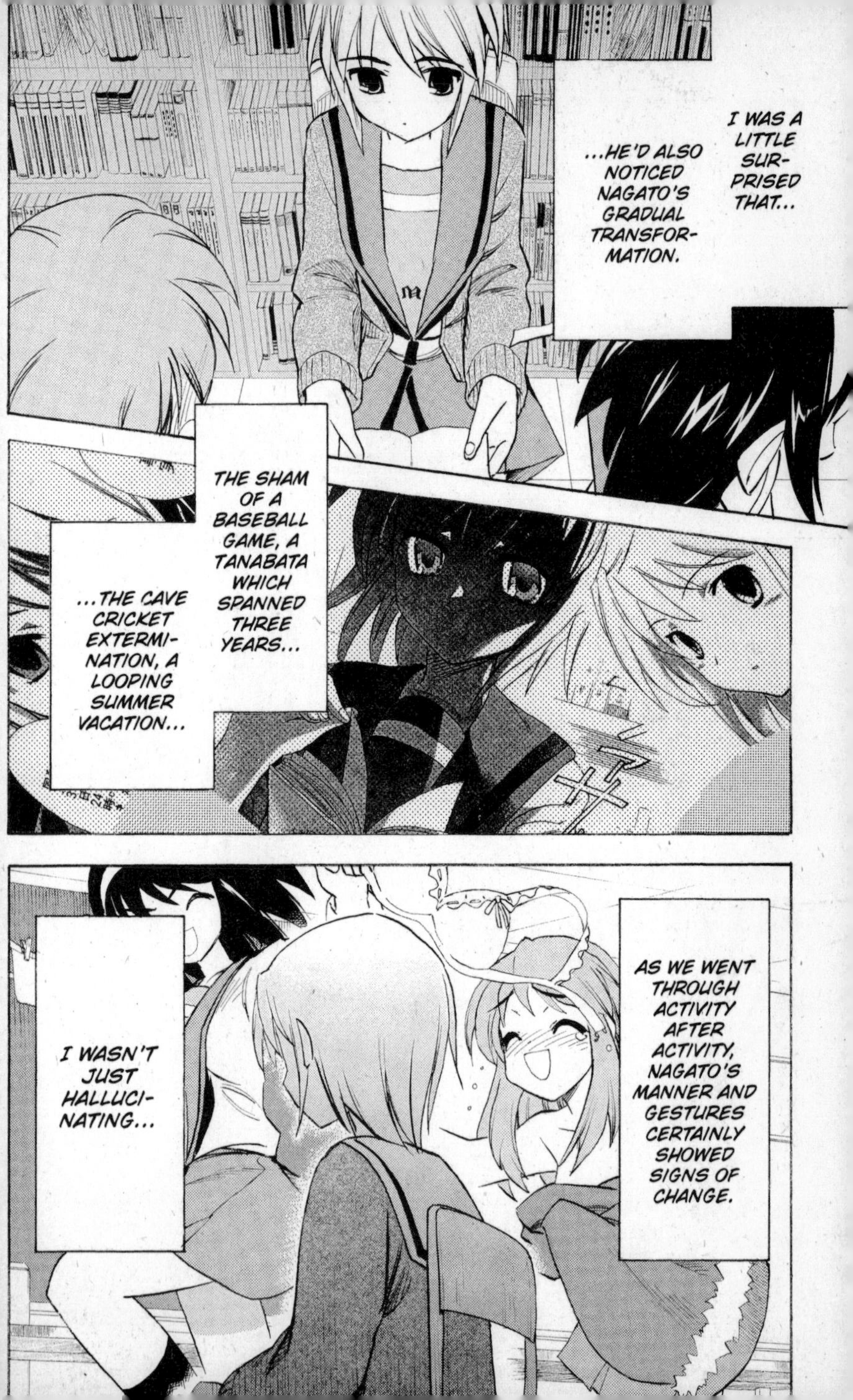
I WAS A LITTLE SURPRISED THAT...
...HE'D ALSO NOTICED NAGATO'S GRADUAL TRANSFORMATION.
THE SHAM OF A BASEBALL GAME, A TANABATA WHICH SPANNED THREE YEARS...
...THE CAVE CRICKET EXTERMINATION, A LOOPING SUMMER VACATION...
AS WE WENT THROUGH ACTIVITY AFTER ACTIVITY, NAGATO'S MANNER AND GESTURES CERTAINLY SHOWED SIGNS OF CHANGE.
I WASN'T JUST HALLUCINATING...

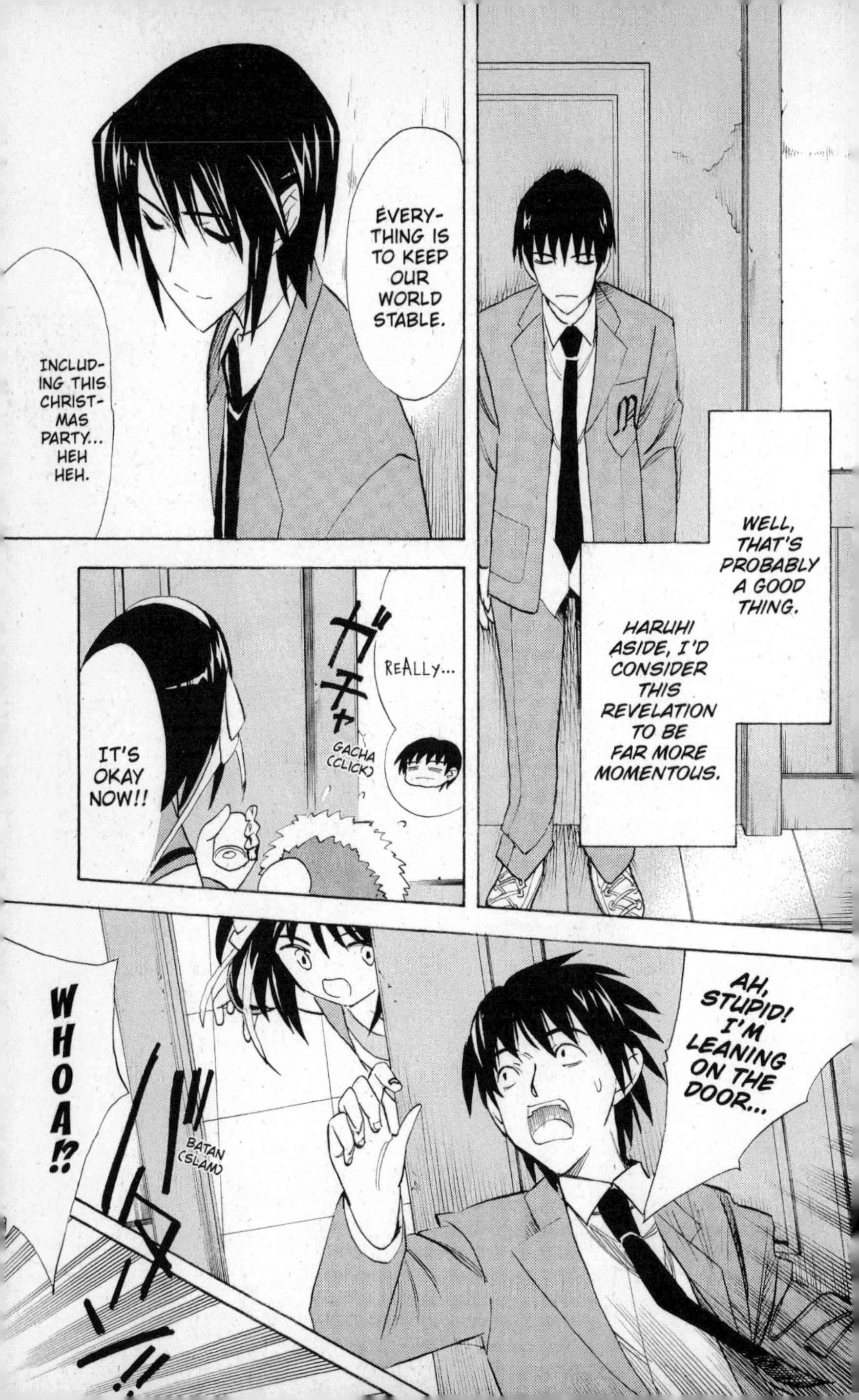
WELL, THAT'S PROBABLY A GOOD THING.
HARUHI ASIDE, I'D CONSIDER THIS REVELATION TO BE FAR MORE MOMENTOUS.
EVERY-THING IS TO KEEP OUR WORLD STABLE.
INCLUDING THIS CHRIST-MAS PARTY... HEH HEH.
REALLY...
ガチャ
GACHA (CLICK)
IT'S OKAY NOW!!
AH, STUPID! I'M LEANING ON THE DOOR...
WHOA!?
BATAN (SLAM)

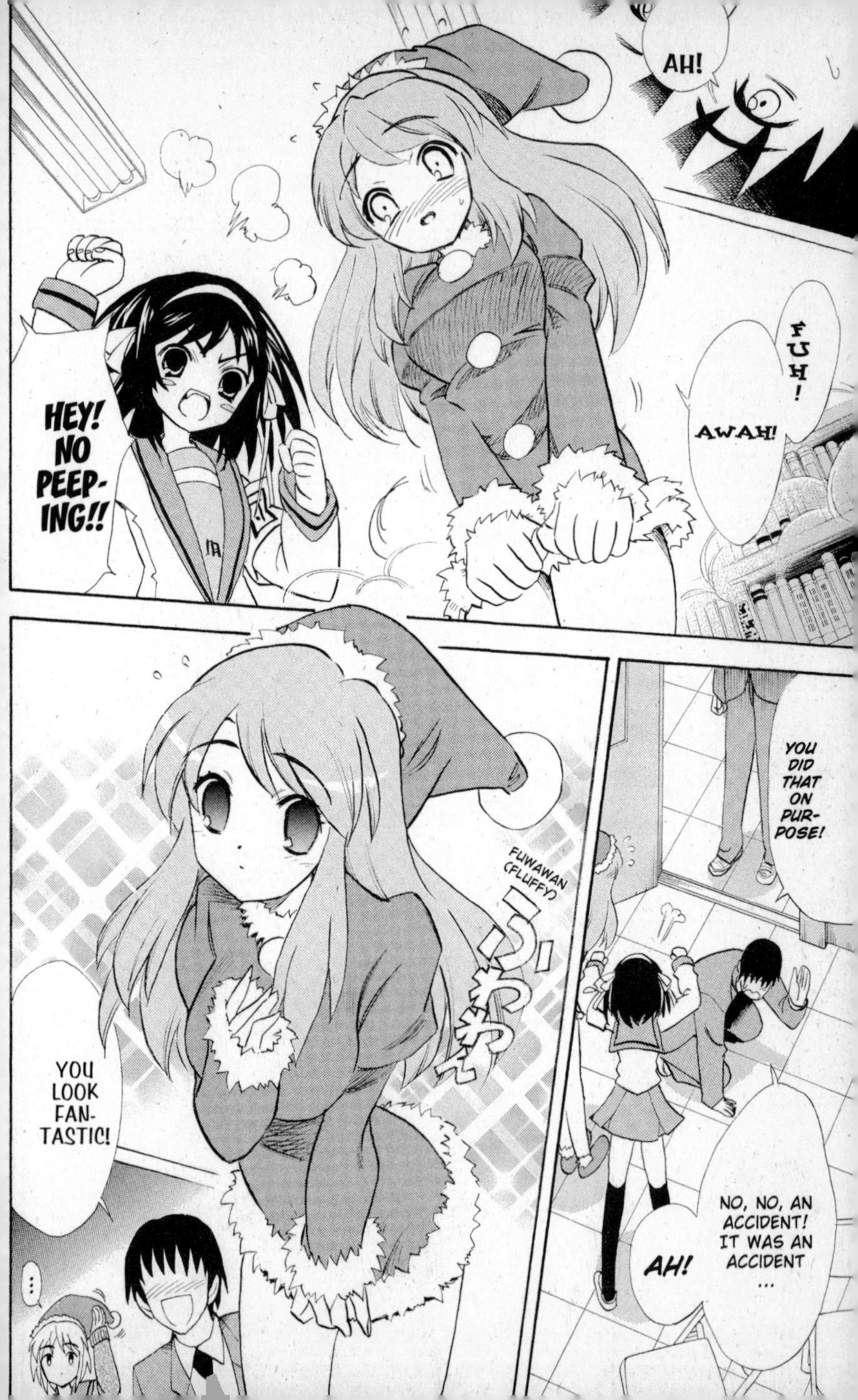
AH!
FUH!
AWAH!
HEY! NO PEEP-ING!!
YOU DID THAT ON PUR-POSE!
NO, NO, AN ACCIDENT! IT WAS AN ACCIDENT ...
AH!
FUWAWAN (FLUFFY)
YOU LOOK FAN-TASTIC!
...

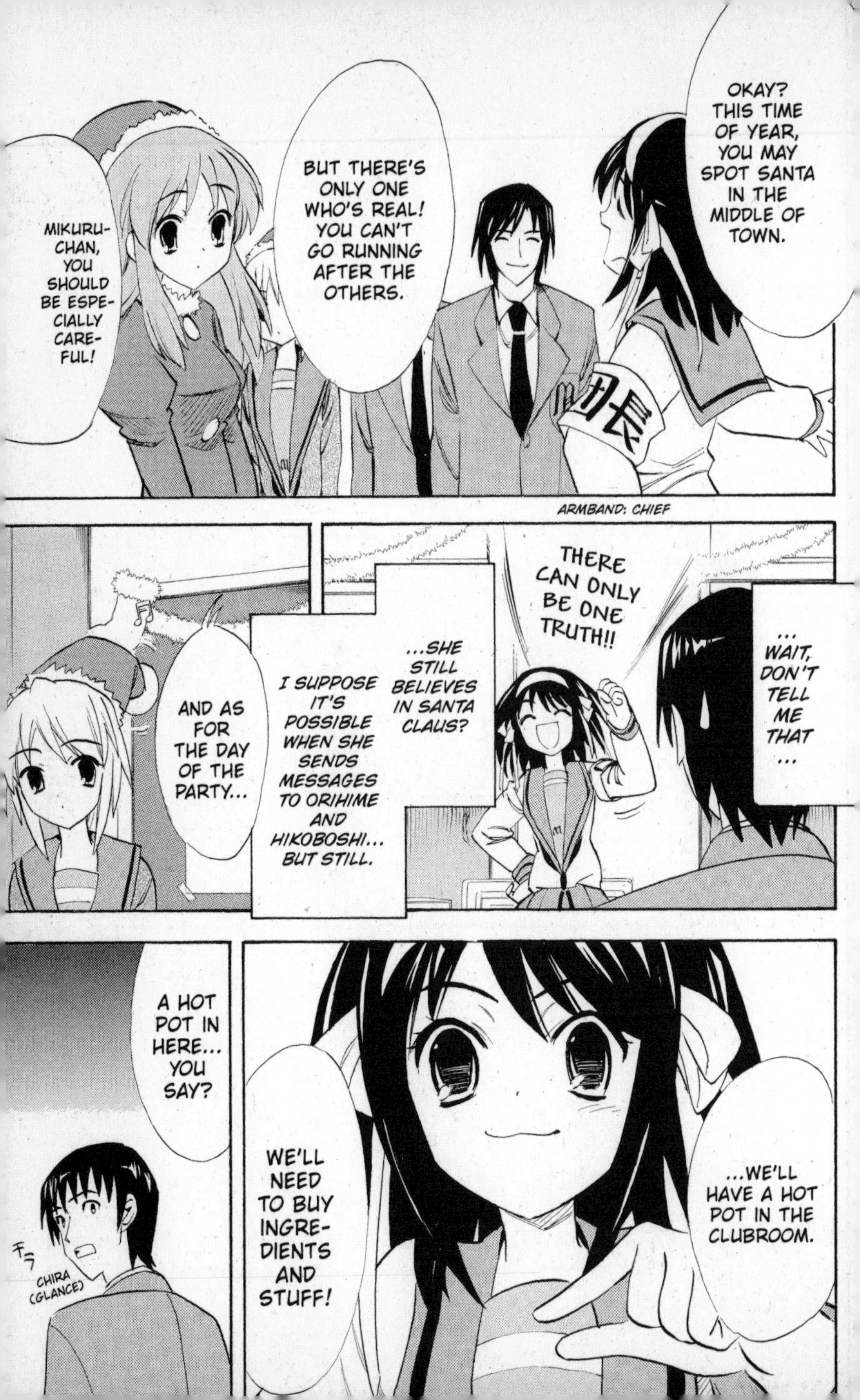
OKAY? THIS TIME OF YEAR, YOU MAY SPOT SANTA IN THE MIDDLE OF TOWN.
BUT THERE'S ONLY ONE WHO'S REAL! YOU CAN'T GO RUNNING AFTER THE OTHERS.
MIKURU-CHAN, YOU SHOULD BE ESPECIALLY CAREFUL!
ARMBAND: CHIEF
THERE CAN ONLY BE ONE TRUTH!!
... WAIT, DON'T TELL ME THAT ...
...SHE STILL BELIEVES IN SANTA CLAUS?
I SUPPOSE IT'S POSSIBLE WHEN SHE SENDS MESSAGES TO ORIHIME AND HIKOBOSHI... BUT STILL.
AND AS FOR THE DAY OF THE PARTY...
...WE'LL HAVE A HOT POT IN THE CLUBROOM.
WE'LL NEED TO BUY INGREDIENTS AND STUFF!
A HOT POT IN HERE... YOU SAY?
チラ
CHIRA (GLANCE)

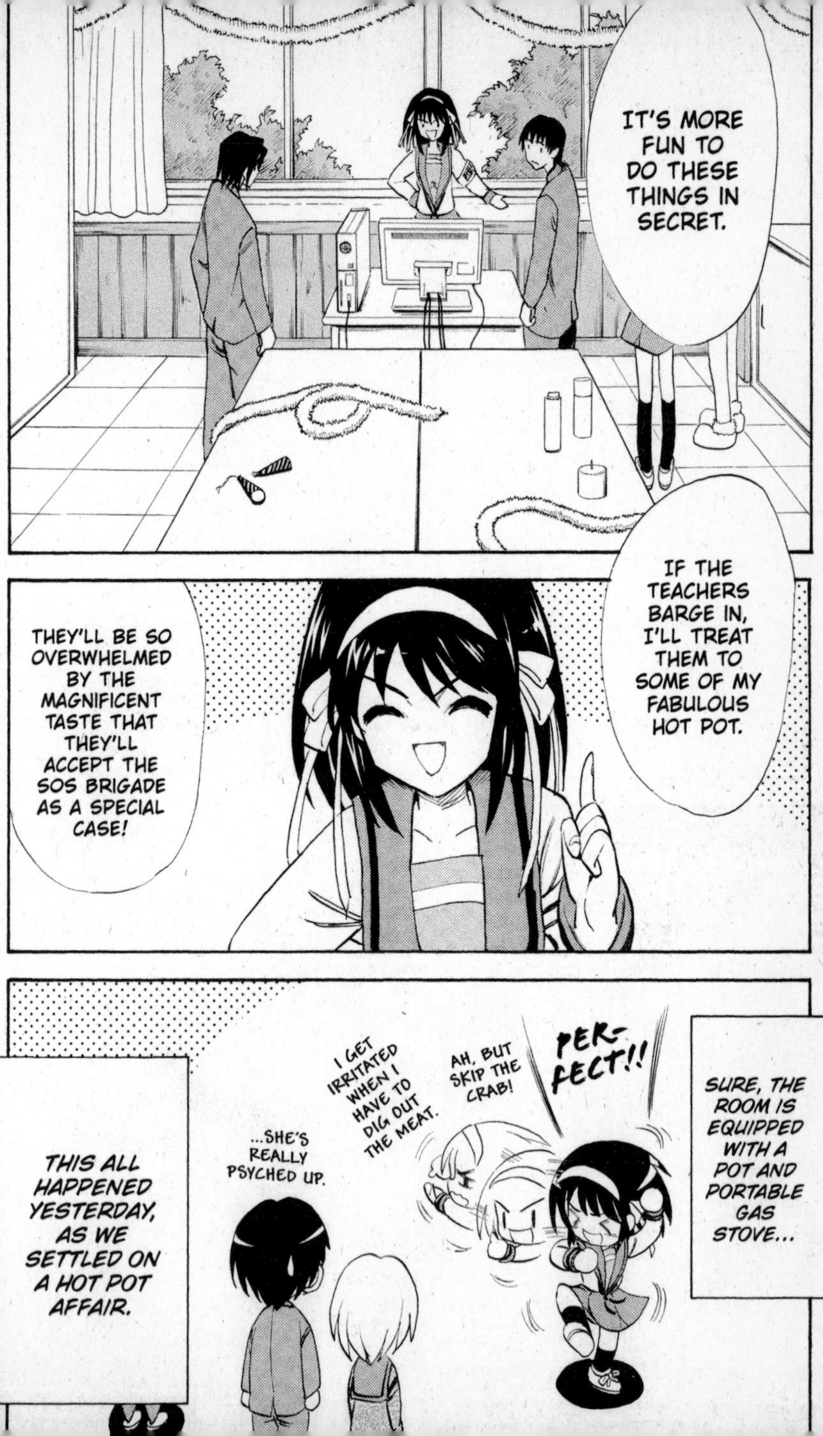
IT'S MORE FUN TO DO THESE THINGS IN SECRET.
IF THE TEACHERS BARGE IN, I'LL TREAT THEM TO SOME OF MY FABULOUS HOT POT.
THEY'LL BE SO OVERWHELMED BY THE MAGNIFICENT TASTE THAT THEY'LL ACCEPT THE SOS BRIGADE AS A SPECIAL CASE!
SURE, THE ROOM IS EQUIPPED WITH A POT AND PORTABLE GAS STOVE...
PER-FECT!!
AH, BUT SKIP THE CRAB!
I GET IRRITATED WHEN I HAVE TO DIG OUT THE MEAT.
...SHE'S REALLY PSYCHED UP.
THIS ALL HAPPENED YESTERDAY, AS WE SETTLED ON A HOT POT AFFAIR.

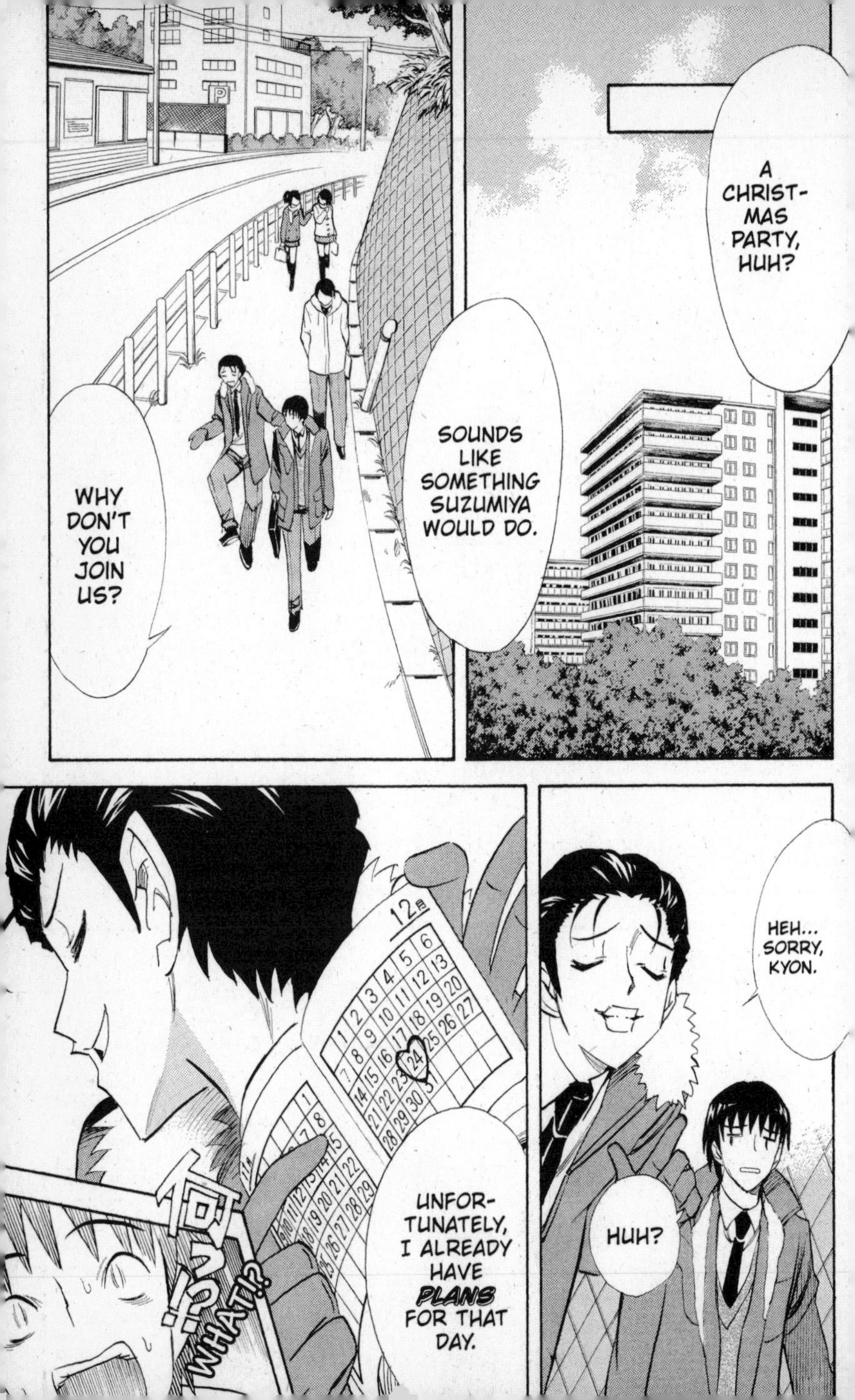
A CHRIST-MAS PARTY, HUH?
SOUNDS LIKE SOMETHING SUZUMIYA WOULD DO.
WHY DON'T YOU JOIN US?
HEH... SORRY, KYON.
HUH?
UNFOR-TUNATELY, I ALREADY HAVE PLANS FOR THAT DAY.
何っ!?
WHAT!?

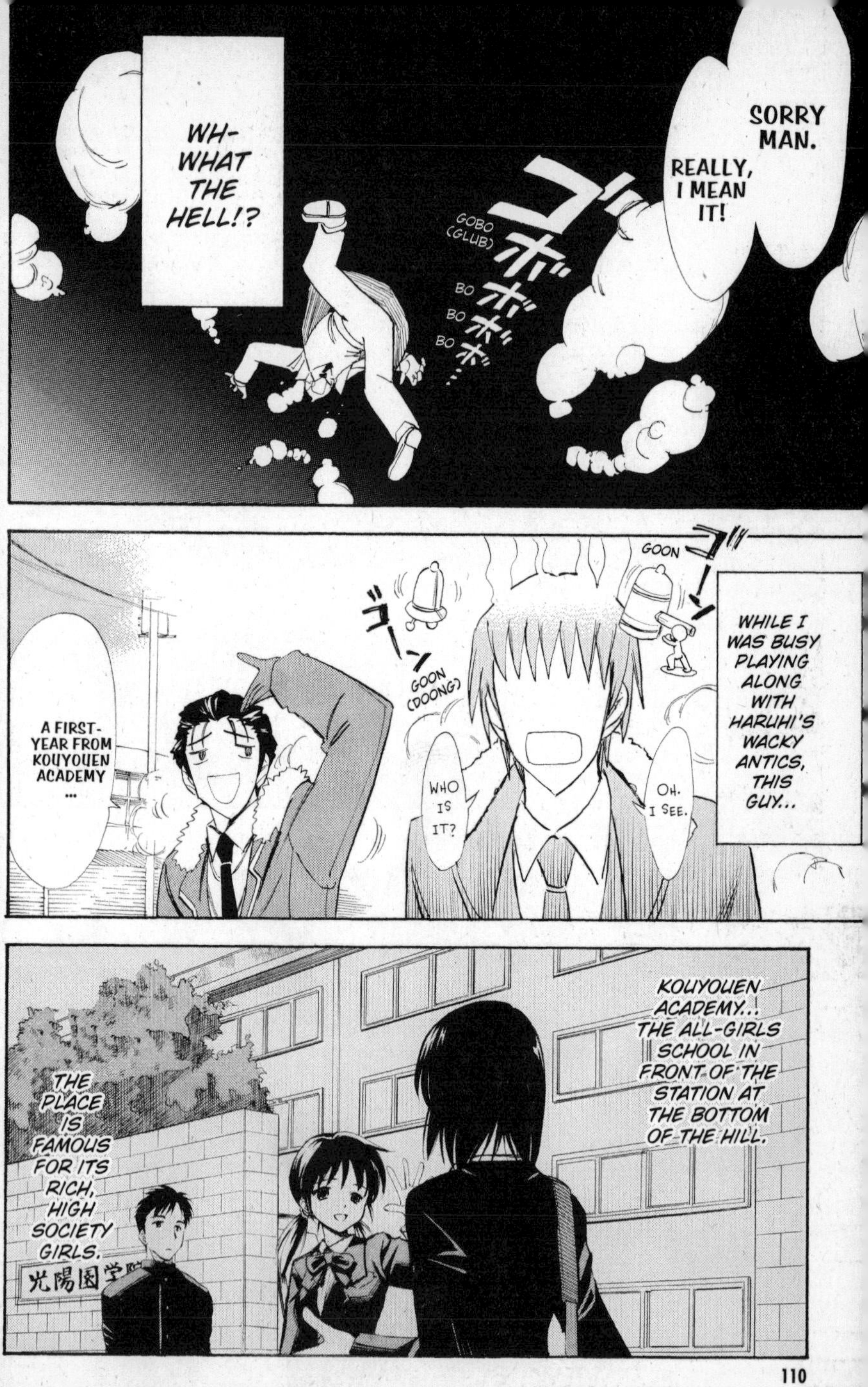
SORRY MAN.
REALLY, I MEAN IT!
GOBO (GLUB)
BO
BO
BO
WH- WHAT THE HELL!?
WHILE I WAS BUSY PLAYING ALONG WITH HARUHI'S WACKY ANTICS, THIS GUY...
GOON
OH. I SEE.
WHO IS IT?
GOON (DOONG)
A FIRST-YEAR FROM KOUYOUEN ACADEMY ...
KOUYOUEN ACADEMY... THE ALL-GIRLS SCHOOL IN FRONT OF THE STATION AT THE BOTTOM OF THE HILL.
THE PLACE IS FAMOUS FOR ITS RICH, HIGH SOCIETY GIRLS.
光陽園学

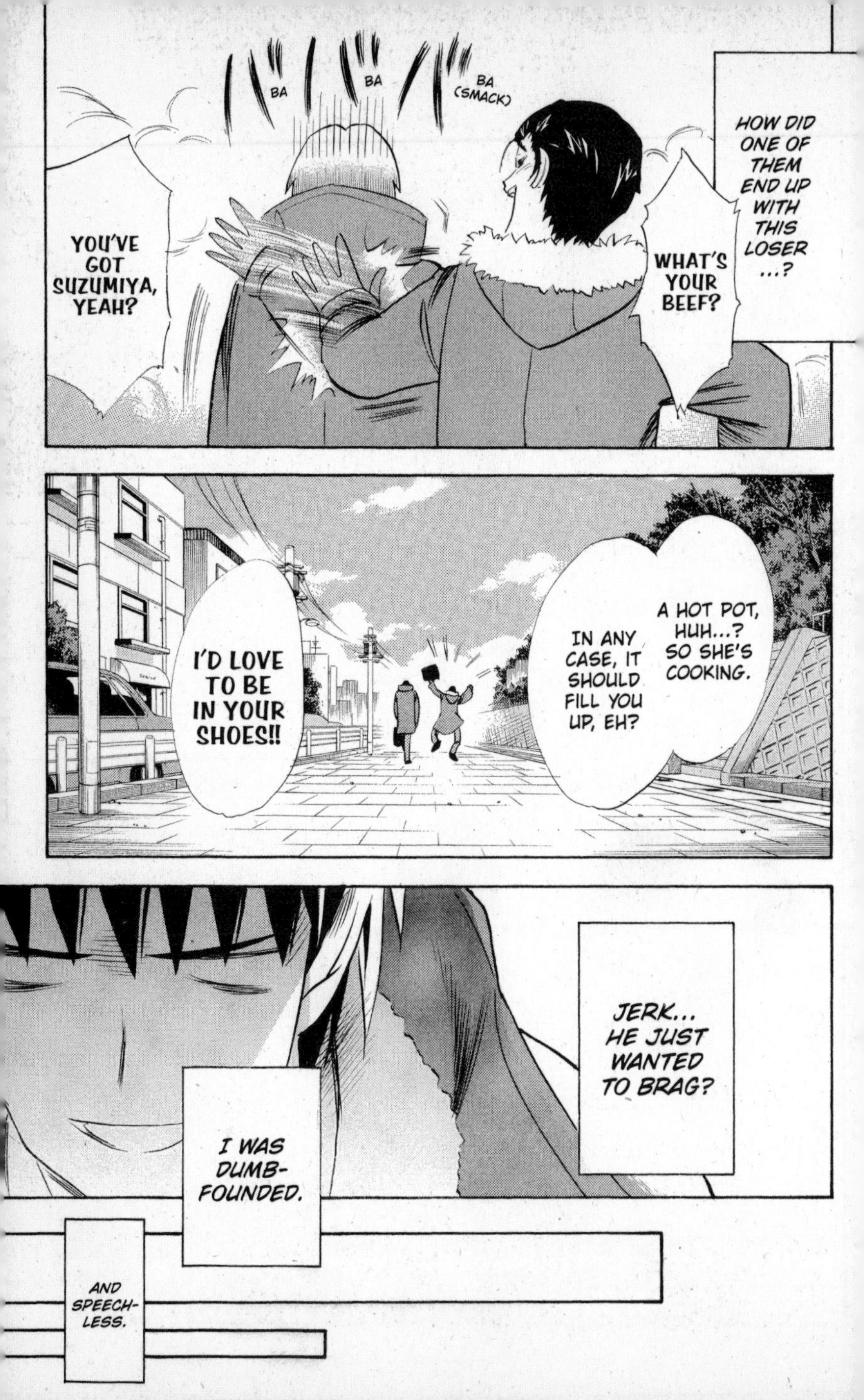
HOW DID ONE OF THEM END UP WITH THIS LOSER ...?
WHAT'S YOUR BEEF?
BA BA BA (SMACK)
YOU'VE GOT SUZUMIYA, YEAH?
A HOT POT, HUH...? SO SHE'S COOKING.
IN ANY CASE, IT SHOULD FILL YOU UP, EH?
I'D LOVE TO BE IN YOUR SHOES!!
JERK... HE JUST WANTED TO BRAG?
I WAS DUMB-FOUNDED.
AND SPEECH-LESS.

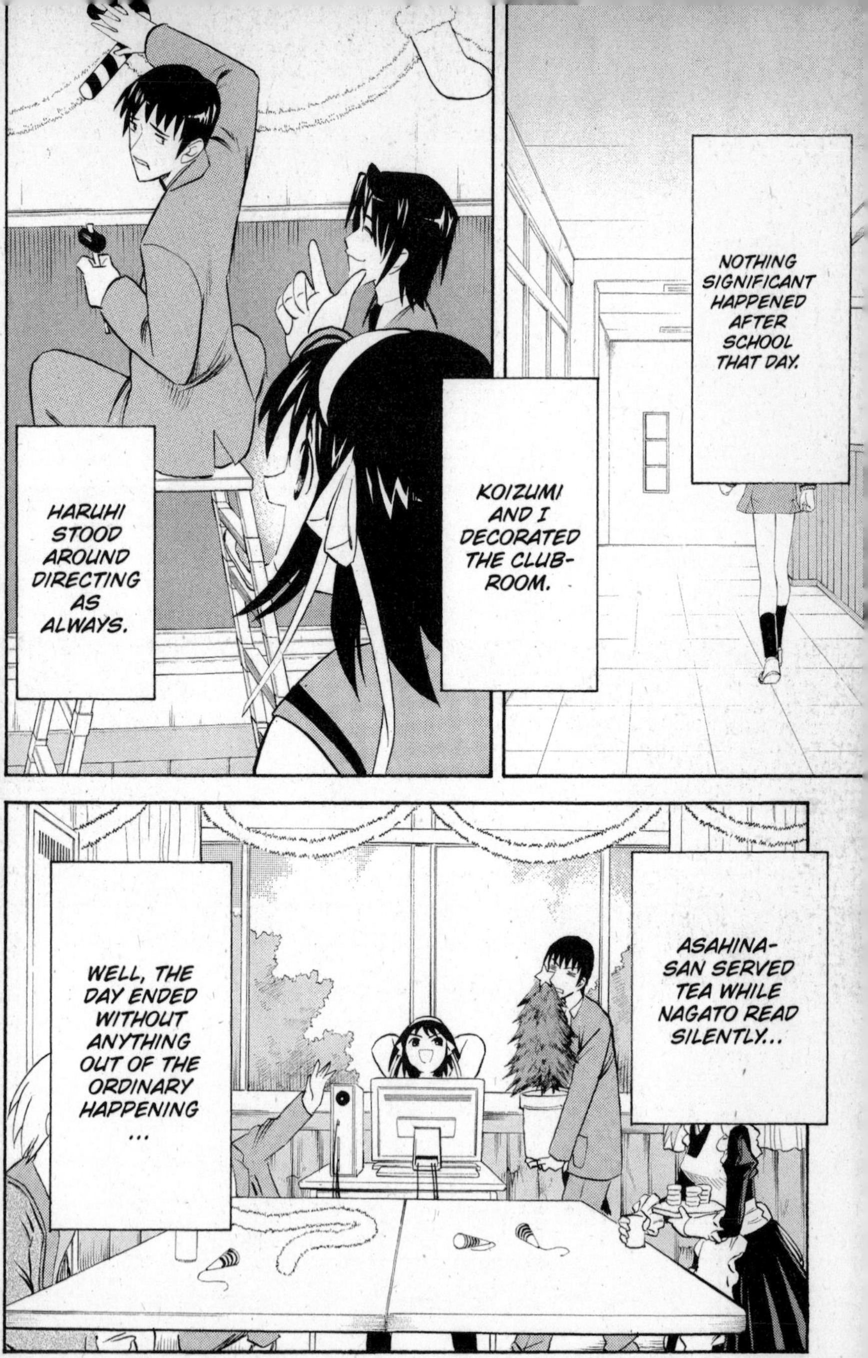
NOTHING SIGNIFICANT HAPPENED AFTER SCHOOL THAT DAY.
KOIZUMI AND I DECORATED THE CLUB-ROOM.
HARUHI STOOD AROUND DIRECTING AS ALWAYS.
ASAHINA-SAN SERVED TEA WHILE NAGATO READ SILENTLY...
WELL, THE DAY ENDED WITHOUT ANYTHING OUT OF THE ORDINARY HAPPENING ...

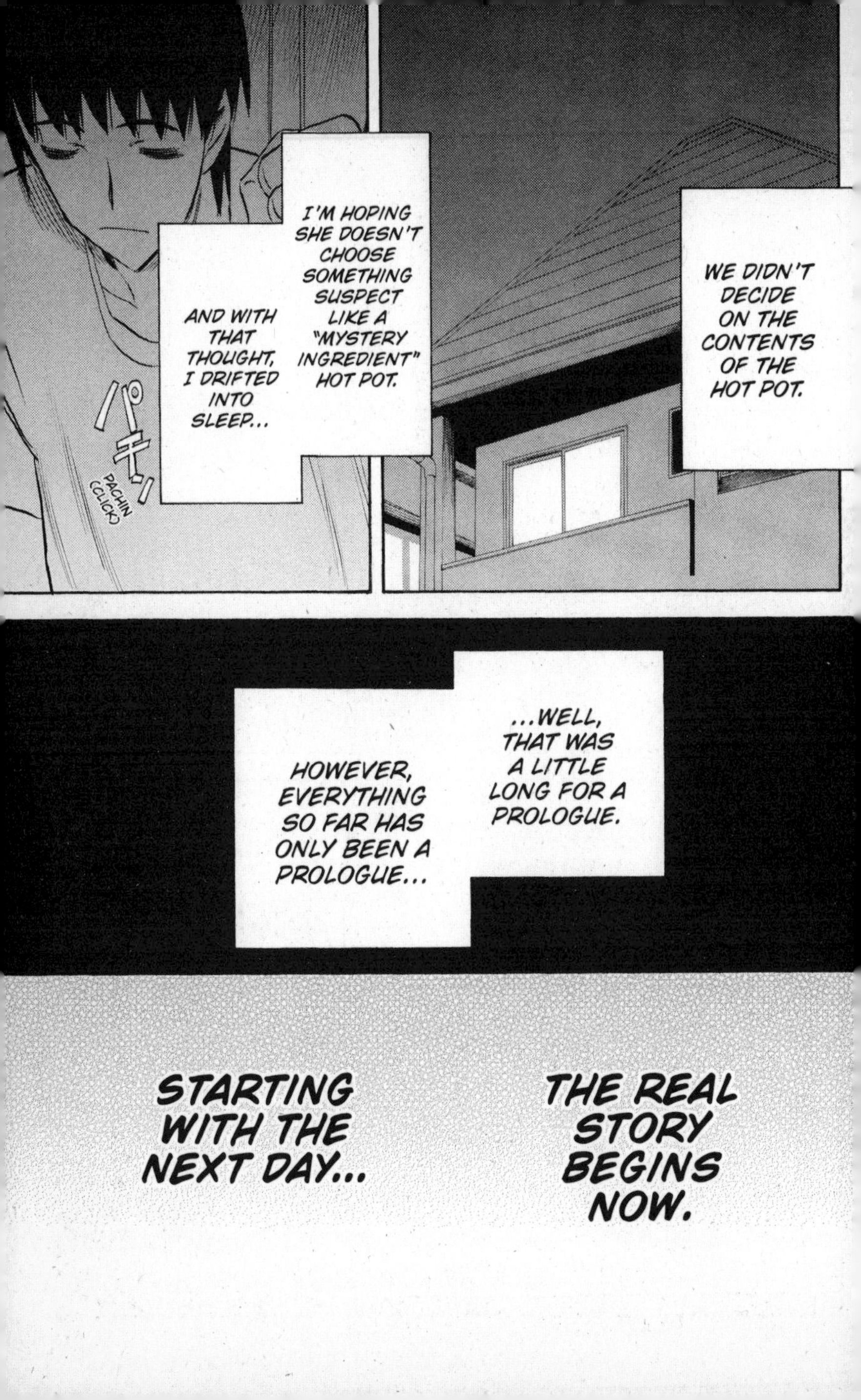
WE DIDN'T DECIDE ON THE CONTENTS OF THE HOT POT.
I'M HOPING SHE DOESN'T CHOOSE SOMETHING SUSPECT LIKE A "MYSTERY INGREDIENT" HOT POT.
AND WITH THAT THOUGHT, I DRIFTED INTO SLEEP...
パチン
PACHIN (CLICK)
...WELL, THAT WAS A LITTLE LONG FOR A PROLOGUE.
HOWEVER, EVERYTHING SO FAR HAS ONLY BEEN A PROLOGUE...
THE REAL STORY BEGINS NOW.
STARTING WITH THE NEXT DAY...

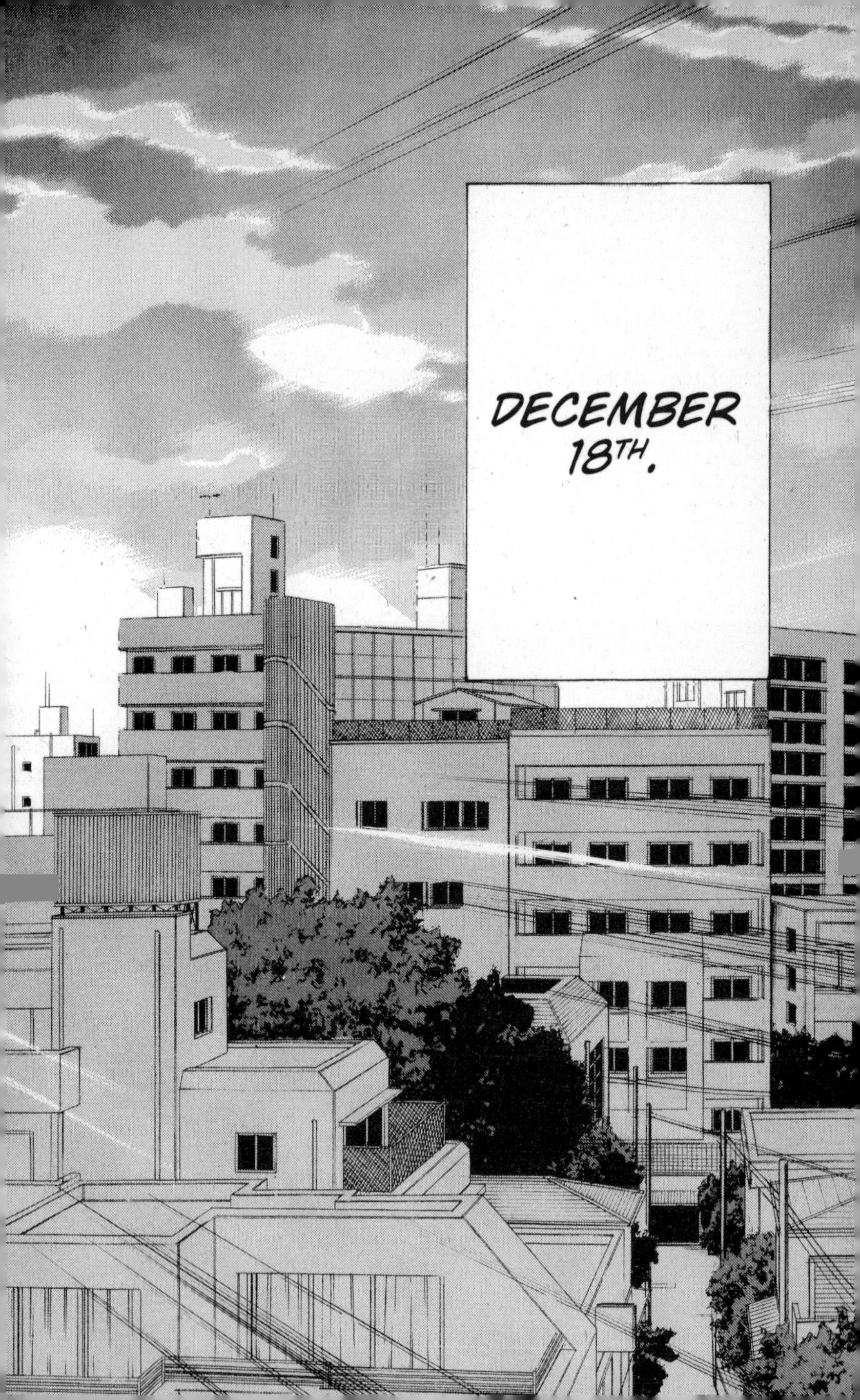
DECEMBER 18TH.

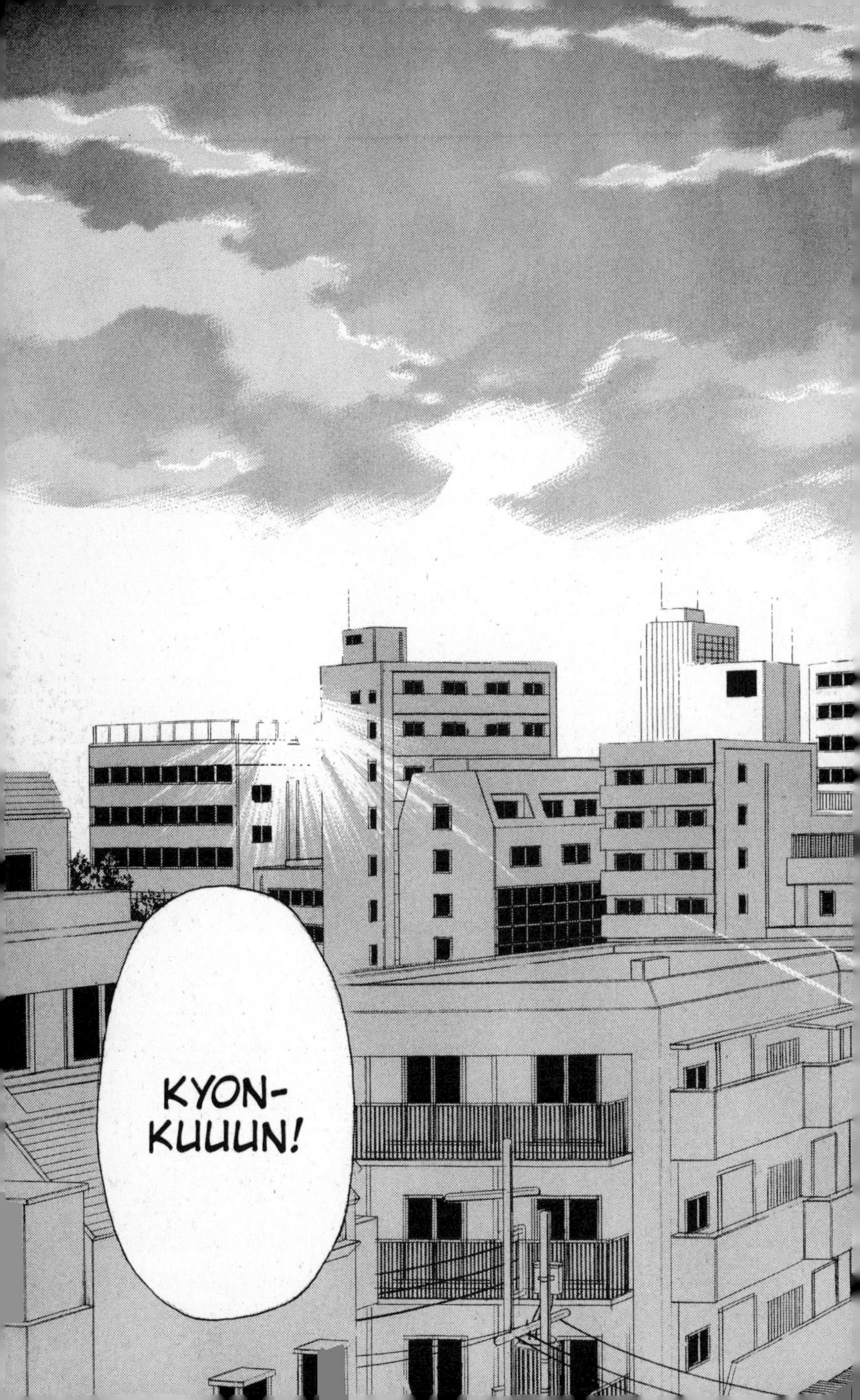
KYON-KUUUN!

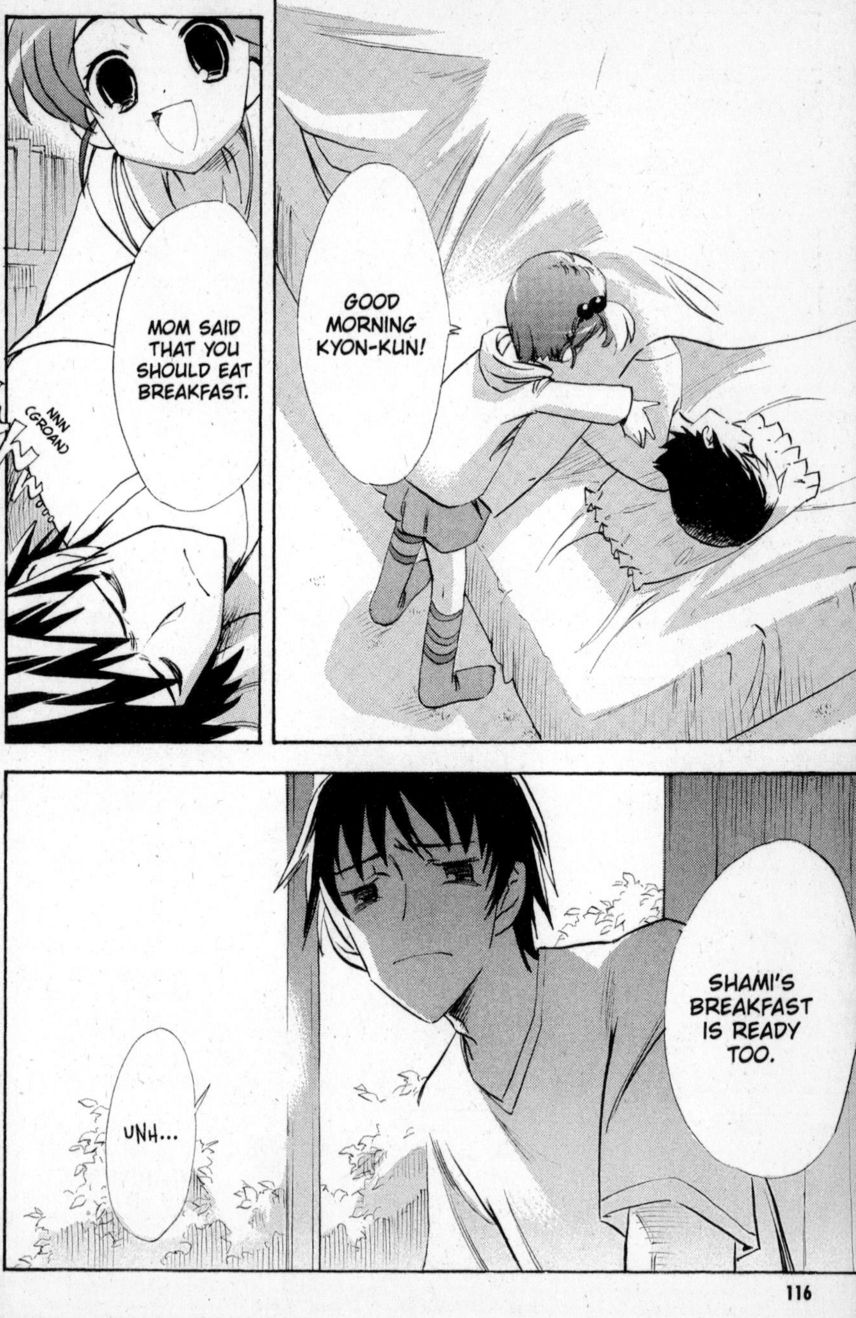
GOOD MORNING KYON-KUN!
MOM SAID THAT YOU SHOULD EAT BREAKFAST.
NNN (GROAN)
SHAMI'S BREAKFAST IS READY TOO.
UNH...

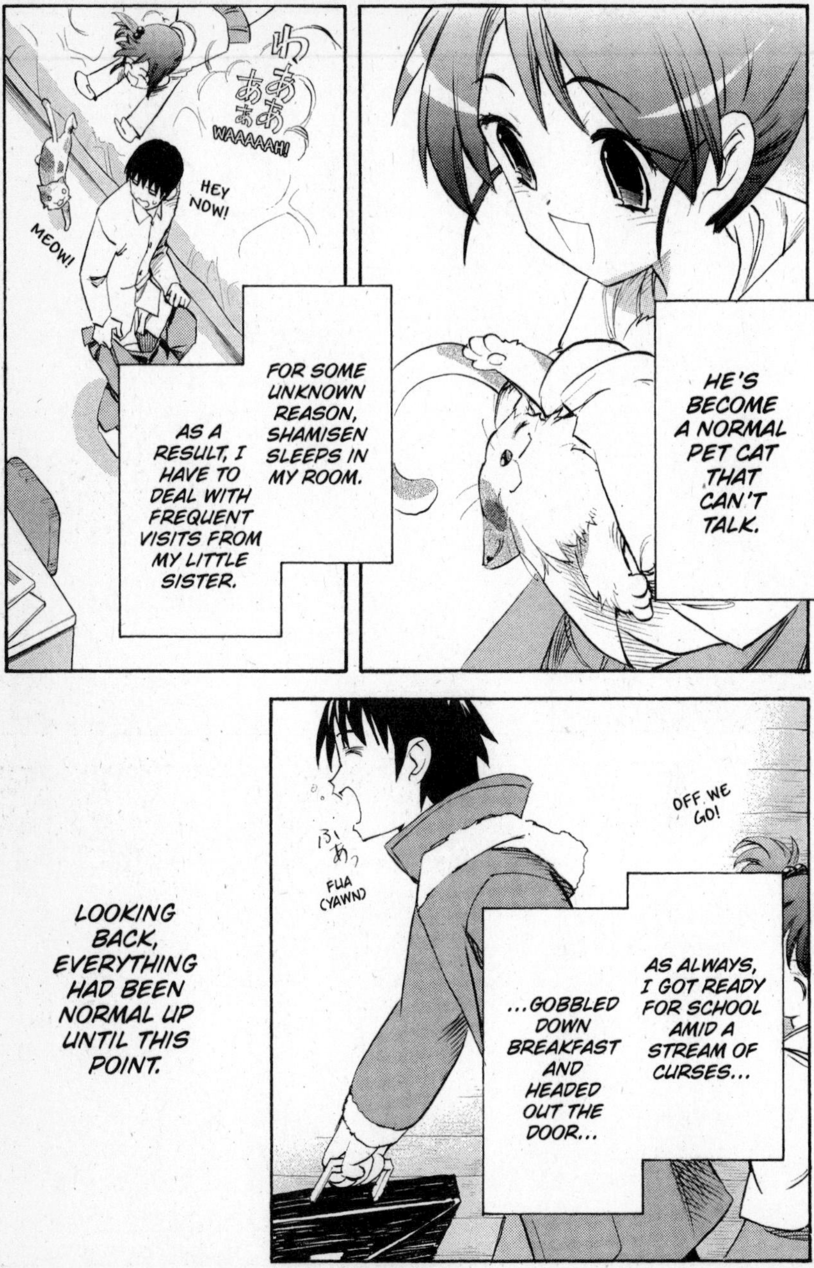
HE'S BECOME A NORMAL PET CAT THAT CAN'T TALK.
わあああ
WAAAAAH!
HEY NOW!
MEOW!
FOR SOME UNKNOWN REASON, SHAMISEN SLEEPS IN MY ROOM.
AS A RESULT, I HAVE TO DEAL WITH FREQUENT VISITS FROM MY LITTLE SISTER.
OFF WE GO!
AS ALWAYS, I GOT READY FOR SCHOOL AMID A STREAM OF CURSES...
...GOBBLED DOWN BREAKFAST AND HEADED OUT THE DOOR...
ふあっ
FUA (YAWN)
LOOKING BACK, EVERYTHING HAD BEEN NORMAL UP UNTIL THIS POINT.

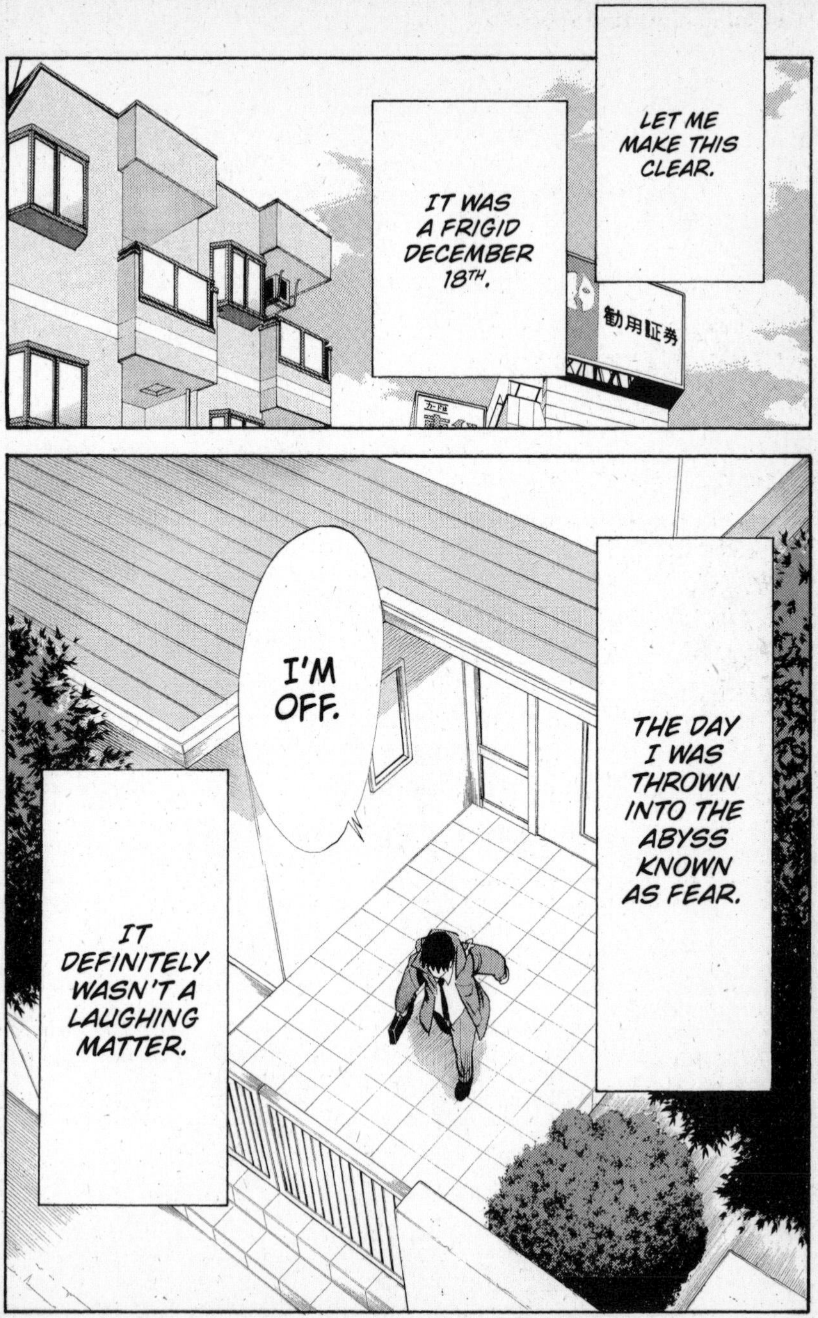
LET ME MAKE THIS CLEAR.
IT WAS A FRIGID DECEMBER 18TH.
勧用証券
THE DAY I WAS THROWN INTO THE ABYSS KNOWN AS FEAR.
I'M OFF.
IT DEFINITELY WASN'T A LAUGHING MATTER.

THE DISAPPEARANCE OF HARUHI SUZUMIYA I : END

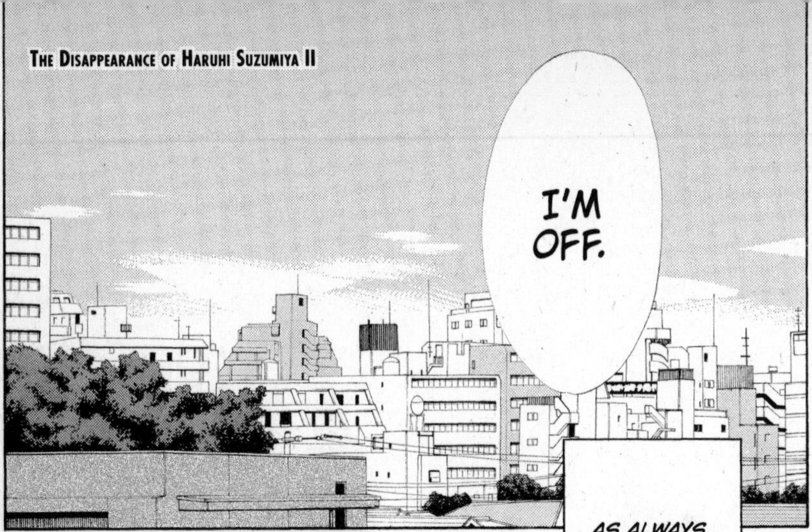
I'M OFF.
AS ALWAYS, I GOBBLED DOWN BREAKFAST AND HEADED OUT...

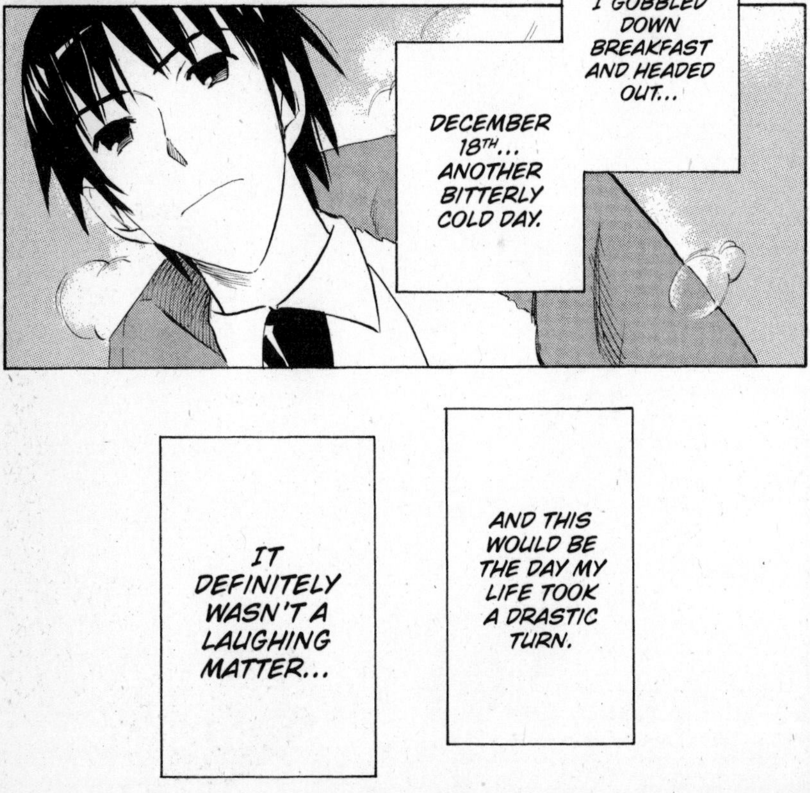
DECEMBER 18TH... ANOTHER BITTERLY COLD DAY.

AND THIS WOULD BE THE DAY MY LIFE TOOK A DRASTIC TURN.

IT DEFINITELY WASN'T A LAUGHING MATTER...

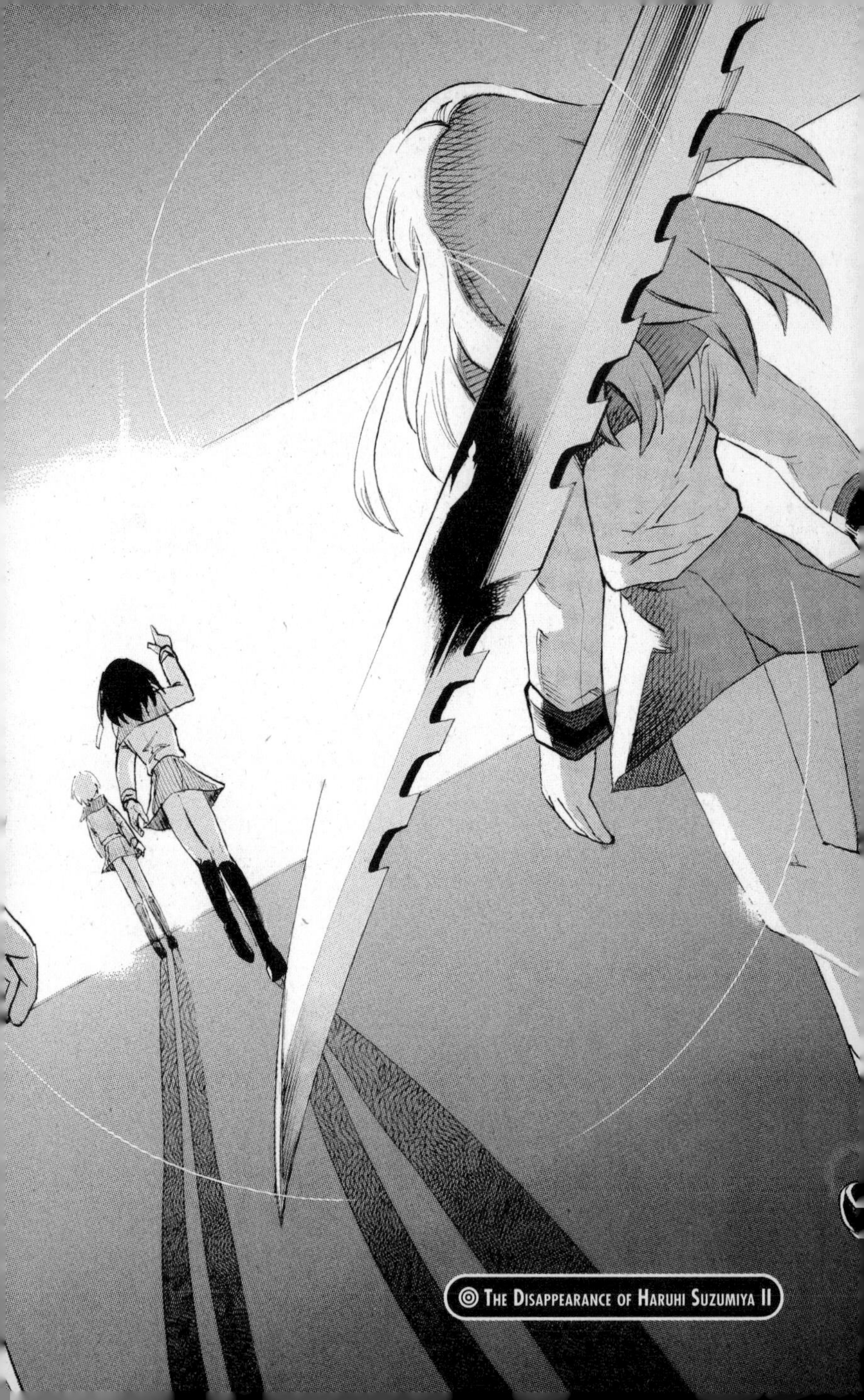

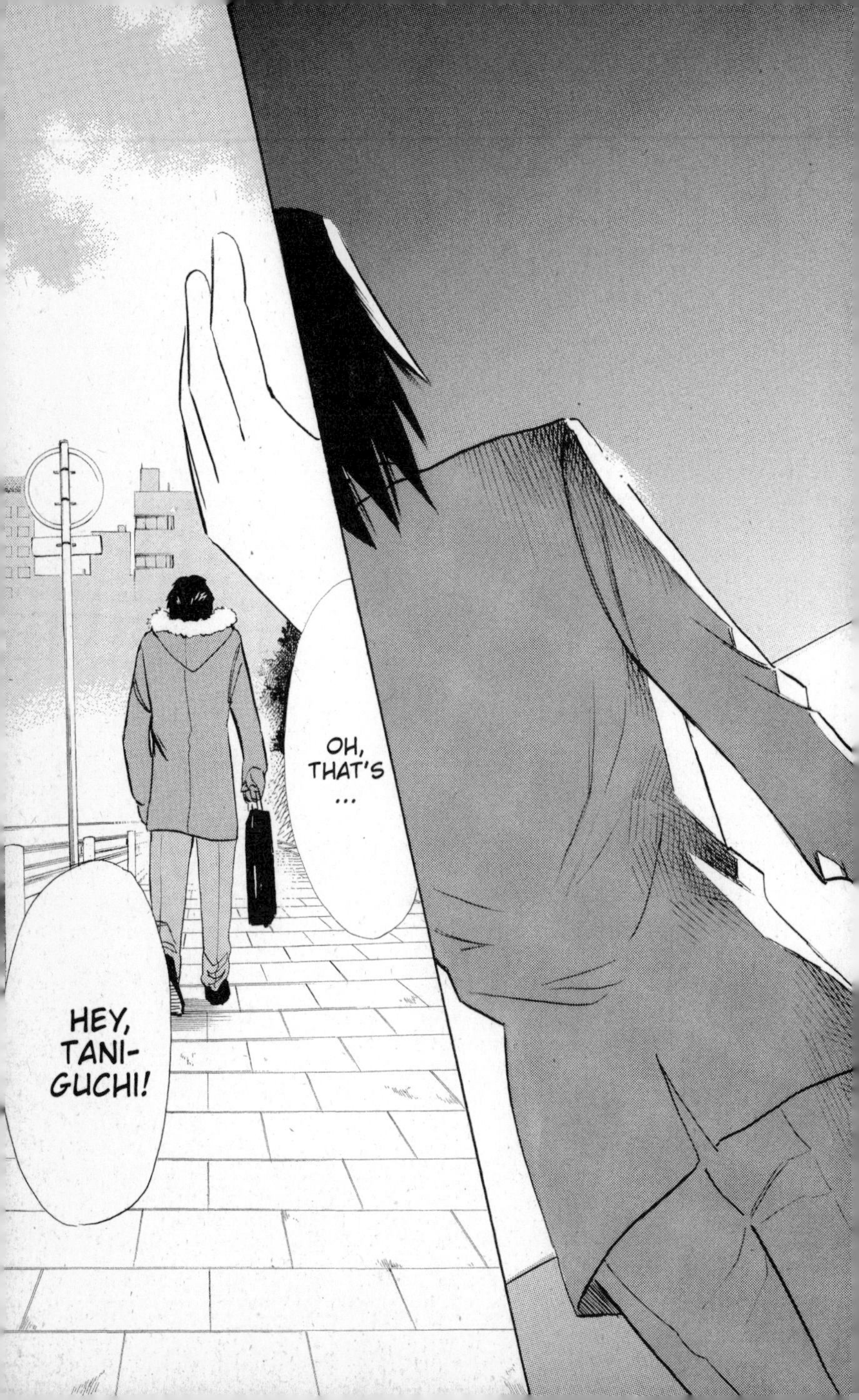
OH, THAT'S ...
HEY, TANI-GUCHI!

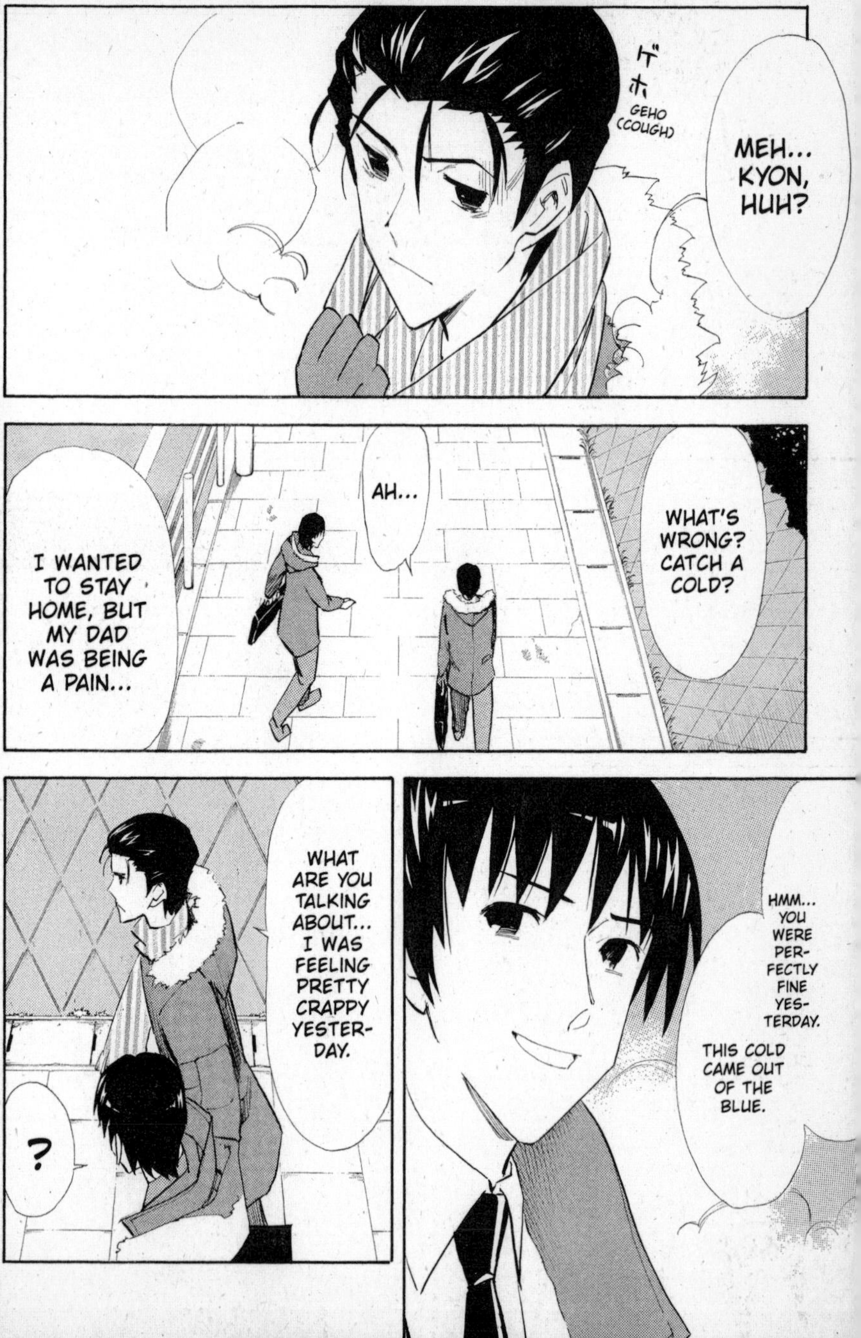
MEH... KYON, HUH?
ゲホ
GEHO (COUGH)
WHAT'S WRONG? CATCH A COLD?
AH...
I WANTED TO STAY HOME, BUT MY DAD WAS BEING A PAIN...
HMM... YOU WERE PERFECTLY FINE YESTERDAY.
THIS COLD CAME OUT OF THE BLUE.
WHAT ARE YOU TALKING ABOUT... I WAS FEELING PRETTY CRAPPY YESTERDAY.
?

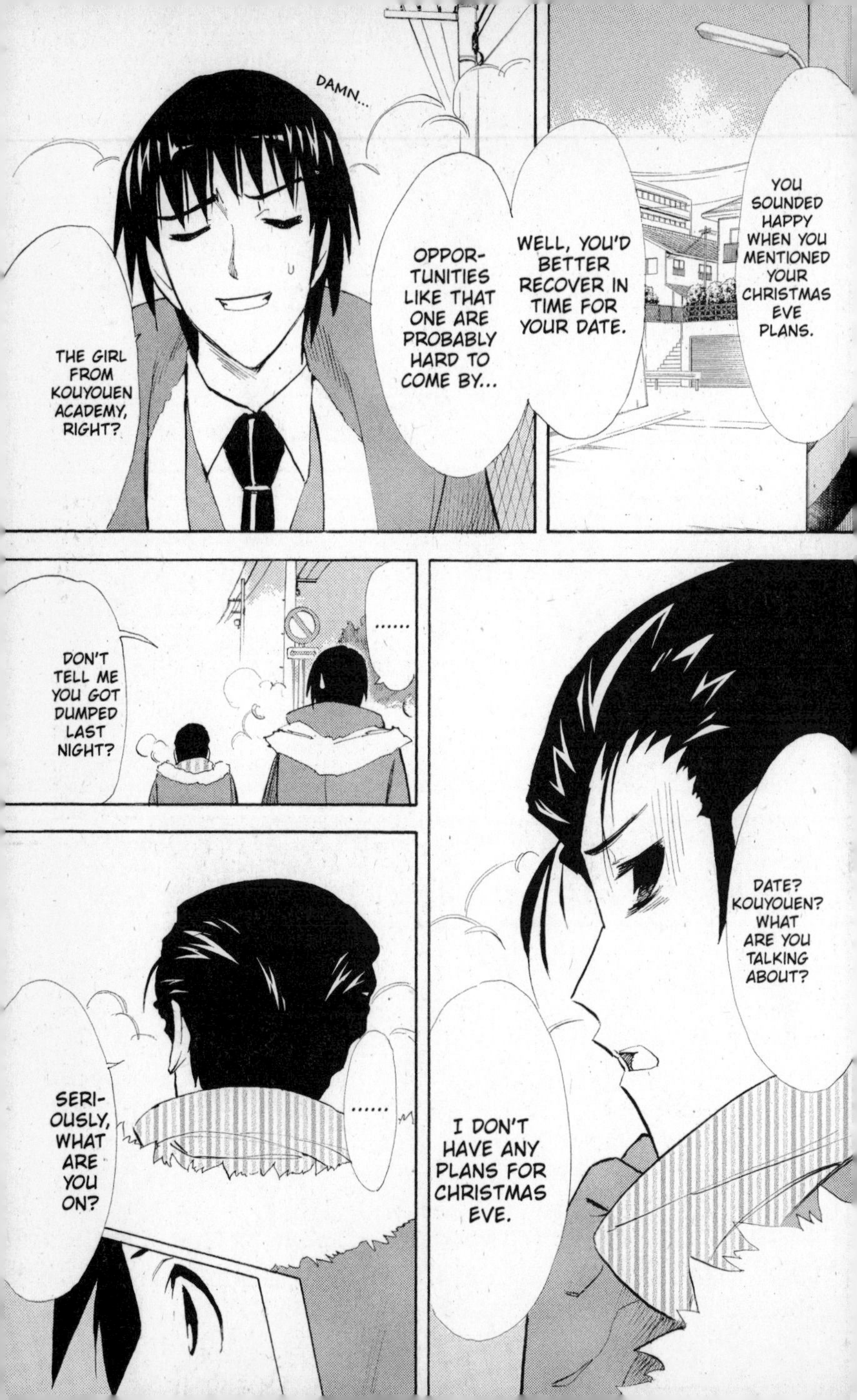
YOU SOUNDED HAPPY WHEN YOU MENTIONED YOUR CHRISTMAS EVE PLANS.
DAMN...
WELL, YOU'D BETTER RECOVER IN TIME FOR YOUR DATE.
OPPOR-TUNITIES LIKE THAT ONE ARE PROBABLY HARD TO COME BY...
THE GIRL FROM KOUYOUEN ACADEMY, RIGHT?
DATE? KOUYOUEN? WHAT ARE YOU TALKING ABOUT?
I DON'T HAVE ANY PLANS FOR CHRISTMAS EVE.
......
DON'T TELL ME YOU GOT DUMPED LAST NIGHT?
......
SERI-OUSLY, WHAT ARE YOU ON?

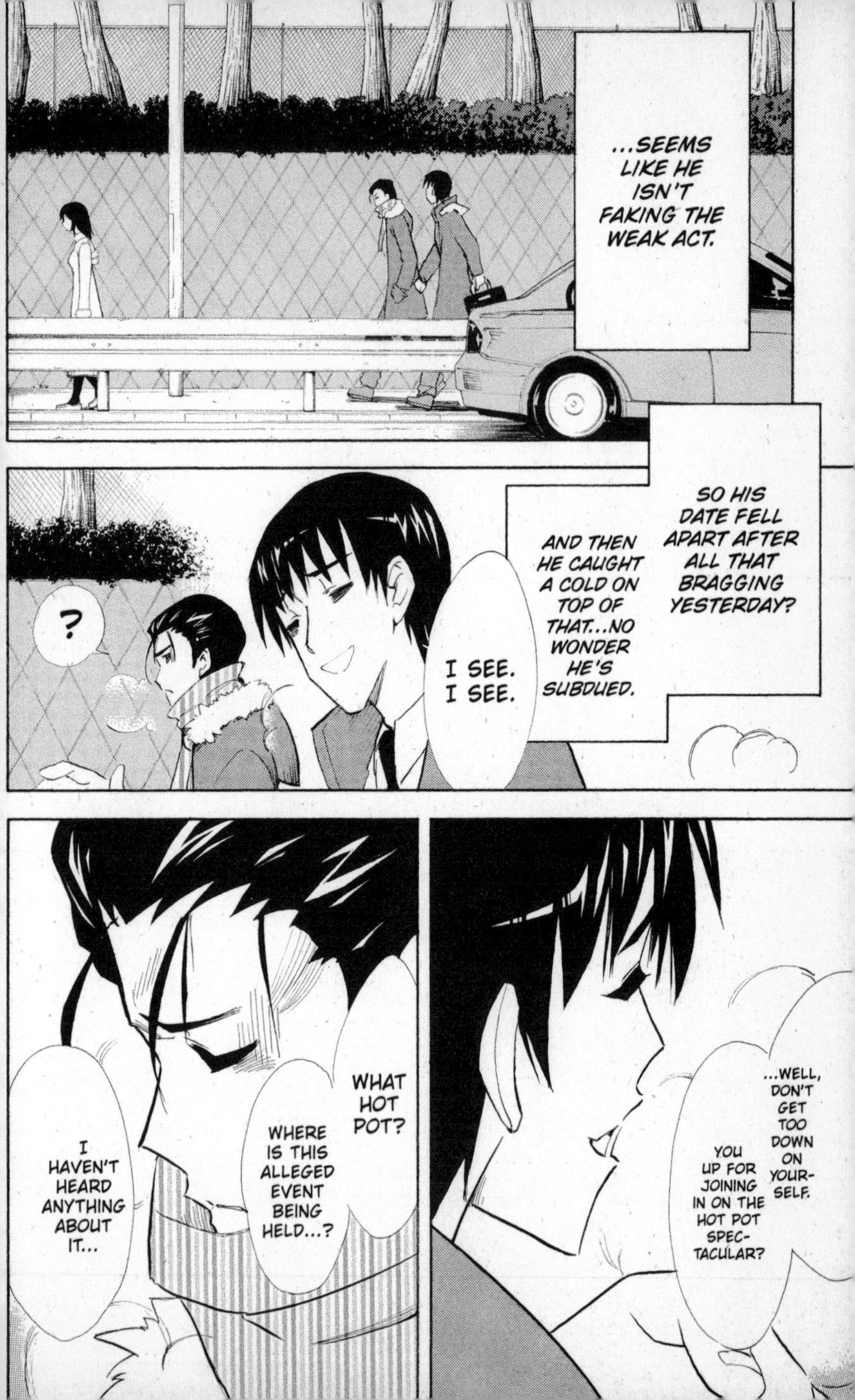
...SEEMS LIKE HE ISN'T FAKING THE WEAK ACT.
SO HIS DATE FELL APART AFTER ALL THAT BRAGGING YESTERDAY?
AND THEN HE CAUGHT A COLD ON TOP OF THAT...NO WONDER HE'S SUBDUED.
I SEE. I SEE.
?
...WELL, DON'T GET TOO DOWN ON YOURSELF.
YOU UP FOR JOINING IN ON THE HOT POT SPECTACULAR?
WHAT HOT POT?
WHERE IS THIS ALLEGED EVENT BEING HELD...?
I HAVEN'T HEARD ANYTHING ABOUT IT...

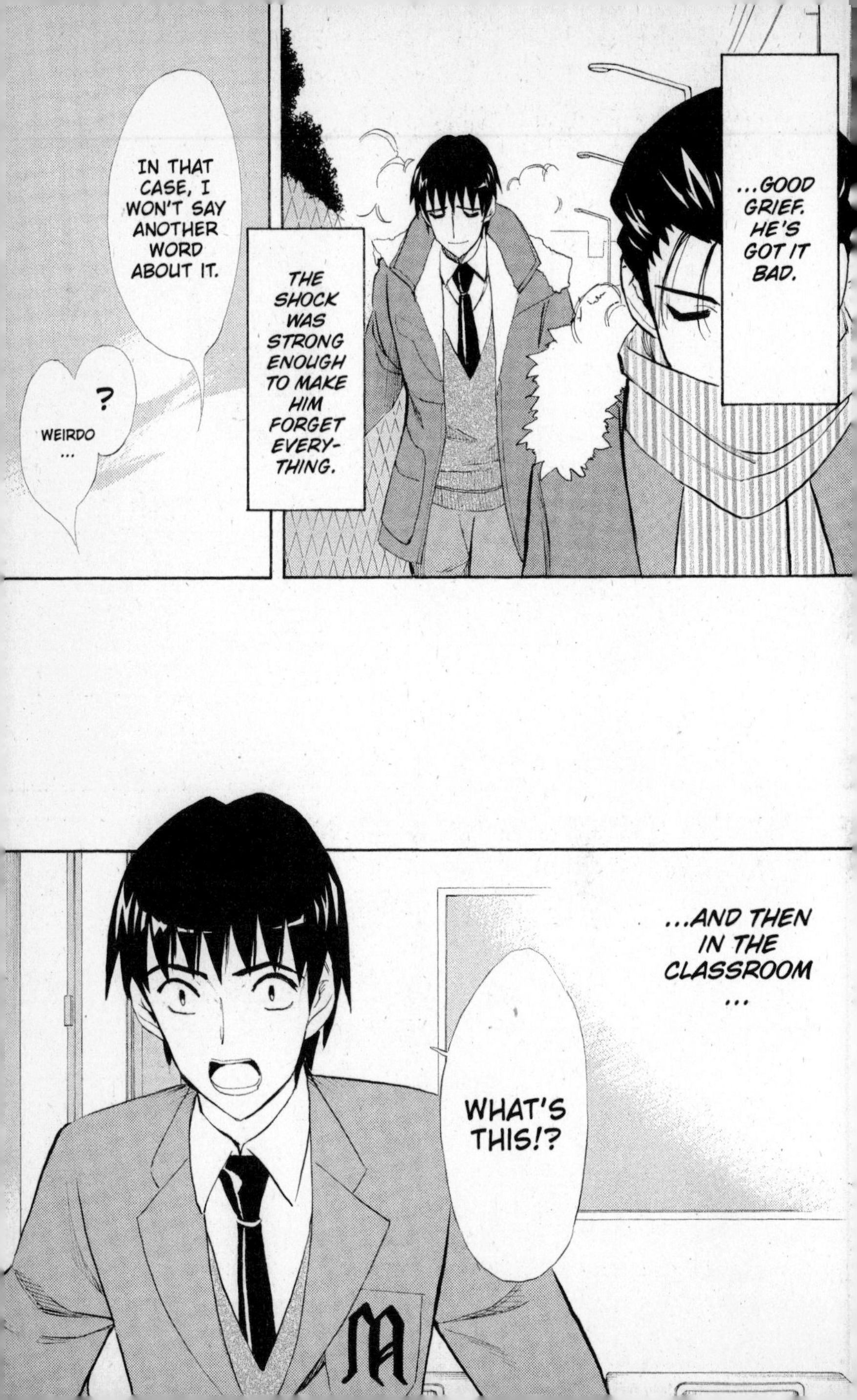
...GOOD GRIEF. HE'S GOT IT BAD.
THE SHOCK WAS STRONG ENOUGH TO MAKE HIM FORGET EVERYTHING.
IN THAT CASE, I WON'T SAY ANOTHER WORD ABOUT IT.
?
WEIRDO...
...AND THEN IN THE CLASSROOM...
WHAT'S THIS!?

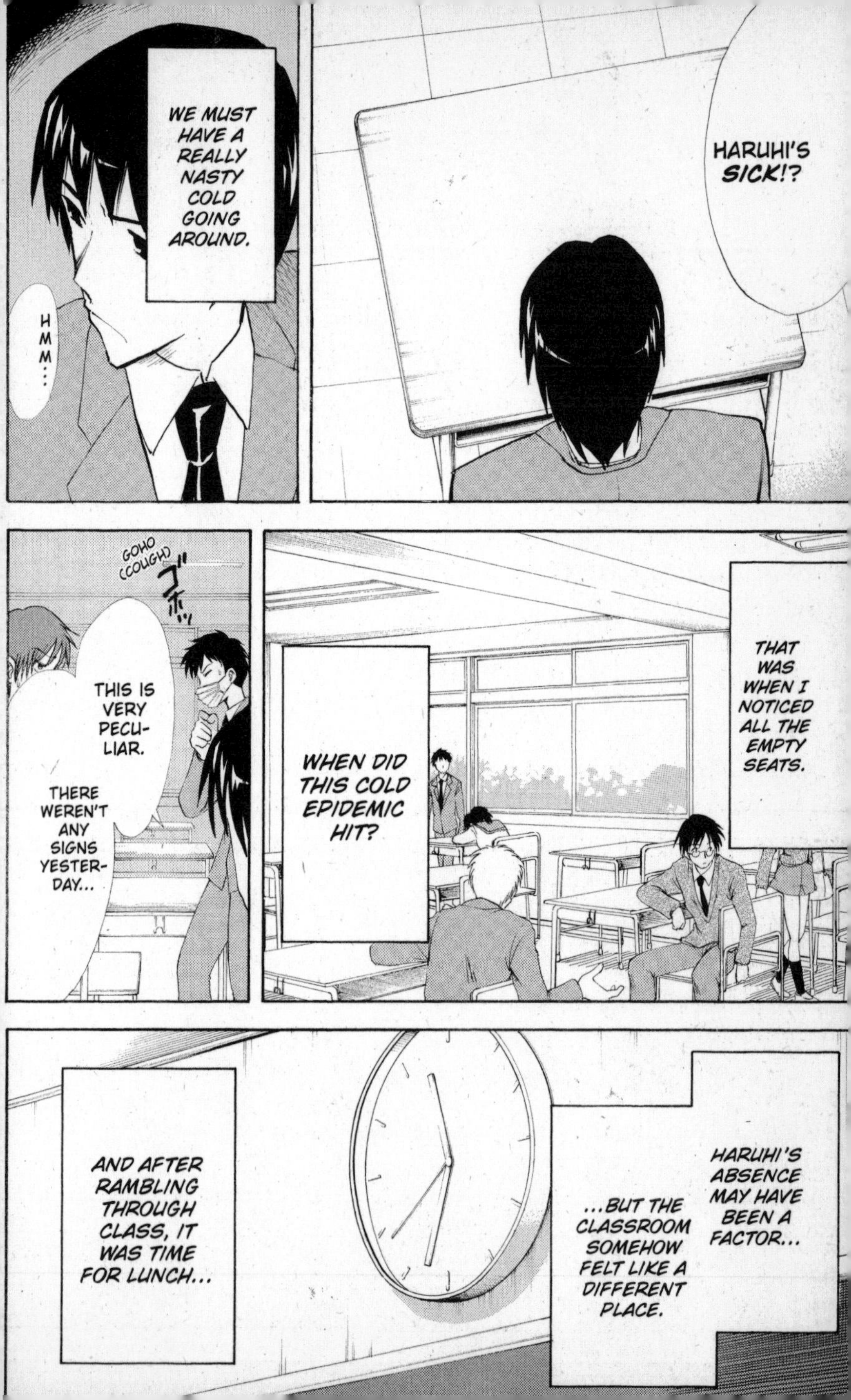
HARUHI'S SICK!?
WE MUST HAVE A REALLY NASTY COLD GOING AROUND.
HMM...
THAT WAS WHEN I NOTICED ALL THE EMPTY SEATS.
WHEN DID THIS COLD EPIDEMIC HIT?
GOHO (COUGH)
THIS IS VERY PECULIAR.
THERE WEREN'T ANY SIGNS YESTERDAY...
HARUHI'S ABSENCE MAY HAVE BEEN A FACTOR...
...BUT THE CLASSROOM SOMEHOW FELT LIKE A DIFFERENT PLACE.
AND AFTER RAMBLING THROUGH CLASS, IT WAS TIME FOR LUNCH...

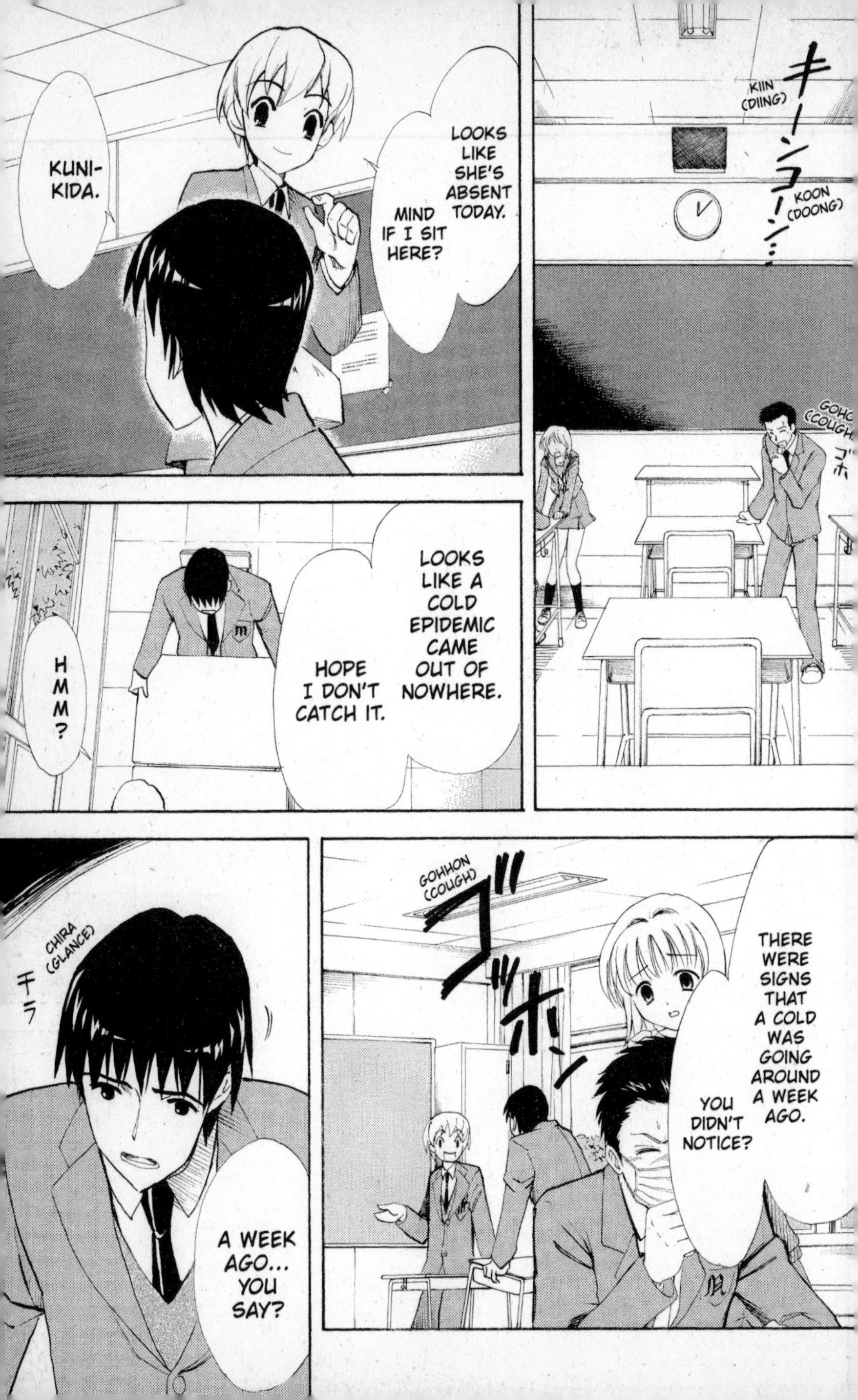
KIIN (DIING)
KOON (DOONG)
GOHO (COUGH
ゴホ
LOOKS LIKE SHE'S ABSENT TODAY.
MIND IF I SIT HERE?
KUNI-KIDA.
LOOKS LIKE A COLD EPIDEMIC CAME OUT OF NOWHERE.
HOPE I DON'T CATCH IT.
HMMM?
GOHHON (COUGH)
ゴホッ
THERE WERE SIGNS THAT A COLD WAS GOING AROUND A WEEK AGO.
YOU DIDN'T NOTICE?
CHIRA (GLANCE)
チラ
A WEEK AGO... YOU SAY?

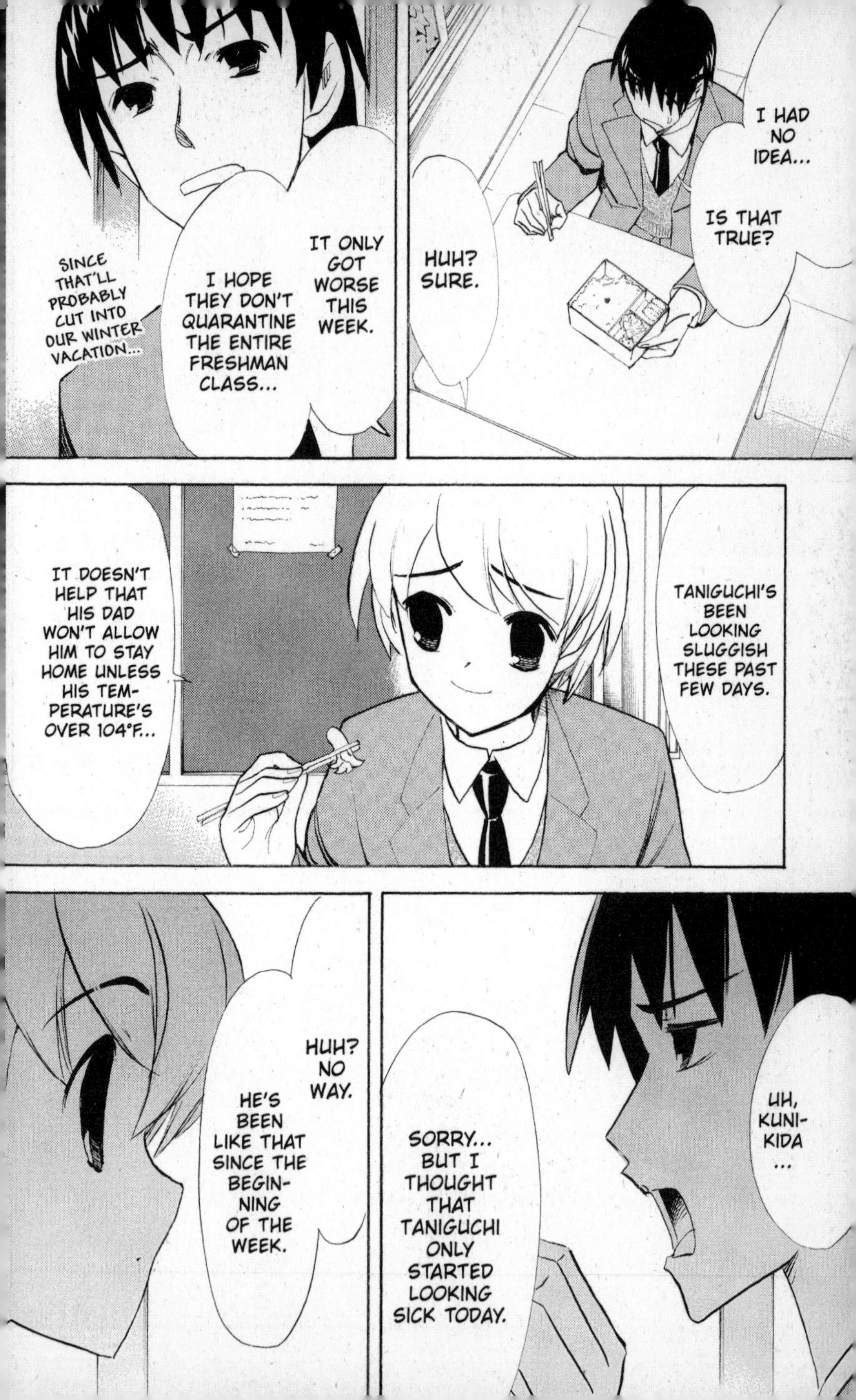
I HAD NO IDEA...
IS THAT TRUE?
HUH? SURE.
IT ONLY GOT WORSE THIS WEEK.
I HOPE THEY DON'T QUARANTINE THE ENTIRE FRESHMAN CLASS...
SINCE THAT'LL PROBABLY CUT INTO OUR WINTER VACATION...
TANIGUCHI'S BEEN LOOKING SLUGGISH THESE PAST FEW DAYS.
IT DOESN'T HELP THAT HIS DAD WON'T ALLOW HIM TO STAY HOME UNLESS HIS TEM-PERATURE'S OVER 104°F...
UH, KUNI-KIDA...
SORRY... BUT I THOUGHT THAT TANIGUCHI ONLY STARTED LOOKING SICK TODAY.
HUH? NO WAY.
HE'S BEEN LIKE THAT SINCE THE BEGIN-NING OF THE WEEK.

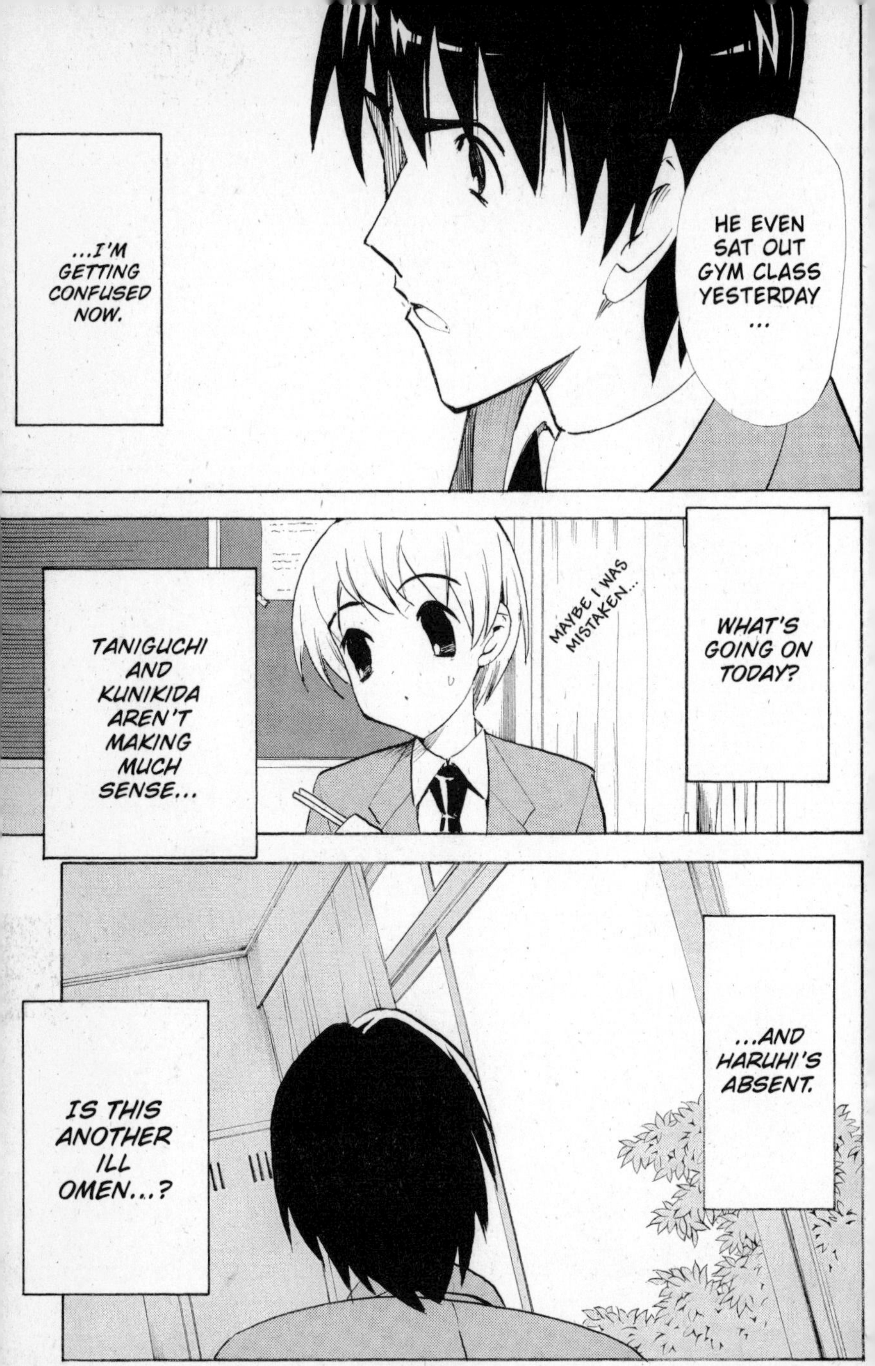
HE EVEN SAT OUT GYM CLASS YESTERDAY ...
...I'M GETTING CONFUSED NOW.
WHAT'S GOING ON TODAY?
MAYBE I WAS MISTAKEN...
TANIGUCHI AND KUNIKIDA AREN'T MAKING MUCH SENSE...
...AND HARUHI'S ABSENT.
IS THIS ANOTHER ILL OMEN...?

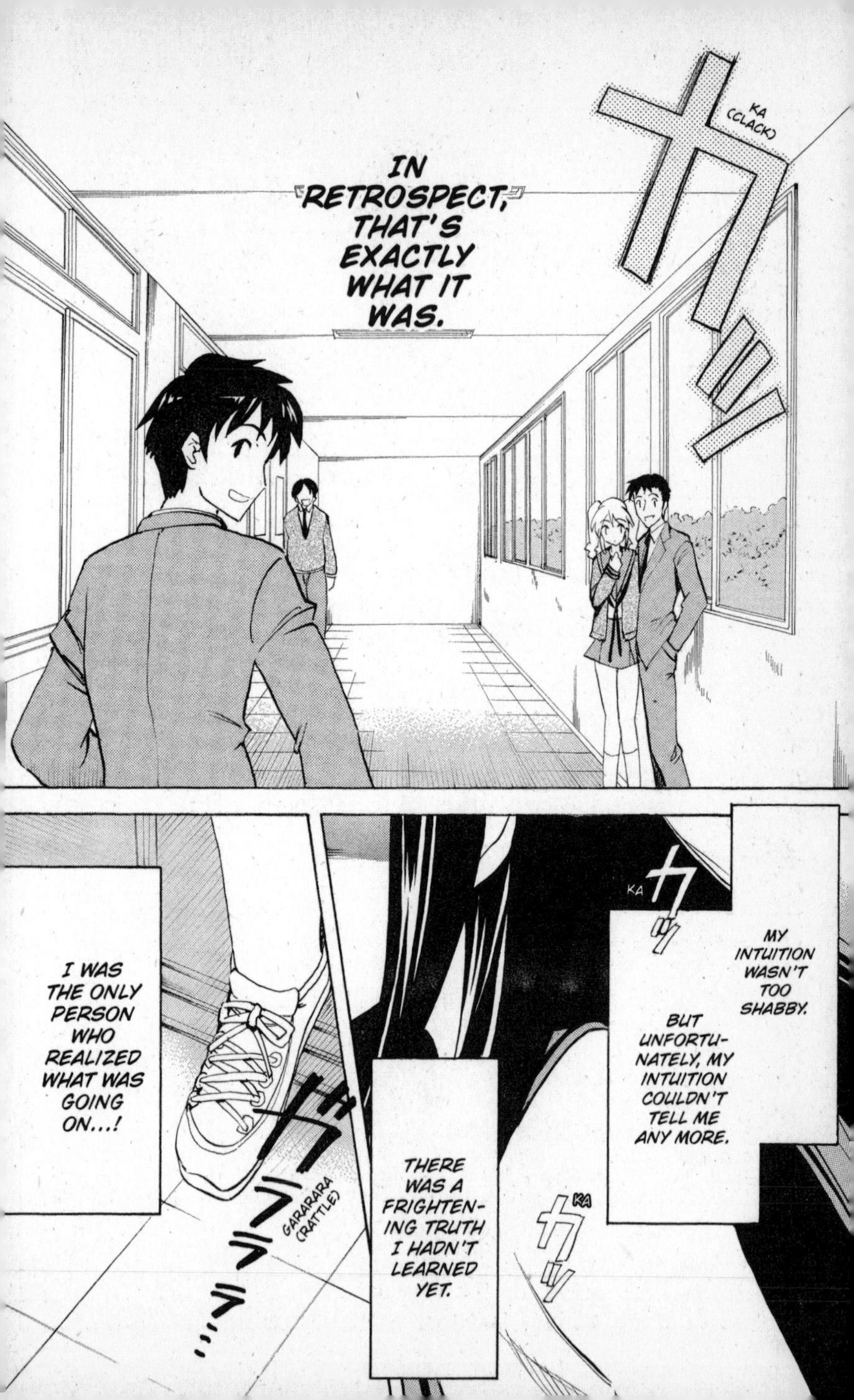
KA (CLACK)
IN RETROSPECT, THAT'S EXACTLY WHAT IT WAS.
KA
MY INTUITION WASN'T TOO SHABBY.
BUT UNFORTUNATELY, MY INTUITION COULDN'T TELL ME ANY MORE.
KA
THERE WAS A FRIGHTENING TRUTH I HADN'T LEARNED YET.
GARARARA (RATTLE)
I WAS THE ONLY PERSON WHO REALIZED WHAT WAS GOING ON...!

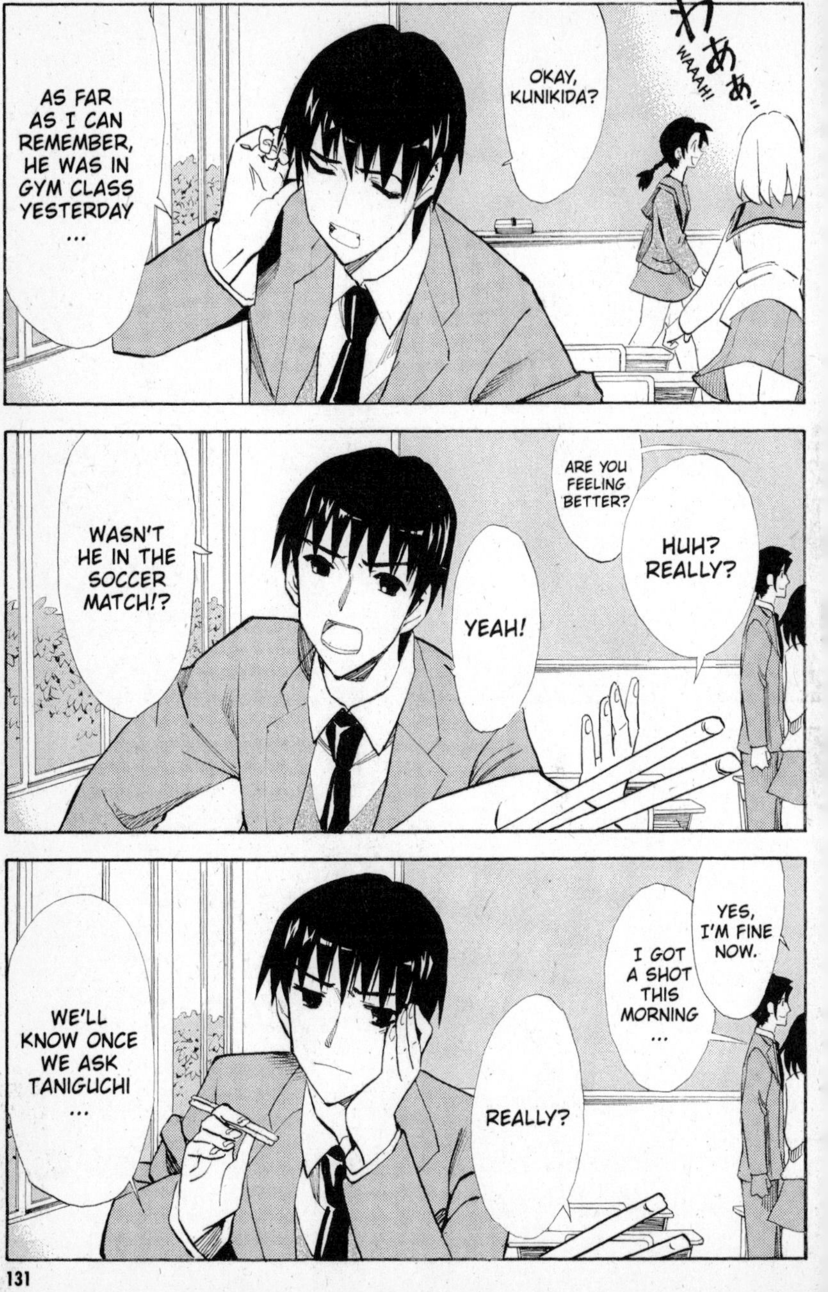
わあぁ..
WAAAH!
OKAY, KUNIKIDA?
AS FAR AS I CAN REMEMBER, HE WAS IN GYM CLASS YESTERDAY...
ARE YOU FEELING BETTER?
HUH? REALLY?
YEAH!
WASN'T HE IN THE SOCCER MATCH!?
YES, I'M FINE NOW.
I GOT A SHOT THIS MORNING...
REALLY?
WE'LL KNOW ONCE WE ASK TANIGUCHI...

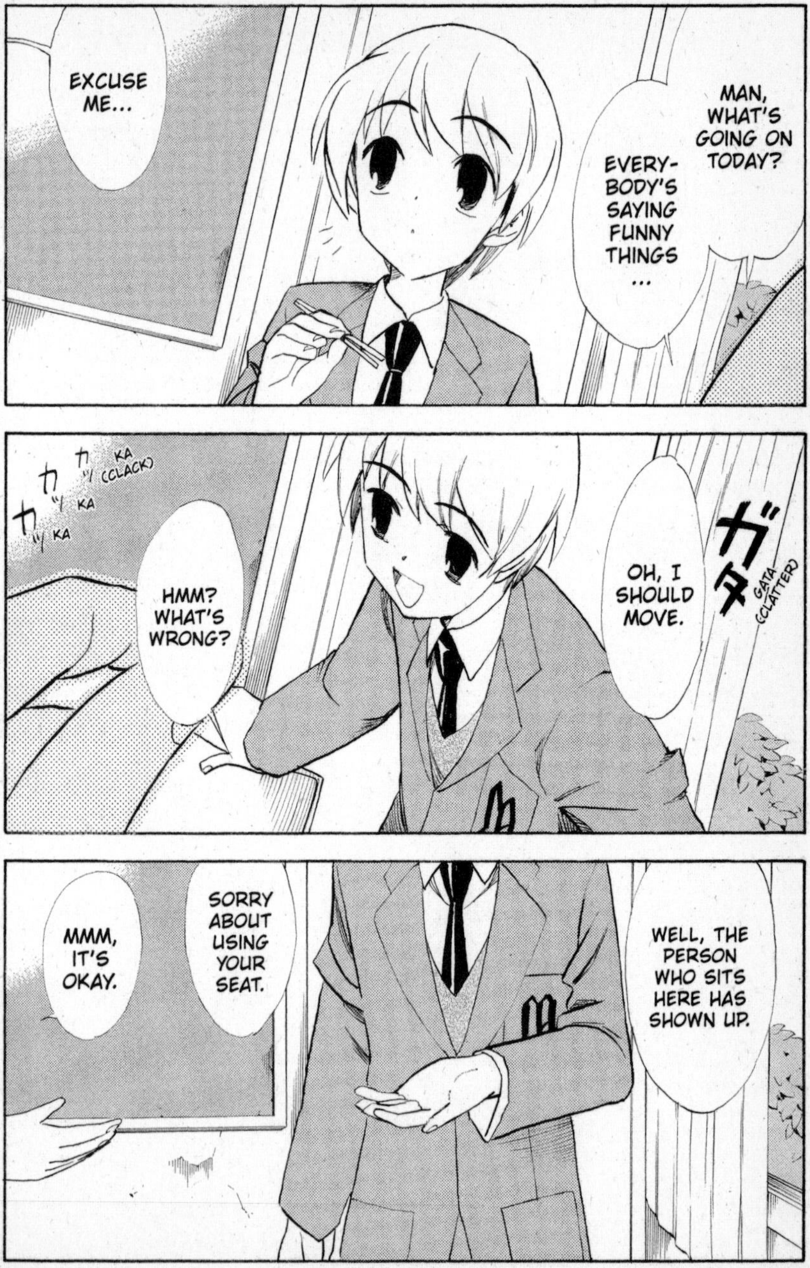
MAN, WHAT'S GOING ON TODAY?
EVERY-BODY'S SAYING FUNNY THINGS ...
EXCUSE ME...
ガタ GATA (CLATTER)
OH, I SHOULD MOVE.
HMM? WHAT'S WRONG?
カッ KA (CLACK)
カッ KA
カッ KA
WELL, THE PERSON WHO SITS HERE HAS SHOWN UP.
SORRY ABOUT USING YOUR SEAT.
MMM, IT'S OKAY.

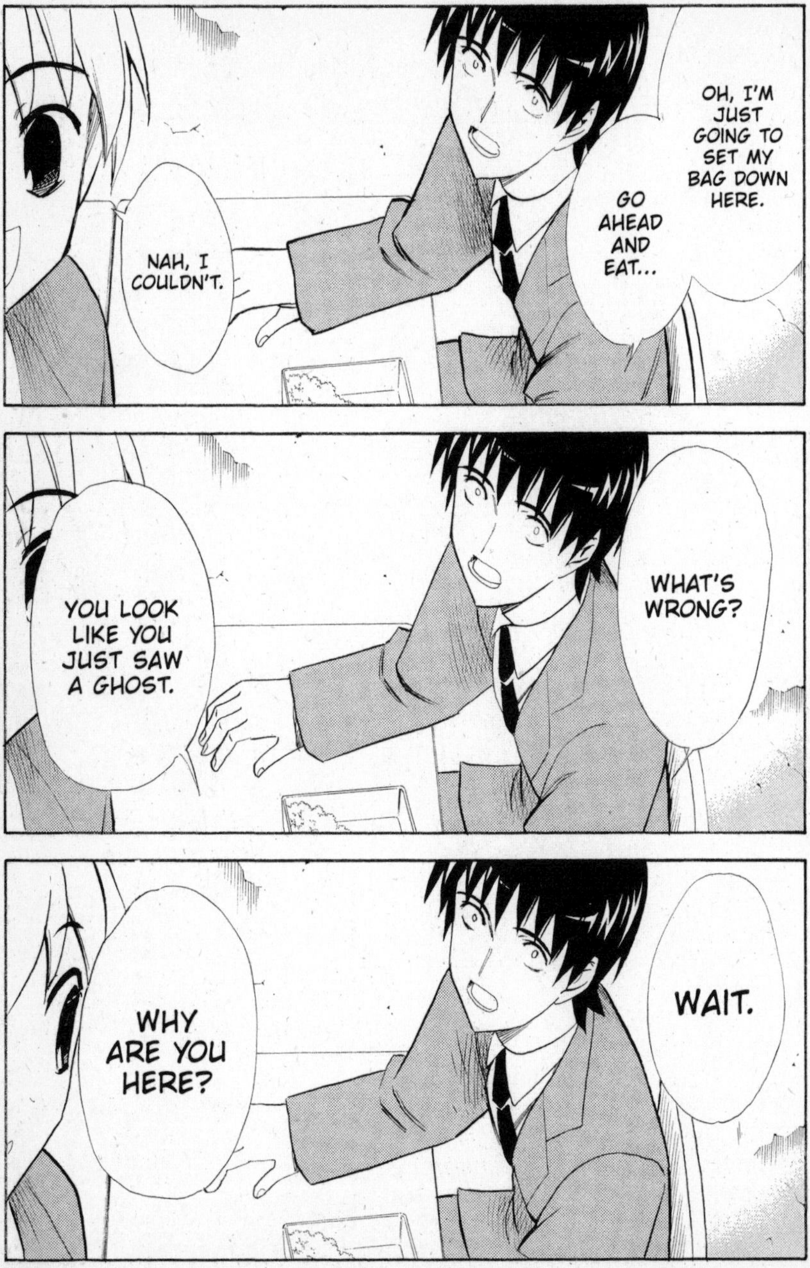
OH, I'M JUST GOING TO SET MY BAG DOWN HERE.
GO AHEAD AND EAT...
NAH, I COULDN'T.
WHAT'S WRONG?
YOU LOOK LIKE YOU JUST SAW A GHOST.
WAIT.
WHY ARE YOU HERE?

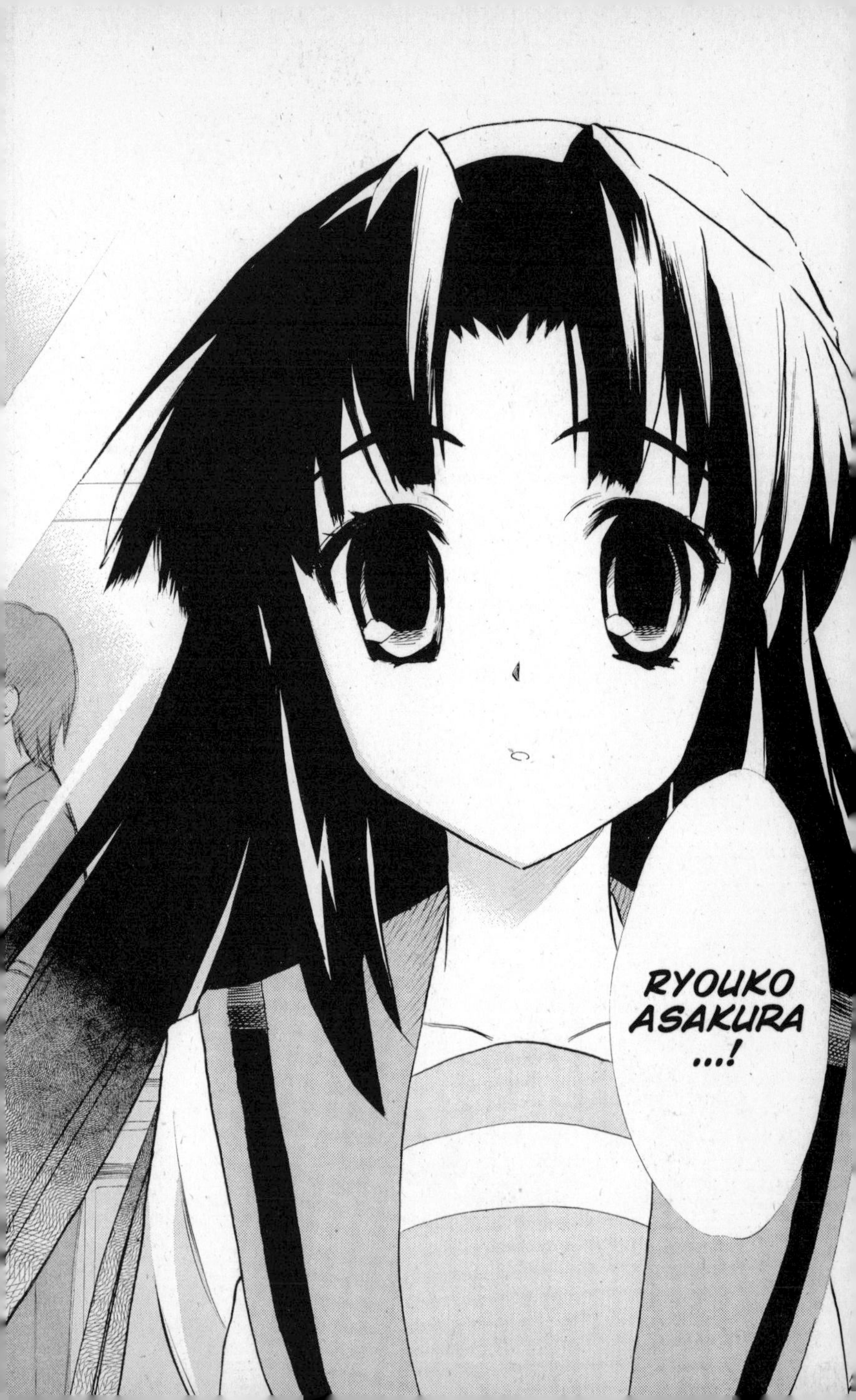
RYOUKO ASAKURA ...!

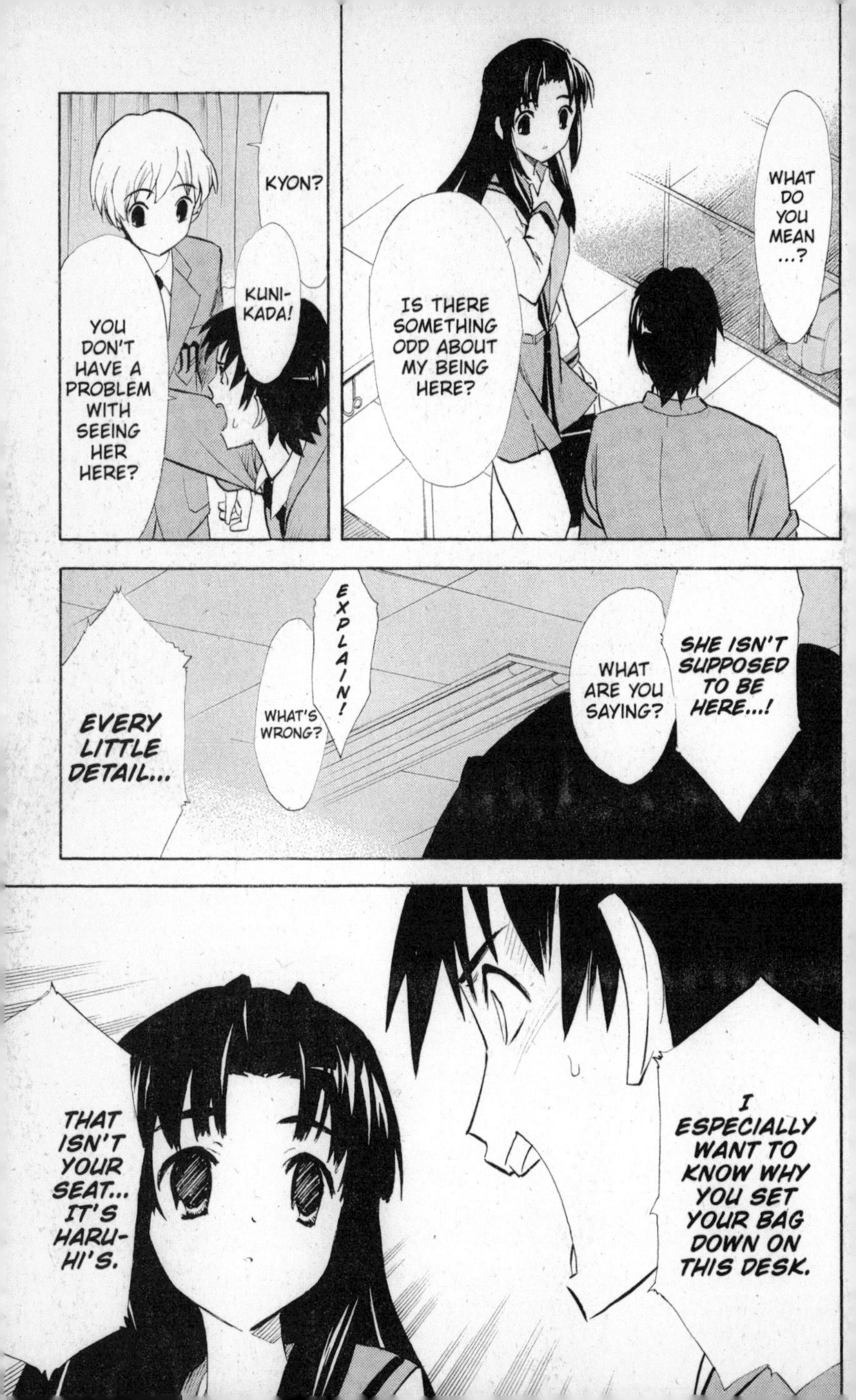
WHAT DO YOU MEAN ...?
IS THERE SOMETHING ODD ABOUT MY BEING HERE?
KYON?
KUNI-KADA!
YOU DON'T HAVE A PROBLEM WITH SEEING HER HERE?
SHE ISN'T SUPPOSED TO BE HERE...!
WHAT ARE YOU SAYING?
EXPLAIN!
WHAT'S WRONG?
EVERY LITTLE DETAIL...
I ESPECIALLY WANT TO KNOW WHY YOU SET YOUR BAG DOWN ON THIS DESK.
THAT ISN'T YOUR SEAT... IT'S HARU-HI'S.

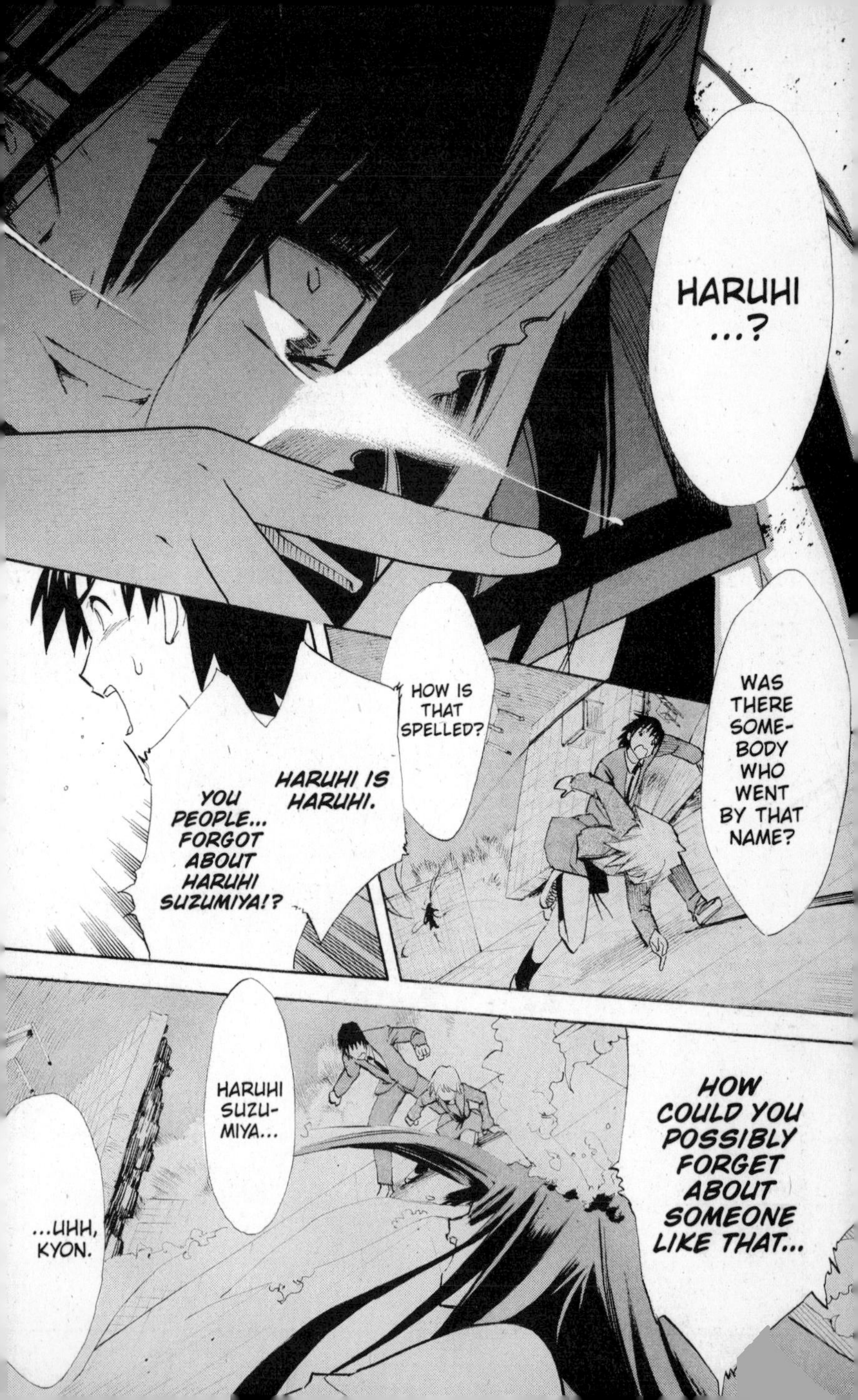
HARUHI ...?
WAS THERE SOMEBODY WHO WENT BY THAT NAME?
HOW IS THAT SPELLED?
HARUHI IS HARUHI.
YOU PEOPLE... FORGOT ABOUT HARUHI SUZUMIYA!?
HOW COULD YOU POSSIBLY FORGET ABOUT SOMEONE LIKE THAT...
HARUHI SUZU-MIYA...
...UHH, KYON.

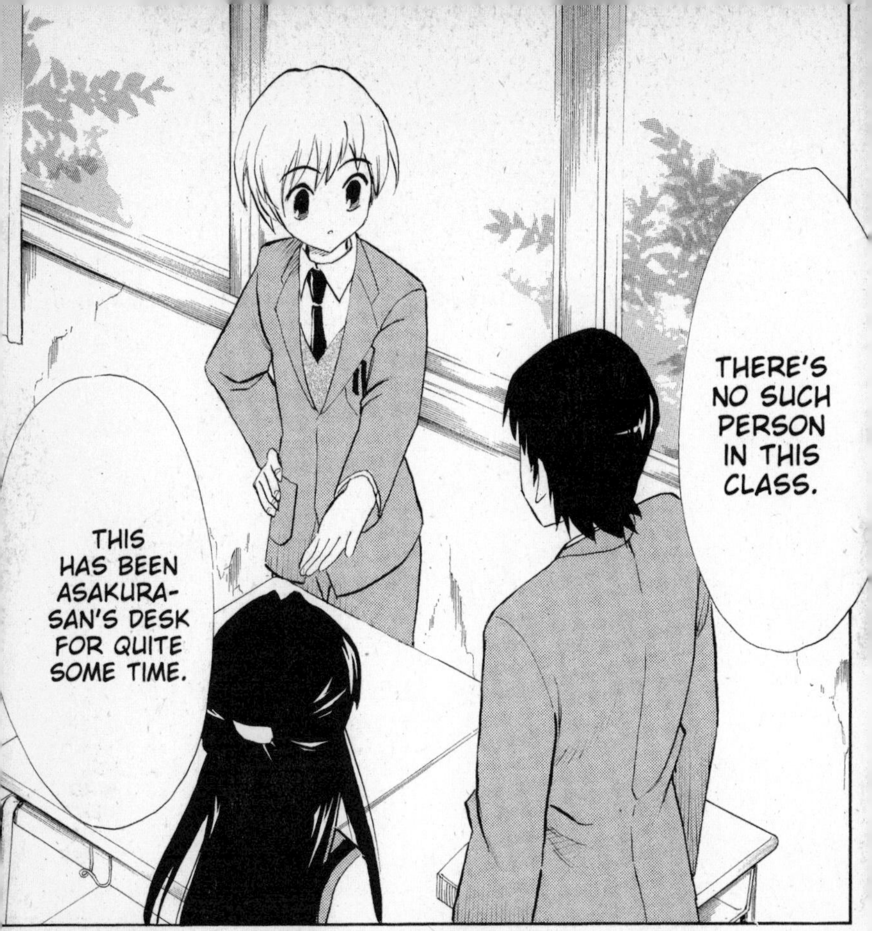
THERE'S NO SUCH PERSON IN THIS CLASS.
THIS HAS BEEN ASAKURA-SAN'S DESK FOR QUITE SOME TIME.

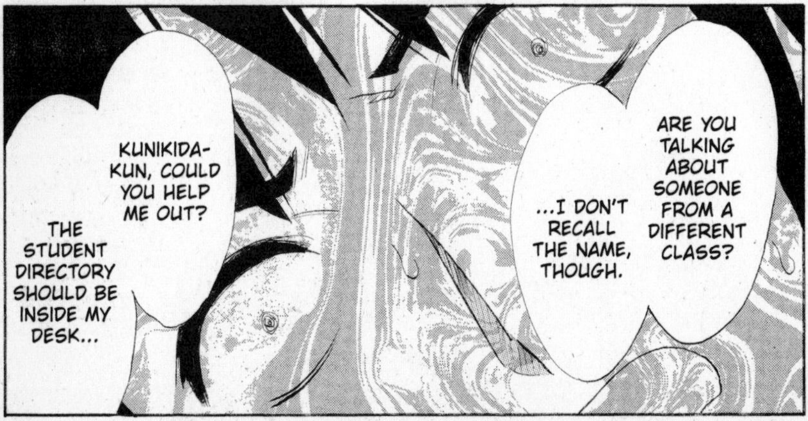
ARE YOU TALKING ABOUT SOMEONE FROM A DIFFERENT CLASS?
...I DON'T RECALL THE NAME, THOUGH.
KUNIKIDA-KUN, COULD YOU HELP ME OUT?
THE STUDENT DIRECTORY SHOULD BE INSIDE MY DESK...

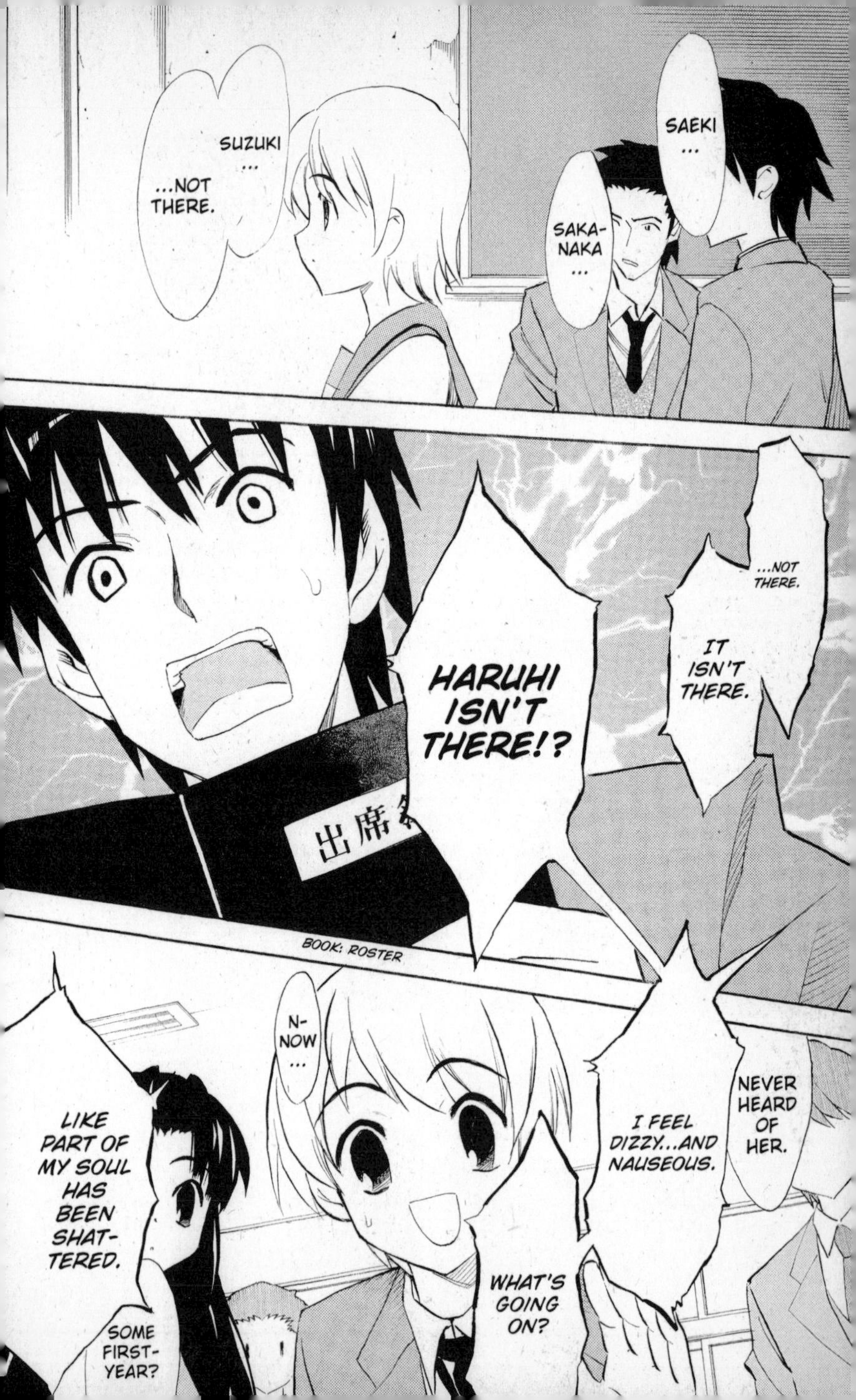
SAEKI ...
SAKA-NAKA ...
SUZUKI ...
...NOT THERE.
...NOT THERE.
IT ISN'T THERE.
HARUHI ISN'T THERE!?
出席
BOOK: ROSTER
NEVER HEARD OF HER.
I FEEL DIZZY...AND NAUSEOUS.
N-NOW ...
WHAT'S GOING ON?
LIKE PART OF MY SOUL HAS BEEN SHATTERED.
SOME FIRST-YEAR?

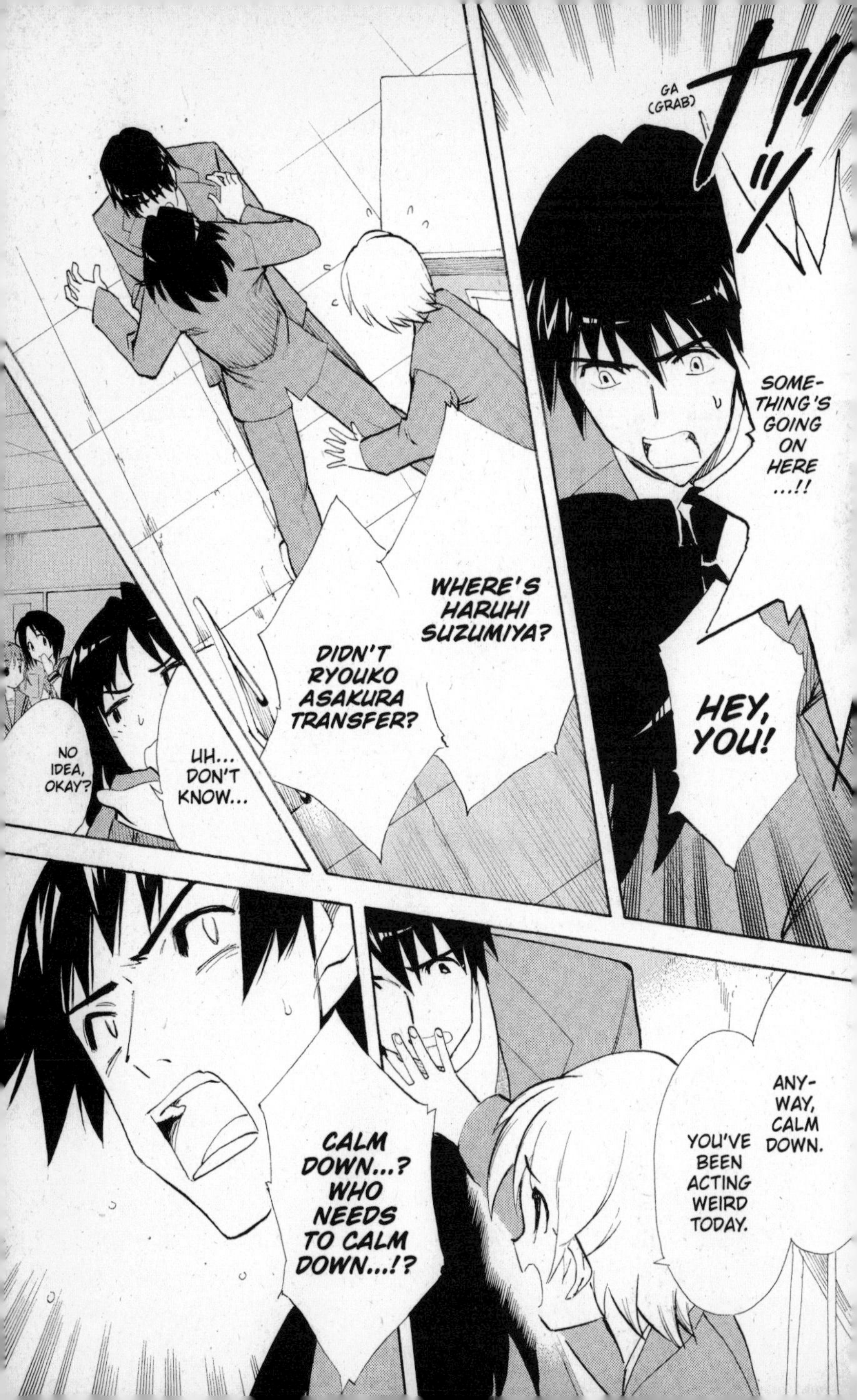
GA (GRAB)
SOMETHING'S GOING ON HERE ...!!
HEY, YOU!
WHERE'S HARUHI SUZUMIYA?
DIDN'T RYOUKO ASAKURA TRANSFER?
UH... DON'T KNOW...
NO IDEA, OKAY?
ANYWAY, CALM DOWN.
YOU'VE BEEN ACTING WEIRD TODAY.
CALM DOWN...? WHO NEEDS TO CALM DOWN...!?

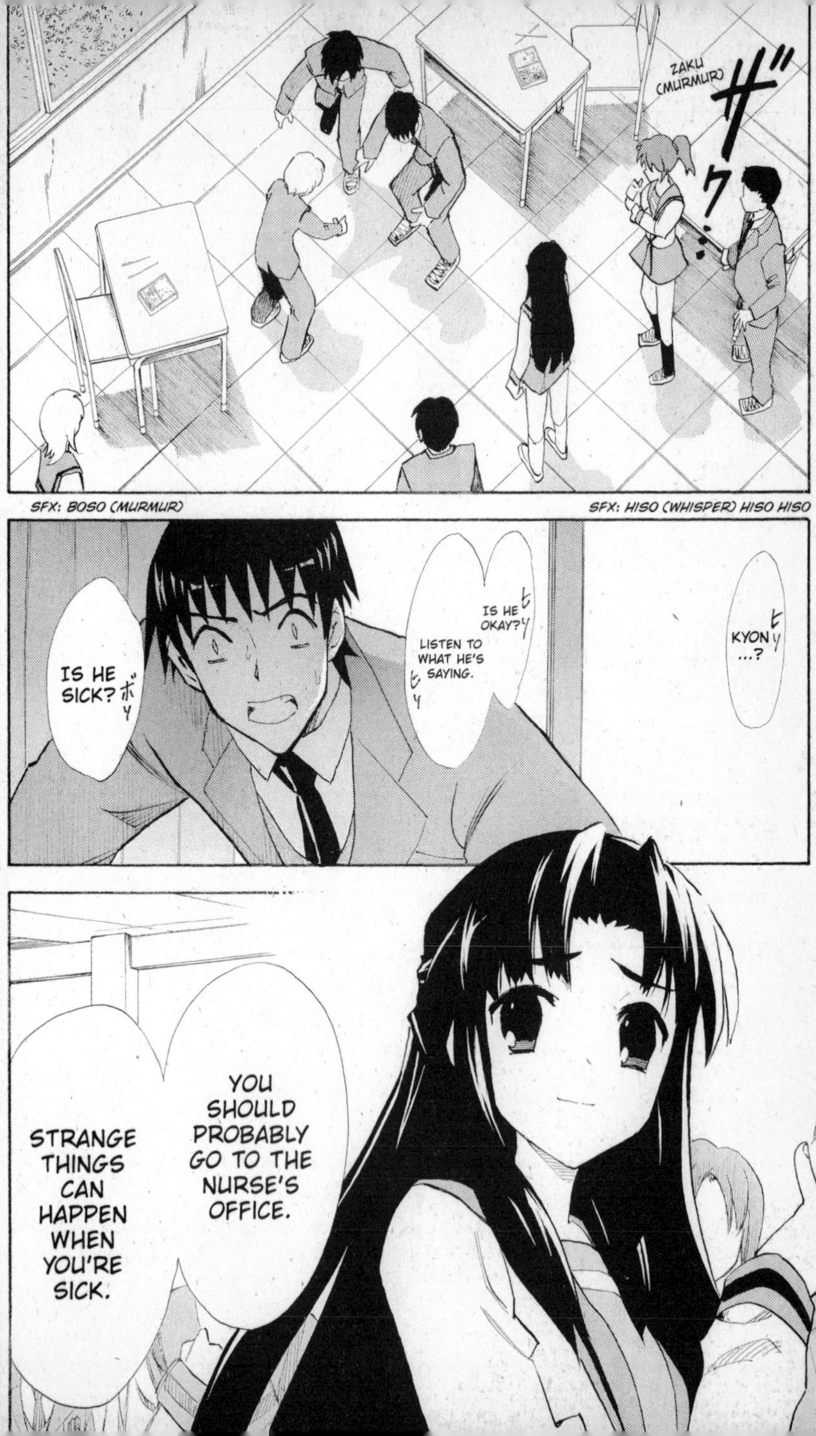

ZAKU (MURMUR)
ザク!
SFX: HISO (WHISPER) HISO HISO
SFX: BOSO (MURMUR)
KYON ...?
IS HE OKAY?
LISTEN TO WHAT HE'S SAYING.
IS HE SICK?
YOU SHOULD PROBABLY GO TO THE NURSE'S OFFICE.
STRANGE THINGS CAN HAPPEN WHEN YOU'RE SICK.

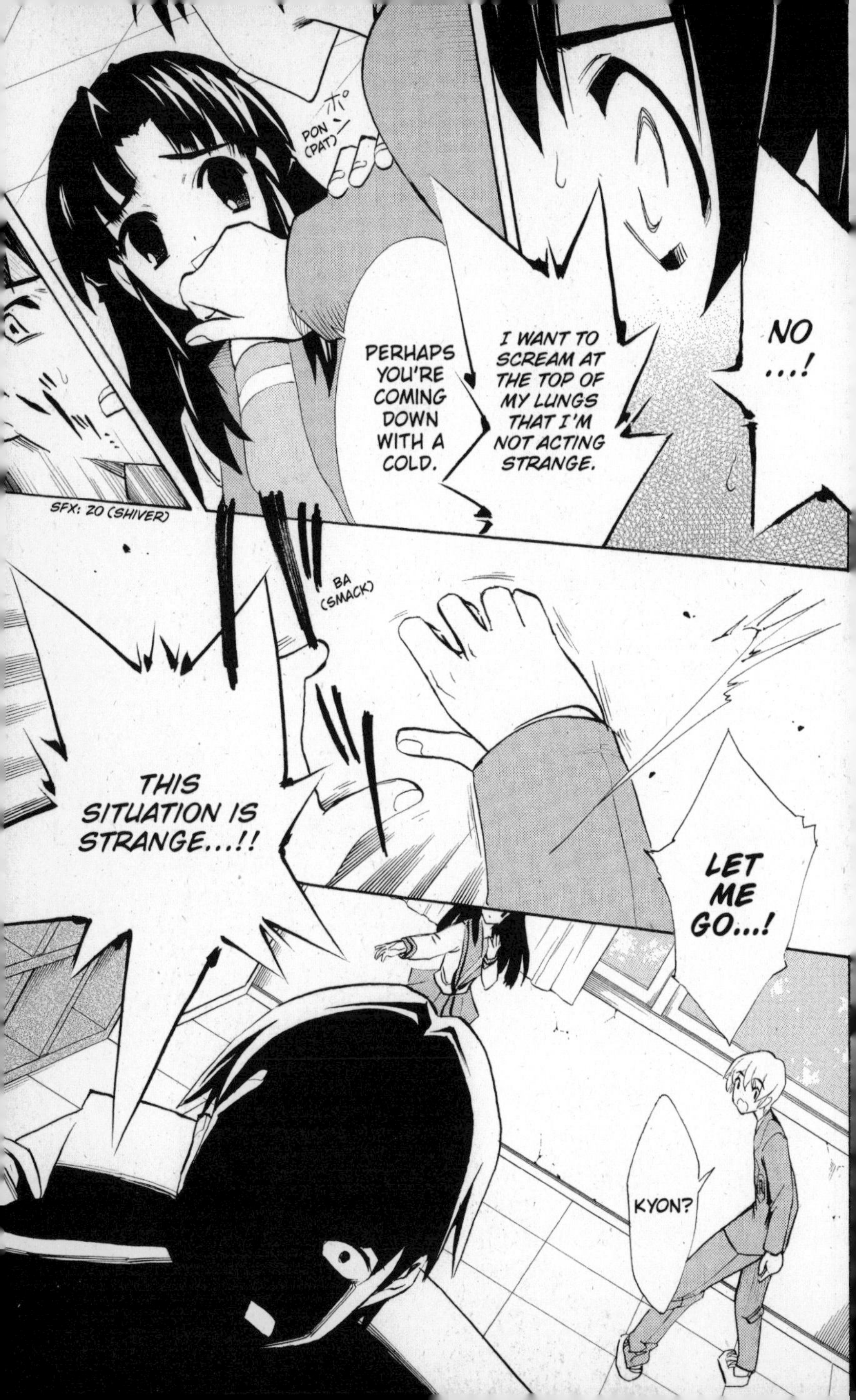
PON (PAT)
NO ...!
I WANT TO SCREAM AT THE TOP OF MY LUNGS THAT I'M NOT ACTING STRANGE.
PERHAPS YOU'RE COMING DOWN WITH A COLD.
SFX: ZO (SHIVER)
LET ME GO...!
BA (SMACK)
THIS SITUATION IS STRANGE...!!
KYON?

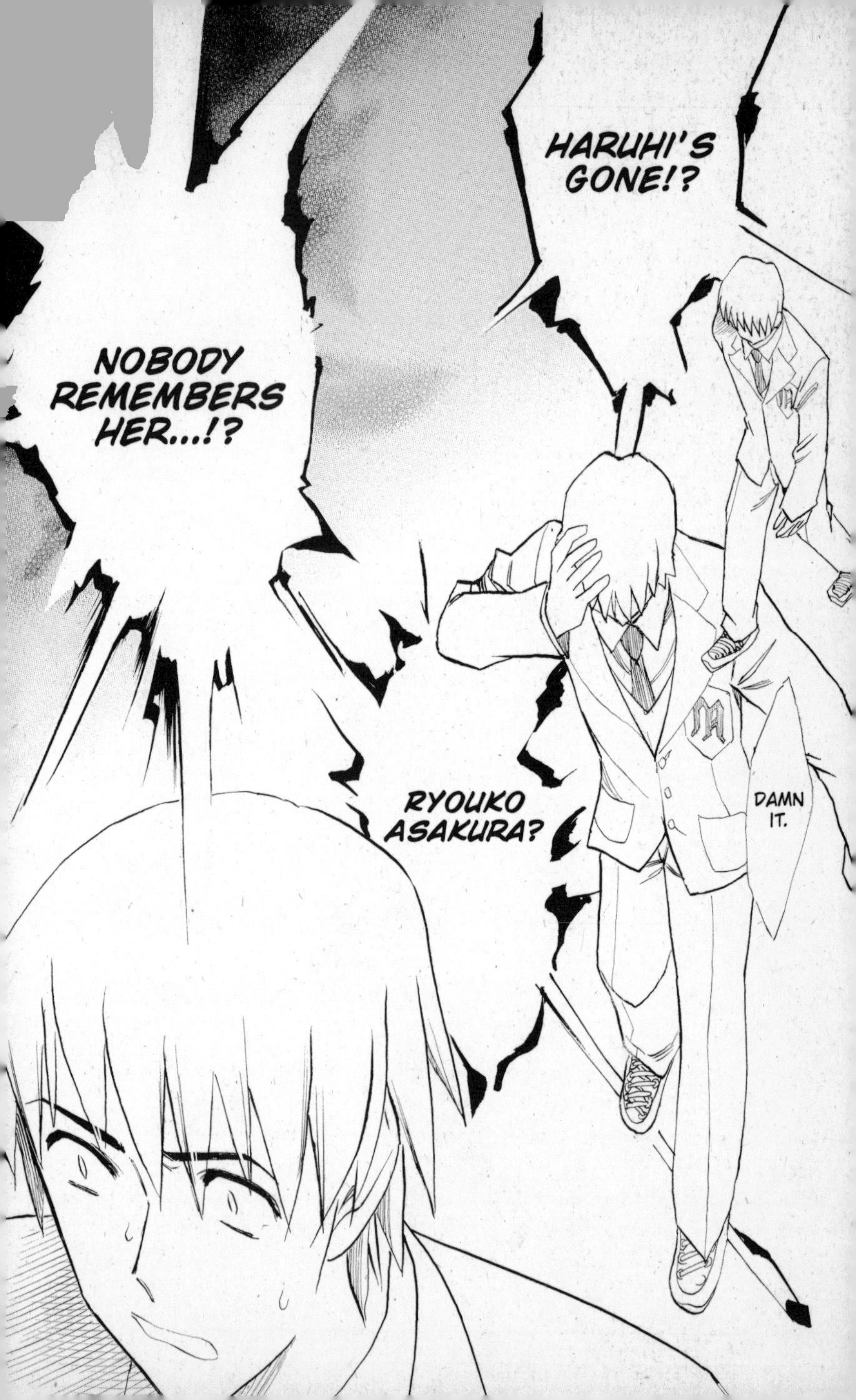
HARUHI'S GONE!?
NOBODY REMEMBERS HER...!?
DAMN IT.
RYOUKO ASAKURA?

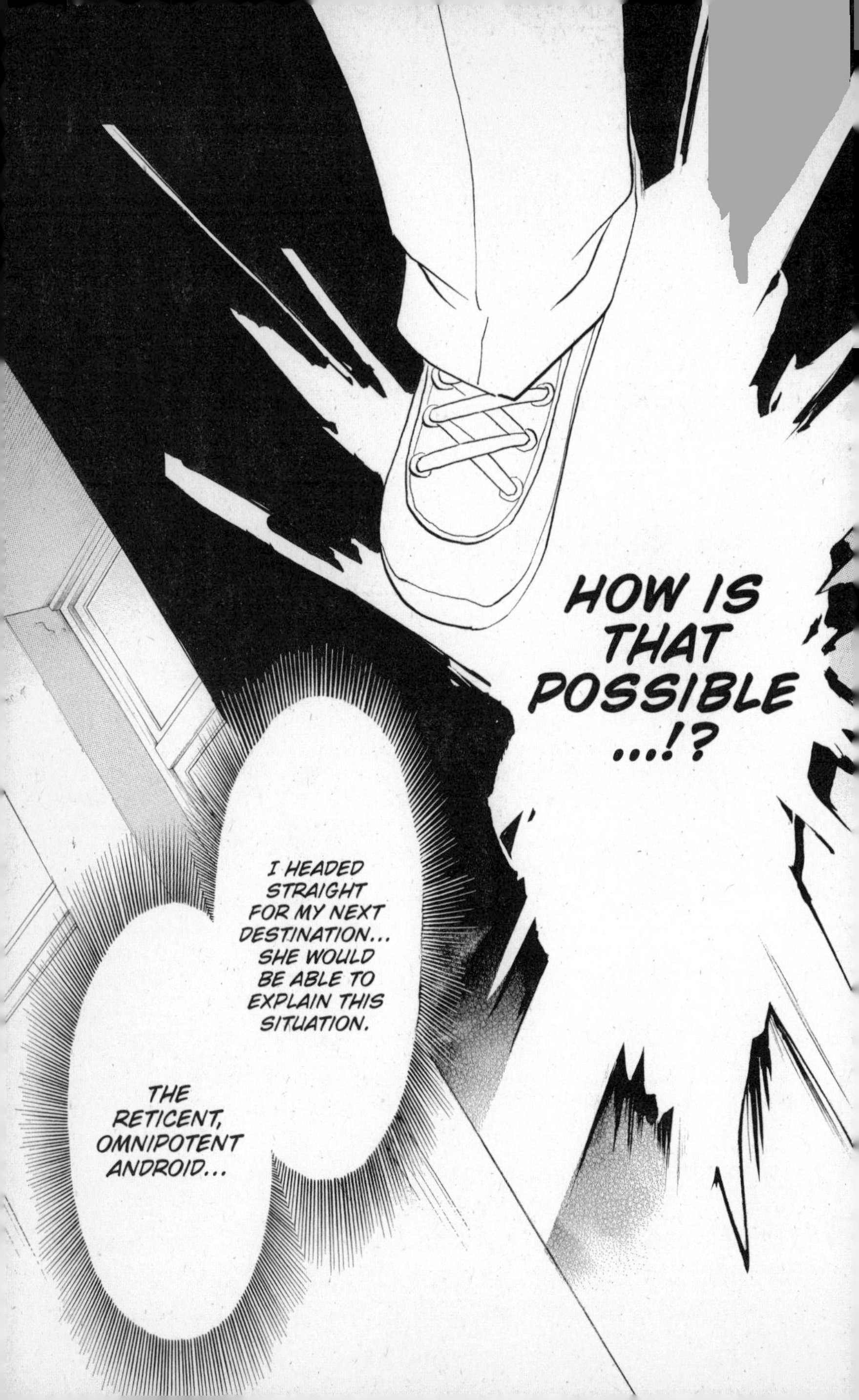
HOW IS THAT POSSIBLE ...!?
I HEADED STRAIGHT FOR MY NEXT DESTINATION... SHE WOULD BE ABLE TO EXPLAIN THIS SITUATION.
THE RETICENT, OMNIPOTENT ANDROID...

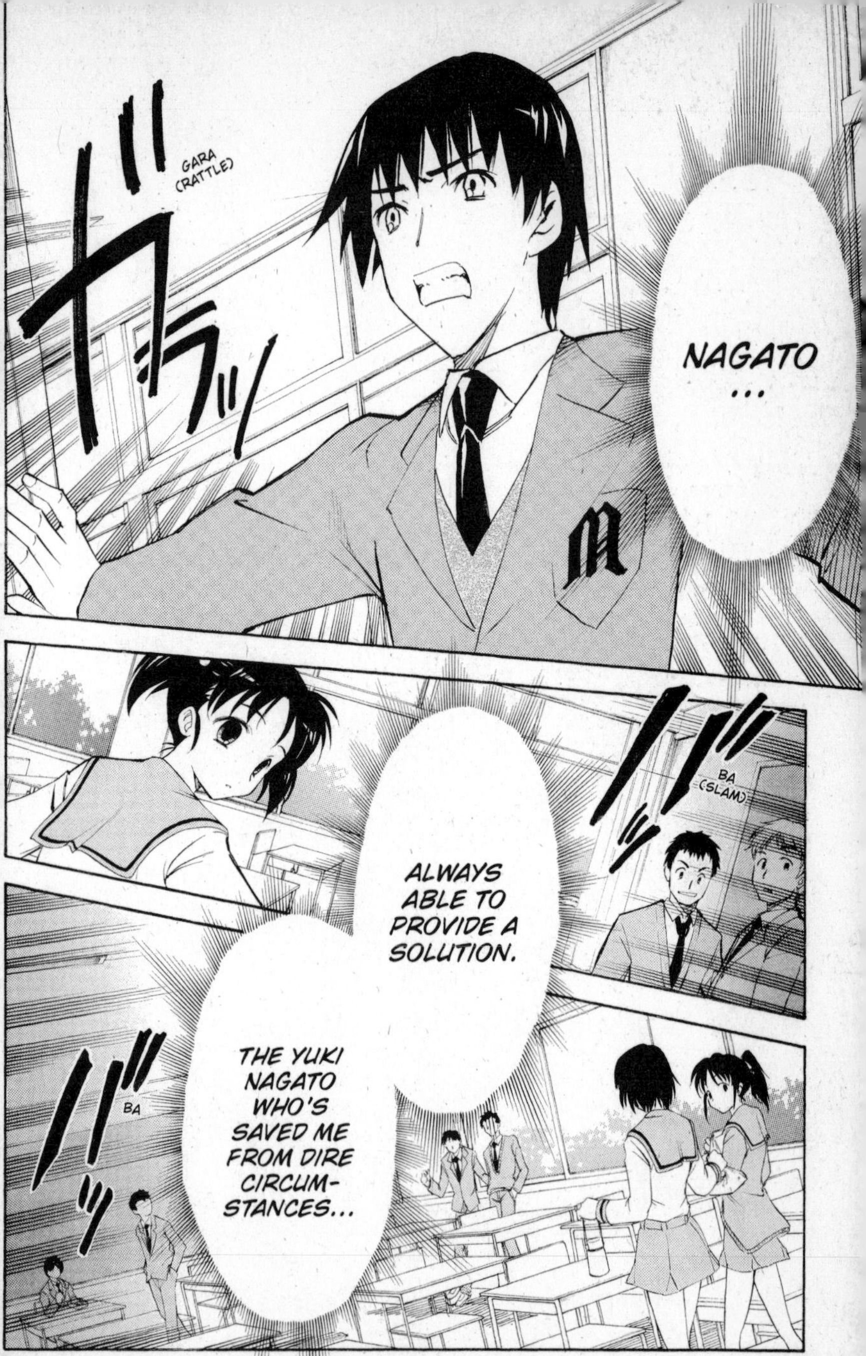
GARA (RATTLE)
NAGATO ...
BA (SLAM)
ALWAYS ABLE TO PROVIDE A SOLUTION.
BA
THE YUKI NAGATO WHO'S SAVED ME FROM DIRE CIRCUM-STANCES...

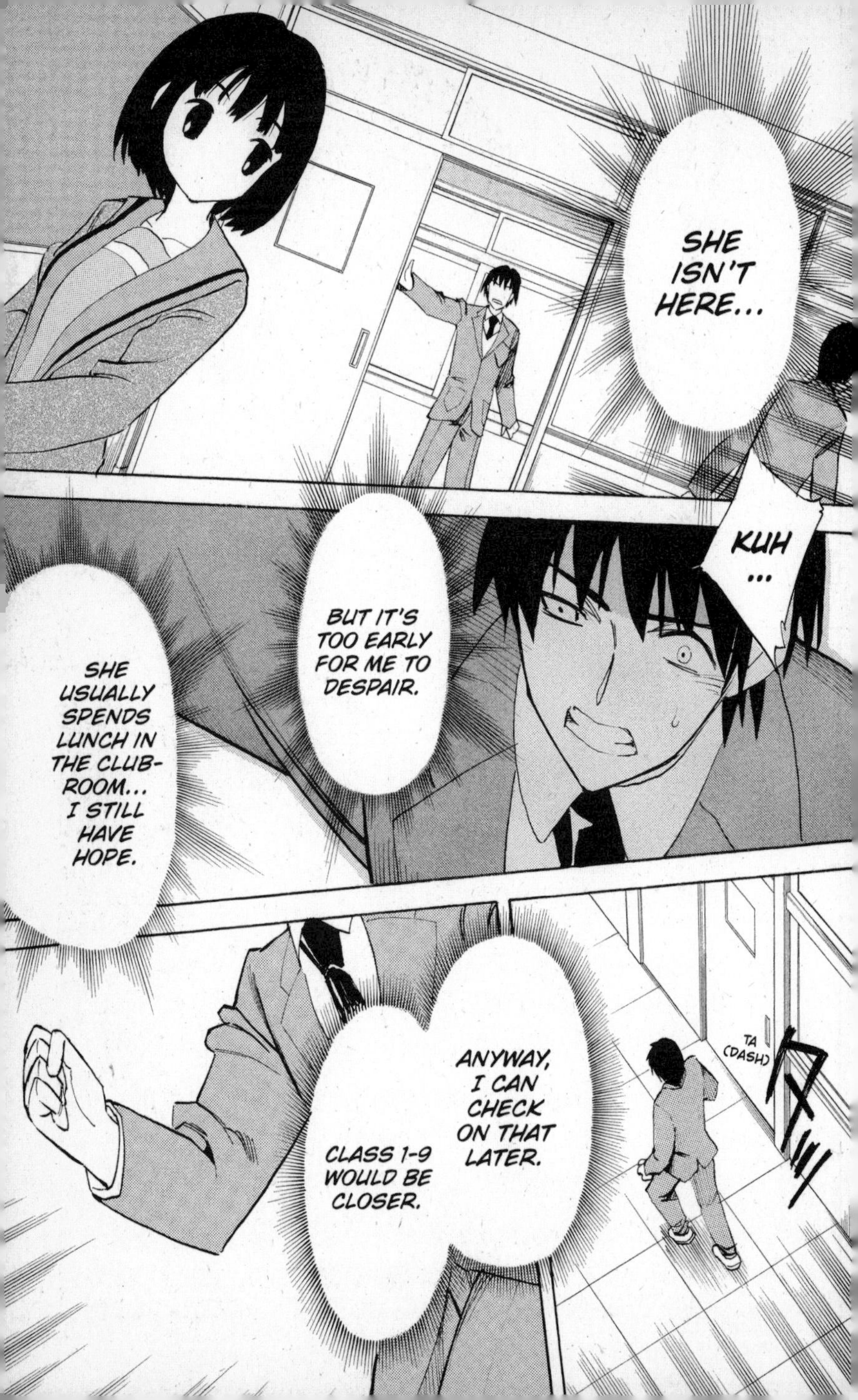
SHE ISN'T HERE...
KUH ...
BUT IT'S TOO EARLY FOR ME TO DESPAIR.
SHE USUALLY SPENDS LUNCH IN THE CLUB-ROOM... I STILL HAVE HOPE.
TA (DASH)
ANYWAY, I CAN CHECK ON THAT LATER.
CLASS 1-9 WOULD BE CLOSER.

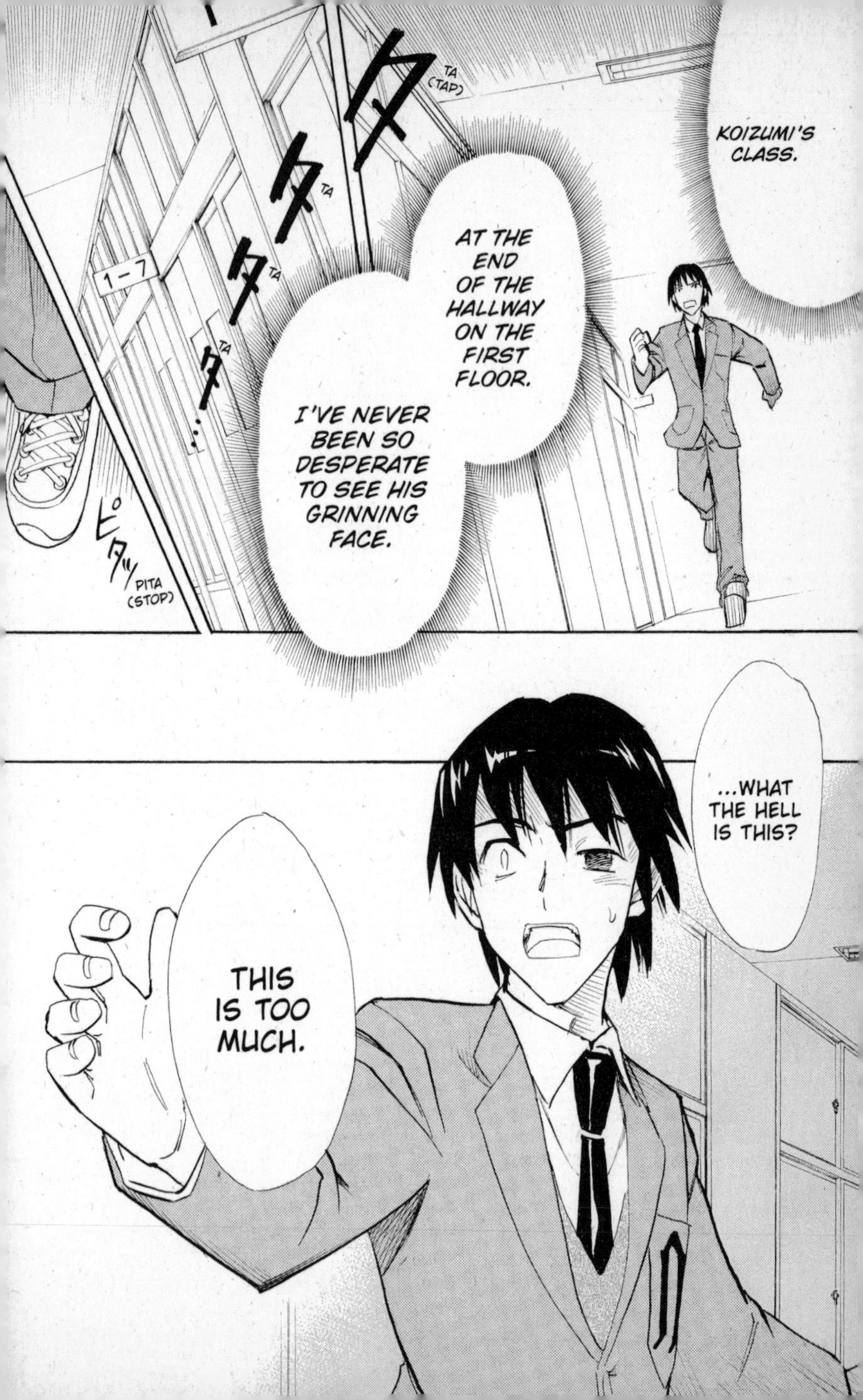
KOIZUMI'S CLASS.
AT THE END OF THE HALLWAY ON THE FIRST FLOOR.
TA (TAP)
TA
TA
TA
1-7
I'VE NEVER BEEN SO DESPERATE TO SEE HIS GRINNING FACE.
PITA (STOP)
...WHAT THE HELL IS THIS?
THIS IS TOO MUCH.

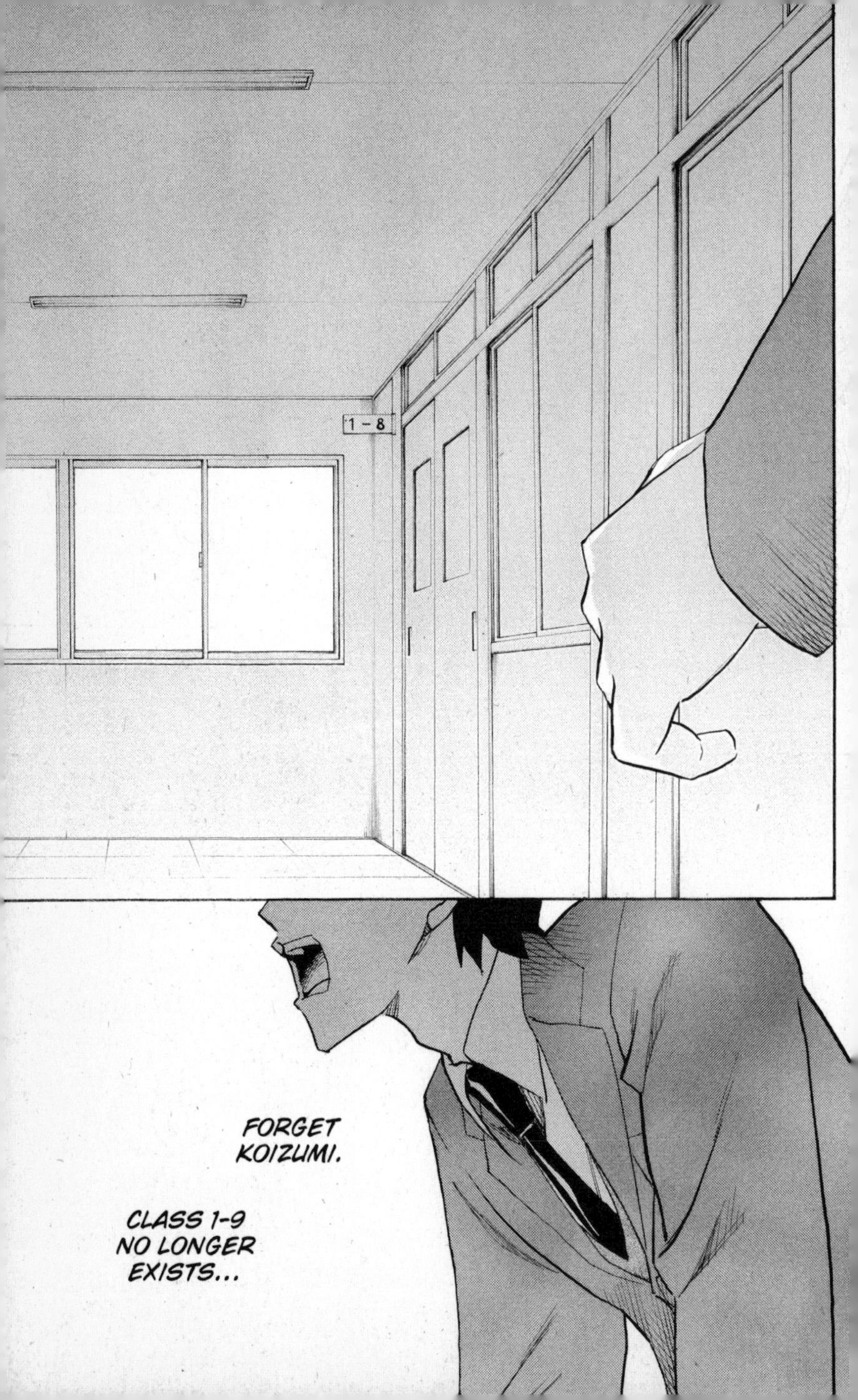
1 - 8
FORGET KOIZUMI.
CLASS 1-9 NO LONGER EXISTS...

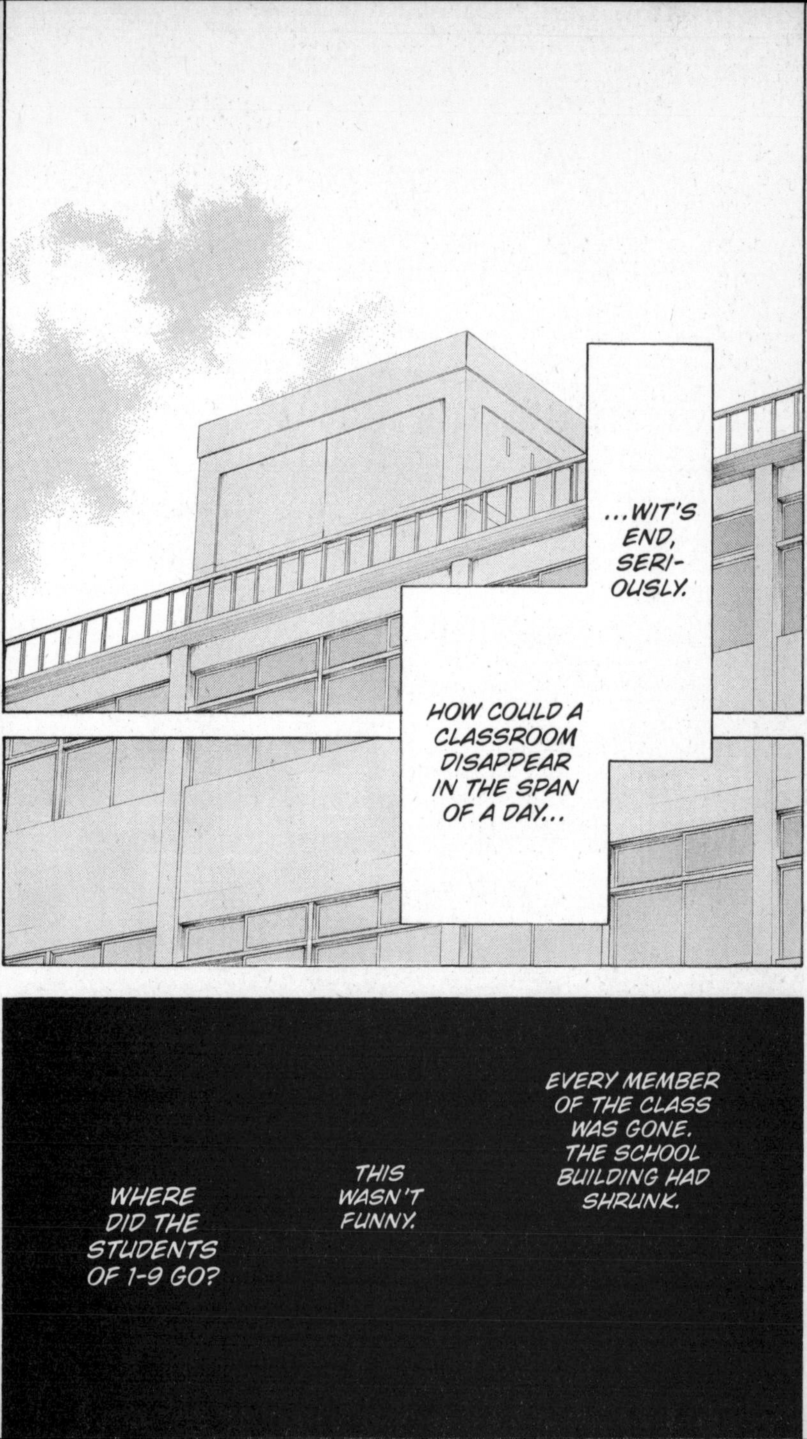
...WIT'S END, SERI-OUSLY.
HOW COULD A CLASSROOM DISAPPEAR IN THE SPAN OF A DAY...
EVERY MEMBER OF THE CLASS WAS GONE. THE SCHOOL BUILDING HAD SHRUNK.
THIS WASN'T FUNNY.
WHERE DID THE STUDENTS OF 1-9 GO?

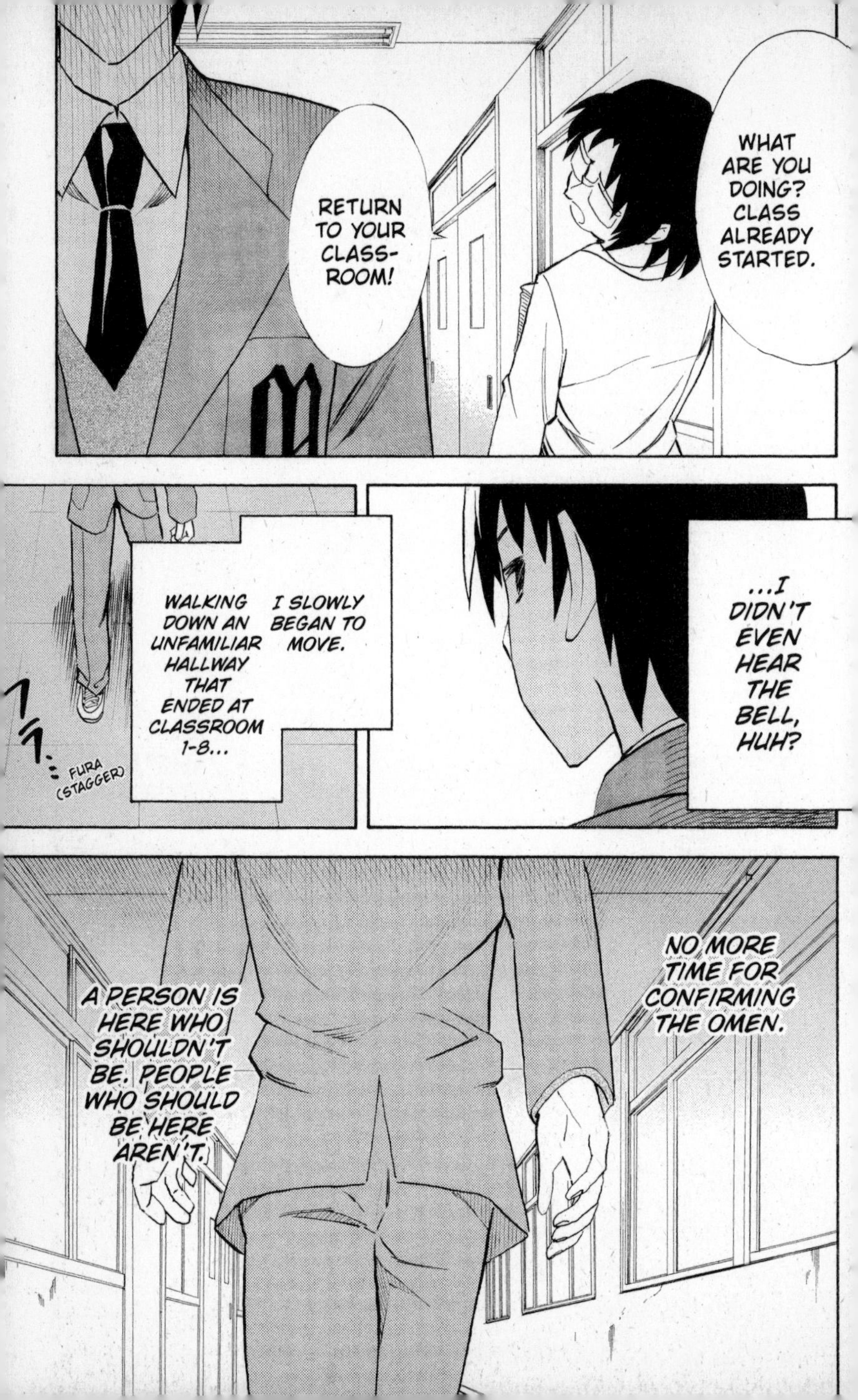
WHAT ARE YOU DOING? CLASS ALREADY STARTED.
RETURN TO YOUR CLASS-ROOM!
...I DIDN'T EVEN HEAR THE BELL, HUH?
I SLOWLY BEGAN TO MOVE.
WALKING DOWN AN UNFAMILIAR HALLWAY THAT ENDED AT CLASSROOM 1-8...
FURA (STAGGER)
NO MORE TIME FOR CONFIRMING THE OMEN.
A PERSON IS HERE WHO SHOULDN'T BE. PEOPLE WHO SHOULD BE HERE AREN'T.

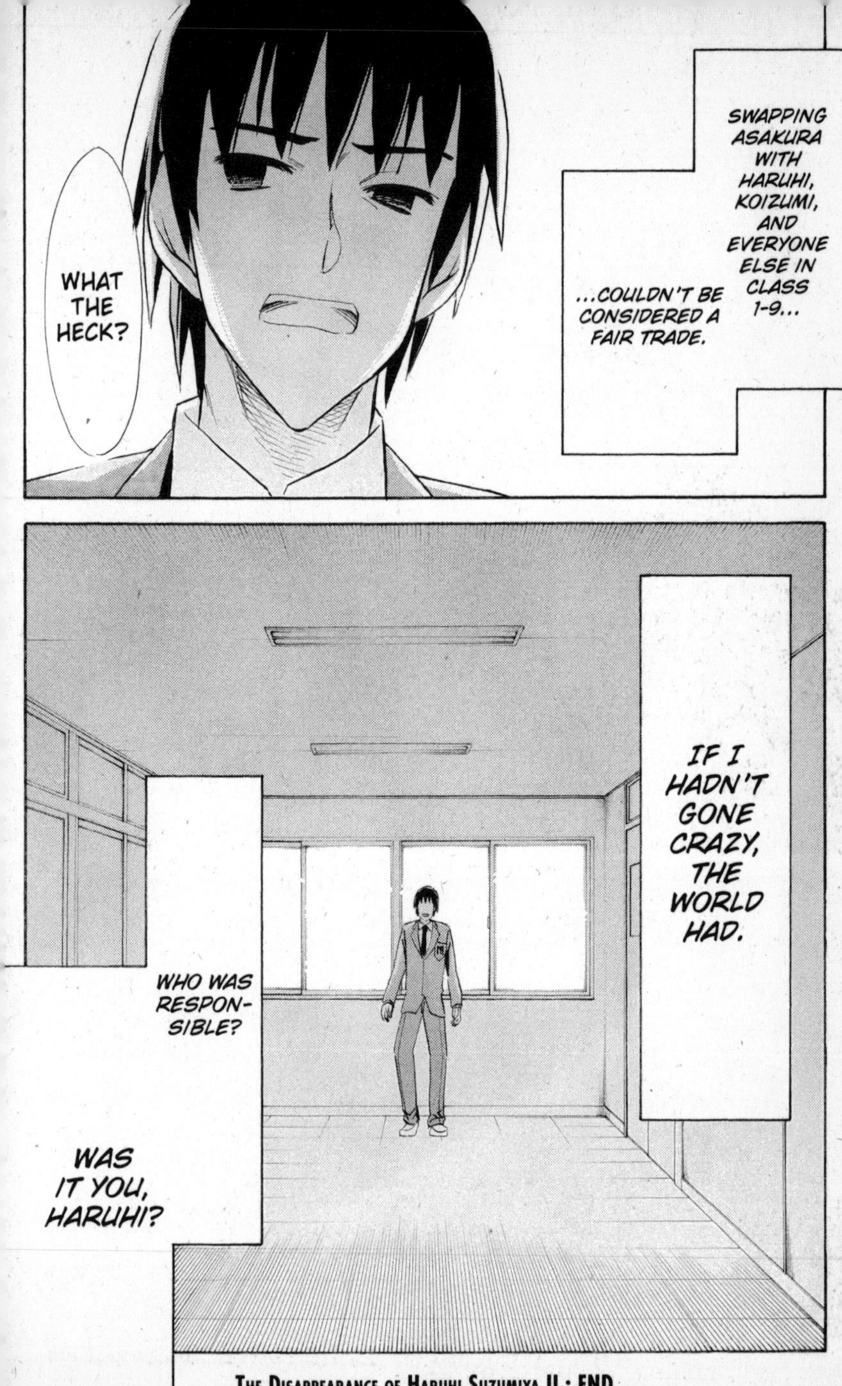
SWAPPING ASAKURA WITH HARUHI, KOIZUMI, AND EVERYONE ELSE IN CLASS 1-9...
...COULDN'T BE CONSIDERED A FAIR TRADE.
WHAT THE HECK?
IF I HADN'T GONE CRAZY, THE WORLD HAD.
WHO WAS RESPON-SIBLE?
WAS IT YOU, HARUHI?

THE DISAPPEARANCE OF HARUHI SUZUMIYA II : END

◎ The Disappearance of Haruhi Suzumiya III

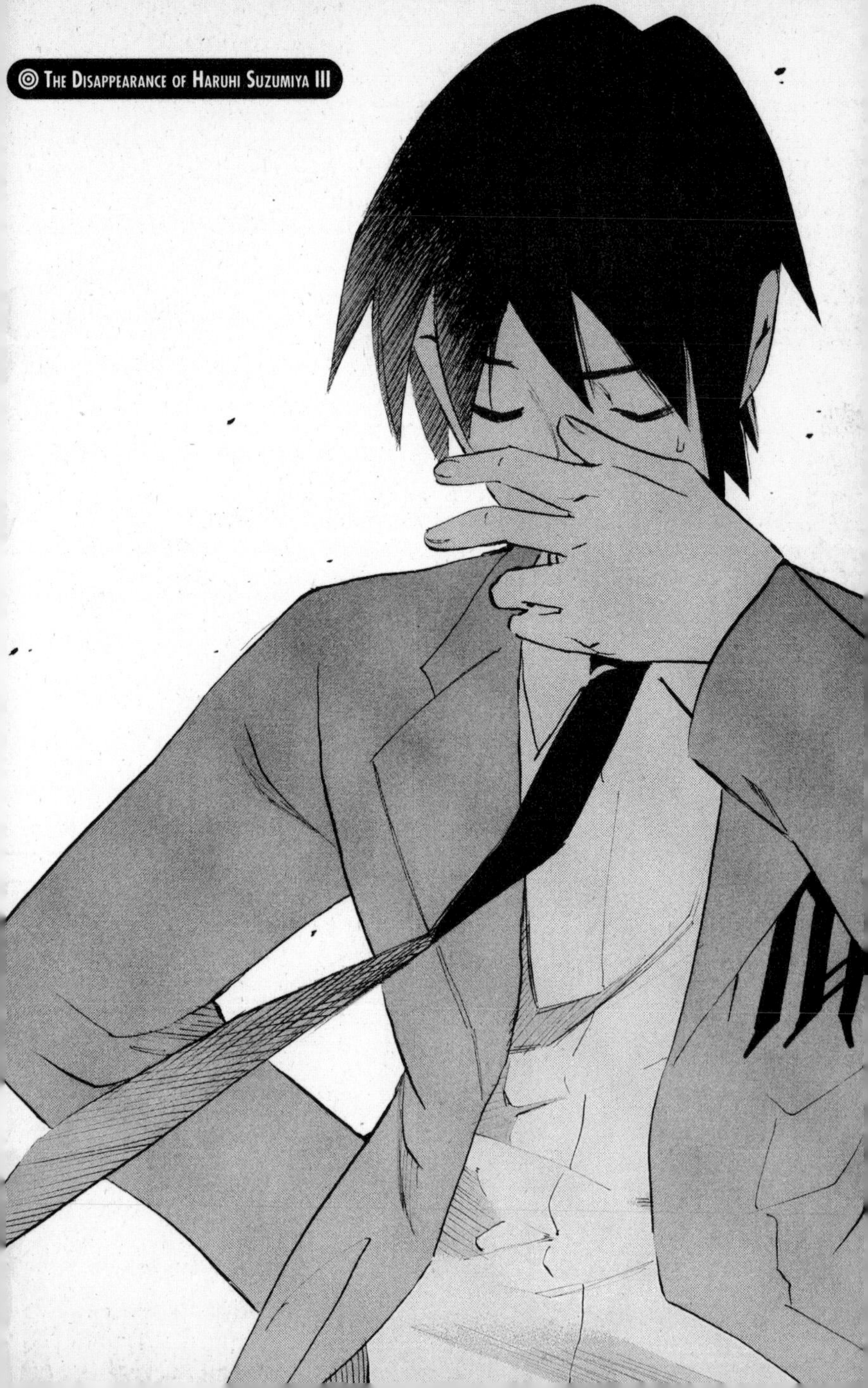

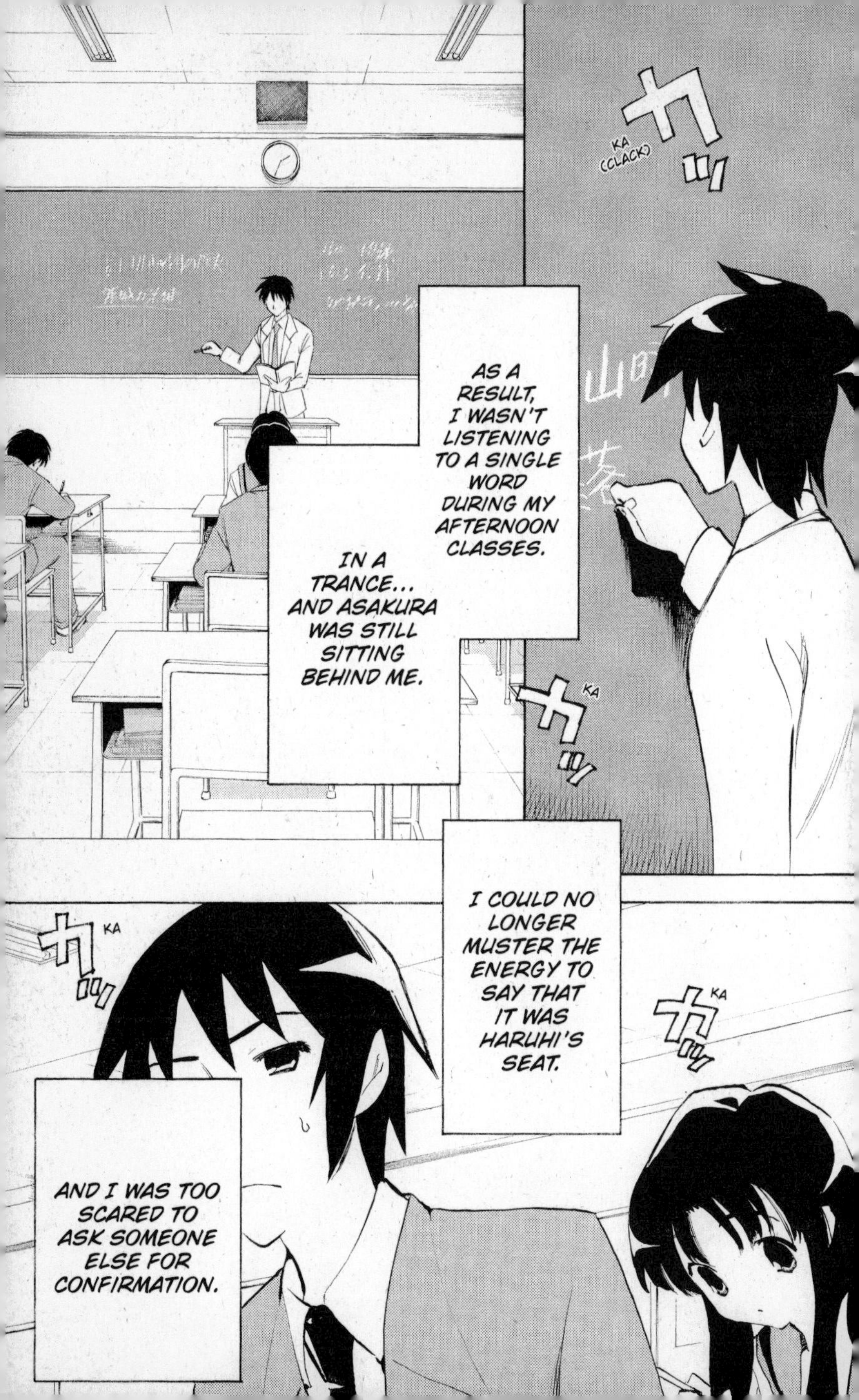
KA (CLACK)
AS A RESULT, I WASN'T LISTENING TO A SINGLE WORD DURING MY AFTERNOON CLASSES.
KA
IN A TRANCE... AND ASAKURA WAS STILL SITTING BEHIND ME.
I COULD NO LONGER MUSTER THE ENERGY TO SAY THAT IT WAS HARUHI'S SEAT.
KA
KA
AND I WAS TOO SCARED TO ASK SOMEONE ELSE FOR CONFIRMATION.

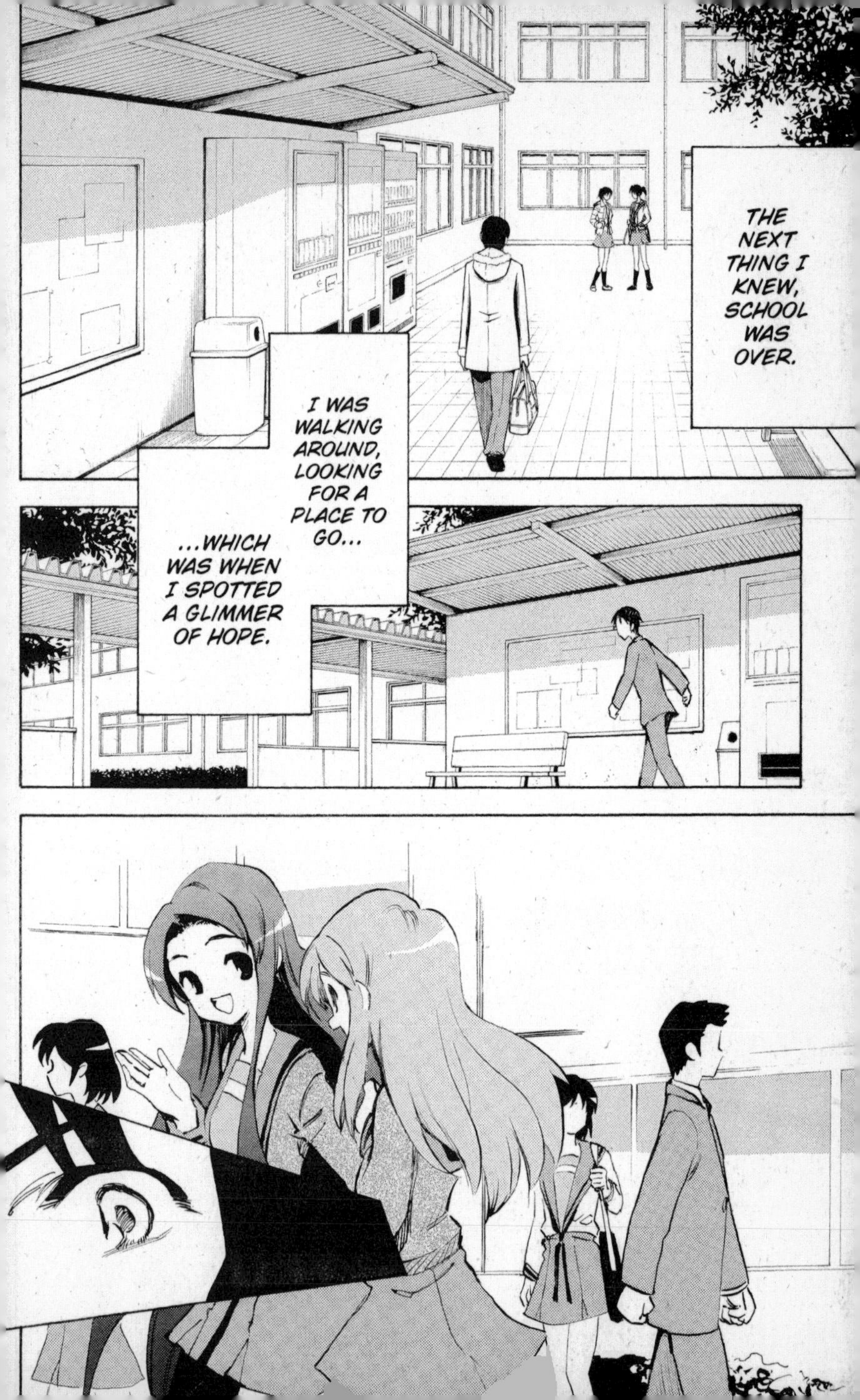
THE NEXT THING I KNEW, SCHOOL WAS OVER.
I WAS WALKING AROUND, LOOKING FOR A PLACE TO GO...
...WHICH WAS WHEN I SPOTTED A GLIMMER OF HOPE.

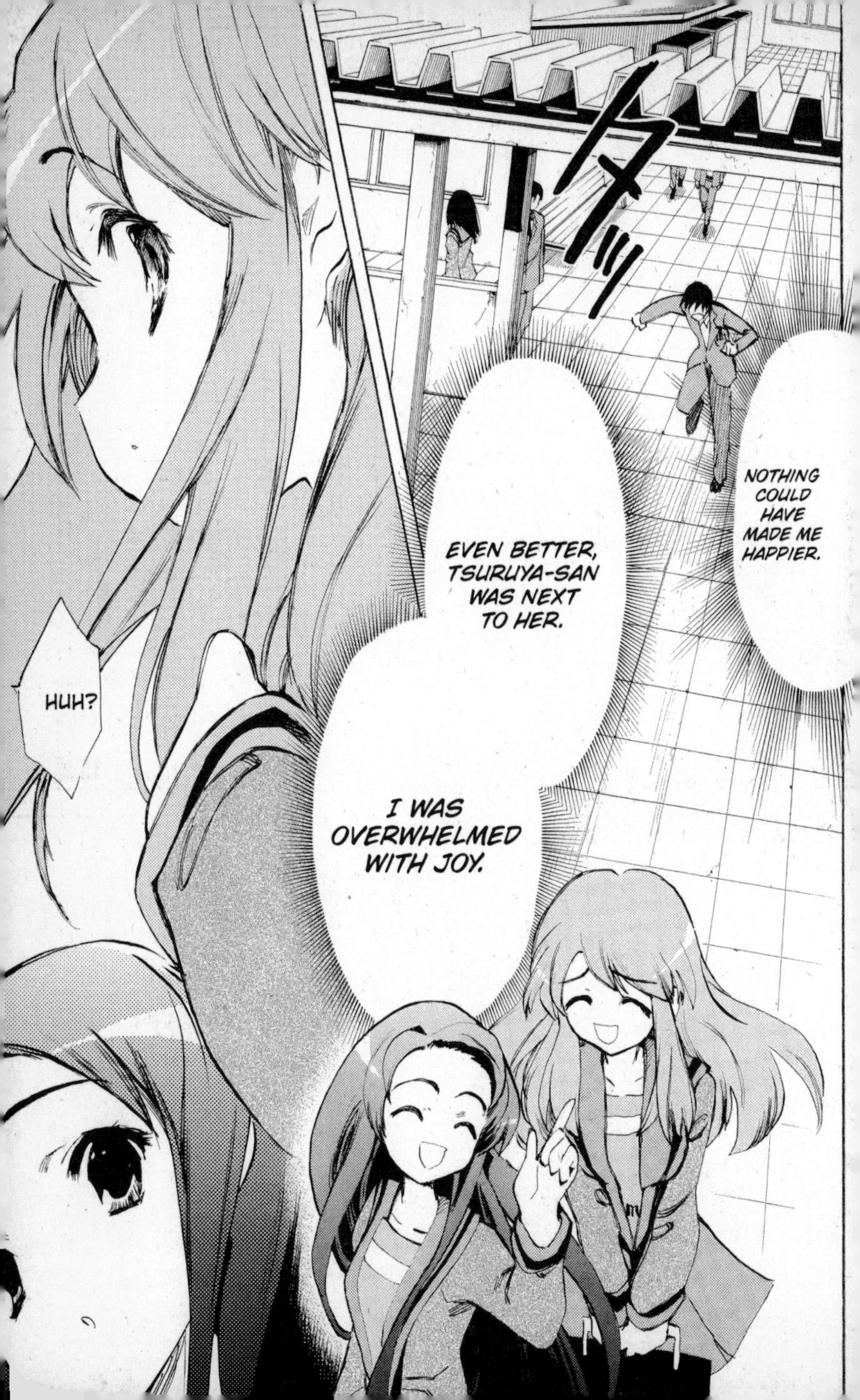
タッ
NOTHING COULD HAVE MADE ME HAPPIER.
EVEN BETTER, TSURUYA-SAN WAS NEXT TO HER.
I WAS OVERWHELMED WITH JOY.
HUH?

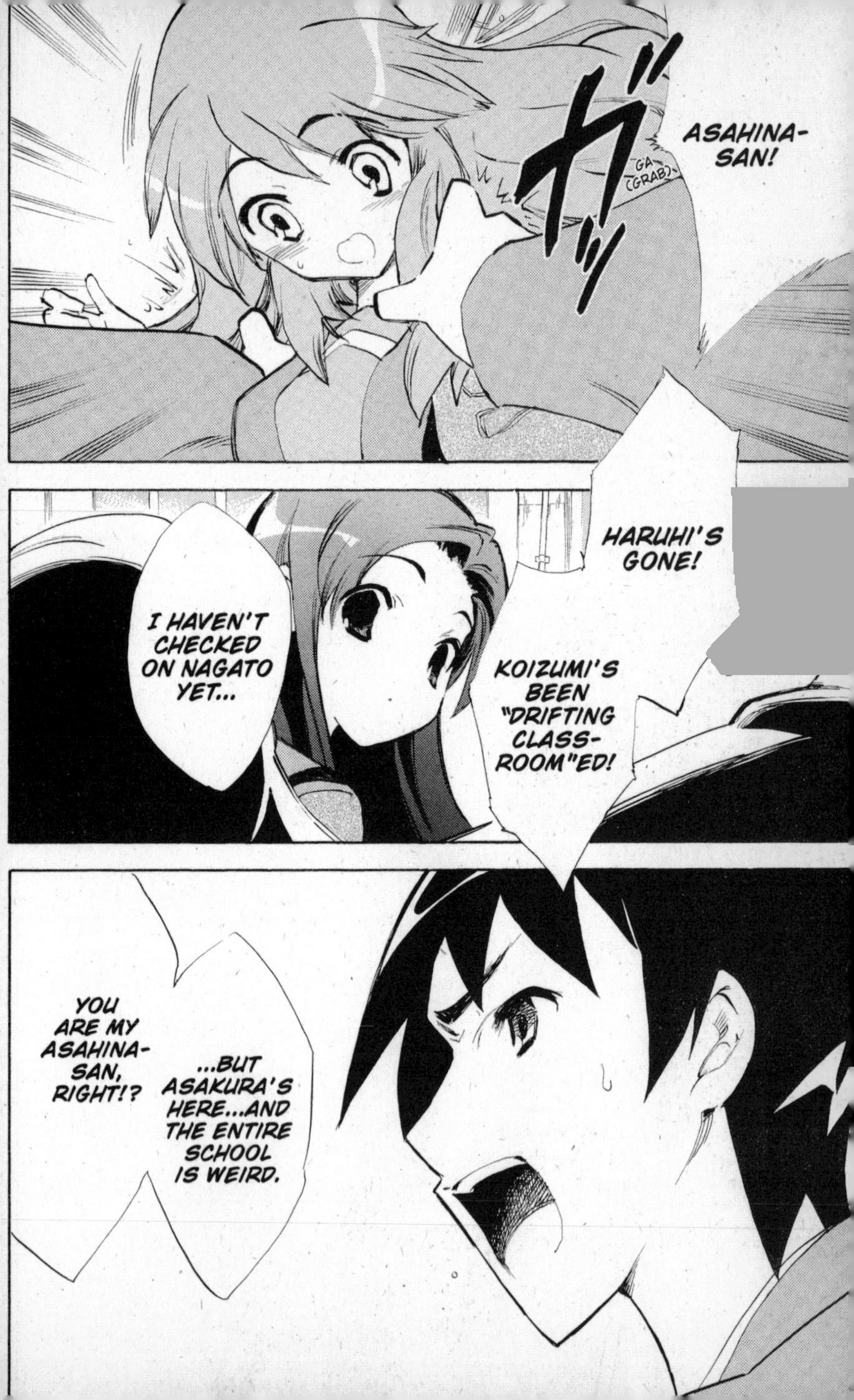
ASAHINA-SAN!
GA (GRAB)
HARUHI'S GONE!
KOIZUMI'S BEEN "DRIFTING CLASSROOM"ED!
I HAVEN'T CHECKED ON NAGATO YET...
...BUT ASAKURA'S HERE...AND THE ENTIRE SCHOOL IS WEIRD.
YOU ARE MY ASAHINA-SAN, RIGHT!?

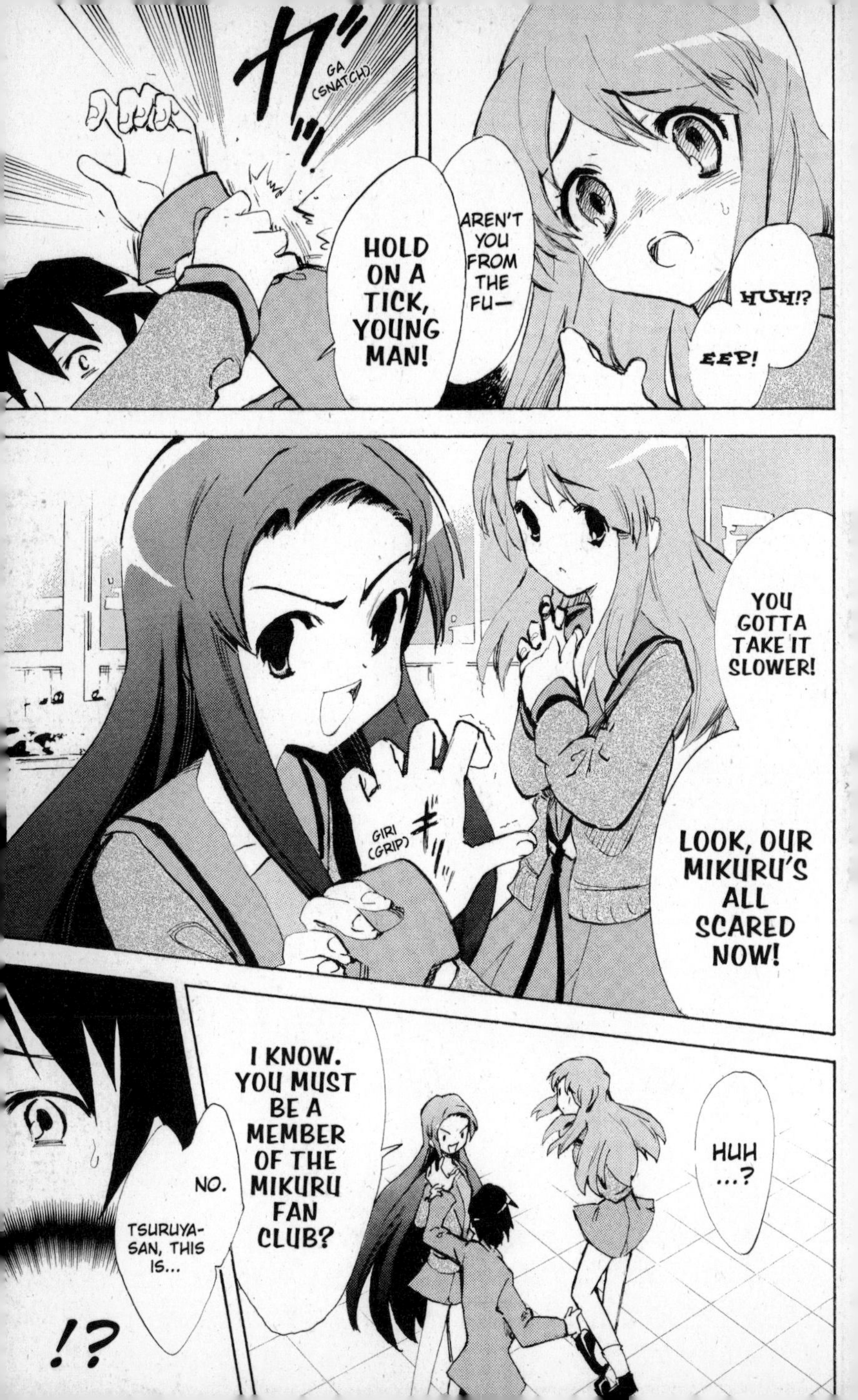
HUH!?
EEP!
AREN'T YOU FROM THE FU—
GA (SNATCH)
HOLD ON A TICK, YOUNG MAN!
YOU GOTTA TAKE IT SLOWER!
LOOK, OUR MIKURU'S ALL SCARED NOW!
GIRI (GRIP)
HUH ...?
I KNOW. YOU MUST BE A MEMBER OF THE MIKURU FAN CLUB?
NO.
TSURUYA-SAN, THIS IS...
!?

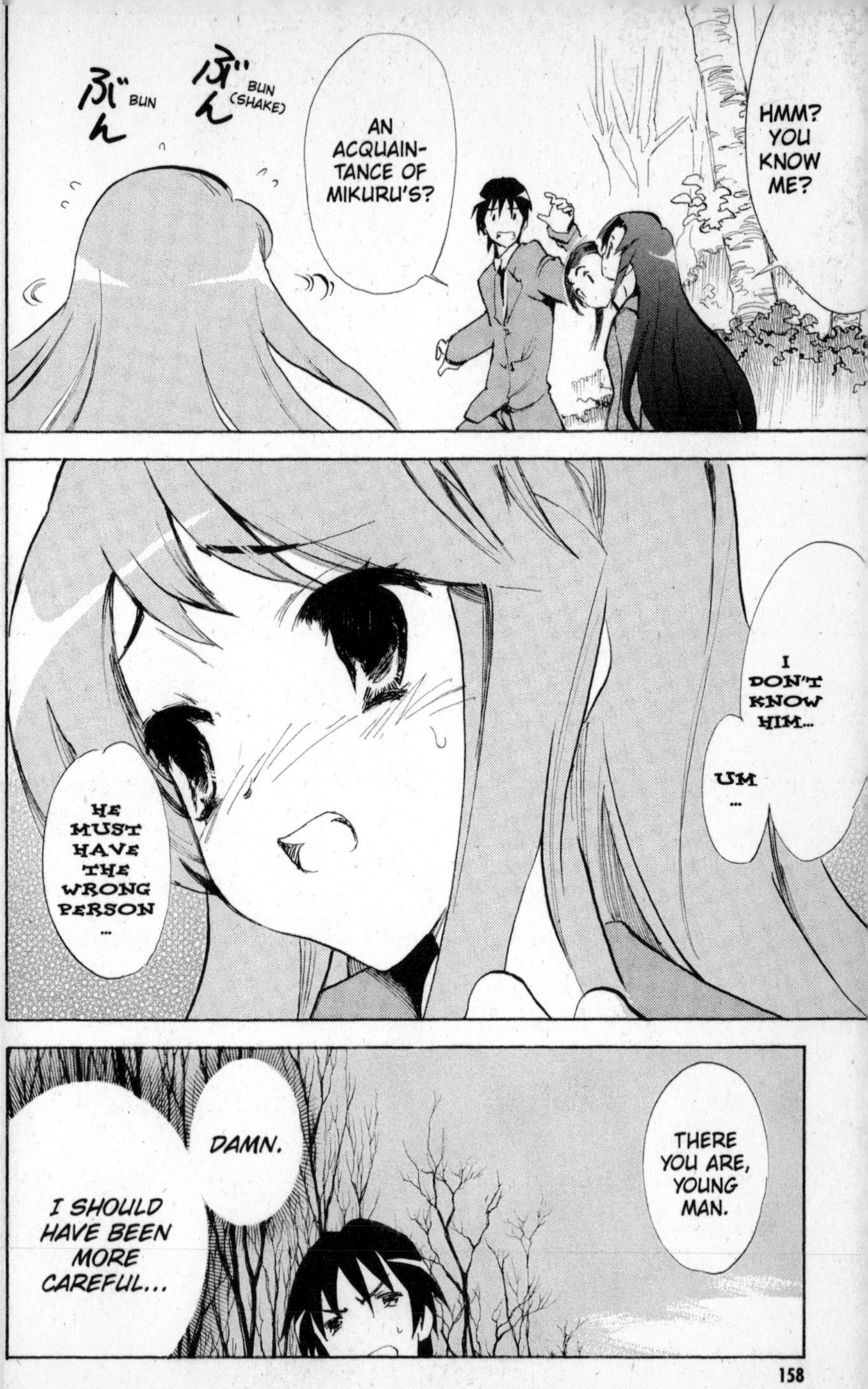
HMM? YOU KNOW ME?
AN ACQUAIN-TANCE OF MIKURU'S?
ぶん BUN (SHAKE)
ぶん BUN
I DON'T KNOW HIM...
UM ...
HE MUST HAVE THE WRONG PERSON ...
THERE YOU ARE, YOUNG MAN.
DAMN.
I SHOULD HAVE BEEN MORE CAREFUL...

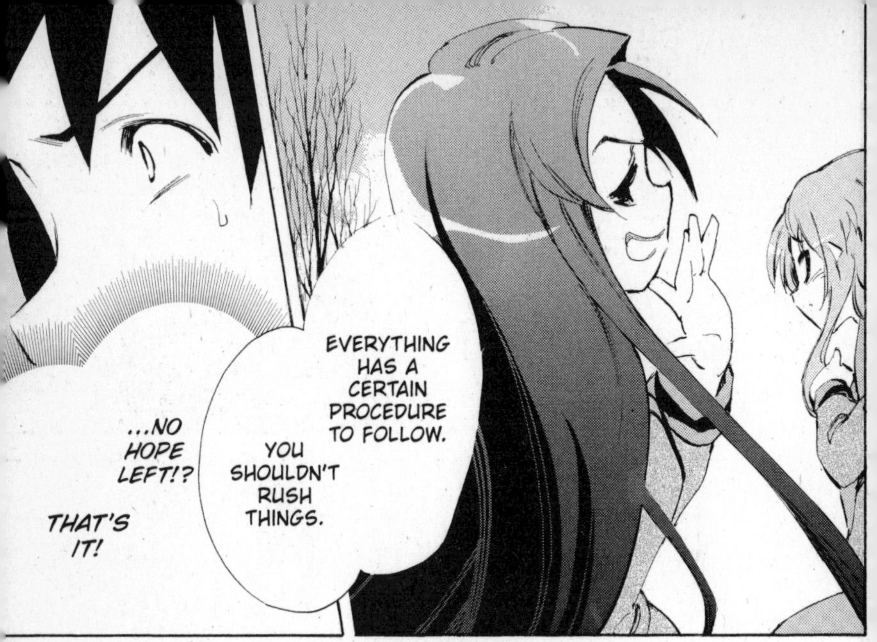
EVERYTHING HAS A CERTAIN PROCEDURE TO FOLLOW.
YOU SHOULDN'T RUSH THINGS.
...NO HOPE LEFT!?
THAT'S IT!

I MUST HAVE BEEN REALLY UPSET.

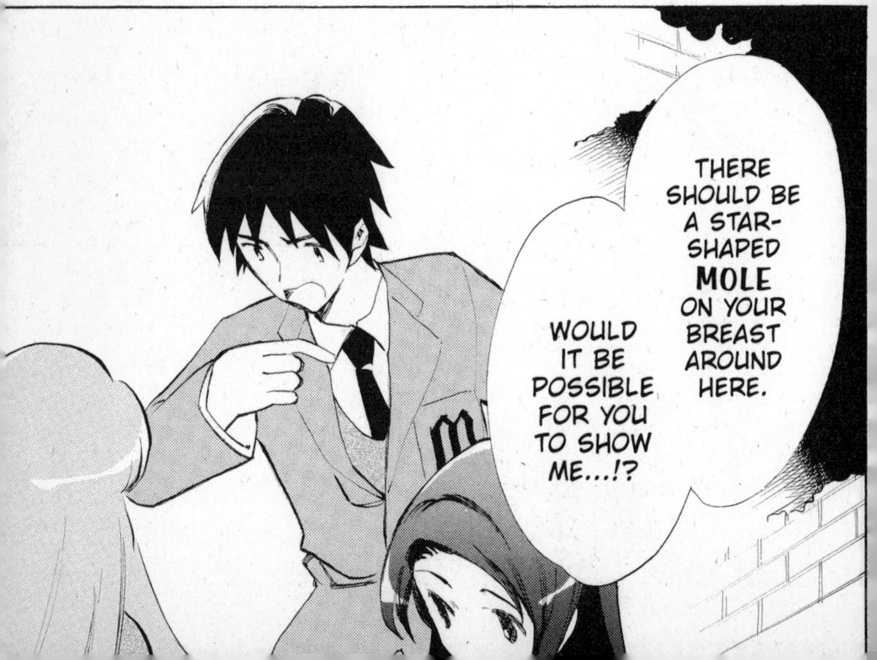
THERE SHOULD BE A STAR-SHAPED MOLE ON YOUR BREAST AROUND HERE.
WOULD IT BE POSSIBLE FOR YOU TO SHOW ME...!?

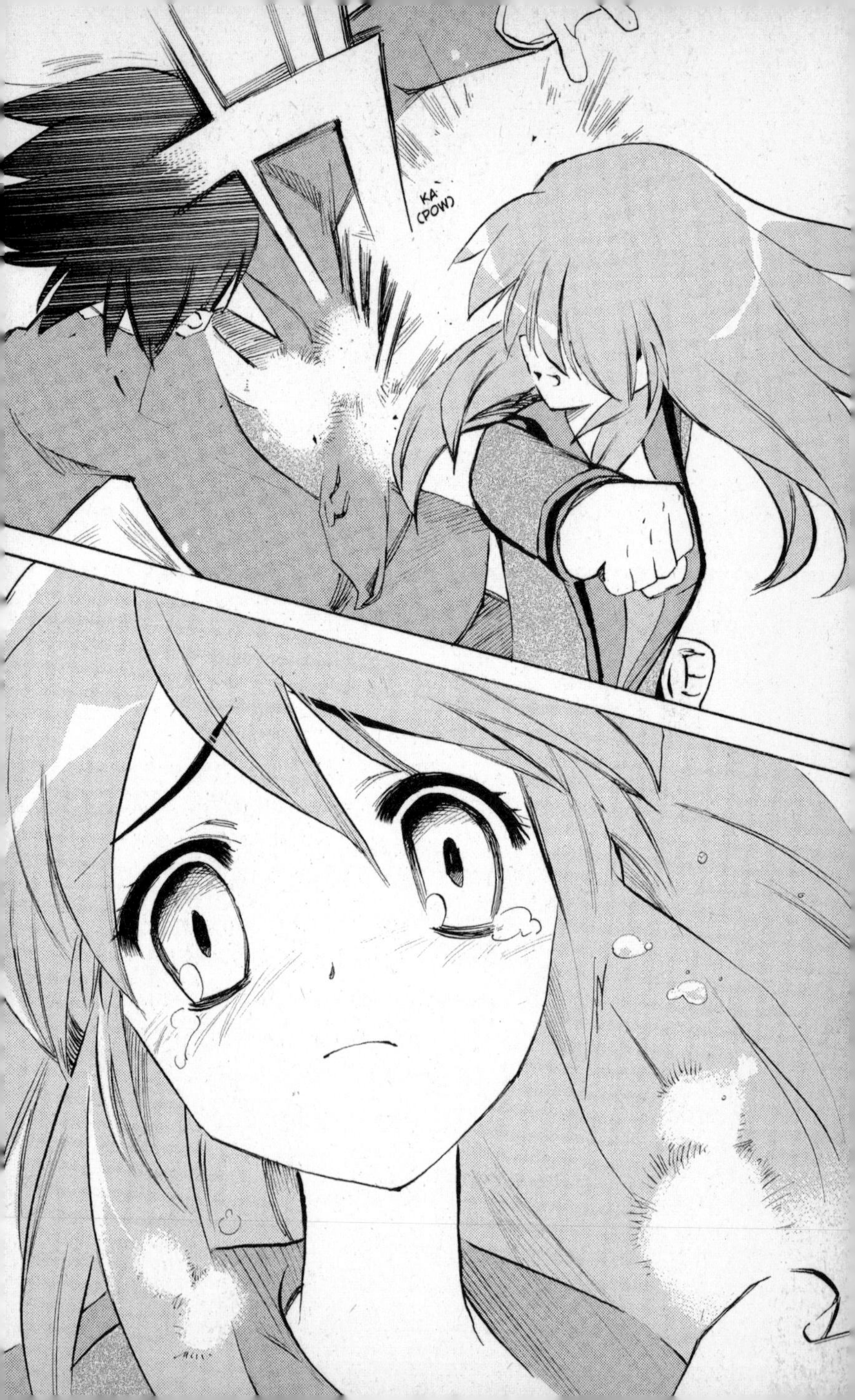
KA
(POW)

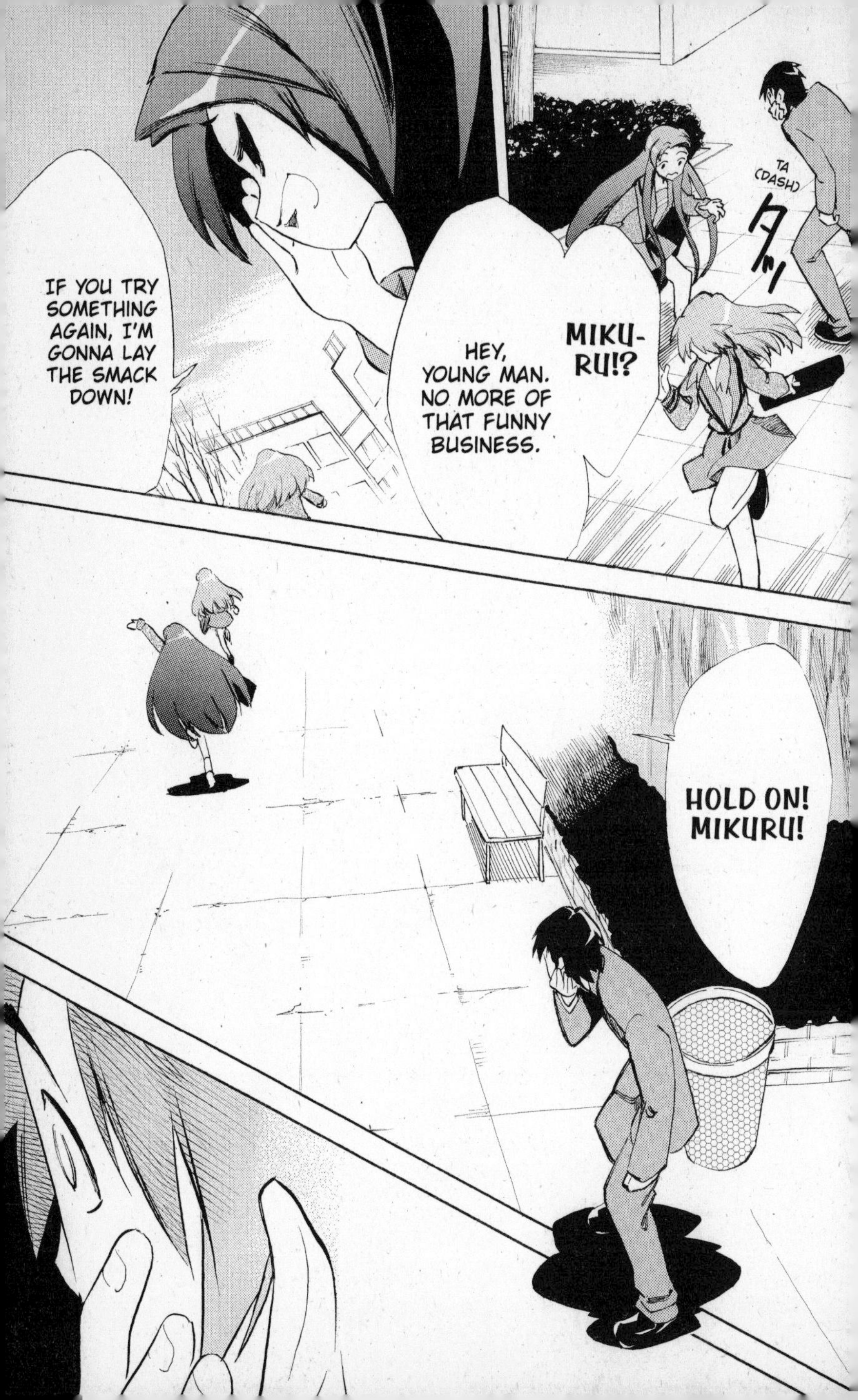
TA (DASH)
MIKU-RU!?
HEY, YOUNG MAN. NO MORE OF THAT FUNNY BUSINESS.
IF YOU TRY SOMETHING AGAIN, I'M GONNA LAY THE SMACK DOWN!
HOLD ON! MIKURU!

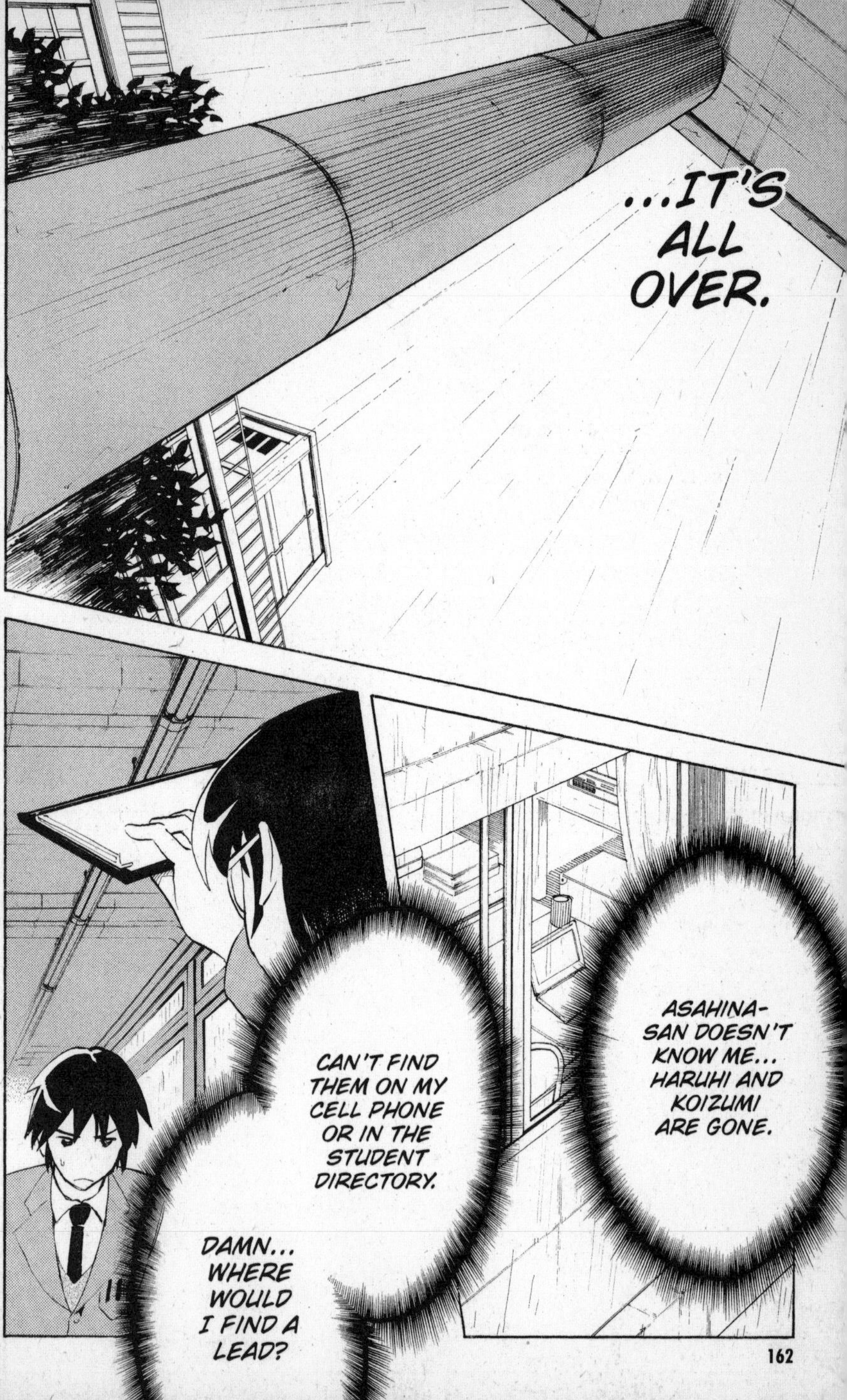
...IT'S ALL OVER.
ASAHINA-SAN DOESN'T KNOW ME... HARUHI AND KOIZUMI ARE GONE.
CAN'T FIND THEM ON MY CELL PHONE OR IN THE STUDENT DIRECTORY.
DAMN... WHERE WOULD I FIND A LEAD?

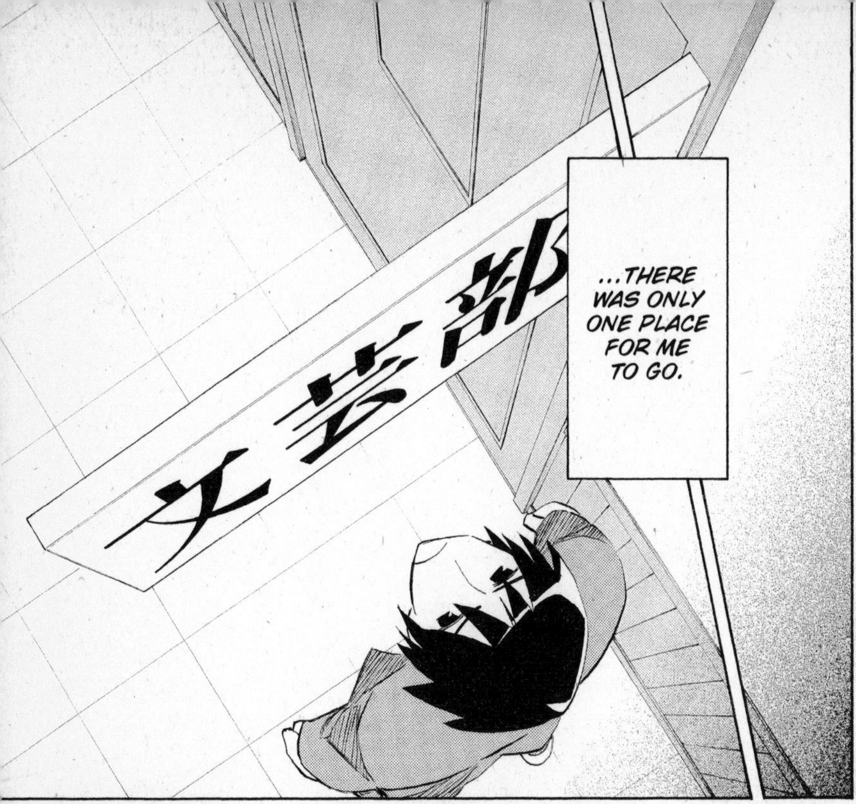
文芸部
...THERE WAS ONLY ONE PLACE FOR ME TO GO.
SIGN: LITERARY CLUB

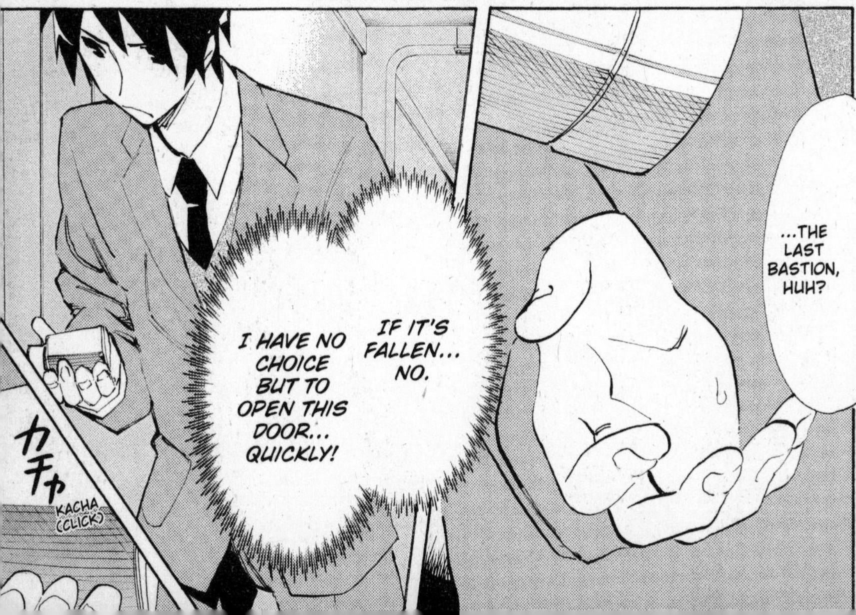
...THE LAST BASTION, HUH?
IF IT'S FALLEN... NO.
I HAVE NO CHOICE BUT TO OPEN THIS DOOR... QUICKLY!
カチャ
KACHA (CLICK)

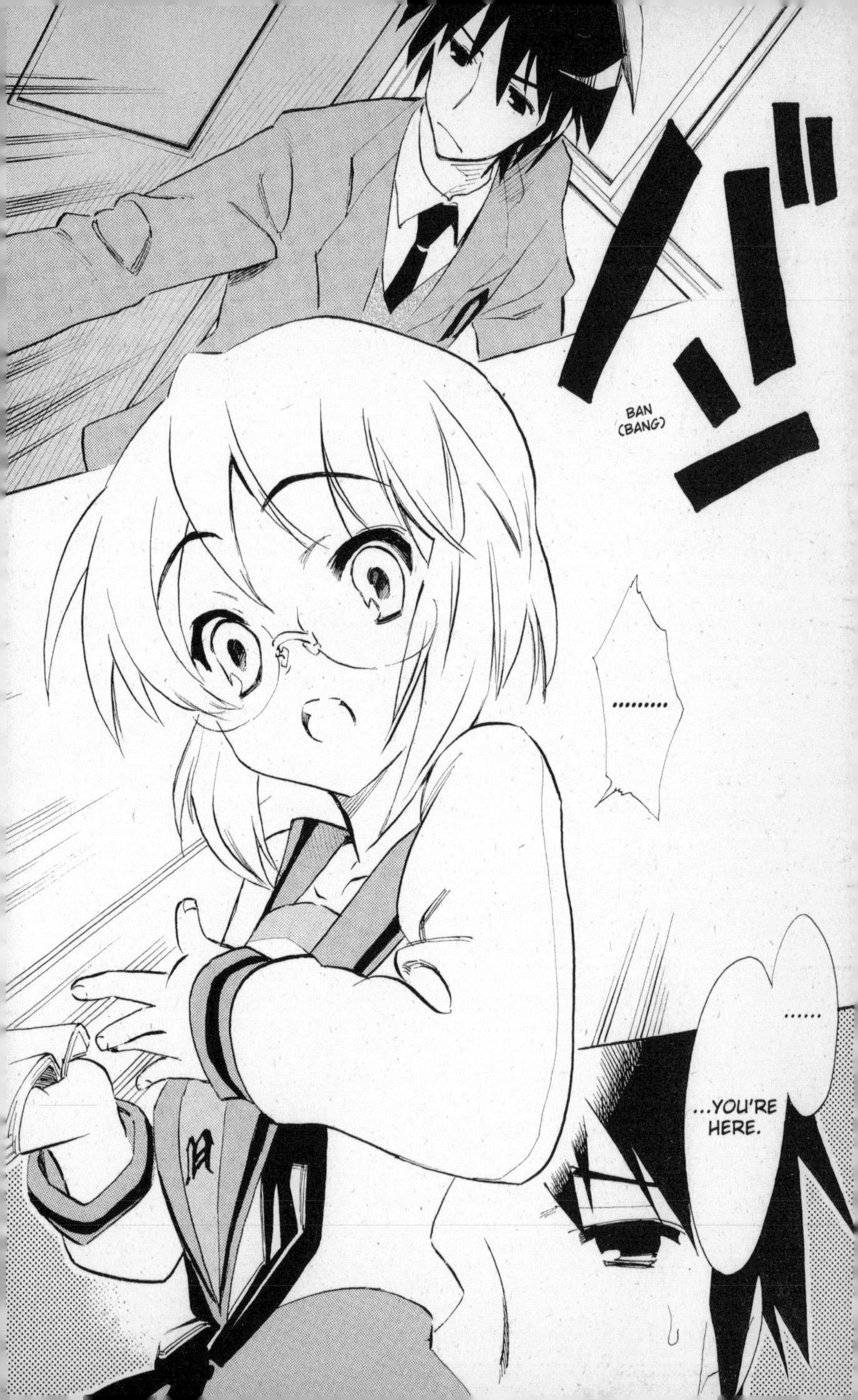
BAN
(BANG)
....
......
...YOU'RE HERE.

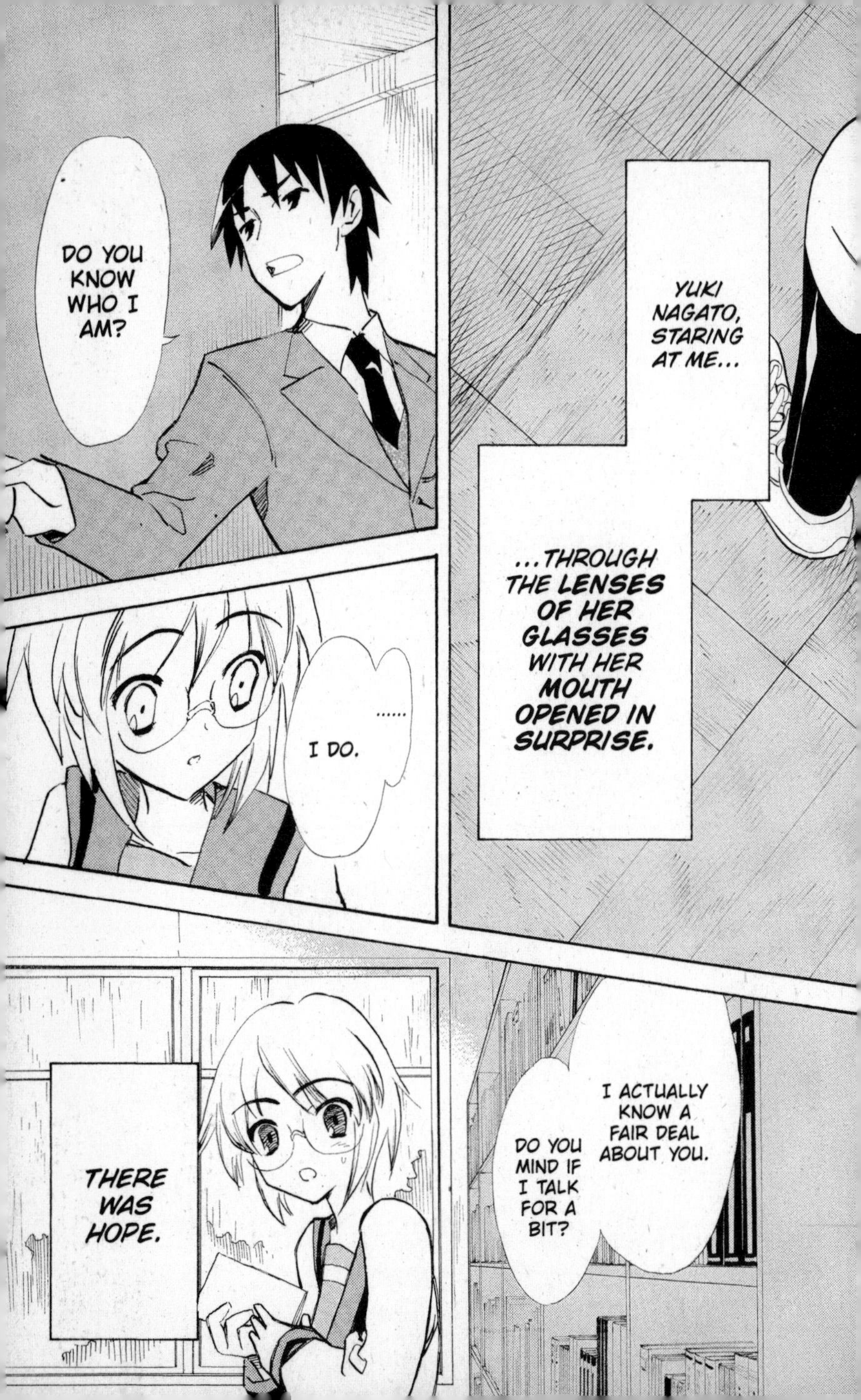
YUKI NAGATO, STARING AT ME...
...THROUGH THE LENSES OF HER GLASSES WITH HER MOUTH OPENED IN SURPRISE.
DO YOU KNOW WHO I AM?
......
I DO.
I ACTUALLY KNOW A FAIR DEAL ABOUT YOU.
DO YOU MIND IF I TALK FOR A BIT?
THERE WAS HOPE.

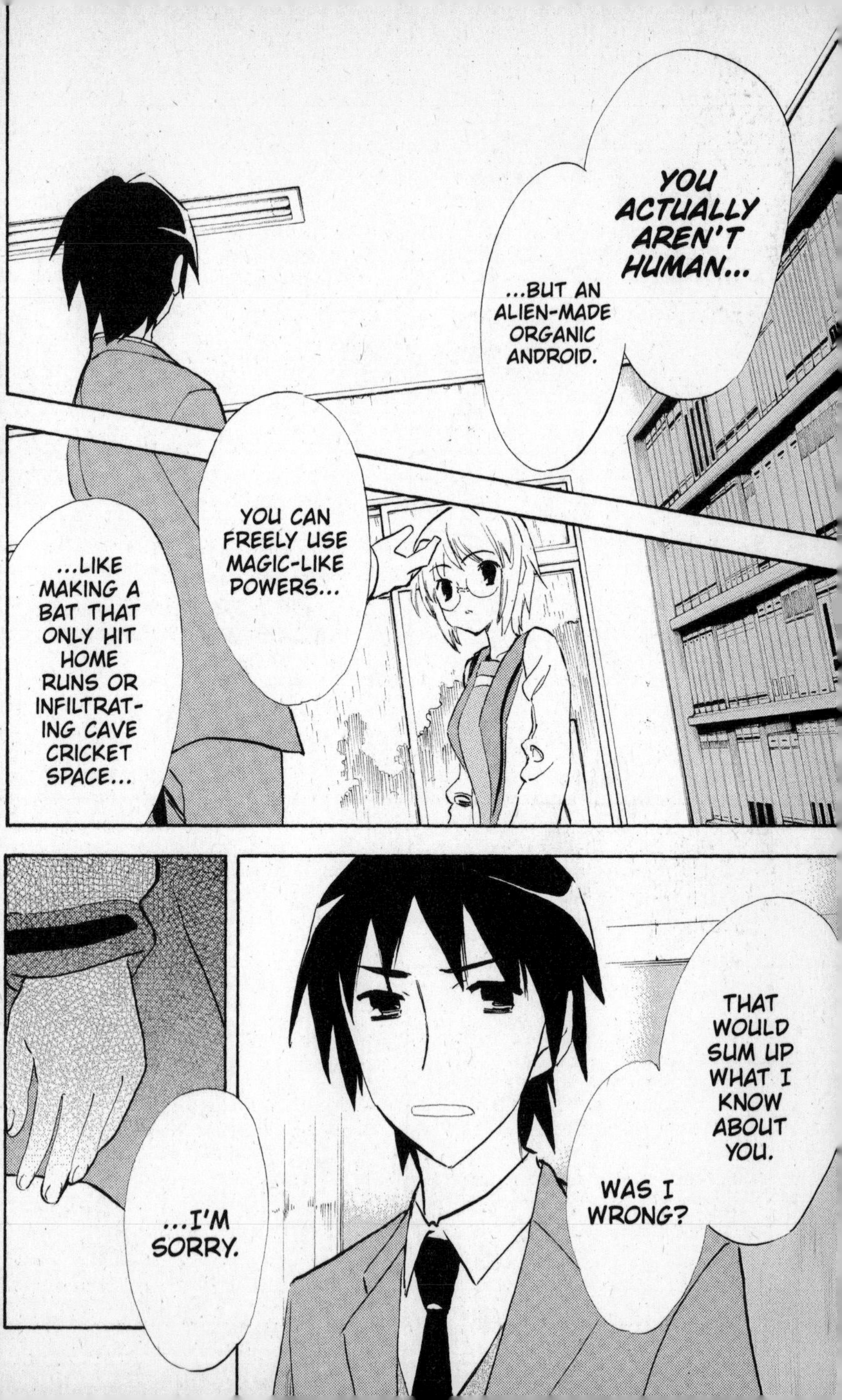
YOU ACTUALLY AREN'T HUMAN...
...BUT AN ALIEN-MADE ORGANIC ANDROID.
YOU CAN FREELY USE MAGIC-LIKE POWERS...
...LIKE MAKING A BAT THAT ONLY HIT HOME RUNS OR INFILTRAT-ING CAVE CRICKET SPACE...
THAT WOULD SUM UP WHAT I KNOW ABOUT YOU.
WAS I WRONG?
...I'M SORRY.

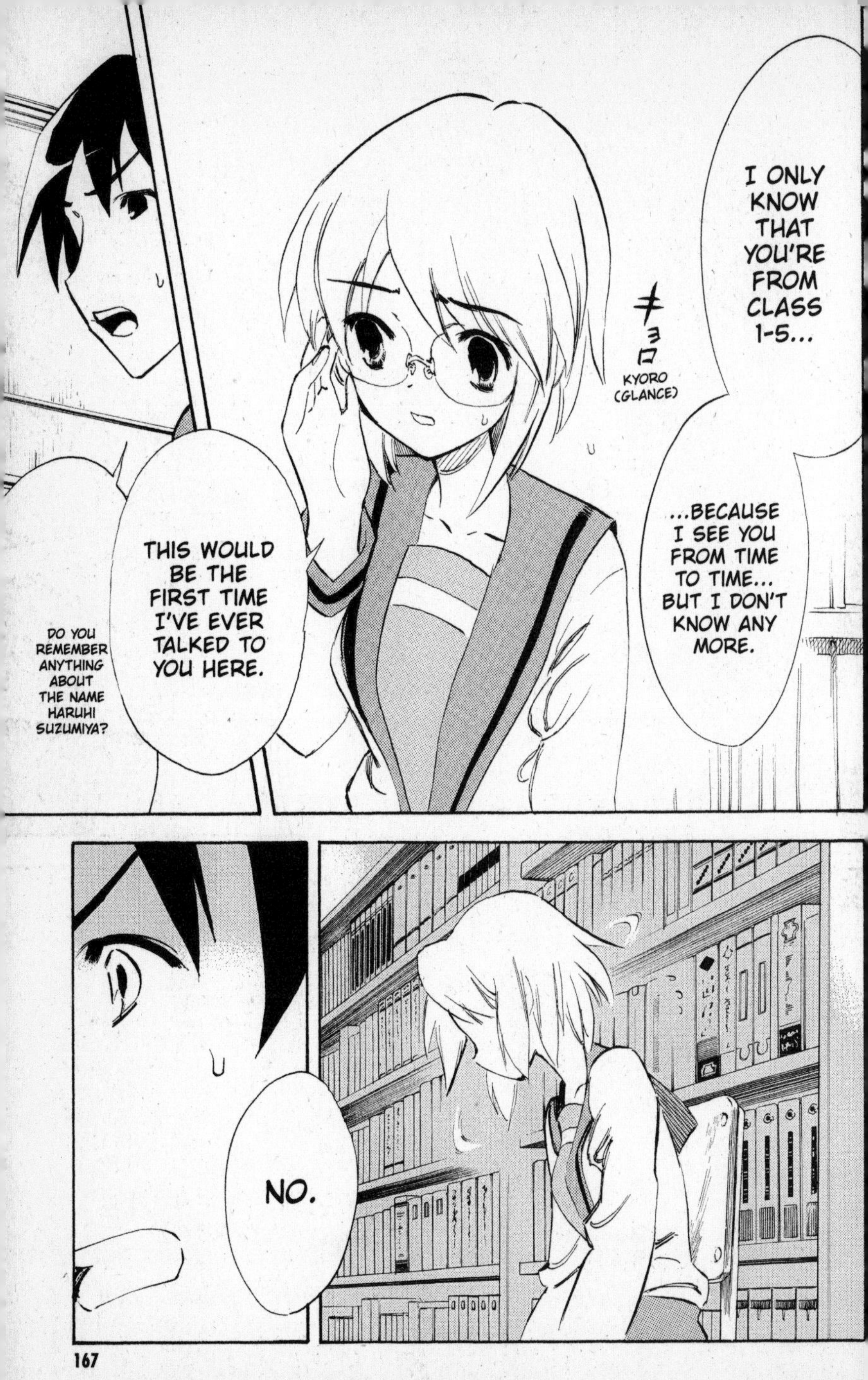

I ONLY KNOW THAT YOU'RE FROM CLASS 1-5...
キョロ
KYORO (GLANCE)
...BECAUSE I SEE YOU FROM TIME TO TIME... BUT I DON'T KNOW ANY MORE.
THIS WOULD BE THE FIRST TIME I'VE EVER TALKED TO YOU HERE.
DO YOU REMEMBER ANYTHING ABOUT THE NAME HARUHI SUZUMIYA?
NO.

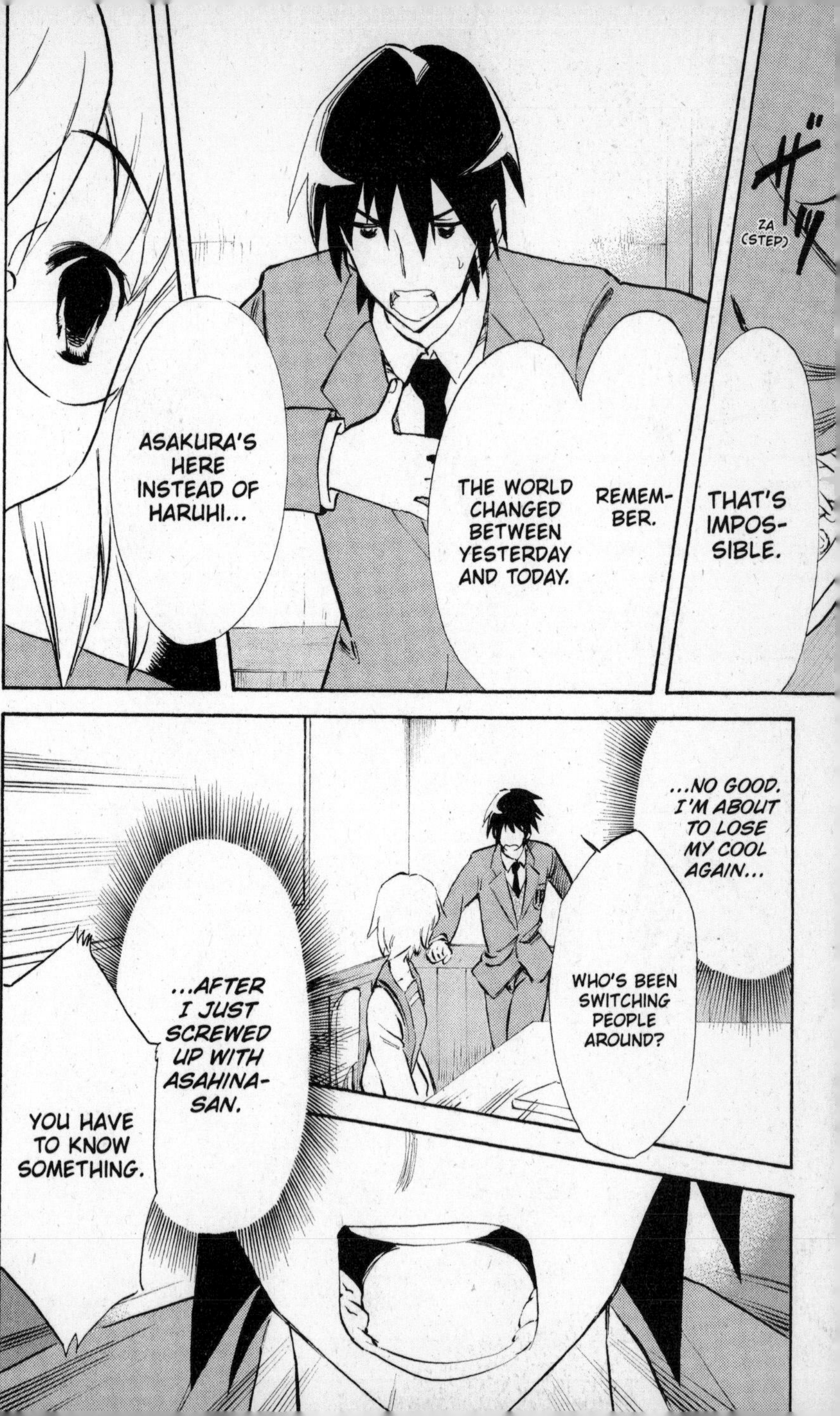
THAT'S IMPOSSIBLE.
ZA (STEP)
REMEMBER.
THE WORLD CHANGED BETWEEN YESTERDAY AND TODAY.
ASAKURA'S HERE INSTEAD OF HARUHI...
...NO GOOD. I'M ABOUT TO LOSE MY COOL AGAIN...
WHO'S BEEN SWITCHING PEOPLE AROUND?
...AFTER I JUST SCREWED UP WITH ASAHINA-SAN.
YOU HAVE TO KNOW SOMETHING.

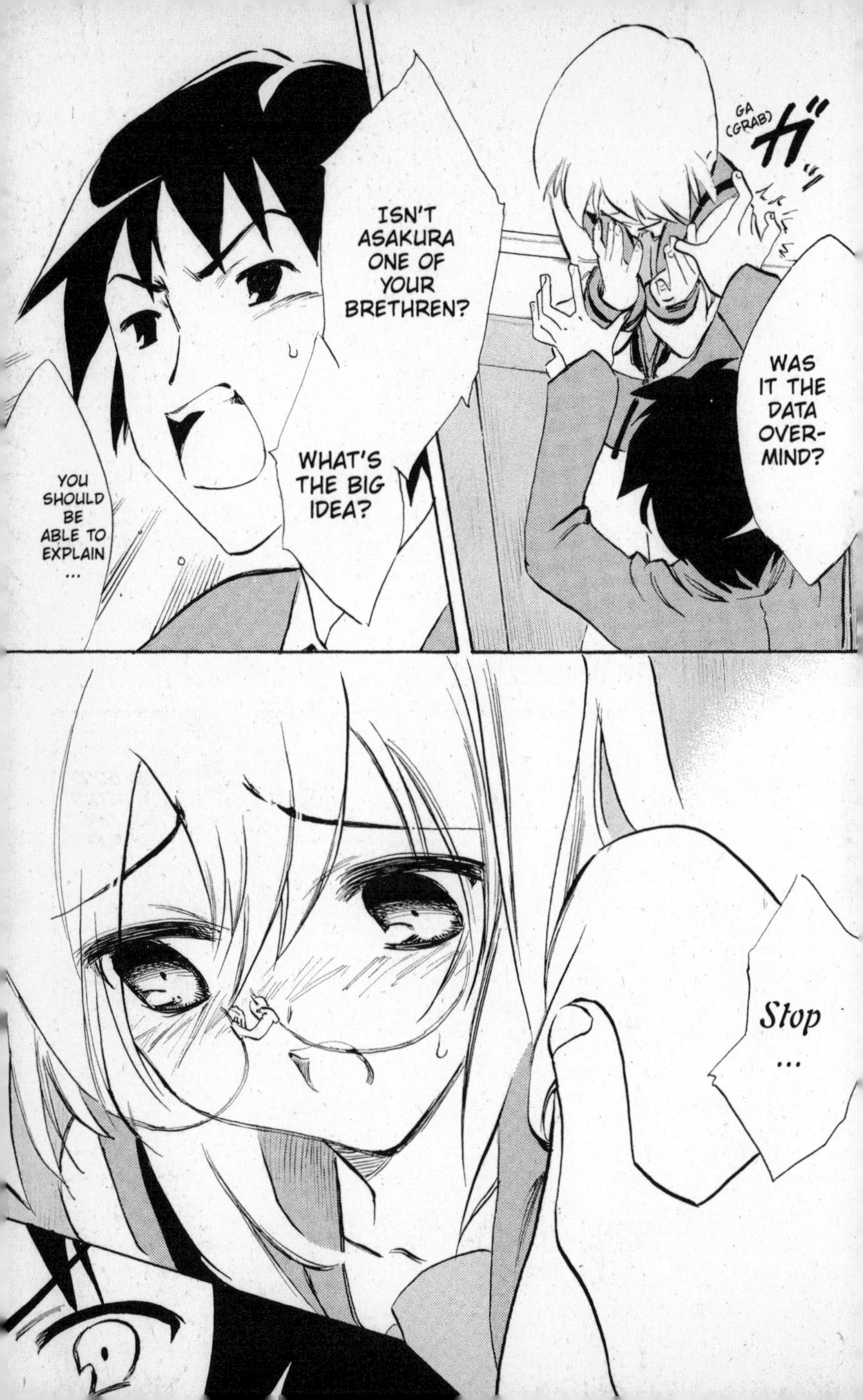
GA (GRAB)
WAS IT THE DATA OVER-MIND?
ISN'T ASAKURA ONE OF YOUR BRETHREN?
WHAT'S THE BIG IDEA?
YOU SHOULD BE ABLE TO EXPLAIN ...
Stop ...

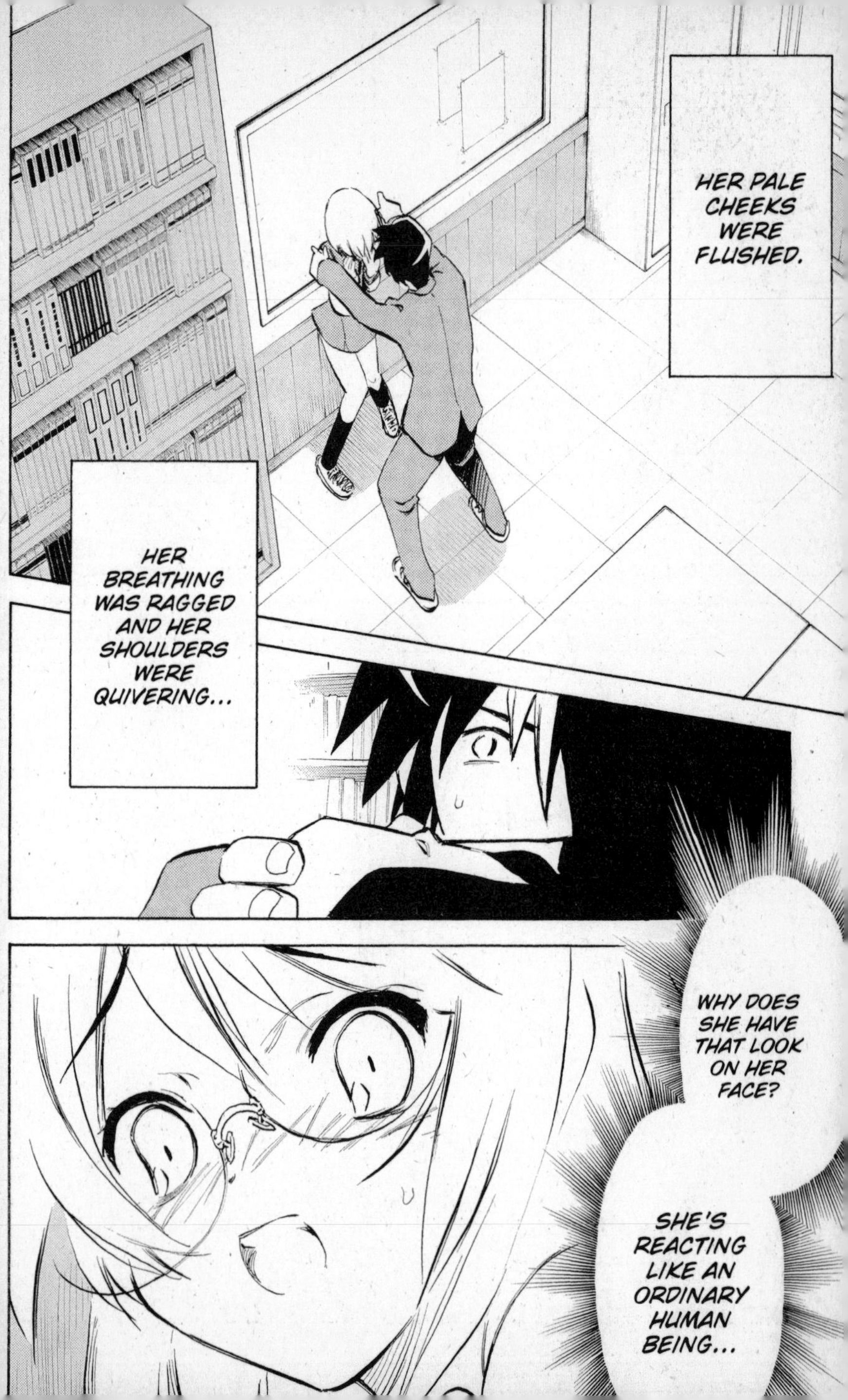
HER PALE CHEEKS WERE FLUSHED.
HER BREATHING WAS RAGGED AND HER SHOULDERS WERE QUIVERING...
WHY DOES SHE HAVE THAT LOOK ON HER FACE?
SHE'S REACTING LIKE AN ORDINARY HUMAN BEING...

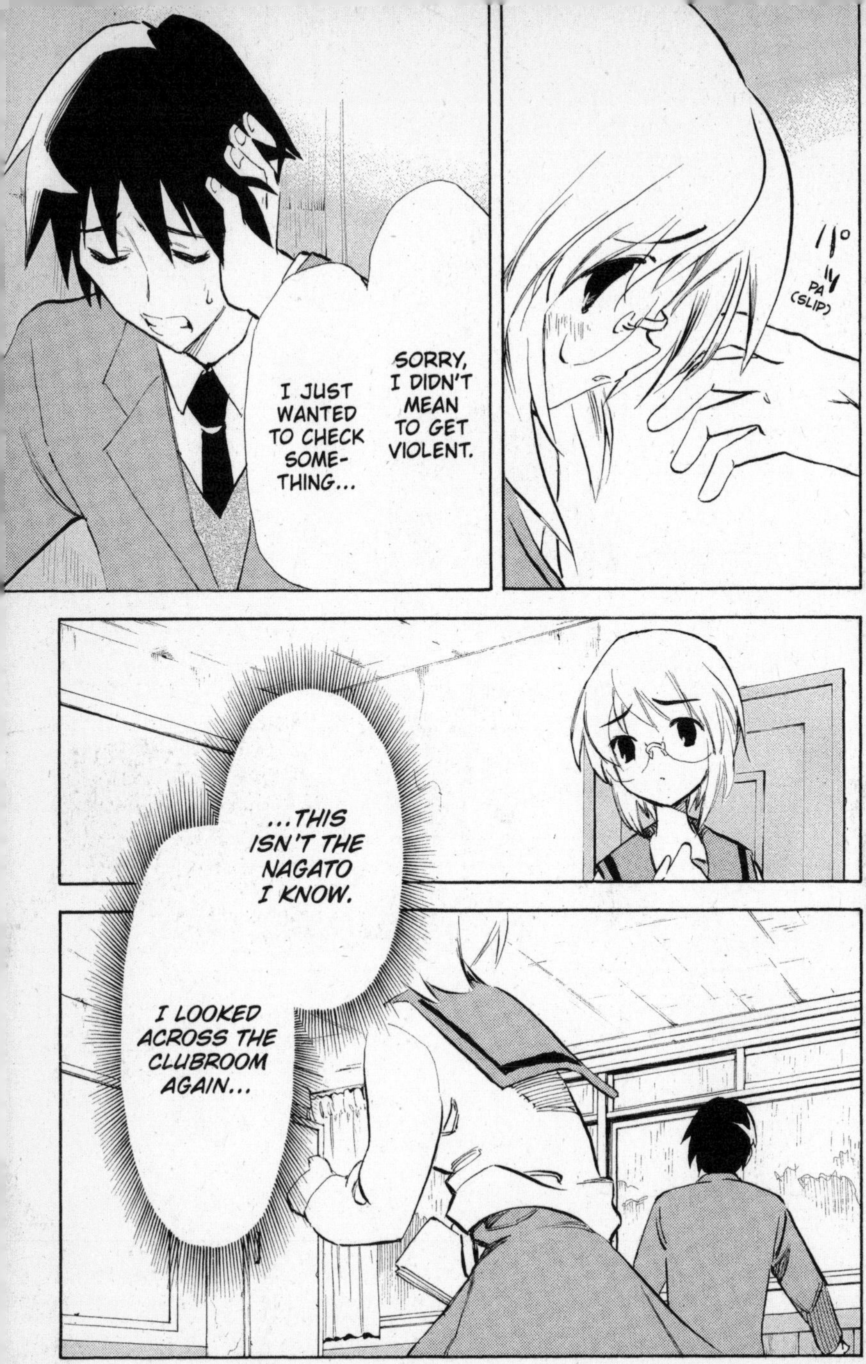
PA (SLIP)
SORRY, I DIDN'T MEAN TO GET VIOLENT.
I JUST WANTED TO CHECK SOME-THING...
...THIS ISN'T THE NAGATO I KNOW.
I LOOKED ACROSS THE CLUBROOM AGAIN...

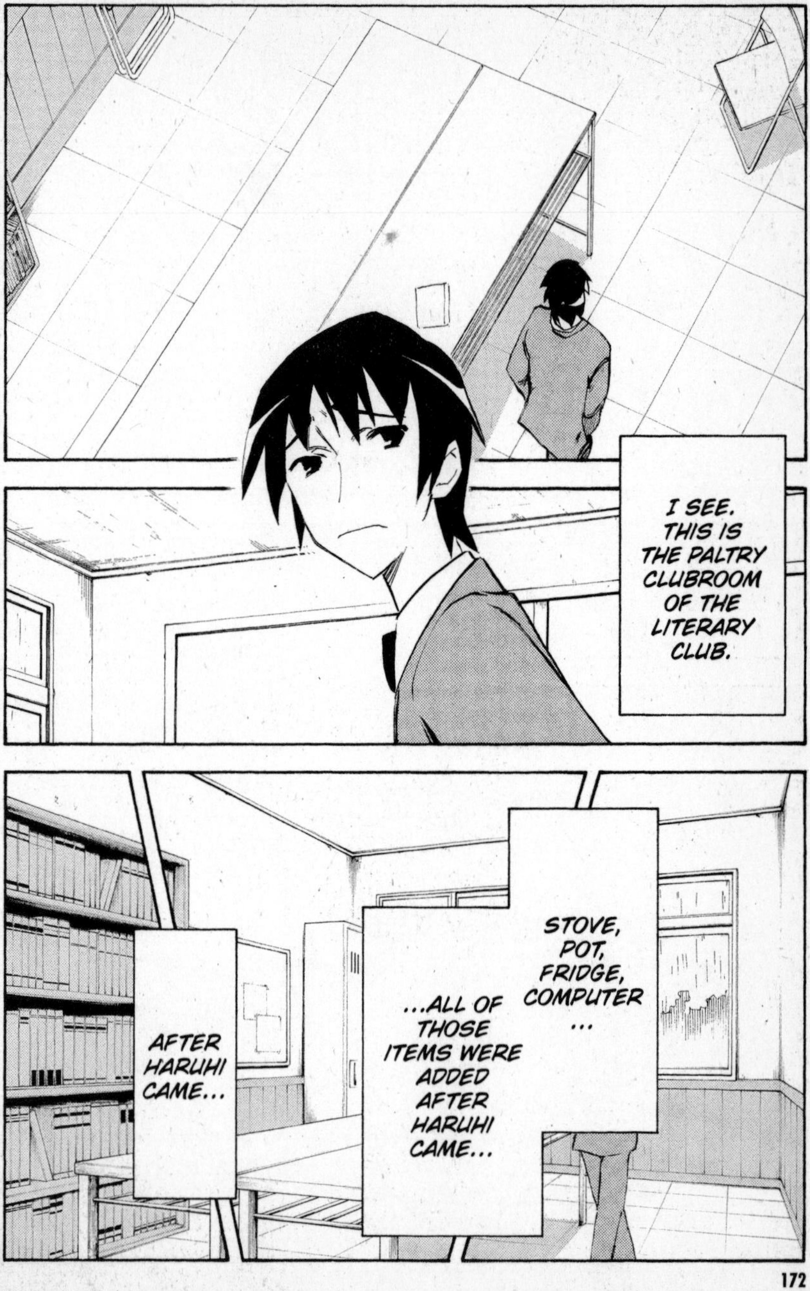
I SEE. THIS IS THE PALTRY CLUBROOM OF THE LITERARY CLUB.
STOVE, POT, FRIDGE, COMPUTER ...
...ALL OF THOSE ITEMS WERE ADDED AFTER HARUHI CAME...
AFTER HARUHI CAME...

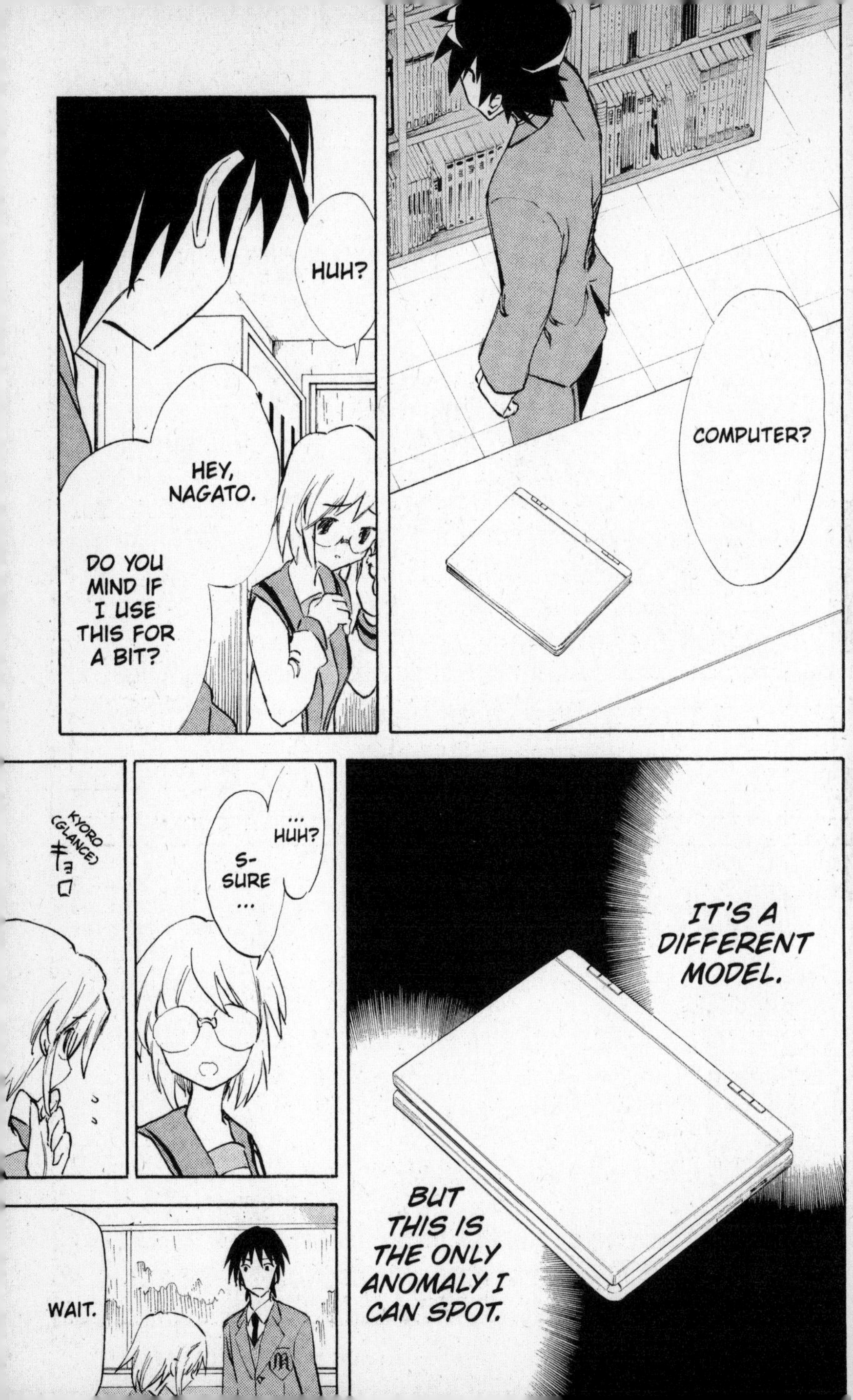
COMPUTER?
HUH?
HEY, NAGATO.
DO YOU MIND IF I USE THIS FOR A BIT?
IT'S A DIFFERENT MODEL.
BUT THIS IS THE ONLY ANOMALY I CAN SPOT.
... HUH?
S-SURE ...
KYORO (GLANCE)
WAIT.

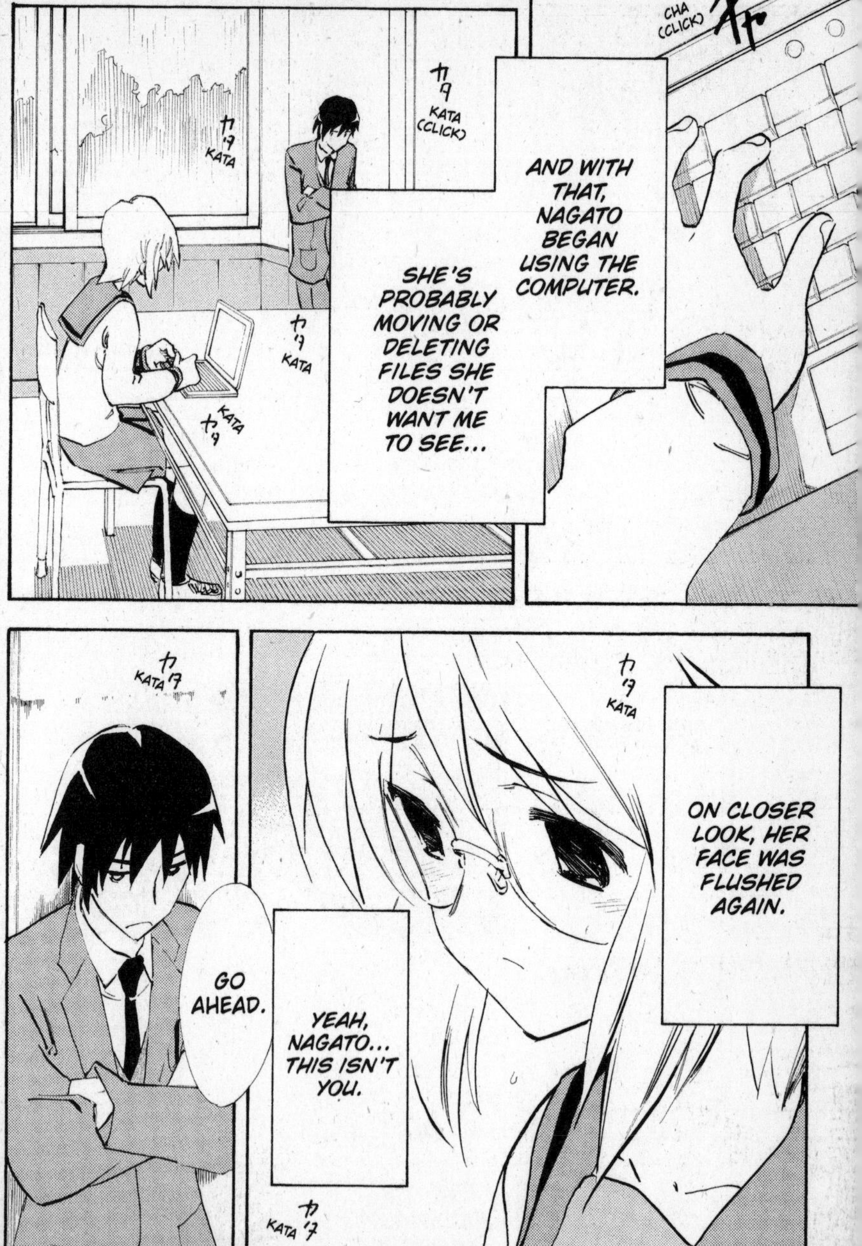
CHA (CLICK)
AND WITH THAT, NAGATO BEGAN USING THE COMPUTER.
KATA (CLICK)
KATA
SHE'S PROBABLY MOVING OR DELETING FILES SHE DOESN'T WANT ME TO SEE...
KATA
KATA
KATA
ON CLOSER LOOK, HER FACE WAS FLUSHED AGAIN.
YEAH, NAGATO... THIS ISN'T YOU.
KATA
KATA
GO AHEAD.

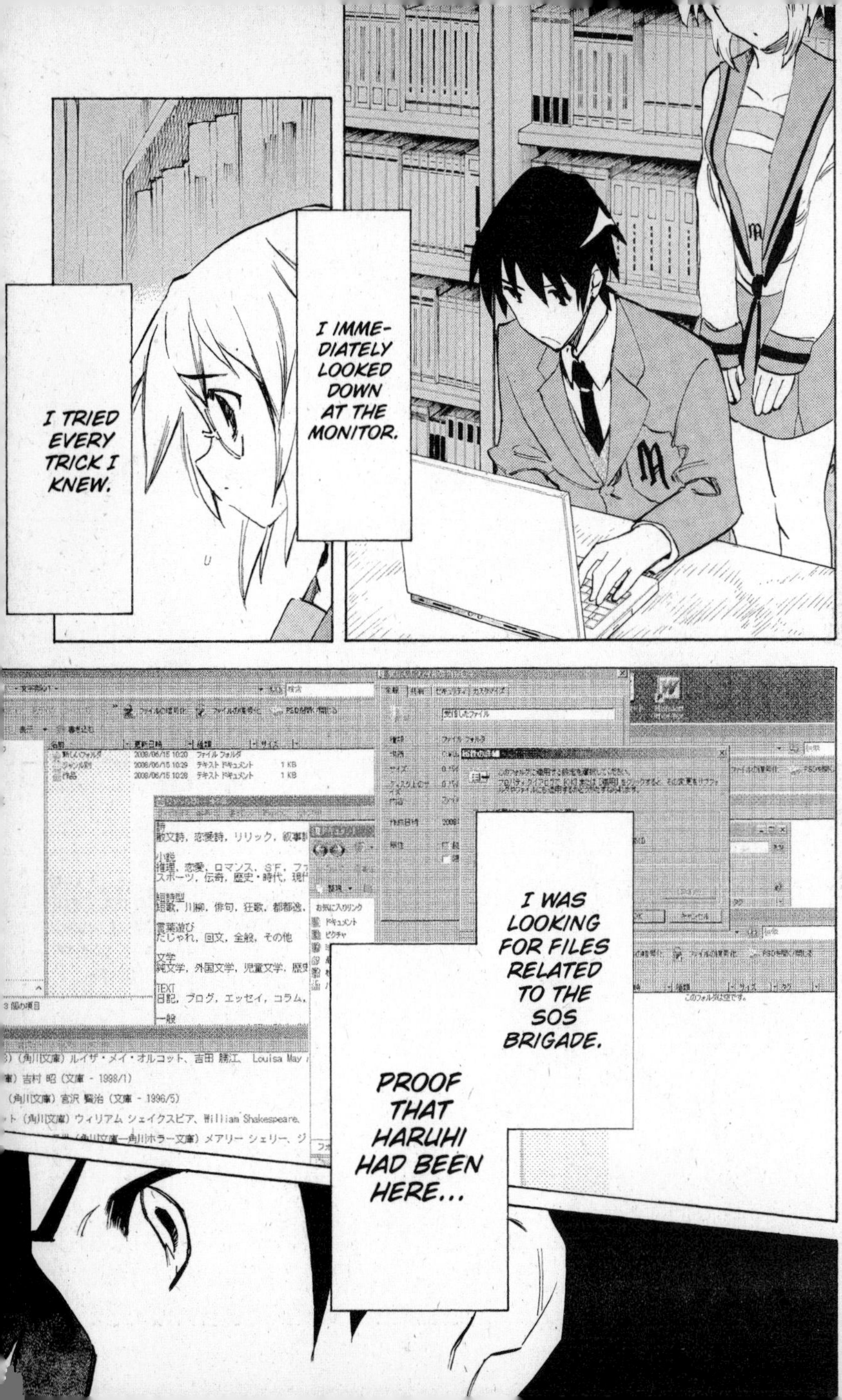
I IMME-DIATELY LOOKED DOWN AT THE MONITOR.
I TRIED EVERY TRICK I KNEW.
I WAS LOOKING FOR FILES RELATED TO THE SOS BRIGADE.
PROOF THAT HARUHI HAD BEEN HERE...

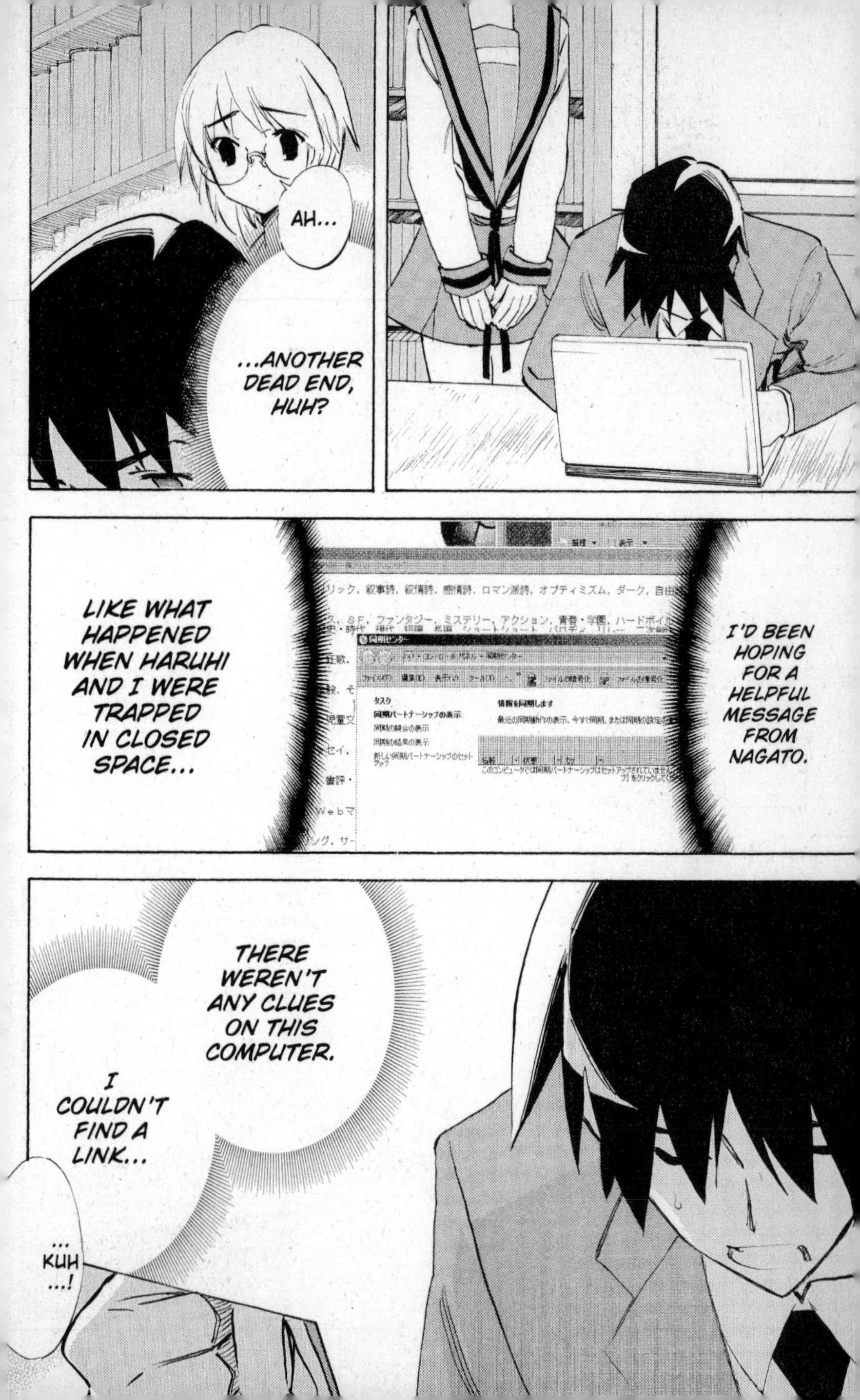
AH...
...ANOTHER DEAD END, HUH?
I'D BEEN HOPING FOR A HELPFUL MESSAGE FROM NAGATO.
LIKE WHAT HAPPENED WHEN HARUHI AND I WERE TRAPPED IN CLOSED SPACE...
THERE WEREN'T ANY CLUES ON THIS COMPUTER.
I COULDN'T FIND A LINK...
...KUH...!

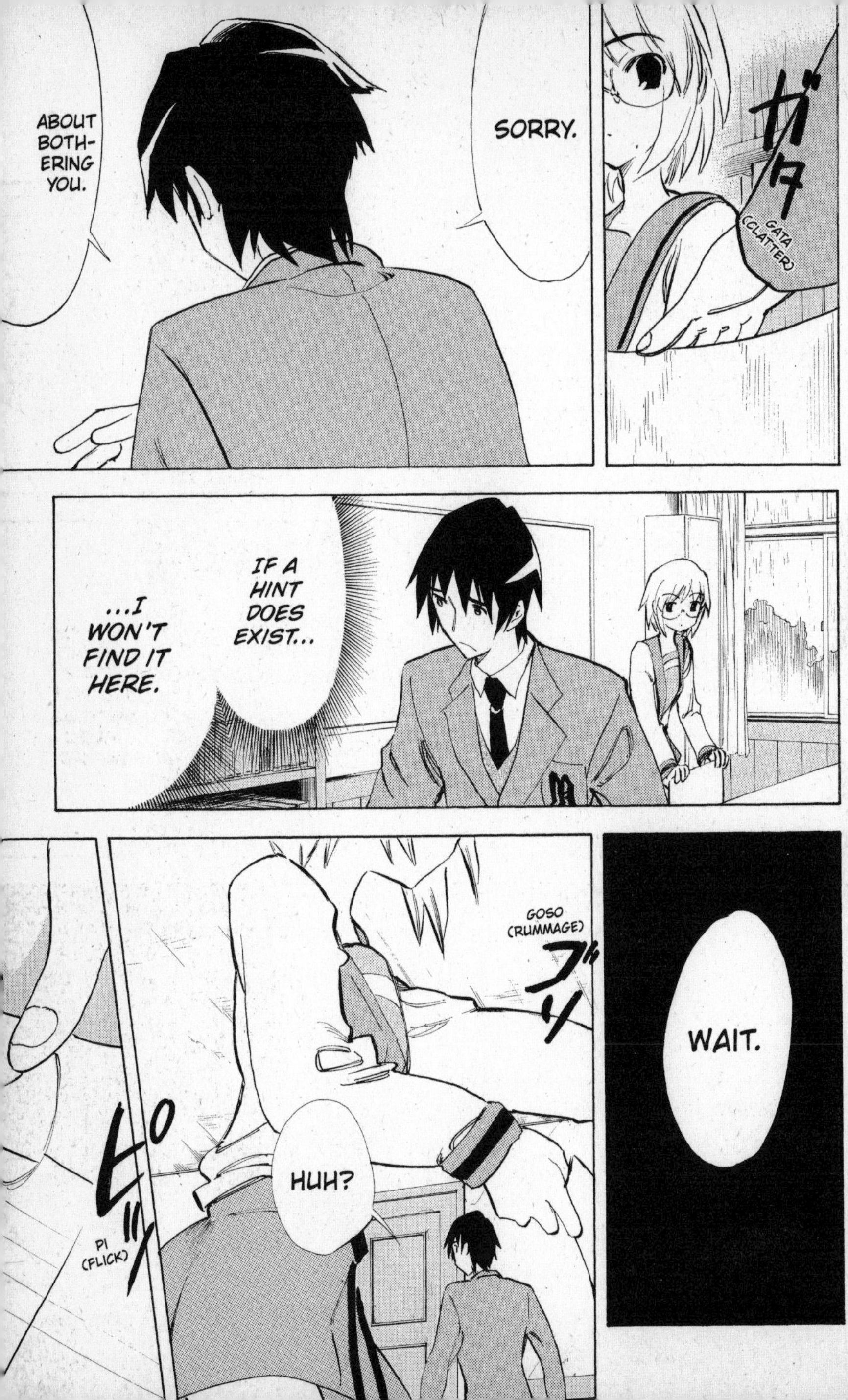
GATA (CLATTER)
SORRY.
ABOUT BOTHERING YOU.
IF A HINT DOES EXIST...
...I WON'T FIND IT HERE.
WAIT.
GOSO (RUMMAGE)
HUH?
PI (FLICK)

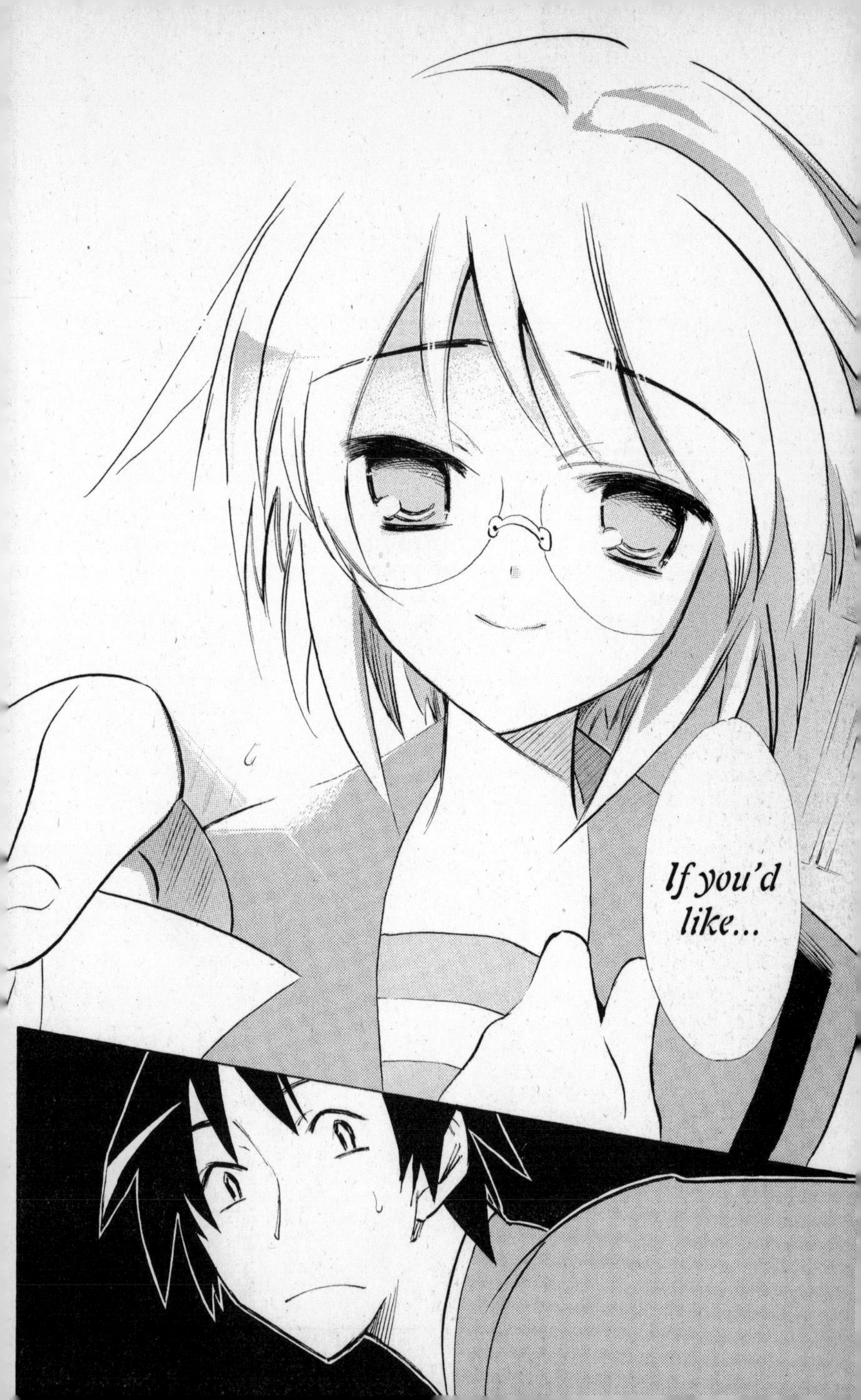
If you'd like...

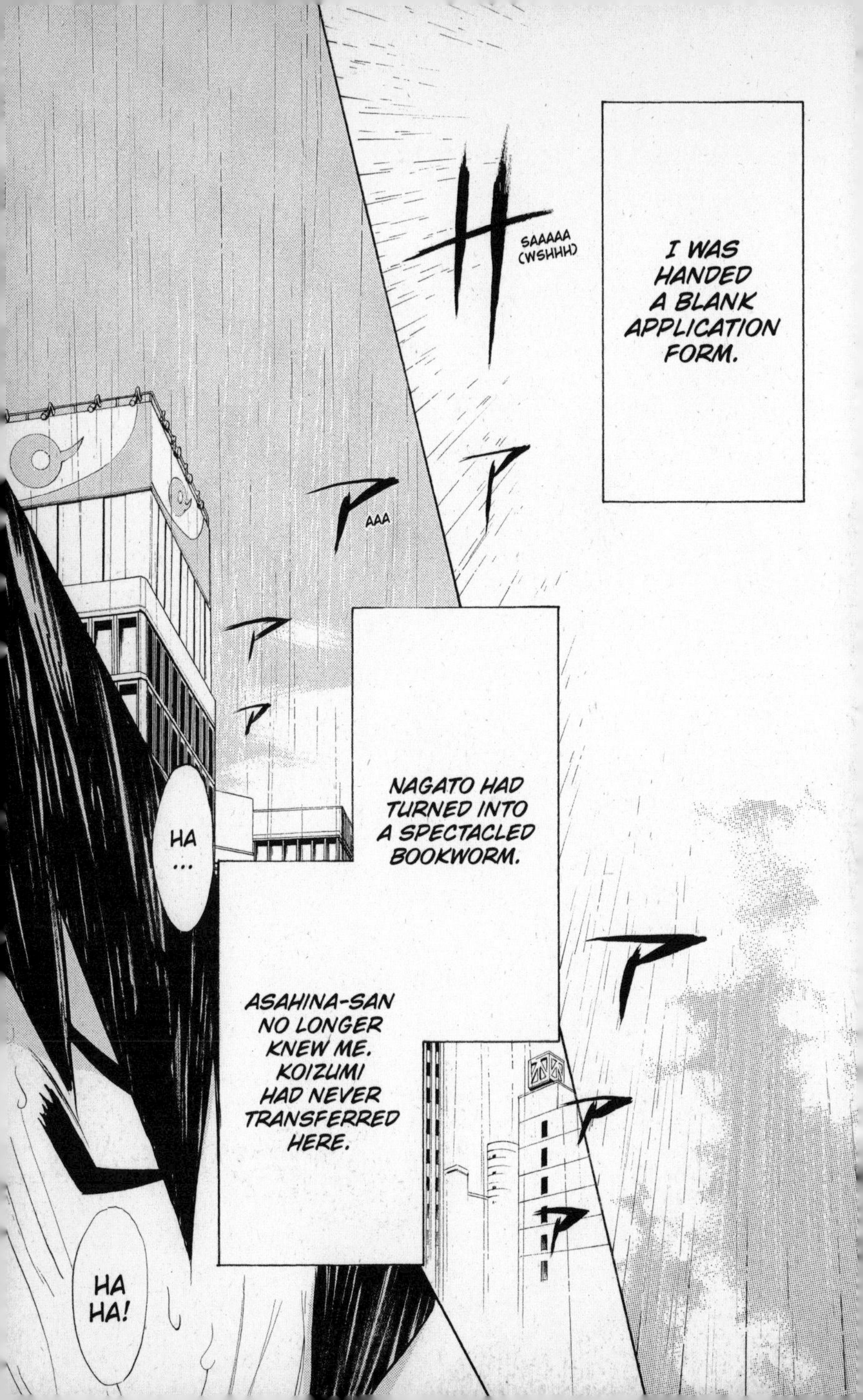
I WAS HANDED A BLANK APPLICATION FORM.
SAAAAA (WSHHH)
AAA
NAGATO HAD TURNED INTO A SPECTACLED BOOKWORM.
ASAHINA-SAN NO LONGER KNEW ME. KOIZUMI HAD NEVER TRANSFERRED HERE.
HA...
HA HA!

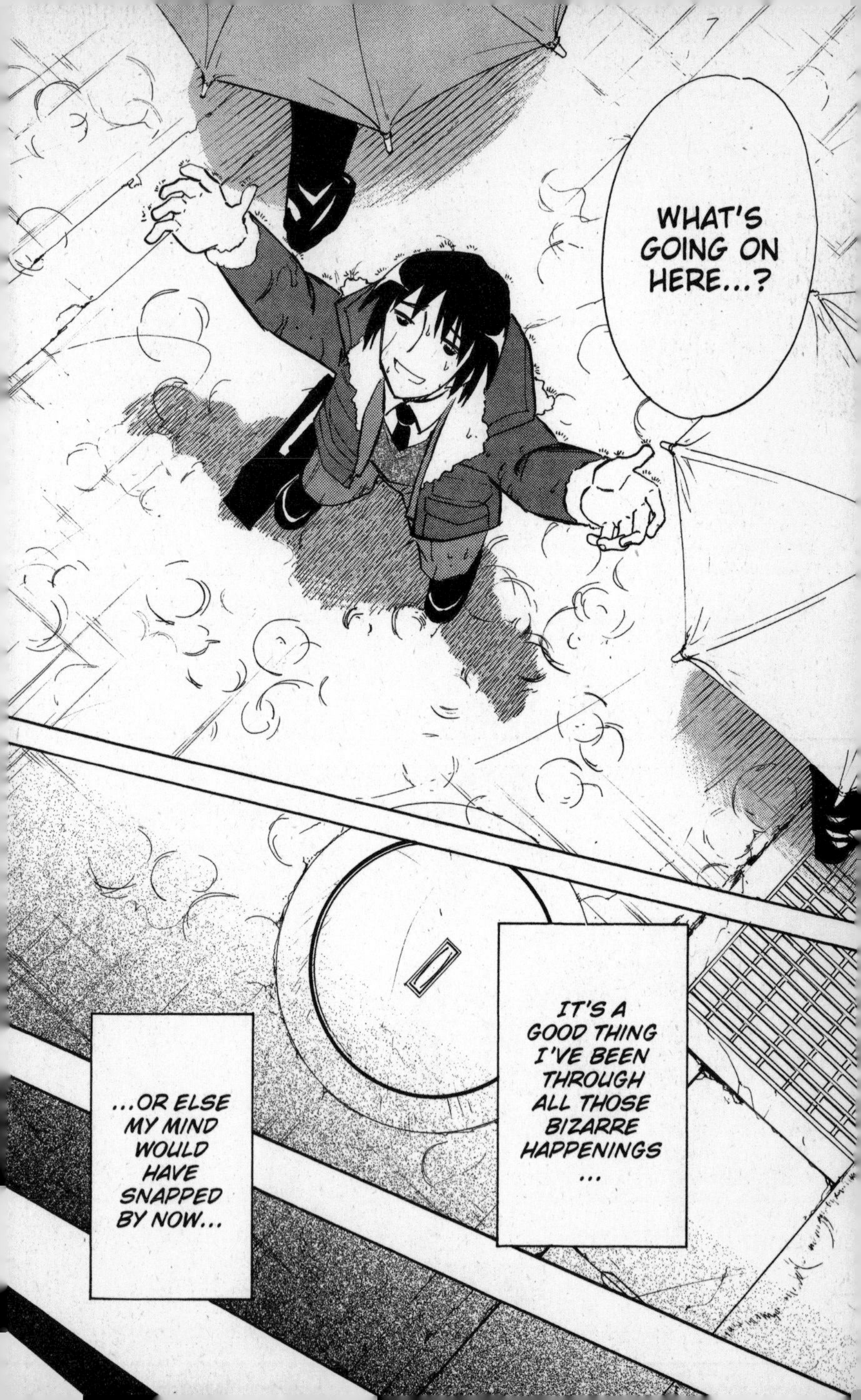
WHAT'S GOING ON HERE...?
IT'S A GOOD THING I'VE BEEN THROUGH ALL THOSE BIZARRE HAPPENINGS...
...OR ELSE MY MIND WOULD HAVE SNAPPED BY NOW...

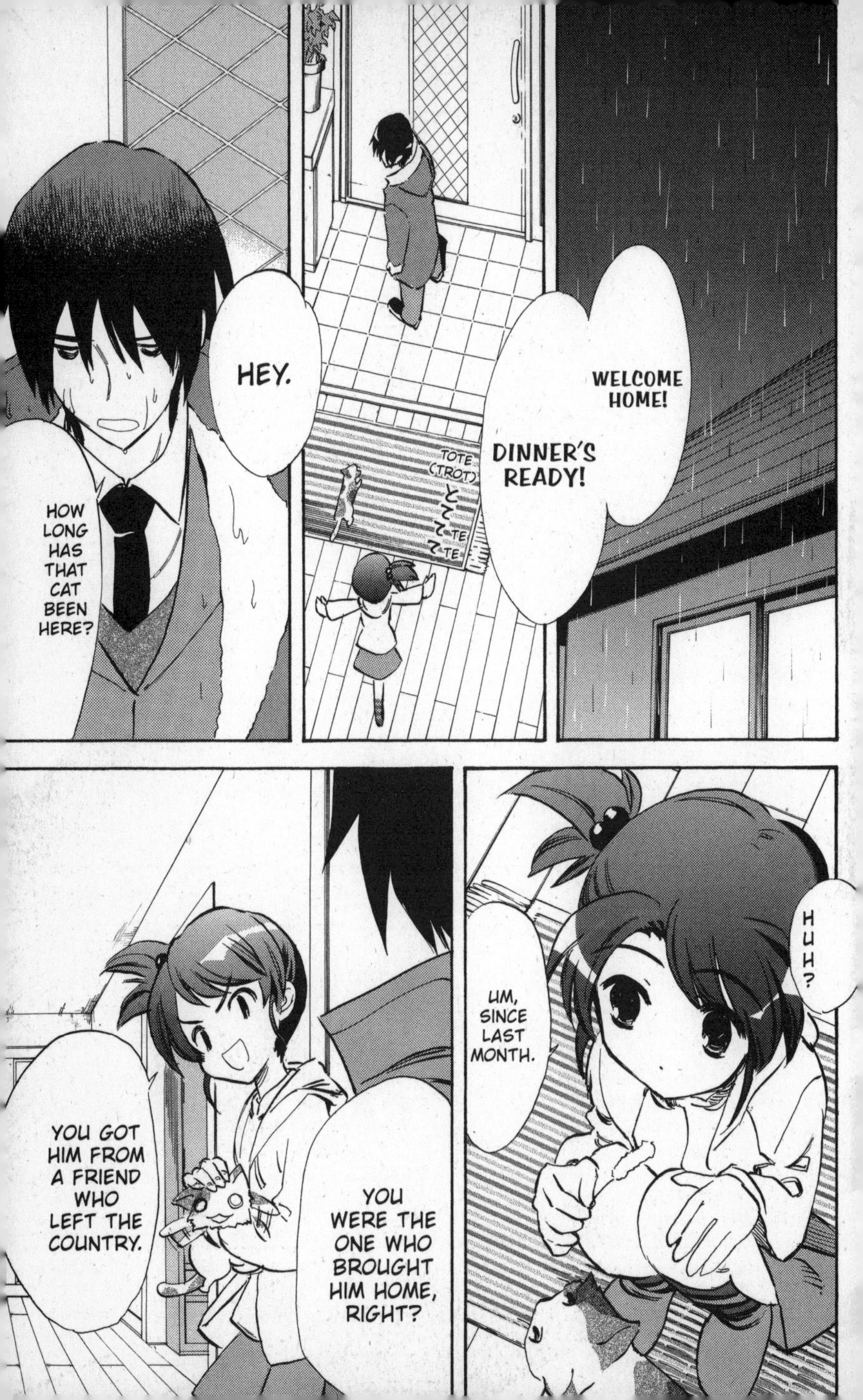
WELCOME HOME!
DINNER'S READY!
TOTE (TROT)
TE TE
HEY.
HOW LONG HAS THAT CAT BEEN HERE?
HUH?
UM, SINCE LAST MONTH.
YOU WERE THE ONE WHO BROUGHT HIM HOME, RIGHT?
YOU GOT HIM FROM A FRIEND WHO LEFT THE COUNTRY.

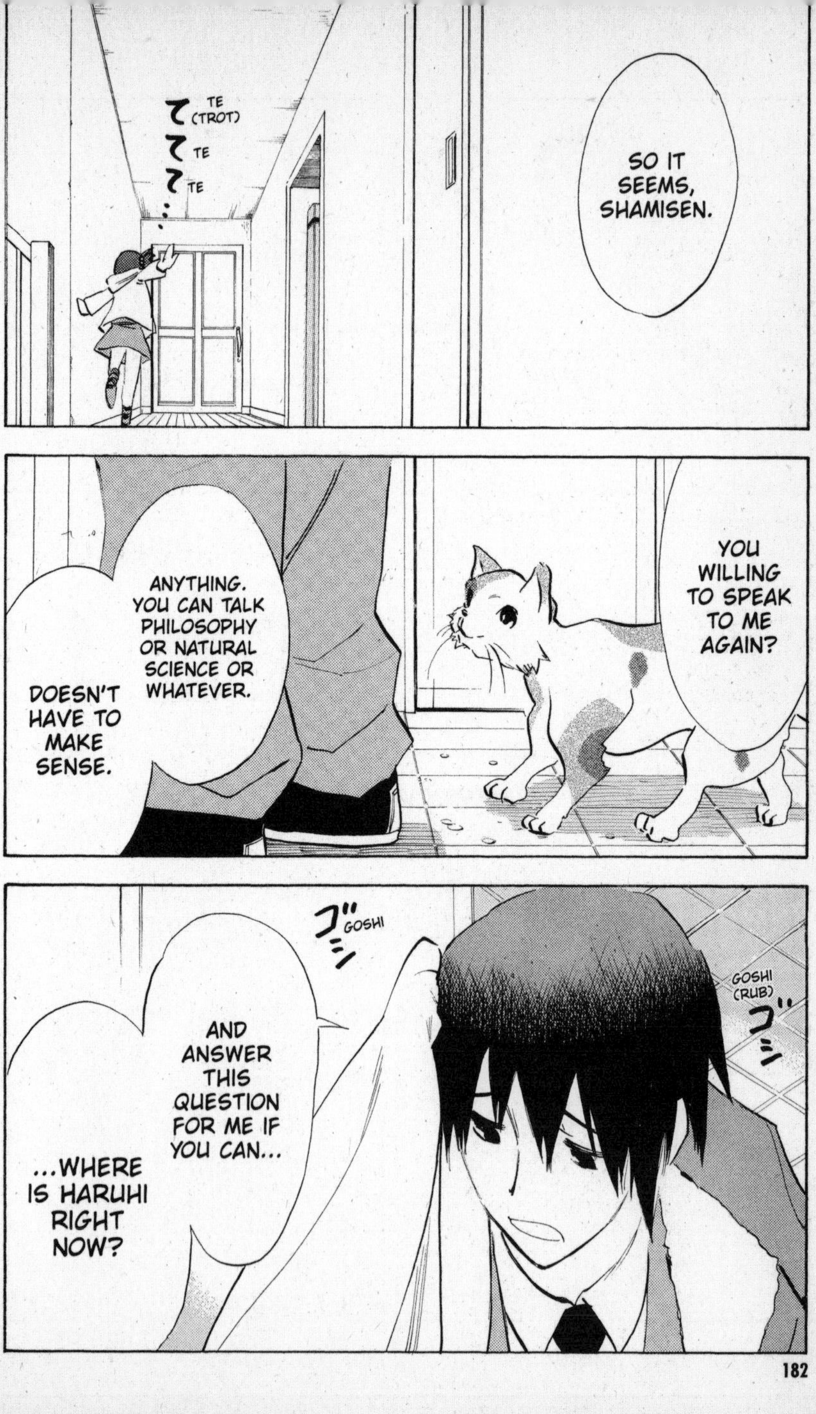
SO IT SEEMS, SHAMISEN.
て TE (TROT)
て TE
て TE
YOU WILLING TO SPEAK TO ME AGAIN?
ANYTHING. YOU CAN TALK PHILOSOPHY OR NATURAL SCIENCE OR WHATEVER.
DOESN'T HAVE TO MAKE SENSE.
ゴシ GOSHI (RUB)
ゴシ GOSHI
AND ANSWER THIS QUESTION FOR ME IF YOU CAN...
...WHERE IS HARUHI RIGHT NOW?

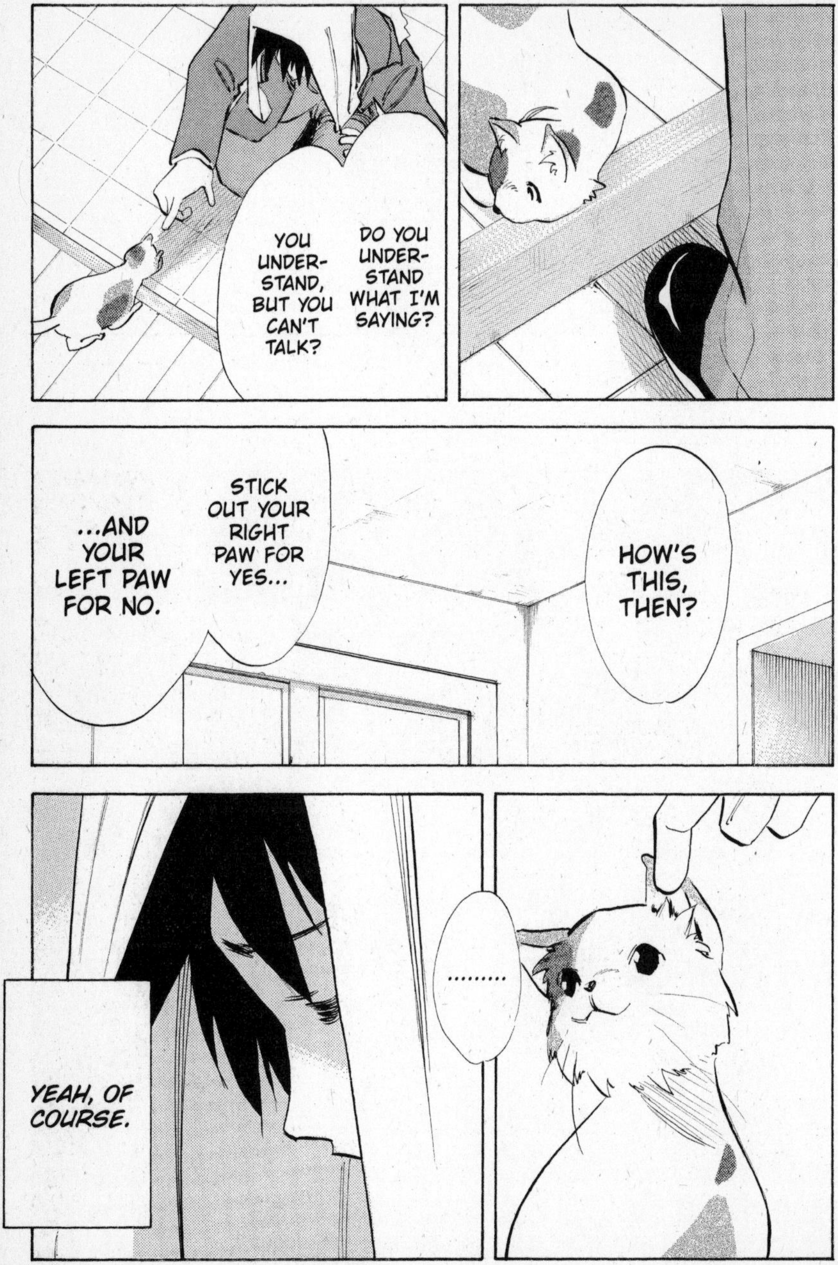
DO YOU UNDERSTAND WHAT I'M SAYING?
YOU UNDERSTAND, BUT YOU CAN'T TALK?
HOW'S THIS, THEN?
STICK OUT YOUR RIGHT PAW FOR YES...
...AND YOUR LEFT PAW FOR NO.
....
YEAH, OF COURSE.

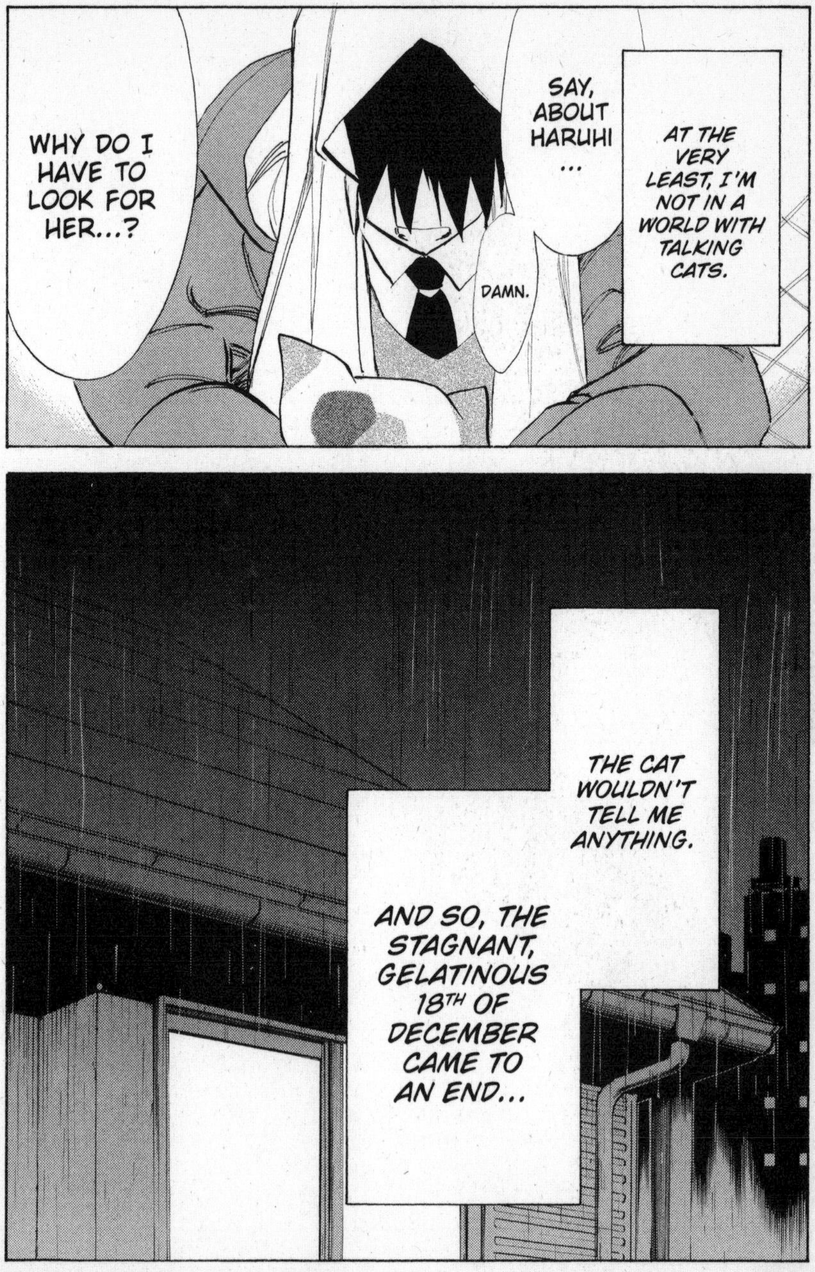
AT THE VERY LEAST, I'M NOT IN A WORLD WITH TALKING CATS.
SAY, ABOUT HARUHI...
DAMN.
WHY DO I HAVE TO LOOK FOR HER...?
THE CAT WOULDN'T TELL ME ANYTHING.
AND SO, THE STAGNANT, GELATINOUS 18TH OF DECEMBER CAME TO AN END...

The Disappearance of Haruhi Suzumiya III : END

TO BE CONTINUED

NOTE: PROGRAM EXECUTE CONDITION. ASSEMBLE THE KEYS. FINAL DEADLINE, TWO DAYS

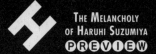

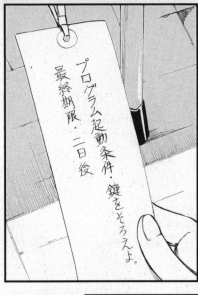

DECEMBER 19TH
A MESSAGE FROM THE NAGATO OF THE FORMER WORLD. "PROGRAM EXECUTE CONDITION. ASSEMBLE THE KEYS." WHAT DO THOSE WORDS MEAN...?

プログラム起動条件・鍵をそろえよ。
最終期限・二日後

AND FINALLY... IS REUNITED WITH...

"HARUHI"!!

DECEMBER 20TH
KYON LEARNS OF THE "HARUHI" IN THIS WORLD FROM TANIGUCHI'S REVELATION.

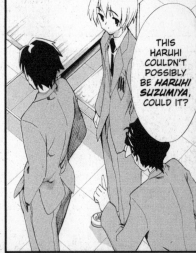

THIS HARUHI COULDN'T POSSIBLY BE *HARUHI SUZUMIYA*, COULD IT?

VOLUME 8 ON SALE SOON!!

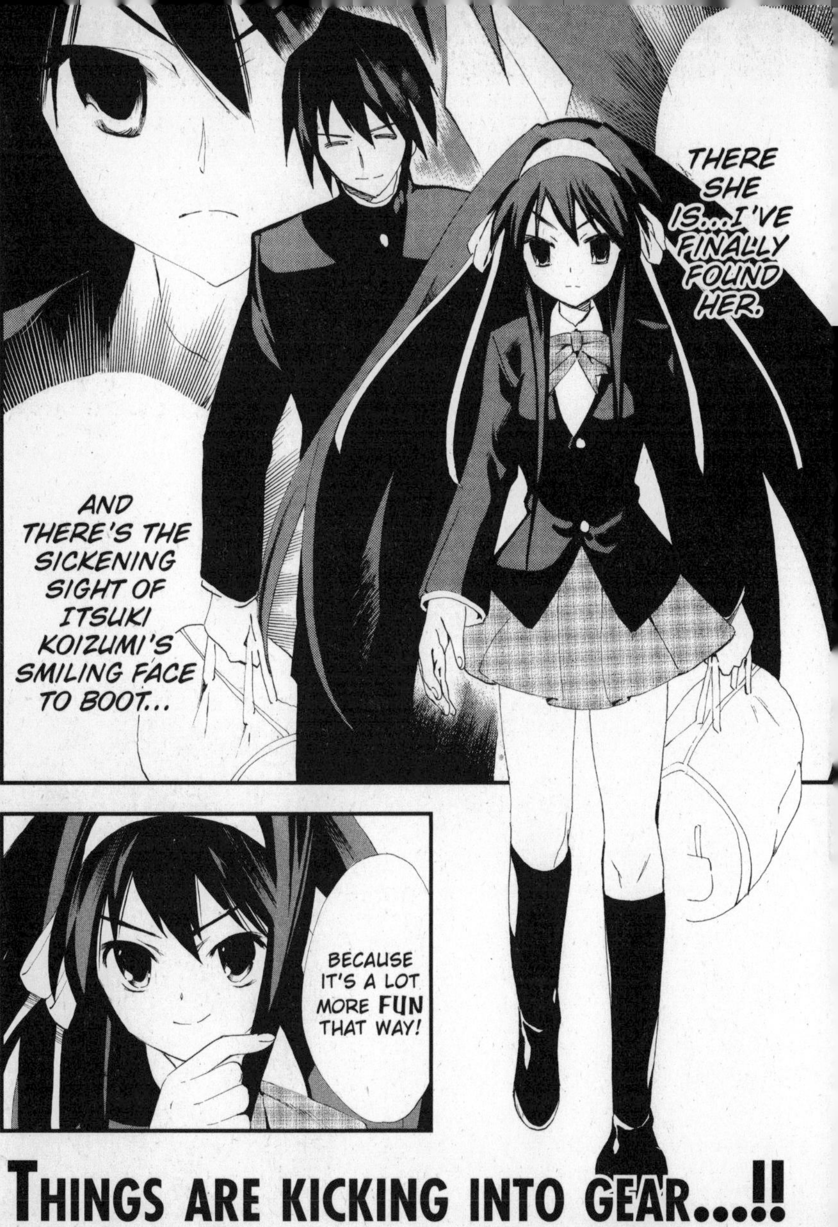
THERE SHE IS...I'VE FINALLY FOUND HER.
AND THERE'S THE SICKENING SIGHT OF ITSUKI KOIZUMI'S SMILING FACE TO BOOT...
BECAUSE IT'S A LOT MORE FUN THAT WAY!

THINGS ARE KICKING INTO GEAR...!!

THE "DISAPPEARANCE" PHASE IS HEATING UP!

BONUS PREVIEW!

THE MELANCHOLY of SUZUMIYA
HARUHI-CHAN
The Untold Adventures of the SOS Brigade

WHOA! CHECK OUT MY NEW SERIES!

STORY: **NAGARU TANIGAWA** ART: **PUYO** CHARACTERS: NOIZI ITO

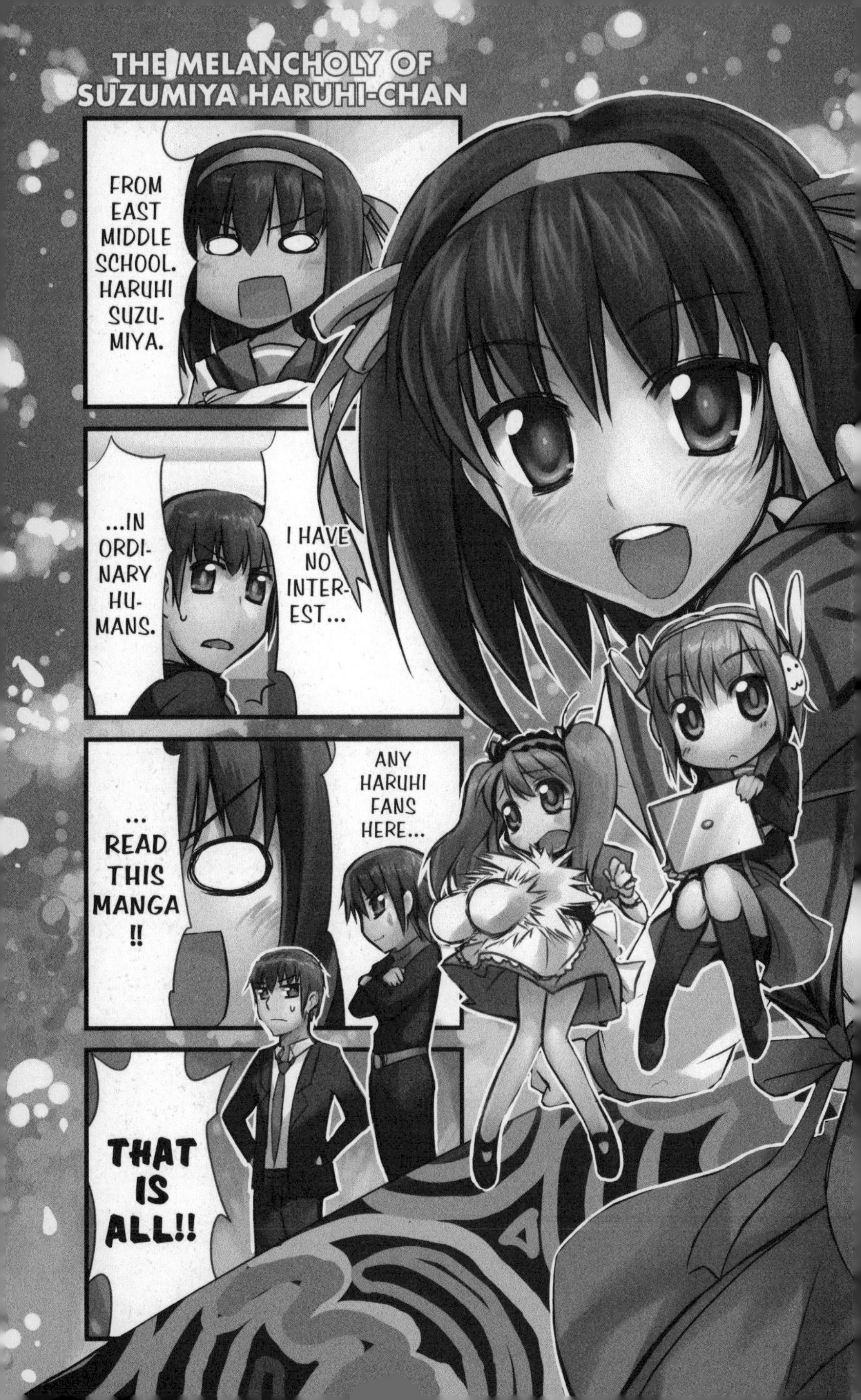
THE MELANCHOLY OF SUZUMIYA HARUHI-CHAN
FROM EAST MIDDLE SCHOOL. HARUHI SUZUMIYA.
I HAVE NO INTEREST...
...IN ORDINARY HUMANS.
ANY HARUHI FANS HERE...
...READ THIS MANGA!!
THAT IS ALL!!

SHOUT

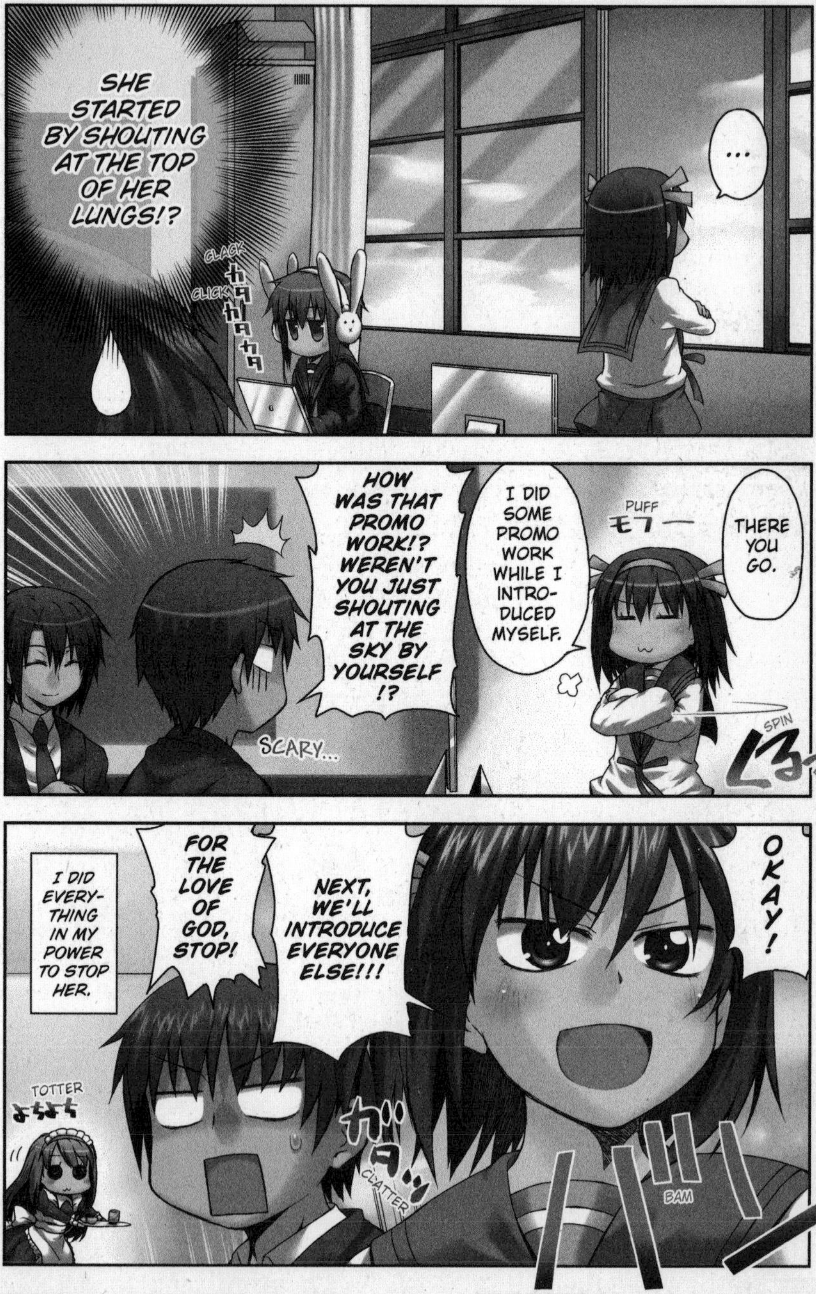
...
SHE STARTED BY SHOUTING AT THE TOP OF HER LUNGS!?
CLACK
CLICK
THERE YOU GO.
PUFF
I DID SOME PROMO WORK WHILE I INTRO-DUCED MYSELF.
SPIN
HOW WAS THAT PROMO WORK!? WEREN'T YOU JUST SHOUTING AT THE SKY BY YOURSELF!?
SCARY...
OKAY!
NEXT, WE'LL INTRODUCE EVERYONE ELSE!!!
FOR THE LOVE OF GOD, STOP!
I DID EVERY-THING IN MY POWER TO STOP HER.
BAM
CLATTER
TOTTER

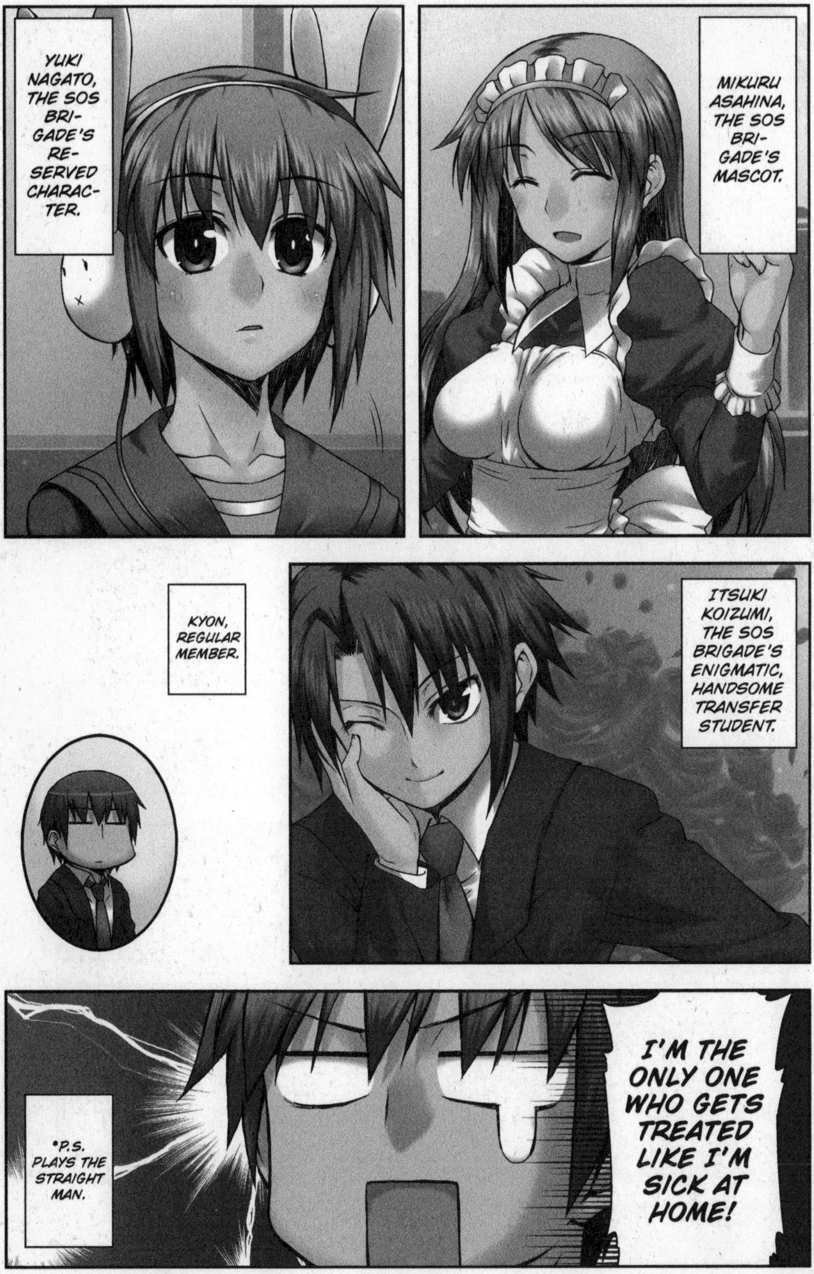
MIKURU ASAHINA, THE SOS BRI-GADE'S MASCOT.
YUKI NAGATO, THE SOS BRI-GADE'S RE-SERVED CHARAC-TER.
ITSUKI KOIZUMI, THE SOS BRIGADE'S ENIGMATIC, HANDSOME TRANSFER STUDENT.
KYON, REGULAR MEMBER.
I'M THE ONLY ONE WHO GETS TREATED LIKE I'M SICK AT HOME!
*P.S. PLAYS THE STRAIGHT MAN.

BELIEVE

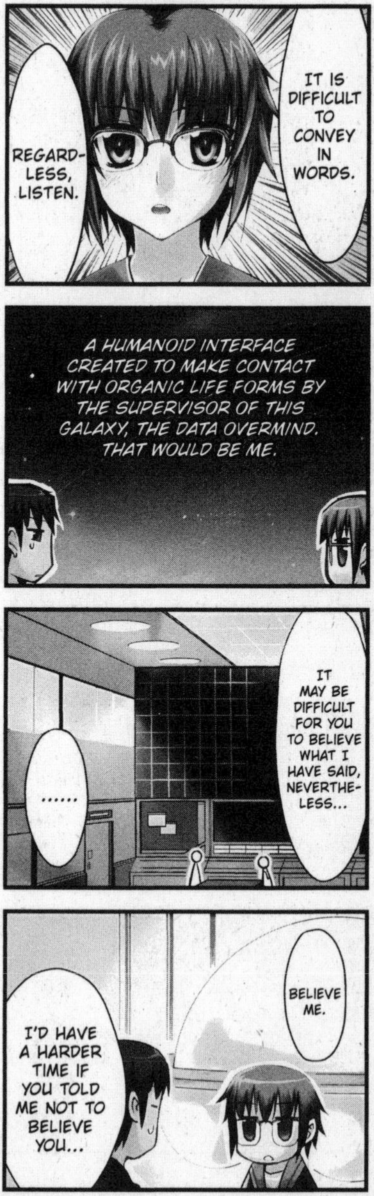

IT IS DIFFICULT TO CONVEY IN WORDS.
REGARDLESS, LISTEN.
A HUMANOID INTERFACE CREATED TO MAKE CONTACT WITH ORGANIC LIFE FORMS BY THE SUPERVISOR OF THIS GALAXY, THE DATA OVERMIND. THAT WOULD BE ME.
IT MAY BE DIFFICULT FOR YOU TO BELIEVE WHAT I HAVE SAID, NEVERTHELESS...
......
BELIEVE ME.
I'D HAVE A HARDER TIME IF YOU TOLD ME NOT TO BELIEVE YOU...

FLIP BOOK

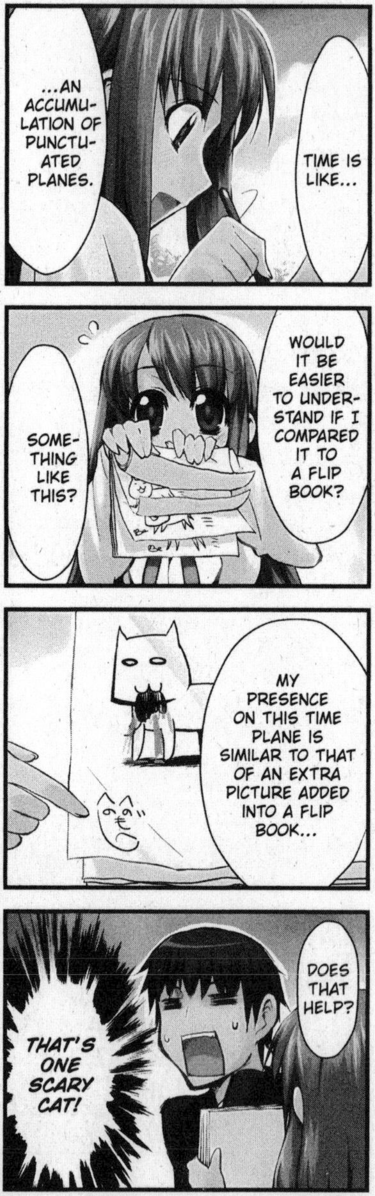

TIME IS LIKE...
...AN ACCUMULATION OF PUNCTUATED PLANES.
WOULD IT BE EASIER TO UNDERSTAND IF I COMPARED IT TO A FLIP BOOK?
SOMETHING LIKE THIS?
MY PRESENCE ON THIS TIME PLANE IS SIMILAR TO THAT OF AN EXTRA PICTURE ADDED INTO A FLIP BOOK...
DOES THAT HELP?
THAT'S ONE SCARY CAT!

ASSIST

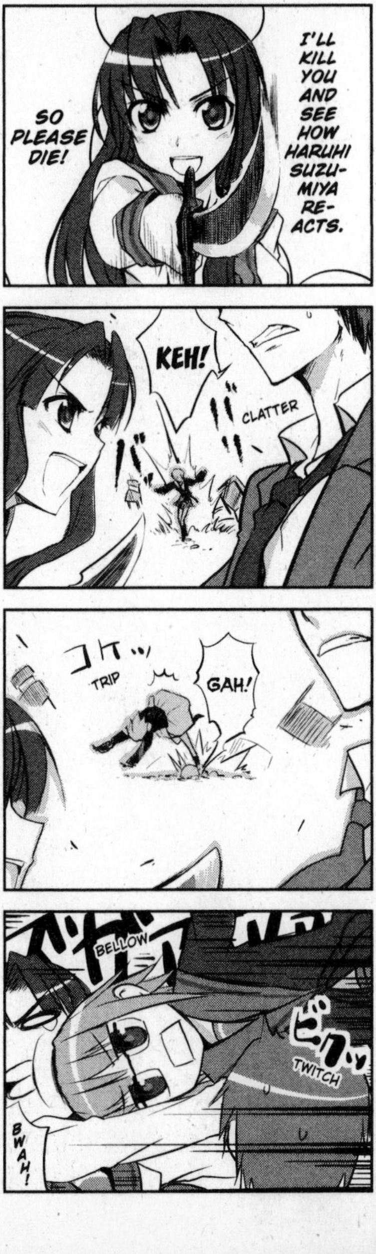

I'LL KILL YOU AND SEE HOW HARUHI SUZUMIYA REACTS.
SO PLEASE DIE!
KEH!
CLATTER
GAH!
TRIP
BELLOW
TWITCH
BWAH!

TWIST

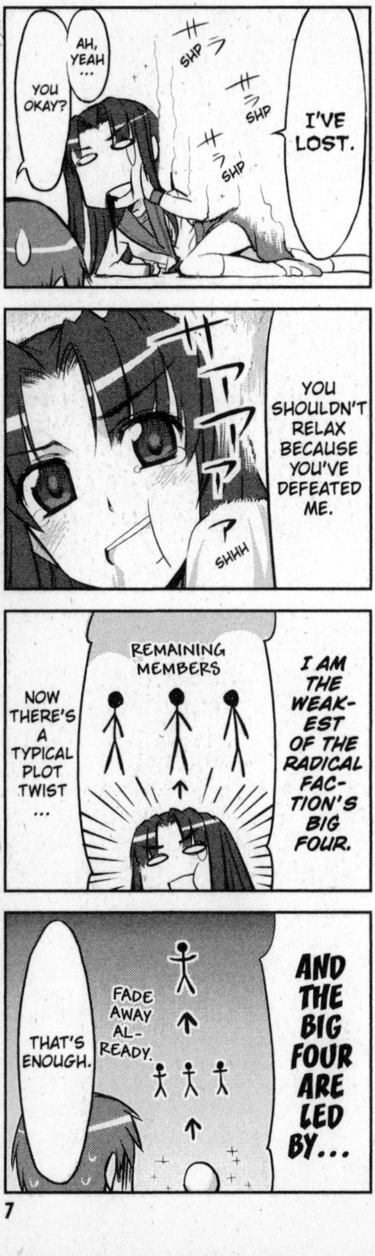

I'VE LOST.
SHP
SHP
SHP
AH, YEAH ...
YOU OKAY?
YOU SHOULDN'T RELAX BECAUSE YOU'VE DEFEATED ME.
SHHH
I AM THE WEAKEST OF THE RADICAL FACTION'S BIG FOUR.
REMAINING MEMBERS
NOW THERE'S A TYPICAL PLOT TWIST ...
AND THE BIG FOUR ARE LED BY...
FADE AWAY ALREADY.
THAT'S ENOUGH.

•Haruhi-chan •SOS Brigade brigade chief. Selfish, pushy, eccentric, and cute.

•Kyon •Supposed to be the main character in this story. Still stuck as the straight man in this work.

•Nagato •A taciturn alien who's always reding. Defeated Asakura-san by head-butting her.

•Mikuru-chan •Actually from the future. An absentminded airhead who's also a wonderful and beautiful girl.

•Koizumi •An enigmatic transfer student who happens to be an esper. A smug and detestable stud who's always smiling.

•Asakura-san •An alien who opposes Nagato. A poor, little thing who was head-butted four panels after showing up.

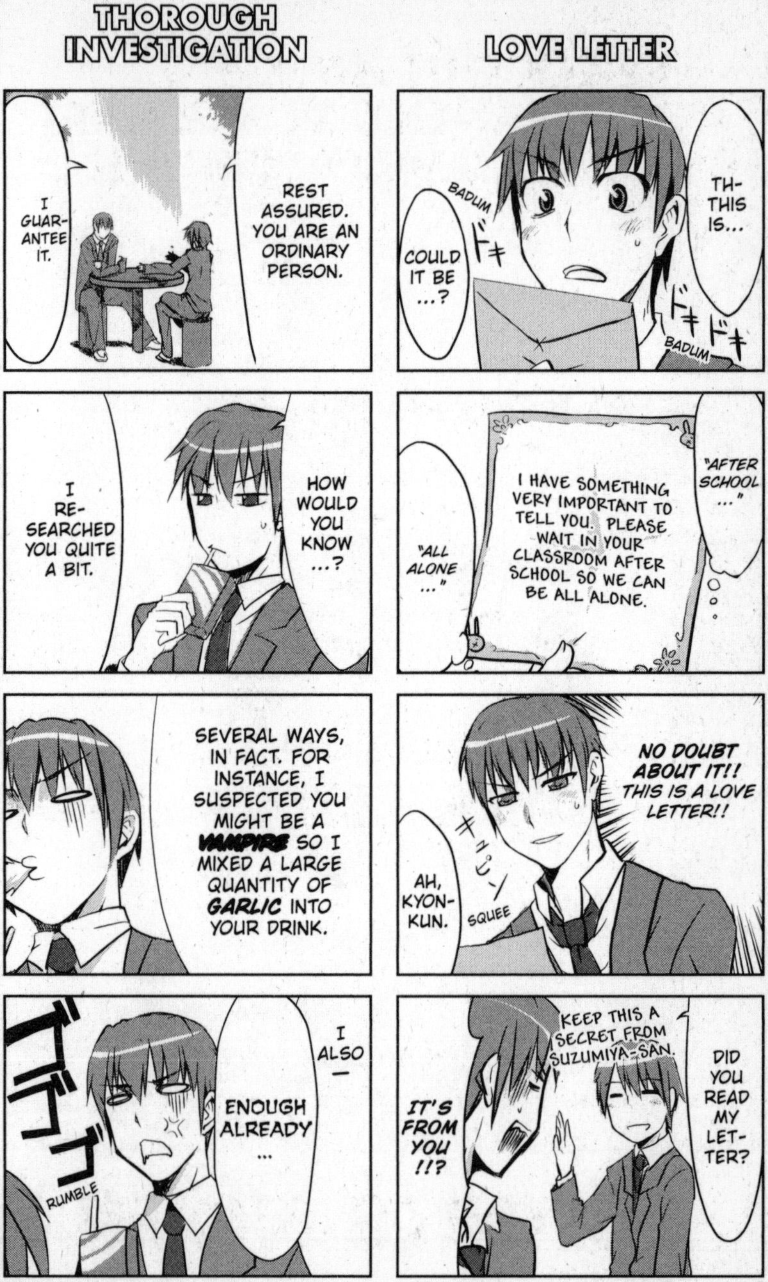
LOVE LETTER
TH-THIS IS...
BADUM
ドキ
COULD IT BE ...?
ドキドキ
BADUM
"AFTER SCHOOL ..."
I HAVE SOMETHING VERY IMPORTANT TO TELL YOU. PLEASE WAIT IN YOUR CLASSROOM AFTER SCHOOL SO WE CAN BE ALL ALONE.
"ALL ALONE ..."
NO DOUBT ABOUT IT!! THIS IS A LOVE LETTER!!
キュピーン
SQUEE
AH, KYON-KUN.
KEEP THIS A SECRET FROM SUZUMIYA-SAN.
DID YOU READ MY LET-TER?
IT'S FROM YOU!!?
THOROUGH INVESTIGATION
REST ASSURED. YOU ARE AN ORDINARY PERSON.
I GUAR-ANTEE IT.
HOW WOULD YOU KNOW ...?
I RE-SEARCHED YOU QUITE A BIT.
SEVERAL WAYS, IN FACT. FOR INSTANCE, I SUSPECTED YOU MIGHT BE A VAMPIRE SO I MIXED A LARGE QUANTITY OF GARLIC INTO YOUR DRINK.
I ALSO —
ENOUGH ALREADY ...
ゴゴゴ
RUMBLE

THE MELANCHOLY OF HARUHI SUZUMIYA

7

Original Story: Nagaru Tanigawa
Manga: Gaku Tsugano
Character Design: Noizi Ito

OCT   2010

Translation: Chris Pai for MX Media LLC
Lettering: Alexis Eckerman

SUZUMIYA HARUHI NO YUUTSU Volume 7 © Nagaru TANIGAWA • Noizi ITO
2008 © Gaku TSUGANO 2008. First published in Japan in 2008 by KADOKAWA
SHOTEN PUBLISHING CO., LTD., Tokyo. English translation rights arranged
with KADOKAWA SHOTEN PUBLISHING CO., LTD., Tokyo through TUTTLE-
MORI AGENCY, INC., Tokyo.

English translation © 2010 by Hachette Book Group, Inc.

Yen Press
Hachette Book Group
237 Park Avenue, New York, NY 10017

www.HachetteBookGroup.com
www.YenPress.com

Yen Press is an imprint of Hachette Book Group, Inc. The Yen Press name and
logo are trademarks of Hachette Book Group, Inc.

First Yen Press Edition: October 2010

ISBN: 978-0-316-08953-1

10 9 8 7 6 5 4 3 2 1

BVG

Printed in the United States of America